DARE
TO BE
A GREAT
WRITER

DARE TO BE A GREAT WRITER

329 KEYS TO POWERFUL FICTION

BY LEONARD BISHOP

CINCINNATI, OHIO

ABOUT THE AUTHOR

Leonard Bishop has proven himself as an authority on writing. A writer, editor, teacher, and lecturer, he taught the first "team-teaching" creative writing class at Columbia University with James T. Farrell. He has also taught at New York University, the University of California, and at writing conferences throughout the country, and Boston University has honored him by establishing a "Leonard Bishop Collection." He has published in several notable magazines including *Esquire*, *The Nation*, and *New World Writing*.

Leonard Bishop's best-selling novels include *The Everlasting* (published by Simon & Schuster under their Poseidon Press imprint and by Pocket Books in paperback) and *Against Heaven's Hand* (published by Random House and made into an ABC "Movie of the Week"). He lives in Kansas.

Dare To Be a Great Writer. Copyright © 1988 by Leonard Bishop. Printed and bound in the United States of America. All rights reserved. No part of this book may be reproduced in any form or by any electronic or mechanical means including information storage and retrieval systems without permission in writing from the publisher, except by a reviewer, who may quote brief passages in a review. Published by Writer's Digest Books, an imprint of F&W Publications, Inc., 1507 Dana Avenue, Cincinnati, Ohio 45207. First edition. First paperback printing 1992.

96 95 94 93 92   5 4 3 2 1

Library of Congress Cataloging-in-Publication Data

Bishop, Leonard, 1922-
  Dare to be a great writer.

  Includes index.
  1. Authorship.   1. Title.
PN145.B54   1988   808'.02   88-5718
ISBN 0-89879-464-1

Design by Christine Aulicino

For Celia:
 who insisted.

ACKNOWLEDGMENT

To all the students in the Monday Night Writing Class conducted mostly in Berkeley and San Francisco from 1968 to 1983. I have been liberal in availing myself of the writing instruction I imparted to them. Much of this book has been based on information and references that were recorded during their class time. Over the years there were more than 150 students who attended the Monday Night Writing Class, and there was only one student I did not like.

Introduction

No one consciously chooses to become a mediocre writer. Their work drifts into obscurity because they do not dare to become great writers. When mediocre writers fail at concocting even mediocre novels, they are either not published or, if published, they are not read. If you boldly risk writing a novel that might be acclaimed as great, and fail, you could succeed in writing a book that is splendid.

The writer of great books does not hide them in attic trunks, hoping that one day they will be discovered by some snoopy descendant who will have them published posthumously, to achieve awards and immortality. Most writers of great books loathe anonymity and despise poverty. They do not cringe away from public acclaim. They are men and women who boldly write for great accomplishment and fame and wealth, IN THEIR OWN TIME.

A great book fulfills this era's writing fashion and current reading preferences, then satisfies the fashions and preferences of readers in the eras to come. A great novel fascinates, enraptures, and absorbs you today—then does the same for your great-great-great-great-great grandchildren.

Writing is done by someone. It is not, like some mythical goddess, a skill that springs forth, full grown from the genes of inspiration. A writer must know what he is doing. Consciously, and with deliberation. Dramatic characters, inventive plotlines, exciting and intense situations are not achieved through accident or "good luck." The writers of great books zealously learn the craft of their profession so they can release the power and depth of their imagination and experience. Any writer who believes in the "lucky creative accident" in writing is pushing elephants on roller skates up greased ramps.

Dare to be a Great Writer offers craft techniques that competently function in the development of scene, plot, character, conflict, relationships, perception, viewpoint, dialogue, overall structure, and hundreds of other insights that will convince the inexperienced writer that unless you support talent with controllable craft, you had better search elsewhere for fame and wealth and awards.

There are also fifty-two comments that deal with attitudes and experiences involved in the career of being a writer. Many of the problems that writers have do not arise from what they cannot do in writing, but from what they do not realize a writer must experience if he is to survive society, and himself.

At the bottom of all intention and purpose: beneath the tinsel, glitter, hocus-pocus, nobility, integrity, public service, and romance of being a writer—the primary purpose and intention of writing is to get the work into a form that someone will want to publish so some people will want to read it. All the rest is legend and fable.

While I have used every technique in *Dare to be a Great Writer* in my own work, I did not originate the techniques. They have existed in the heritage of writing long before I became a professional writer. Other writers have revealed them in their work, in lectures, journals, interviews, articles, and other forms of communication. All I have done is taken some time off from my own fiction writing to bring a portion of them together, and to explain their function as clearly as I could.

Some of what I have written may offend by its bluntness. Some of it may seem cynical as I debunk areas of the fable and mythology in the "lore of writing techniques" and "how writers live." Although my interest is to reach many writers of potentially great books, I have not diluted or compromised any of what I know and believe should be written about writing. I have avoided the fluff and cutey-pie meanderings that are useless to the inexperienced writer and included only those techniques and attitudes that have worked for me and for other professional writers.

In the years I have been writing and instructing, I have been witness to appalling exploitations of inexperienced writers. They are lied to, misled, cheated, humiliated, and scandalously disregarded—by publishers, literary agents, university instructors, private instructors, and cunning professional writers who have abandoned their empathy and humaneness to gain support for their own vanities. The exploitation of inexperienced writers has become a new American industry.

This exploitation of the inexperienced will always occur. The innocent victim either creates the scoundrel, or the villain will always find an inexperienced writer to victimize. By drawing on the criteria for what defines an "inexperienced writer," I would comment that I was the most inexperienced of all when I began writing.

After being let out of high school, I became a drifter, a bum. Around 1949, I returned to New York City after a long stretch of being a hobo. I quit the road because I was feeling jinxed. I had almost been crippled, or killed, too many times. If you believe in luck, you know she's an ill-dispositioned lover. You never know when she'll cackle, "You've had it, baby—beat it!" and spit in your face.

I decided to clean up and begin relating to "respectable" society. My only possessions were a cigarette lighter, a clogged pocket watch, thirty-two dollars, and a clunky typewriter I had won in a dice game. I moved into my mother's apartment in Astoria and began looking for a job.

The only work I could do was donkey work, given to dummies. I became a shipping clerk for Bond Clothes, in their warehouse near the East River.

Then one night my older brother discovered my father hiding in a dark hallway, gun in hand, waiting for my mother to return so he could kill her. We calmed him down, dumped the gun, and did not report him to the police. With his criminal record, he would have been locked away for life. He was still on heroin and always in a junkie depression, always brooding—believing that when my mother left him, she had stolen his children. We promised to visit him every Saturday morning, buy him breakfast, and talk about "Duh good ol' days, see," if he would stop attempting to kill our mother. He agreed.

I was deeply shocked. Not because he was trying to kill my mother (he had tried it several times before) but because I could see myself ten years from now, standing inside my father's skin. I was younger and taller, sure—but there I was—a beaten down old junkie with no place left to drift but some hell where rages and hatreds and violences jeered you to sleep. Just a grim dead bum waiting to be hauled off by the garbage truck.

I was against the wall, clawing for an opening to hide in. I could hear the shovels of hell clattering at me, feel the opened ovens searing my soul, and I was terrified. It was then that I decided to use my typewriter to become an author.

There is no logic to the choices a man makes when he is fixed into a state of terror. All he knows is that he must choose, he must act. Thinking holds you in a grip of paralysis, taking an action changes things. Come on, come on, do it. What've you got to lose?

The phrase "I'll become an author" was like a great ram battering my mind. I didn't think: "I'll become a *writer*!" because I believed that all writers ever did was practice their handwriting and then teach penmanship. No. I have a typewriter. I'll become an *author*.

I was almost twenty-seven years old and little more than semiliterate. I rarely read even a newspaper, and when I did, I had to carefully trace my finger under the words and say them aloud to understand some of what I was reading. I was a glowerer, a brooder. I was in a constant state of rage. I was big, muscular, and crude, and few people liked me. Everybody I looked at knew I hated them. To the intellectual, the academician, the objective examiners of human behavior, I was an "interesting, challenging case."

I located a university-type school (The New School of Social Research) that did not require a conventional academic background. My high school diploma, fortunately, did not inform the New School's admissions office that almost all my credits were in woodworking, sheetmetal, electrical wiring, printing, bookbinding, carpentry. I had been an indifferent, troublesome student who was happiest prowling the streets of the Lower East Side of New York City. The system was preparing me for the "trades" so I could be removed from the streets before I became a social menace.

I enrolled in a creative writing class and was immediately overwhelmed by the erudition of the other students, and the writing instructor. I met writers like William Styron, Mario Puzo, Joseph Heller, Norman Mailer, James Baldwin, Vance Bourjaily, Harvey Swados, Hiram Hayden, Jack Kerouac, Thomas Berger. They knew so much. They spoke so clearly, as though they were actors in a British movie. They made me feel like a damp grub. To me they were soft: snails civilization had deprived of a shell.

I worked in the daytime and read books and wrote at night—then typed the handwritten pages and submitted them to Dr. Charles Glicksberg, the writing instructor. I developed a direct, tight manner of writing. I knew that if I kept my sentences short, no one would suspect I was ignorant. Short sentences couldn't contain much grammar. The words I used were abrupt, jab words. My concept of how to write a short story was to take a lot of loose bricks and some buckets of mortar and bring them to an interesting, dramatic sight everyone wanted to see. Then begin building a high and solid brick wall in front of the sight and force the people to climb the wall to see what was hidden behind it.

The stories were just scenes, sketches, fragments about the days I had lived, and the people I had hurt and the people who had destroyed me—they were raw, almost formless stories—all nerve and no tooth. But they vibrated. The instructor said, "Crude, yes. You might even say they were ill-mannered, and vulgar. But they stink with power!"

It wasn't intelligence, it wasn't imitative cunning, or academic razzle-dazzle, or style. It was content. It was the dynamic that came from the Great Depression starvation and the scrabble to stay alive. The other students wanted to hear what I wrote. Dr. Glicksberg was a proper Ph.D. scholar and would replace the obscenities with asterisks. "Go (asterisk) yourself, ya (asterisk). Take your no good (asterisk) and (asterisk) and shove it up your (asterisk) (asterisk) (asterisk)." Sometimes it was difficult to understand my stories because so much of the meaning was concealed behind asterisks.

Around 1950 Dr. Glicksberg was able to get funding for a paperback book of the students' writing. Some of the writers were William Styron, Mario Puzo, Thomas Berger, Jack Kerouac. A story I had written was put into the collection, which was mailed to hardback publishers. My story was titled "Death While Drinking Coffee," about a woman who tells her former lover that when he left her she tried to commit suicide. He tells her, "Nobody's worth dyin' for, ya dumb (asterisk)."

About three weeks later the writers began getting letters from editors, complimenting them on their work, and setting up appointments to discuss their "writing careers." I received a letter from George Joel, of Dial Press.

George Joel was a nattily dressed short man, with black hair combed straight back and delicate features that seemed crowded into the center of his small face. He was not intimidated by my rough manner (I was chewing a toothpick and smoking a cigarette). He had the pale blue paperback book on his desk. I pointed to it. "I'm in it." He nodded and told me he liked my writing.

"It has savagery, an undiluted power to it. What you write has obviously been lived. Are you working on a novel?"

I had never considered writing a novel. I was still trying to read my way through short stories without nibbling my tongue to shreds before falling asleep. But I sensed an opportunity. I was a dummy, but I was not stupid. Survival is gripped in the instincts: sniffing the "lucky break" is in your animal intuition. I was being challenged by Opportunity. Dare to live big—to be an author—or grub through life in the mediocre, in the penny-ante. I nodded to Mr. Joel.

"Sure, yeah, I'm writin' a novel."

"Excellent, Leonard. Why don't you bring some of it in so I can read it. If I like it, I'll offer you a contract, and an advance."

"Sure, okay. I'll bring it in next week."

I was now living in a $12-a-month cold water flat (no hot water, toilet facilities in the hallway) on West 60th Street. I stayed in the rooms for one week, writing until I was tranced with fatigue, and just slumped into sleep. This was an opportunity and I was bucking the mega-odds, taking the big dare. I had a chance of not being a criminal, a drifter always living on the knuckle.

I wrote about violence, poverty, booze and drugs; brutality, and fleeting times of love and courage and humor. I used myself as the major character. When I was done, I had seventy-five typewritten pages of a first novel.

I went to the offices of Dial Press and flung the manuscript onto the receptionist's desk, "Give this (asteriskin') book to that guy Joel, an' don't screw me up, or I'll twist off your (asterisk) head, see!" She was so astonished and afraid, her eyes rolled like someone about to faint.

Four days later I received a letter from George Joel, asking me to come to his office. He liked what I had written. He offered me a contract and $1000 advance—I signed, and I became an author.

From that day on, I laid it all on the line and went for whatever "being an author" could bring me. To me, the character of a man is determined by how he fixes himself into the "risk dimension" of life. Straining to live exactly the way others live, aping the manner and morality and being interchangeable with everyone who walks your street might bring you security and some safety—but there is no reward: no heart-slamming love, no gut-aching laughter. No rainbow of bubbling colors to climb along and be bright and glaring and let yourself be changed by the marvel of rich experience. You don't get what you earn; you get what you risk, what you dare.

After leaving George Joel's office, I remember standing on the corner of 5th Avenue and 42nd Street, during the hectic lunch hour, holding the contract on my chest, above my heart. I was pushed and shoved and stepped on but I stood and silently wept, and prayed: "Hey, God, gimme a break, okay? I'll give it all I got—and if what I've got's not enough, help me, will ya, okay? Will ya help me?" My tears were hurting and sweet.

In the spring of 1952, almost exactly one year and six months from when I signed the contract with Dial Press, my first novel *Down All Your Streets* was published. It achieved national critical acclaim and became a moderate best seller.

I was no longer a low bum, a hobo, a loser. I had faced down the challenge of Opportunity and dared to claim it for my life. "Hey, God, look at me, I'm gonna live, I'm an author!" I was an author. I would dare to become a great writer, and keep taking that dare no matter how many books I would have to write. You get what you dare, baby, and if you want big, you dare big—or you piddle away in a nickle-and-dime existence.

I am not engaged in some evangelical crusade which claims that "writing is the way to worldly salvation." I believe that if a writer can return to the world more than what the world has given him, then he has earned his keep, not only as a writer, but also as a human being. I also believe that whatever saves my life must be good. I have lived a God-blessed life, and I want to pass it on.

Dare To Be a Great Writer is not meant to be read page after page, from beginning to end. It is structured to be read on any page you open to.

If you are looking for help with a particular problem you've encountered with your own writing, the topic index at the end of this book will help you locate specific subjects covered in the text.

Coincidence

If the writer decides that coincidence (a startling shift of events independent from any action on the hero's part) is acceptable, he should use the coincidence *against* the hero.

When an act of coincidence is used against the hero, it is an unanticipated, but believable, misfortune. When the coincidence is used *in favor* of the hero, it becomes an obvious gimmick used by a writer who has exhausted his resources for invention.

Story Mark is building an irrigation system that will turn an area of Nevada into an immense oasis. He is being funded by the government.

Example (coincidence for hero) The newly elected president is a violent anti-ecology fanatic. He cuts off all funds for ecology projects. Angrily, Mark stabs a shovel into the ground. He hears an odd sound. He begins digging and finds a treasure chest of diamonds left by a wandering tribe of Incas. Mark uses the wealth to finance the project.

This is an obvious ploy by the writer to conveniently extract Mark from the crisis. Also, there is nothing heroic on Mark's part to overcome the insurmountable odds against finishing the irrigation system. No exorbitant demands are placed upon his character to sustain his stature.

Example (coincidence against hero) Mark is doing well with the irrigation project. The new anti-ecologist president stops the funding. Mark's crew is dedicated and works without pay. Then one man, while digging, uncovers a fortune in buried Inca treasure. He divides it with the others on the crew, and they abandon Mark and the irrigation project.

Because the coincidence works against Mark, it becomes another setback he must overcome if he is to remain heroic. Characters with good luck are blessed. They never achieve, they merely garner blessings.

Information Planted in Dialogue

When the writer uses dialogue as a plant for information, rather than speech, the dialogue becomes unbelievable. The reader sees the information, rather than hearing the sound of people speaking.

Example A husband and wife are in the living room. He is upset. He has a dreadful confession to make. He wrings his hands. He begins.

"Susan, I have a dreadful confession to make. Now that we've been married for seventeen years and three months, and we have three children—Nathan, Will, and Martha—and our home, which is a three bedroom, two bath and double garage hacienda-type structure, is almost paid for, except for $8,956 that remains, I want to say that for years now, I have been an undeclared drunk."

The information in his dialogue is obviously planted. She knows most of it—so should the reader. This background information should be brought in through other techniques, or devices, which are not obvious. Usually, a line of description follows to allow Susan to speak.

Example Susan rubbed her forehead and sighed forlornly.

"Well, Benjamin, you know that when we met at the high school prom and I was wearing the corsage you gave me—two red roses and a white carnation—and my ambition was to become a nurse which I sacrificed that I might marry you, but I was a Fundamentalist Lutheran and had to obey your wishes—I have been aware now, for years, of your drinking."

The content of dialogue should refer to the immediate topic between the speakers. There can be references to the past, but they should be brief. This material about the past is sneaked in during the dialogue because it is not important enough to warrant a scene or a long recollection. If past material is made too prominent in "present" dialogue, the present dialogue becomes inauthentic. If the dialogue of the characters lacks credibility, the characters become unbelievable.

Start at the Center of the Scene

After fifty pages of the novel, the writer can begin using "writing-saving" techniques. With fifty pages already accepted by the reader, there is some assurance that he will continue reading. It is now that the writer can consider beginning in the "center" of critical scenes, without including the beginnings.

Scene (after 50 pages) A sixty-year-old man is in love with a younger woman. He has grandchildren. He is willing to divorce his wife to marry the younger woman. He is gravely troubled about disrupting everyone's life.

This can be a critical scene in the novel. An old relationship ends, a new one begins. There is the traditional way of writing the scene.

Outline of scene The man goes into a bar. He thinks. Remembering the past, planning the future. He imagines the scene that will occur with his wife. His desire for the younger woman is intense. He leaves the bar. He will confront his wife. He hesitates at the door. He goes into the house. He hesitates, then begins the confrontation. This is the CENTER OF THE SCENE. It begins pleasantly and ends with hatred and violence.

The introspections of the man can be distributed through earlier scenes—as the old and new relationships are being developed. By page fifty the reader knows the major characters: their conflicts, motives, character. The preparation in the bar is wasted. START THE SCENE AT THE MOMENT OF CONFRONTATION.

Example He walked into the living room and draped his coat on a chair and breathed deeply. Emily sensed he was troubled. He leaned over the chair and glanced at her, then looked down. "Emily," he muttered, licking his dry lips. "I have something to tell you. I met a young woman and . . ."

The beginning of the scene (in the bar) is mere preparation for reaching the center where the first intense thrust toward the climax happens. Quite often the preparation for reaching the center of the scene is the writer's way of *feeling* himself into the scene. The reader does not want to read preparation. The reader wants to get right to the content and continue reading.

Economy in the novel does not always mean the elimination of unnecessary writing. It can also mean not imposing unnecessary reading (excessive use of details, rambling introspection, etc.) on the reader.

Simplistic Story Lines

When developing a short story, avoid SINGULAR, one-dimensional stories that move from one moment to another, without deviation. They are predictable. There are no distractions or surprises. They lack suspense and excitement.

Example (singular story line) Frank's business is failing. He decides to burn his factory for the insurance money. He vows to begin again. He plans to pay back the illegally gained money by donating it to charity. He plans the arson, then performs it. He is caught or he is not caught.

The only suspense the writer can create in this singular story line is through the mechanics of how Frank commits the arson and if he does or does not avoid detection. To keep those mechanics interesting, the plot must become bizarre, contrived. There is a high risk of becoming unbelievable.

Example (complicated story line) Frank's business is failing. He enrolls in a fire-prevention school to learn how to set fires without leaving traces. He asks particular questions which arouse the instructor's suspicions. Frank learns what he must know for his arson, and leaves the class. He prepares a fire bomb and sets it. The instructor, who is following him, sees Frank leave the building. He rushes in to defuse the bomb. It explodes. Frank, knowing the instructor will be killed, charges in and rescues him.

The ending is optional. Frank can abandon the instructor and collect his money or he can rescue him and face indictment for arson.

A complicated story should always contain two plot lines. The major plot line, through which the major characters play their parts in the events. The secondary plot line, or supporting plot, creates the handicaps, distractions, added conflicts, additional suspenseful situations.

A singular story is always obvious and uninteresting. Its predictability eliminates intensity and suspense. A complicated story with two plot lines is suspenseful and compelling. The reader knows the story will end—but the way it will end cannot always be predicted.

Heroes Against Villains

If the villain is a pushover, then the hero who defeats him is not truly heroic. He is merely struggling against an average handicap. Villains should be equal to the hero in character strength and should have more resources for asserting victory. Both must have monumental strength and stature.

Good and *Evil* are moral judgments based on the interests of those who regulate society. Depending on the century being written about, the writer selects a spectrum of moral values for the hero and villain to function with. As the story justifies the hero's effort to succeed, you must also explain the villain, through his personal values. They should be brought together many times for the purpose of clashing.

Example (hero) He wants to clear out the ghettos and build low-rent apartments for welfare families. Though he will gain celebrity for his efforts, his first interest is humanity. A woman loves him.

Example (villain) Born in an Egyptian slum, he fought his way out with dedicated ruthlessness. He has murdered some enemies who tried to stop him. He owns the land the hero wants. He intends using it for a toxic dump for his chemical factories. He loves the hero's woman. By destroying the hero he believes she will love him instead. He must have her.

The sooner the writer brings the enemy into the hero's life, the greater the opportunities for merging both stories. To create suspense and excitement, the villain should be winning the battle for the greater part of the novel, pitting his enormous resources against the hero's few. It should appear impossible for the hero to triumph.

Then, as the hidden weaknesses (evil) of the villain begin to gain tyranny over his reason, the indomitable character (good) of the hero begins to shift the balance in the hero's favor. The longer you sustain the villain's evil strength, the more sympathetic the hero becomes. So when the hero finally triumphs, it is a triumph indeed!

The Anecdote as Model for a Short Story

If short story writers would analyze the structure of an effectively told anecdote, they would clearly understand the traditional short story form. A typical anecdote contains all the techniques present in the competently crafted short story. It is an idea that has become a story developed through a plot line. There is narration, foreshadowing, dialogue, motivation, characterization, description, suspense, crisis, and a conclusive end.

> **Example (anecdote)** A drunk is driving up a mountain road during a rain storm. He smashes through the rail and is flung from the car. He grasps a loose branch in the mountainside and hangs in the air. "Dear God," he prays, "Save me!" An angel appears. "God will help you." The man is afraid.
> "I'll do anything, just have Him save me."
> "God wants to know if you trust Him."
> "Yes, I trust Him. I'll do anything to prove it. I'll never drink again."
> The branch loosens. The man looks down. He is 3,000 feet above a roaring river. Only the light from the angel is present. "Do you really trust God?" the angel asks again. "I trust Him, I'll do anything to prove it." The angel nods. "All right, let go of the branch."

The *situation* and *characterization* are in the opening sentence: a drunk driving in a rain storm. *Action:* crash through rail. *Opening suspense:* grasping branch. *Motivation:* to stay alive. *Secondary character:* the angel. *Plot line:* possibility of rescue. *Informational dialogue:* help is available. *Sustained suspense:* ". . . if you trust Him." *Foreshadowing:* "I'll do anything to prove it." *Inner revelation* and *character change:* "I'll never drink again." *Description of danger:* loosening branch; roaring river below. *Continued suspense:* "Do you really trust God?" *Mystery:* how will angel save him? *Heightened suspense:* "I'll do anything . . ." *Crisis and story point:* "Let go of the branch." (*Added mystery:* does he or doesn't he let go?)

Just as there are a variety of anecdotal forms, so are there a variety of short story forms. Inside a lean anecdote is a fat short story ready to be written.

Characters Writing Themselves

Writers must not be intimidated by myths about writing. They must only be concerned about the *realities* of writing.

A myth that has been around for many years is that a writer has not reached the core of a character until that character starts writing for the writer. That is a romantic and unrealistic precept. It was probably originated by the gropings of some literary critic trying to explain how Dostoevsky, Proust, Tolstoy, Dickens, Joyce, and other great writers were able to explore the characters they wrote about.

It was later picked up by writing instructors who had studied all the theories about writing and writers, but had no intimate, experiential workaday insights into its procedures.

Characters are dead images. Characters have no minds, no relationships, and do not cavort about the pages in a self-motivated, self-energized search for a story. They cannot analyze, interpret, reveal, or create themselves. Characters think, feel, speak, and act only when the writer decides on their function, and when it is their suitable time. The writer is always in control of his writing. He can never legitimately claim, "The character made me do it!"

A writer is not some bogus medium sitting in a dumb, wordless trance, biding time until the *spirit character* whacks him, demanding, "Hey, wake up, I'm ready to write you!" If characters were floating around the cerebral realms in some incorporeal state until they located a wishy-washy writer to express them, they would want to dominate the novel. They would obsess on being the "stars," and overwrite themselves. They would gobble the action and talk endlessly.

This concept of a story or novel "being written by the characters" is a cheap bid to promote a mystique about writing. Writing is something that someone does. Day after day after day. The writer reaches the depths of a character because he has skills and know-how.

There are no "one-novel" writers. There are only novelists who have stopped writing.

Use Introspection Sparely

If writers are concerned about the value of *introspection* (a character's thoughts), they have cause to be. The function of introspection often depends upon the time (publishing era) in which you are writing. Perhaps beginning with Marcel Proust's *Remembrance of Things Past* introspection achieved prominence. Yet writers do not realize that if Proust submitted his fiction to a publisher today, it would be rejected for two reasons: (1) not enough story, (2) excessive introspection. Today's publishers would also reject *Moby-Dick, The Brothers Karamazov, War and Peace,* for the same reasons.

You are writing in an era where story line and events dominate. Introspection, though important, must be used sparingly and selectively. Introspection reveals information about situations and relationships that the reader cannot gain through a clinical description of activity. It is also used for demonstrating the changes happening in your characters and their relationships.

Example John hurried about the airport terminal searching for his wife. He looked for a woman wearing a red angora hat.

This description merely shows John's activity. It does not offer information about his attitudes, or his feelings.

Example John hurried about the airport terminal searching for his wife. He would demand that she stay at home. *Our children are more important than her pointless medical convention.* John looked for a woman wearing a red angora hat. *God, how I hate her ridiculous hats.*

You now know why he is searching for his wife. You learn something about their relationship, his wife's profession, that they have children, and what he thinks of her taste in hats.

Activity is a sequence of actions that reveals only a minimum of information. The reader has no clear insight into what this activity might mean. The character's introspection offers this explanation.

Information from Secondary Characters

A writer cannot always allow the major character to know everything about himself. Characters, like real humans, have perceptual limitations. Yet, if important information that the character cannot know about himself is vital to the story or relationships, this information must be included for the reader. An effective technique is to provide this information through the viewpoint of another character.

What a secondary character assumes or judges as meaningful about a major character becomes factual or at least possible.

Example A bank president devotedly loves his only daughter. To him, the relationship is wholesome, though slightly indulgent. But his attachment to the girl is more than the conventional father-daughter relationship. In the novel, it is imperative that he be unaware of this.

If the major character is not allowed to realize this "unwholesome" attachment to his daughter, the reader might not perceive that it exists. The writer may not want to impose this information onto the president's characterization lest it appear as some glib psychological explanation. By using the viewpoint and interest of a secondary character, the writer can gain a qualified access to establishing this information.

Example The bank president and his daughter are lunching at a restaurant. They are chatting in whispers and muted laughs. Three bank executives, seated at a table in another part of the restaurant, observe them. One mutters, "They look more like lover and mistress than father and daughter." His scandalous remark causes the others to become silent. The executive then has a brief moment of introspection about the unwholesome nature of the relationship.

This information that the character cannot know, and which the writer doesn't want to impose through narration or exposition, is now part of that father-daughter relationship. Though the executive's observation is only a speculation, the observation becomes a possibility.

General Sex Scenes

Whatever is natural to human desire and behavior should not be alien or exiled from the writer's examination.

General sex scenes—lovemaking, copulating, coupling, lust or passivity—are used for specific reasons in a story or novel. A sex scene should be used to cause change in character, relationship, and event. The assortment of protuberances, cavities, and contours of the human anatomy and how they are employed is never more important than what happens within the people involved in an act of sex. Whether two people of the opposite sex, the same sex, or several people of assorted sexes are engaged in this activity, the purpose of the scene is to strike change in them. As the result of these changes, opportunities are opened for changes in the story, through events or situations.

If a man and woman have been married for thirty years and you depict them during sex, you must use that scene either to affect their present relationship, or to expose an aspect of their relationship that was not known before. Otherwise why bother describing an activity they (presumably) have been conducting for thirty years?

Example (long-standing relationship) They lay beside each other, gasping. She waited, tensely. When she heard his muffled snores, she grinned, happily. After thirty years of making love he finally went to sleep without first smoking a cigarette.

When two or more people are viewed in a sex scene for the first time, the scene must serve as an interval that changes them, individually, and in their relationship. There is no other reason for bringing them to this intimate point. They must be changed.

Example (their first time together) They lay beside each other as though hiding in the darkness. He yawned, "Your name is Sharon, isn't it?" She shifted away from him, disliking the odor of his cologne. And he was the president of a perfume company. She said, "No, it's *Charon*." She would never prostitute herself again, just to get a job. Never. He edged onto his side, squinting at her. "Having a good time, Ms. Charon?" Though she hated to lie, she needed the job. "You were overwhelming." He yawned again, "But of course."

Unless you are writing for a readership of voyeurs, the athletics of sexual action eventually become tedious. So do descriptions of anatomical possessions already owned by most people. Lust, passion, sensuality, pleasure, impotence, virility, failure, accomplishment, all serve to impose uncommon *pressure* on the participants. This pressure is used to provoke insights and realizations the characters could not acquire under different circumstances. Sexual pressure is unlike any other pressure.

Narrating the Small Scenes

An appropriate time for *narration* is when the writer wants to include a group of small, individual scenes that are not particularly dramatic. They are scenes that are little more than a statistical detailing of the present. They convey the passage of time, changes of place, the activity of daily living. They are unexciting, but necessary. The information must be included, but must not interfere with the motion, the pace of the story.

Story thus far A family has been forced to migrate to America.

The scenes (a) The family is taken in by relatives (b) The parents find jobs in the city (c) The children attend public school (d) The parents earn enough money to rent their own apartment (e) The assimilation period continues with bland regularity (f) They are accepted into the community (g) During a birthday party the police demand entry and arrest the son for first degree murder.

While this period of assimilation is necessary for authenticating the family's background in America, dramatizing each scene would require too many pages. The technique of *narration* is appropriate at this time.

Example Their first months passed as gradually as the appearance of seasons. David and Miriam attended public school, quickly learned the language and began instructing their parents. Sarah's seamstress work became recognized as artistic, and people brought their worn clothes to be mended. In April, Benjamin was promoted from shipping clerk to junior salesman. Everyone worried about the rebellious streak in Reuben who refused to attend services in the synagogue.

By grouping these undistinguished scenes together into a collective narration, the reader gains an awareness of the family's social progress without having to read an itemized invoice of undramatic scenes. The writer maintains the flow of the novel without irreparably damaging the pace.

"Find-and-Stop" Novels

Beginning in the mid-1960s, a novel structure that has been accorded stature by the public is the *find and stop* extravaganza. Its momentum is a 'forward thrust' that never slows. The reader rarely becomes involved in the characters. The novel is designed for rapid, forgettable reading. The structure is mainly episodic. It is essential that the writer become familiar with this structure. It requires skill.

Story A fanatic leader of zealous but misguided patriots plans to assassinate a president, or a pope, or to destroy the world.

Structure: plot line They either notify the authorities or their plan is discovered. The hero, or heroes, are assigned to "find and stop" the villains. Until the three-quarter mark in the novel, the villains become stronger, the heroes are in a constant state of failure.

They are confronted by sexually electric women (or men) who either help or betray them. The "good" agents always sacrifice their "sex/love" relationships to uphold their patriotic integrity. At the three-quarter point of the novel, the villains begin failing, the heroes begin succeeding. Just before the trigger is pulled, or the bomb is set, or the lethal bacteria is released, the president, or the pope, or the world is saved. At the novel's end, some heroes are allowed to die to accomplish their cause.

The novel is unadulterated adventure. The characters are unimportant as people. The predesigned plotting dominates. The technical competence of device, mayhem, and plot complication keeps the novel moving forward.

The "find-and-stop" structure should be studied for use in all forms of writing. To use it effectively, the writer must be surgically selective with his content. The reason why people do what they are doing must be revealed through their actions—without the techniques of narration or introspection to explain. The explanations are incorporated in the actions of the characters.

"Make-It-or-Else" Deadlines

All unpublished writers have, at one time, declared, "If I don't make it in one year (or two, or three), I'll stop trying to become a writer. At least I know *I tried.*" This is a pointless, limiting deadline. There is no recognizable or even vague sign that appears to reveal that the writer should continue, or quit. The two most valued attributes in the writer's character are faith in self and dogged persistence.

Publication attitudes, publishing conditions, and public preferences are unstable. The writer is not struggling against known resistances. Circumstance in every phase of publishing jumps like a berserk checker game. If the writer persists, his time will come and he will be prepared to accept its rewards.

When William Saroyan believed he was ready to be published, he composed a list of publications he assumed would accept his stories. With methodical persistence, he began sending them to one publication after another. When he had reached the end of his list, and *all* of his stories were rejected, he began sending them out again, *to the same publications*. On the second time around he began acquiring acceptances. Happily for American letters, Saroyan did not set himself a "make-it-or-quit" deadline. He believed in himself, and he persisted.

If all that was required of a person to achieve the stature of professional writer was to study the craft, put in time practicing, and then begin sending material out to be published—then anyone could become a professional writer. It would not be a profession, it would be a mundane form of employment.

In almost all instances, the greatest enemy the writer must continually confront is his own character. A writer does not work in the same time frame as the average person. He is contending with indefinable and quixotic shifts in circumstance. To overcome such tyrannizing odds, the writer must have faith in himself, and take his time.

Character Changes After Long Absences

Any time a character disappears for more than ten pages or so, even if the passage of time is only for two hours or two days, he should be redescribed, *from another aspect*.

Story Three young men have graduated from medical school. Albert is a pediatrician. Carl, an internist. Milton leaves the profession.

In an episodic novel, the writer often uses the viewpoint of three different major characters. He alternates their appearances, ascribing to each character a sufficient space to work out their individual roles. In a well-integrated story, Milton and Carl will appear in the sequences given over to Albert. Albert will appear in Milton's or Carl's sequences. Their lives are closely intertwined.

Example Albert gains a position in a hospital. In his sequence he has an affair with Carl's wife. Milton borrows money from Carl to open a pharmacy. When Carl's "viewpoint" takes over, a part deals with his disrespect for Milton, his reverence for Albert. Carl does not know of the affair Albert is having with his wife.

When one of the three major characters is absent from many pages—in his own viewpoint—he must be redescribed to reveal character changes so the story can be advanced. It is not to refamiliarize the reader with the character. It is only to gain an opportunity for revealing character changes (moral, physical, emotional, etc.) at each reappearance of the character. The writer does it quickly.

Example (after three days and a thirty-two-page absence) Milton no longer appreciates the high grades Carl had earned. They disproved his own progress, his own qualifications. He never realized how much he disliked Carl.

Example (after another twenty-six page absence) Milton knew that Albert was having an affair with Carl's wife. He would tell this to Carl, just before his most important exam. That would cut down his pride.

After one absence Milton has become disgruntled about becoming a doctor. After another absence, he is seen to be morally vicious.

False Limitations on First-Person Narrators

There is a misleading limitation placed on the use of the "first person," the "I." Writers are advised to use it only in short stories or short novels. The "single vision" of the narrator, it is said, makes it impossible to enter into the mind of another character.

To overcome this supposed limitation the writer should use a subtle shifting in the prose, which is developed in three stages.

Move from the *immediacy* of the first person, to a remoter focus of *objective* narration. Sustain this objective narration long enough to allow it to develop into another form of "third person."

Example (immediacy) I was afraid to let them bring me into the pre-operating room. I would be alone. I would be in bed, feeling the needles and tubes piercing my flesh. I would imagine all the cruel and heartless work that would be done on my ailing body.

(Objective narration) Dr. Ching came in and grinned at me. "This will be a piece of cake, Jerry. I've done two hundred operations of this type, and they were all successful." He patted my shoulder. I liked him. He never cared that other doctors hated his being Chinese.

(Like third person) He was born in a small province in South Korea. During the war he was left for dead in a ditch. An American soldier found him almost frozen stiff. He was taken to a hospital where he recovered. He swore that he would show his gratitude by becoming a doctor. He thought Americans were strange people. They always worry.

In the last paragraph the first person narrator has entered the mind and background of the Chinese doctor. If different material is desired—emotional, intellectual—the writer merely changes the content. When he has achieved the effect he desires he can then shift back to the hospital room, to the immediate—the first person.

Don't Use Static Openings

Do not open a short story or novel with a character sitting and thinking. It is not dramatic. It is static. A story should *happen* to a reader.

Example Martin Gilmore sat in his room, thinking. He did not like his thoughts. If he told his wife she would mock him. He thought, I will not tell her I'm leaving her. He kept thinking of excuses.

This is *preparation* for drama. It may pique the reader's interest for a moment, but it will not cause his participation. You cannot dawdle.

Example Martin Gilmore flung clothes into a valise. He would not tell his wife he was leaving her. She would stop him. He pushed down the valise lid. Suddenly, a rock smashed through the closed window. He cringed back. His wife already knew.

This opening is more effective. Your character is engaged in behavior that allows the reader to become involved. His thinking is directly related to the action. The situation is dramatic.

In a static opening, your descriptions appear forced and become inactive.

Example (static) A note was attached to the rock. Martin began reading the message. He was a short man with tufts of gray hair circling his baldness. He had slumped shoulders and trembling hands. The bedroom was elongated. The bed was mussed.

You are describing too much AND NOTHING IS HAPPENING.

Example (active) Martin picked up the rock and tore off the note it held. Sweat glistened on his baldness. His hands trembled as he read. His slumped shoulders tensed. "Your wife won't let you leave her." He rushed across the elongated room and snatched the valise from the mussed bed. Nothing on earth could make him stay.

Your descriptions are now part of the action. When descriptions flow with the action, they are given vitality. You are using details that contribute to the scene not merely describe the setting.

Research

Writers spend many hours researching the costumes, artifacts, food, armaments, and fixtures indigenous to the historical novels they are writing. Using all of this research, merely because you have it, is not advisable. To become a skilled writer you learn to make sacrifices.

Example (poor use of research) Sir Galavant slashed his Persian *Quaddara* sword at Sir Treleway's *escuffa*, the extra plate usually worn over the helmet when tilting. Sir Treleway, fighting with a long and narrow quadrangular blade, the *estoc*, dodged the blow, losing his *espalliers*, his shoulder guards.

Period details are used for authenticating the particular time and place. They are supports. They promote the writer's authority. They create atmosphere and credibility. They do not contain drama. They establish believability. The writer of a historical novel should decrease the use of authenticating details as the novel progresses.

Example (in the novel's beginning) The long Godstad ship skimmed through the calm waters. The sixteen oarsmen on each side pulled their oars in rhythmic regularity. Circular shields were fastened by ropes tied to the wooden grips inside the rail.

As you get further into the novel, you merely have to write: "The Godstad ship moved smoothly through the water." You do not have to overauthenticate by continually piling on the details of time and place.

In historical novels you first gratify the reader's desire to leave this present time (intellectual curiosity), then keep them from returning to the present time by the emotional content of your story. Research is fascinating only to the writer. The reader wants the substance of relationships and story events.

Italics in Introspection

Through a selective use of "flash insights" the writer can inject fragments of a character's past or thoughts in an action scene without slowing the pace. The technique utilizes typefaces—italics.

Scene In a territorial battle during the Civil War, a soldier is commanded to race across an open field to rescue a fallen general. Near the general is a copse of trees where there are two snipers waiting for someone to try the foolhardy, but courageous rescue.

The traditional technique for this pure action interval is to describe the soldier's rescue of the general in objective description.

> **Example** Billy raced in a zig-zag crouch. His arms were pistons pumping his body harder. Two bullets snapped dirt near his feet. The men behind him shouted encouragement. His breath kept bursting in his body. Two more shots cracked the air. Pain slashed across his neck. His boots kicked up dirt as he kept running to the general.

That is a competent, acceptable description of action.

The writer, constantly alert for an opportunity to resolve a character's problem, to define a deep feeling, to implant or reaffirm an attitude, will use this pure action scene for added information. It can be done through the use of short, one-sentence italics.

> **Example** Billy raced in a zig-zag crouch. His arms were pistons pumping his body harder. Two bullets snapped dirt near his feet. *If they give me a medal for this, I can go into politics.* The men behind him shouted encouragement. His breath kept bursting in his body. Two more shots cracked the air. Pain slashed across his neck. *Good. People vote for soldiers who were wounded rescuing generals.* His boots kicked up dirt as he kept running to the general.

The italicized sentences are too short to block the pace of the action. The scene is enriched with the soldier's humanness—a depth is dramatically revealed: a pressing ambition is emphasized.

Interlocking Episodes

Interlocking episodes are connected to each other, not only by their placement, but by how the closing end of one episode contains the beginning of the episode that follows. This structure can aid the writer in avoiding tedious preparation for the next scene. Get right into the next scene.

> **Story** Eddie, a petty thief, is deeply in debt to loan sharks. If he doesn't pay up on Tuesday he will be badly beaten. Eddie decides to rob a wealthy man known for always carrying large sums of cash.

Fulfilling this section of the novel will require three episodes.

Episode 1 Eddie knocks the wealthy man unconscious. While searching for the man's wallet, Eddie thinks about Charlie, the friend he is trusting to provide him with an alibi so he won't be accused of robbing the wealthy man. Charlie is viciously greedy.

There is now no need for "writing Eddie into" the next scene with Charlie. The last part of the robbery episode (Eddie's worrying about Charlie's loyalty) sets up immediate entry into the next scene.

Episode 2 Eddie and Charlie are arguing about money. Charlie won't establish Eddie's alibi unless he gets half the robbery money. While Eddie is counting out the money to Charlie, he knows he won't have enough left to pay off the loan sharks. Afraid of a terrible beating, Eddie decides to pack a suitcase of clothes, and leave town.

There is now no need to "write Eddie into" the next scene. The end of the previous episode contains the beginning of the episode that will follow. You have eliminated some tedious scene-preparing.

Episode 3 Open with the contents of Eddie's suitcase scattered on the bed. A bloody Eddie is lying on the floor while a loan-shark thug is counting out the remainder of Eddie's money. It's not enough.

All three scenes are interlocked because before each scene ended, a connecting factor was provided to lead into the next episode. The technique has eliminated the amount of writing needed to prepare the beginning of scenes. You get into the next episode because it is prepared for by the ending of the previous episode.

The interlocking episode structure will not work if the episodes do not immediately follow each other. The pre-preparation is too frail, too faint, to remain in the reader's mind if the related episode does not immmediately appear.

Don't Fear the Novel's Size

It is not the lack of talent, skill, will or time that stops a writer from beginning a novel. It is the fright that overwhelms him when considering the *entire* novel he wants to write. He considers all the plot lines, characters, backgrounds, motivations, and conflicts that must be accomplished, and the task becomes an awesome tyranny.

A writer should compare the creating of a novel to repairing a dilapidated house. He is like a carpenter with the tools, the time, and the know-how to begin. He does not attack the entire house, *all at once*. He works on it, portion by portion. He can fix a crooked doorway, tighten a squeaky floor—find an opening situation, create a character. He has repainted a wall before—written a ten page scene before. Novels, like houses, are tangible. They are not abstract, mysterious entities.

The carpenter knows that each part of the house he repairs belongs to the entire house. The writer knows that each scene he writes has a relationship and continuity to the entire novel. The entire novel is in him. He brings it forth in short parts.

The novel is not a living entity that must be conquered. The novel is a work of parts that must be put together. The writer builds one portion at a time.

There are splendid examples the writer can use for overcoming this fear of beginning a novel: THE EXISTENCE OF OTHER NOVELS. Millions of novels have already been written by millions of other people. Writers are not great men or great women. They are not exceptional, superhuman beings. They are only men and women who have created great writings.

Writers should never be so awed by the public relations legends promoted about the lives of writers that they are frightened by their extraordinary accomplishments. They are only writers. It is what they decided to become: it is the profession they constantly work at.

Start your novel today, *a little bit at a time.*

Physical Descriptions as Transitions

"Transition: Passage from one place, state, stage of development, type, etc., to another; change; also, the period, place, passage, etc., in which such a change is effected . . ." *(Webster's New Collegiate Dictionary).*

In writing, a transition is used to shift viewpoint, place, time, and tone. One basic type of subtle transition is the physical description.

Many writers either do not understand or appreciate the secondary use of a physical description. Physical descriptions not only establish a physical reality (sound, sight, smell, taste, touch), they also have transisting value. They are tiny, unnoticeable bridges.

To change viewpoint: Lila's viewpoint Lila thought the house was decrepit and frightening. While she slept, a ghost might cut her throat. (transition) *She brushed a cobweb from her cheek. It flicked through the dark and stuck to Ralph's face.* (Ralph's viewpoint) He snatched it from his nose, thinking, *Tonight, I'll pretend I'm a ghost and cut her throat.*
To change character mood: good mood Farley awoke suddenly. He laughed happily. He had dreamed that forty bikini-clad women were massag-

ing his scrawny torso. (transition) *He sat up and moaned with pain. The arthritis in his body felt like hardening cement.* (Bad mood) He moaned, "Rotten, no good, raunchy, mean body I got!"

To change from one place to another, then back again: living room Fred stopped reading and leaned back in the rocking chair. *He listened to the tick-tick-tick sounds his wife was making in the kitchen. He knew Bella was dicing onions for his omelette.* (Kitchen) Bella hurried to the stove. *Why do I always let the coffee boil over?* She lowered the flame under the coffee pot. (Living room) *Fred listened to the gurgling coffee pot and grinned. Why does she always let the coffee pot boil over?*

The descriptive phrases that serve as a transition should be selectively chosen. The beginning of the description should be related to the sentence before it: the end of the description should be related to the sentence that follows.

Example Marty dropped the wine glass and jumped back as it shattered. The noise was surprisingly loud. "What was that noise?" his wife called from the bedroom.

A transition is like a small bridge spanning a space. It is used for getting from one place to another without interrupting the motion forward.

The Adventure Novel and The Tragedy Novel

At times, it is wise to remove the weighty, intellectual aura from a literary form and view it as a working possibility to be used in the creating of a novel. The differences between *tragedy novels* and *adventure novels* is an example of this. To clearly understand these forms, they should be compared to each other.

Both adventure novels and tragedy novels contain major characters who are engaged in a life-or-death struggle. The major character of the adventure novel cannot be tragic, because he enters upon external adventures voluntarily. He consciously chooses to struggle against the evils of the world outside himself. His life or death may be tragic to himself, but the reader shares only his adventure. Although he may die, his death happens only after the evil has been destroyed. If he defeats evil, and lives, he is cheered. Because the evil he chooses to defeat is outside of him, he is heroic, but not tragic.

Adventure novel A cunning lawyer, trying to bilk Jeffrey Cane of his inheritance, has him committed to an insane asylum. Jeffrey escapes and kills the lawyer. He begins a crusade to kill all crooked lawyers.

In the adventure novel, the motivation for Jeffrey's killing of lawyers is obvious. Any additional information only broadens the explanation of the original motives. Jeffrey's motives never change or deepen. He is on a consciously chosen crusade. His joy in killing those he believes are evil is greater than the guilt he feels for committing evil. His struggle is not to stop himself, but to keep from being caught until all the crooked lawyers in the world are killed. The reader admires his cunning and gains excitement while he is being pursued. The reader pities the innocent victims, but enjoys the adventure.

The major character of the tragedy novel is compelled, by the content of his character, to become part of world events that will destroy him. His struggle is from within. His struggle is spiritual. He is driven as though by a terrible compulsion, which he tries to control, but cannot. The reader hates what he is compelled to do (his adventure) but joins in his inner struggle.

Tragedy novel Robert Dorn has the desire to murder young blondes who wear fake diamond earrings. He knows it is immoral, illegal, and a dangerous venture. Yet, though he wants to stop himself, he cannot.

In the tragedy novel, the reader becomes involved in Robert Dorn's struggle to stop murdering. Though the reader witnesses the murders, he has pity for Robert. HE CANNOT HELP HIMSELF. Readers sympathize with Robert's uncontrollable drive. (They have many such drives of their own.) Robert is possessed of a fierce compulsion, and it is tyrannizing him. The reader is sorrier for the murderer than for the anonymous victim. The reader does not know the victim, but is focused on the intimate, agonizing character of Robert.

When Robert prowls the city for another victim, the reader knows Robert's inner torment and how he is fighting the compulsion within him. "Don't do it, Robert," the reader pleads—and hopes this time he will not kill. When Jeffrey hunts another crooked lawyer to kill, the reader merely wonders how Jeffrey will elude the police. There is no torment in Jeffrey when he kills. Otherwise he would stop. Robert cannot stop himself. Jeffrey can.

Robert continually tries to understand why he is compelled to act in such a homicidal manner. His motivations are not fixed. They are constantly deepening. His soul and spirit are exposed. His contest is with the evil, the compulsion in himself. Only when he finally has an "enlightenment" that reveals his true motives—his individual type of compulsion—is he allowed to be caught or killed. Though he understands the flaw which has turned his life tragic, he cannot stop his own destruction. The reader loves and pities him.

These are general differences between the tragedy and adventure novel. Yet they share a basic similarity. Toward the three-quarter point, both major characters must experience changes in character and a drastic turn of events.

In the adventure novel, Jeffrey must begin realizing he is fully purged of hatred for crooked lawyers and swears to stop killing. The writer must then devise another surprising circumstance that will not allow him to stop killing.

Example A corrupt lawyer has been studying and following Jeffrey. He then calls on Jeffrey and shows him irrefutable proof that could convict Jeffrey as the Crooked-Lawyer Killer. The corrupt lawyer wants money for his silence. Though Jeffrey has sworn to stop killing, he must get the damning evidence by killing the corrupt lawyer.

In the tragedy novel, Robert must begin gaining control over his need to kill. He finally dominates his compulsion to murder by turning away from a victim who is a young blonde wearing fake diamond earrings. But his peace of soul does not last long. His victory over the compulsion to kill was only temporary. He must keep killing and suffering, until he is killed.

Example In a desperate attempt to stop himself from killing blondes wearing fake diamond earrings, Robert goes to a hypno-psychiatrist who puts him under. He remembers that his younger sister, a vicious blonde nine-year-old who had a murderous temper, stole her mother's earrings, and was caught. To avoid being punished, the girl smashes her mother's head with a brass table lamp. The mother returns home from the hospital, totally paralyzed. Robert realizes he hated his sister and has been killing blondes as a substitute for killing his sister. He is now free of the desire to kill his sister. But the hypno-psychiatrist happens to be a blonde woman wearing fake diamond earrings. Robert cannot control himself. He kills her. Now he knows he is beyond help and is an irrational murderer. He goes to a high building and hurls himself off.

Although readers are heartbroken over Robert's tragic end, they are happy he is no longer around to keep killing blondes.

Stylized Prose

Though the novel is a demanding form, it does have some mercies. Every writer fashions himself to be a "prosist," a talent capable of lyrical flights, able to use prose in a style so grand that he can make great poets seem like senile doodlers. As he becomes more professional, he works to control this vanity. Professionalism is the beginning of writing wisdom. Yet there are intervals when he can sneak this grand writing into the functional writing, without debilitating or diminishing its function.

Example (functional prose) Paul gripped the sides of the chair as Mr. Rogers shouted that he was an incompetent fool. He did not look at the older man. He was ashamed for having lost the bank a $3,000,000 account. After he was dismissed as chief loan officer, he would quietly commit suicide.

The prose is not distinguished. It is functional. Its purpose is to establish a situation, some attitudes, a possible future action. Yet it is also a moment that is vigorous with emotion and intense with drama. It is strong enough to absorb some "arty" prose without being too weakened.

Example (stylized prose) The rage in Mr. Rogers' voice roared against Paul's consciousness, causing him to press himself to the wall, feeling faint as he imagined his years of loyalty to the bank, the love affair he was having with Mr. Rogers' wife, his aspiration to ascend to the throne of the vice presidency, smashing, shattering against the stones of disappointment now amassing in the president's disgust for his incompetence. The sighs of truth softened in him and in languid silence Paul saw a gun touching his temple. . . .

Such "lyrical" or stylized writing is permissible only when the intensity of the situation is strong enough to withstand the invasion of artistry. This grandiose prose often contributes to the disposition without maiming the content. But it must be used effectively and without such frequency that the display of being talented in writing stylized prose becomes more important than the content. The reader should first read the content, then notice the prose.

The Montage Novel

The montage story is one of the most difficult forms to accomplish. It requires an undeviating control and clever interlocking of different stories, plot lines, recollections/flashbacks, and viewpoints. It is a story form which has a character-puzzle the reader must piece together.

"Montage: Any literary . . . composite combining and blending more or less heterogeneous elements usually superimposed or overlapping each other . . ." (*Webster's New Collegiate Dictionary).*

Example Four women are playing bridge. They are biding time, waiting for billionaire Simon Firshman to arrive. He will name the woman he has chosen to marry. Each woman has a reason for wanting to become his bride.

The montage story is done in fragments, selectively shuffled and arranged to create suspense and drama. It is written through the viewpoint of each player. The writer shifts from viewpoint to viewpoint, bringing out more of the story and plot as the four viewpoints unfold.

Example Sandra wants his wealth. Myra wants to kill him for having ruined her father's bank. Lois is a secret hypnotist who will entrance him into signing over his money. Judy loves him.

In the conventional multiple-viewpoint story, the writer can use the viewpoint of major, secondary, tertiary, and even incidental characters. In the montage story, viewpoints are limited to only the major characters. Any other viewpoints might clutter the puzzle with too many small pieces of information that could keep getting lost, or become distracting.

The primary type of transition from one viewpoint to another is dialogue that appears as "passing-the-time-of-day-talk," but should contain a portion of each character's story or attitude, to reveal more of their characters.

Example Lois hoped the others did not notice her hands tremble as she thought of Simon Firshman's physique. She muttered, "I'll bid two no trump," hating the lust she was feeling. Judy said, "I'll pass," and sighed. "I think what Simon's putting us through is really cruel." Myra shrugged, "Simon's done worse things to us. And I'm not the only one who has scars to prove it." Sandra snickered, "He tried beating me once. I kicked him where the sun don't shine." Myra's lips trembled, "He deserved more," and stared dully at her cards. They looked like the tombstones around her father's grave. *Dad, Dad, I'll ruin Simon, you'll see, just as he ruined you.* Listlessly, she played her cards, remembering the morning she met Simon. . . .

The paragraph began in Lois's viewpoint, continued on to carry the viewpoints of Judy, Myra, and Sandra, and ended in the viewpoint of Myra. All through dialogue—leaving bits of information as it is spoken.

The women should not be strangers to each other. What they know of each other should provide hidden information. Each viewpoint brings out this information and reveals hidden information about the billionaire.

Example (Judy's viewpoint) She despised Sandra. Always flaunting her body like a flag. Come, salute me. Simon wanted more than sex from a woman. He wanted friendship. Myra said, "My, I have a terrible hand." Judy almost snickered. You also have a terrible soul. Simon did not ruin your father. Your father tried to ruin Simon. Judy clenched her cards. He will pick me.

The billionaire's story is the secondary story. Since he appears only at the end of the story, he cannot reveal his own plot line. All of his story must emerge through the information, attitudes, and memories each woman has about him. The billionaire's plot line is written through the women. Each reveals an enlightening facet of his character that none of the others knows. The reader pieces the parts together. It is the reader who develops the drama and impact of the billionaire's story.

The levels of tension are derived from the suspense in the present. Which woman will he select? Does the reader know before he enters? There is little action in what is happening *now*. The action and drama occurs through the short recollections and short flashbacks that each woman has about her own past and how it is related to the billionaire's story.

If the writer desires to reveal some of the billionaire's viewpoint, it must be accomplished during the flashbacks of the women. But this is not advisable. The billionaire is interesting and complex only as long as he remains mysterious, or a segmented character whom the reader must fit together into a whole. It is through piecing these fragments of the billionaire together that the reader decides upon which woman he chooses, and why. The writer should use distraction devices and false leads *to mislead the reader.*

The Alchemy of Writing

None of what you are writing makes sense, right? The characters have the depth of cellophane. The story staggers like a convulsive drunk. The plot line lacks logic, there is just no point in going on. Becoming a professional writer is just a delusionary dream.

Good. Now you are really into your writing. Now you are about to reach the ability you have not touched before. You are into the dark, almost arcane dimension of the writing process that no one can explain. But before you can grow as a writer, you must touch this unexplainable dimension.

This is where the character of the writer is tried.

It is in this dimension that the *alchemy* of writing happens. Just as the alchemists of old labored to transmute lead into gold, and could not, so the writer labors to turn tripe into treasure. The alchemist fails—the writer succeeds.

All of a sudden, in time no quicker than a toad's blink, your writing changes. It is marvelous, exactly what you wanted. But why does it take this suddenness so long to happen? The reason eludes analysis, but the method of achieving it is comprehensible. It is the writer's tenacity, his persistence, his faith.

The writer does not always recognize his own progress. He is so concentrated on bringing his work to "rightness" that he does not realize all the skill he has already accumulated and is using. He is not only developing more complicated techniques, but is also, unknowingly, creating an administrator within his own writing process. This administrator is always shuffling, arranging, bringing it all together in seeming suddenness. And then the writer goes on. He keeps writing, because that is what a writer does.

Sometimes a writer's year is used writing from one suddenness to another—from one alchemy to another alchemy. But only if he persists, and has faith in himself, does this sudden alchemy happen.

The General Purpose of Foreshadowing

Foreshadowing is a technique used in *present* situations that points to what may happen in the future. It is a buffer device, a deliberate preparation the writer uses to set up the reader for accepting and believing future changes in relationships, character, plot, and events. The foreshadowing can be subtle, obvious, or stated.

Subtle A forest ranger, making his rounds, notices a cave he has not seen before. Before he can look into it, he hears a scream. He spurs his horse to the person screaming, leaving the cave uninvestigated.

Obvious While idly watching television, a man is shown cleaning his revolver. He looks to the wall. There is a photograph of the police commissioner. He aims the gun and giggles, "Boom, you're dead."

Stated Tomorrow he would resign his office of governor.

In relating a story, the writer's objective is to create a group of fascinating characters engaged in a sequence of events that form a compelling tale. At no time should the writer allow the reader to be unduly surprised or shocked out of the reading experience. Shock or surprise, in writing, is meant to draw the reader deeper into the lives and events in the story. Foreshadowing is like a casual whisper, "Don't be surprised if this happens," or a demanding shout, "Don't be shocked if this change in character or plot line or relationship happens."

Example If a child is going to suddenly grow a third eye in the center of his forehead, sometime before that development occurs, it is wise to have the child in a laboratory, toying with a vial of green pills. Before his father, the mad scientist, chases him from the laboratory, the child should have swallowed one of the pills.

The *type* of writing (moody, harsh, tense, etc.) can foreshadow the disposition of the scene that follows. The description of a character can foreshadow how he will function.

> **Example** Gary had a narrow face and always rubbed his hands when he was in the presence of money.

Opening Chapters

A first chapter not only begins the novel, it also prepares the reader for the many techniques the writer will use throughout the novel. The presence of these techniques in the first chapter allows the reader to accept them in longer, more complicated forms, as the novel continues. For example, if the novel is episodic in structure, develop the first chapter through a series of separate incidents. There should be at least three "breaks"—a time break, a place break, a viewpoint break.

> **Example** You open with a crisis: A diplomat is negotiating with an enemy to pay ransom to a terrorist group that has kidnapped the ambassador. (break) You shift to the leader of the terrorists who is instructing his men on how to pick up the money when it is paid. (break) You shift to the ambassador's wife who is busy arranging the pageantry for her husband's funeral. You have three stories, characters, situations.

If you intend to use multiple viewpoint throughout the novel, then establish in the first chapter a sequence of viewpoints within each of the scenes you use to establish the structure of the episodic novel.

> **Example** The enemy agent smiled as the diplomat telephoned the ambassador's wife. These people were happy only when tyrannized, he thought. The diplomat said, "I assure you, Mrs. Thurmaine, we are doing all we can to hasten Lawrence's return." Her whining voice was irritating. The ambassador was probably happier with the terrorists. "Why did they have to take him now?" Mrs. Thurmaine asked. "We have guests coming for the Fourth." She nibbled her lower lip, annoyed. The diplomat didn't care, and Lawrence never enjoyed her fabulous parties.

Using the techniques in miniature that you will be using later on in bulk keeps the reader's attention from being jogged by the sudden appearance of new techniques. Never allow the reader to put the novel down to wonder, "Now why did the writer do that?"

Using Dialogue to Foreshadow

Dialogue is often used for foreshadowing. Characters speak in order to communicate, to express themselves, to persuade. They can also plant future story and relationship possibilities in the present action.

> **Example** Two murderers are talking. "Looks like a bad storm's comin' in. You think it'll cause Jimmy to pop outta the water?"
> "No. I wrapped fifty pounds of chain around him."
> "Shoulda made it a hunnred. A bad storm might pop him up."

Any competently written scene serves a dual purpose. (A) It advances the present story. (B) It foreshadows a later, more important event.

> **Example** An alcoholic airplane mechanic is warned that if he's caught drinking on the job, he will be fired. He is assigned to check a cargo plane that will carry high explosives. He fights a heavy desire for drink while performing his job. His hands shake as he fills emergency oxygen tanks, tightens bolts, greases bearings. He finishes the job and is happy he conquered his desire to drink.

The primary purpose of the scene is to show that the mechanic can fight his alcoholism. The secondary purpose is to reveal that in his struggle with a desire to drink, he is careless. Later on, the cargo plane crashes.

Foreshadowing has a linkage effect in establishing *continuity* throughout the story or novel. As one scene suggests the later appearance of another scene, the later scene causes a recollection of the earlier scene. This brings the past and present together in a continuing flow. It aids in creating the impression that the story, though emerging a little at a time (as it is being read) is happening all together in the fullness of experience.

Using Images to Describe Attitude

Use images, including similes and metaphors, to enhance the reality of a setting. They emphasize detail that might ordinarily be lost among other details. By "imagizing" a detail you imply the existence of other details. *"Arrows, like a storm of sleet, burst from the castle parapet."* You need not describe the arch and flight of the arrows, the archers, the castle. Images give sparkle to ordinary prose. Images also express character attitudes without an intrusive explanation from the writer.

"The clouds moved across the sky," is not as interesting as *"The clouds dragged along the sky like gray laundry bags."* You have made a common detail more interesting and created a mood.

"The man's nose was a thick finger poking at you when he spoke," is more graphic than *"The man's nose was thick,"* or *"He had a thick nose."*

Use images sparingly and selectively. *"Albert glanced to the corner. The lamp post stood on the sidewalk like an underfed hobo."* Albert's mood is obviously low, depressed. Change the image and you change the attitude. *"The lamp post stood on the sidewalk like a lean clown balancing a bright globe,"* and Albert's disposition is cheerful, merry. Since a lamp post is a common fixture on a city street, you don't have to describe the remainder of the street: the mailbox, the curb, the house stoops and doorways, to make it a convincing street. The reader fills in what you have implied.

Using a physical detail in one sentence and defining a character's mood in the following sentence can cause overwriting and a separation between the setting and the character.

Example (physical detail) Albert glanced to the corner and saw a lamp post. (Character's mood) He felt depressed.

Using the physical detail and the character's mood in one sentence, through the use of an image, brings them together in a shorter form.

Example Albert saw a lamp post that stood on the corner like an underfed hobo.

By blending the physical detail with the character's mood in one sentence, you make the character and the setting one. You have allowed the image to reveal the physical detail and to explain the character's disposition, and used one sentence rather than two. When you can eliminate an unnecessary sentence, do not hesitate.

Reintroducing "Dead" Characters

To reintroduce characters who have disappeared from a novel for about 100 pages or more and many years, adapt an "old-fashioned" movie serial technique.

In the 1920s, the serial heroine was always tied to railroad tracks. A monstrous train was seen rushing to mangle her. Just before the train struck, the installment ended. The next week's installment would open with a review of last week's ending. A voice-over narration would explain what had happened. Then the new installment would begin, and the heroine was rescued from certain death, so the serial could continue. This technique can be used for characters who disappear for many years (and pages) and, because of the story demands, must reappear again.

Example Little Peter is trapped in a burning building. His uncle, John Page, charges in and drops the boy out the window to someone below. The building collapses. John Page is obviously killed.

But the writer intends a reappearance for John Page. His return will have an important effect on the story and relationships. To make his resurrection credible after twenty years, the writer uses a "superimposed narration" to reintroduce him.

Example (writer's narration) On that horrible night, twenty years ago, John Page had not been killed in the burning building. The explosion flung him through a gap in the floor. He fell two stories onto a mound of laundry bags and debris piled over him, forming a hollow structure which kept him alive. The explosion caused a concussion, followed by deep amnesia. He had crawled from the building and for twenty years wandered about the country. Three weeks ago, after being struck by a bus in Philadelphia, his memory returned. He hitchhiked home to . . .

It is imperative that the scene in which John Page was presumably killed, be dramatic and memorable. Then, 100 pages later, when the burning building scene is recalled and it is learned that he did not die, his reappearance will be credibly accepted, and his story continues.

Characters with Unclear Motivations

There are short stories in which the writer chooses not to have the major character clearly motivated. The character does not, through his own statements or introspections, reveal the motives underlying his actions. The character may not be particularly interesting in himself. He may be exciting because of his effect on other people. The events he causes may be more significant and dramatic than who he actually is. Keeping him unknown keeps him interesting.

Story A neighborhood resident walks into the local bank and holds it up with a shotgun. The alarm is sounded. He uses nine people as hostages. He demands freedom, money, and an airplane trip to Brazil.

Why has this man, whom everyone knows as a quiet, gentle man, who lived alone after being abandoned by his wife and three children, suddenly taken this criminal action? The writer remains outside the character, motivating him externally. He allows the other characters in the story to provide the motivation while the action proceeds.

> **Example (inside bank)** "Why is he doing this crazy thing?"
> "Remember that nurse who used to work in the hospital? She went to Brazil, I heard. They had something going between them."
> "Yes, I remember. And Steve was a patient of hers, yes."
> The bank manager suddenly pleaded, "Steve, taking this money won't get your wife and children back." Steve tightened his grip on the shotgun. "You're on drugs, aren't you, Steve?" The pale fingers touched the trigger.
> **(Outside the bank)** "Chief, I just got a read-out on him. He's a Vietnam vet. He has some psychiatric history. He went berserk once."

The reader may never learn the full and true motivation behind Steve's act of robbery. It does not matter. Steve is interesting and dramatic only so long *as he remains unknown*. Penetrating his consciousness might reveal that he is a drug addict, a philanderer, or perhaps just a dullard. It is only in his remaining unknown that he maintains his stature. The true story has to do with the other characters and how Steve's action changes their lives.

Cultivate Writing Habits

Few writers, either professional or inexperienced, have a continual desire to write. For every desire to write *today,* there are multitudes of distractions to draw you from that creative disposition—family, employment, depressions, entertainments, feelings of futility, drinking, drugs, bowling leagues, church picnics, television, etc.

The only way to stop these distractions from stopping you from writing is to deliberately fortify yourself within an impregnable structure of writing habits. *There is no other way.*

Unless you write every day, with undeviating persistence, you will not achieve the life-long career of a professional writer.

The writer is his own employer. The writer's character gets him to work every day. While the benefits of his enterprise are *eventual,* they are as real as the promise of corporate benefits and promotions.

Writing must be done every day, outside of a few legitimate, catastrophic emergencies. Writers do not receive paid vacations.

If possible, write at the exact time and in the same place every day. The place where you write must become your sanctuary, the realm in which you ignore the existence of the world. This writing time must become so vital and intrinsic to your life that whatever attempts to distract you should be regarded as a vicious threat to your welfare. This may seem fanatic, inconsiderate, ruthless. It is not. If anyone tried to prevent a lawyer, doctor, plumber, pastor, or musician from going to work, they would be dealt with mercilessly.

The writer must develop such strict, unchangeable writing habits that he compels the writing habit to "write" him. It must become more difficult for him NOT TO WRITE.

Mystery, Detective, Suspense, and Spy Novels

The mystery, detective, suspense, or spy story did not originate with Edgar Allan Poe. This story form has its origin in ancient mythology. It has been carried through the Odyssey and the Bible, and continues today. Theseus rescuing Ariadne from the beastly appetites of the Minotaur. King David lusting for Bathsheba and sending Uriah to his death. Many of Chaucer's tales, many plays of Shakespeare (*Hamlet, Macbeth, Othello*) are in this genre. The writers of these stories used writing techniques that are still being used today.

The form is simple, although the techniques and plotting devices used within the limitations of the form can be complicated. There are some fundamental guides that should be followed, then modified to personal skills, then improvised upon as the need arises. Guides are not Laws. Guides are merely carry-over traditions that have worked through the ages.

A. Whatever happens in the story, major or trivial, must be related to the plot. Superfluous, irrelevant, even interesting background facts should be omitted. *All* material must contribute to the story and plot.
B. The hero or heroine (detective, investigator, or innocent bystander) must have a connection or relationship to the setting, for the purpose of credibility. Detectives: police background. Doctors: hospitals. Lawyers: courtrooms. Insurance investigators: big business, wealthy clients, etc. This avoids fumbling for familiarity by the protagonist and the reader.
C. Trivial crimes are no longer spellbinding or shocking. The newspapers publish more violence and gore than writers can invent. The crime novels of today cannot deal with petty crimes. Murder and mega-millions should be the basis for the crime. Homosexuality, marital infidelity, and even incest have been reduced to inconsequential infractions. MANY murders must happen. The resurgence of fascism or terrorist factions that threaten conservative governments is an acceptable story. The betrayal of national interests, or the destruction of

the world through thermo-nuclear bombs are both agreeable stories. The more outrageous and catastrophic the crime, the greater is its chances for being published.

D. Begin with a frightening murder or a horrifying threat to the world. Always establish a pressuring time limit by which the crimes or world dangers must be resolved. Without a time limit, the protagonist(s) could be unhurried, deliberate. They must be harried, scurrying frantically.

E. The protagonist(s) does not have to be immediately sympathetic or effective. This is also an era of the antihero/heroine. At first, the protagonist may be merely more acceptable than the villain(s). Only a little later on, when the impact of the crime and the reason why the protagonist(s) is involved in the chase is revealed, does the protagonist need to become sympathetic. It is always an effective plot-line device to have the hero/heroine's life threatened. The hero can even be seriously injured—but he always recovers.

F. The horrible crime should be premeditated. A woman who kills her husband during a drunken brawl is not complicated. A hit-and-run driver who has to be found is not complicated. Premeditation, which is an act of deliberation, carries many complications which can develop into interesting plot lines.

G. Suspense should be equal to surprise. Although the identity of the murderer or world destroyers may be known while they are being sought, the question should be "Who will he murder next?" or "Will he destroy the world, anyway?" When the reader learns the answer, change the victim and the reason why he was killed: bring up another stalling tactic to save the world. Often, suspense is based on what is expected, although the reader doesn't know how the event will happen. If the hero/heroine is to die, let it be at the end.

The success of the mystery, detective, suspense or spy story depends upon how convincingly the writer makes the reader believe that the killer is living next door or that unless these gross villains are stopped, there might not be another tomorrow.

Universal Feelings

Whether you write a historical novel or a contemporary novel, the characters must be motivated by universal feelings with which the reader will be able to sympathize. Universal feelings are those human emotions that never change, no matter what century people are living in. They bring the reader into an identification with the past.

A novel cannot be competently crafted if universal parallels are not emphasized. Nor will the characters working out their conflicts and relationships be believed.

The thoughts of characters are always modified by the times in which they live, depending upon the prevailing philosophy and morality of that culture But universal human feelings transcend time and are unchanging from century to century. The passion, lust, hatred, love, ambition, jealousy, fear, and worship of the ancient Peruvians or Romans are no different in quality or intensity than what is felt today. The only difference would be in what provokes these universal feelings within the characters.

The writer's basing the emotional content of his characters upon these feelings is what connects today's reader with every time period.

Example When Julius Caesar was assassinated he was killed by political men who were ambitious and obsessed with power. When Abraham Lincoln was assassinated he was killed for the purposes of political men who were ambitious and obsessed with power. When Indira Ghandi was assassinated she was killed for political purposes by men who were obsessed with power.

Many centuries separate these assassinations—yet they were committed by people who were politically ambitious and obsessed with gaining power. The political ambitions, philosophy, and morality may arise from the circumstances of the particular culture, but the drive of passions is exactly the same. The costumes and table manners of the people living in another century may be strange to the reader, but the reader can always identify with what the characters are feeling. The reader has the same universal feelings in this century.

Chapter Breaks

Chapters are emphatic separations within a novel. They shift the story from one place and time to another.

Space breaks (about half an inch between sections, on the same page) used for the same reason, are less emphatic. There is no substantial separation between the sections they disconnect.

If a writer wants to omit five years in his story, a chapter break is more convincing than a space break. It makes the reader turn the page, or look to the next page. *There is a full visual change.*

A space break between two scenes five years apart does not divide the scenes sufficiently. The dramatic energy of the first section "jumps the gap," and the separation is not emphatic. A space break functions best when a separation between scenes is necessary but must not interrupt the flow of writing, the continuity of action.

Chapter breaks do not only occur where large blocks of time are going to be omitted. You can have a three-minute interval between chapters. This kind of chapter break can be used to alter the direction of the story emphatically; to begin new situations.

Example A passenger train cannot be stopped. It is plunging toward the depot where another train is parked. A crash is inevitable. There is panic, fear, scrambling among the passengers.

If the writer wants each of the passengers to tell his own story, he flicks from one to another, through a series of quick space breaks. This rapid change of characters and story keeps pace with the speeding train.

If the writer wants to change the place and time, he slows the train by having it reach a slight incline. He then uses another *chapter* to show what the terminal supervisors and medical teams are doing. Once the new scene (in the start of a new chapter) is over, the writer can return to using space breaks to describe the more hectic activity on the train.

Overlong Speeches

Lengthy blocks of dialogue by a single character are tedious to read and diminish the possibilities for drama. If any character speaks for too long, the language of speech assumes the appearance of the "written word."

Example A candidate for the presidency is addressing a hostile audience. He has lost twice before. This is his last chance. He must pound home five campaign promises and also turn the audience to his favor. If he fails, he will be dumped by the party and end up as a drunk.

Forced to read the entire speech as it is offered, the reader is not hearing spoken dialogue. He is reading written prose. The physical reality of the audience fades. The political issues being expressed flatten into a monotone, as the writer creates the authentic speech patterns. The elements of character and situation are set aside for too long a period. The writer cannot develop a mobile focus and shift about the convention hall to pick up other events that are occurring there. The writer cannot show the effects the speaker is having on the audience.

The writer can use "break-ins" to work in the speaker's five campaign promises—and yet avoid tedious lengthy speeches.

Begin with several lines of speech to establish that someone is speaking. Then break into the dialogue form and *tell* what the speaker is saying. Provide one promise in the dialogue (speech) and another in the description of the speech (exposition).

Example "Ladies and gentlemen, I stand before you humbled by the awesome task of having to bring this nation up from its economic knees to once again stand tall behind the fortress of internal security. This is a time for unity in our. . . ."

The thousands of faces were blurred in his vision. I haven't got them yet, he thought, as he told them his first progressive action would be to stop all welfare programs in the private sector and establish work camps for those citizens who could prove indigence. He heard a quick tapping noise behind him. His campaign manager was signaling him to stop drawling and increase the pace.

". . . and you know I stand for the founding father traditions of our nation. Family, sanctity of home, respect for motherhood, and all the verities taught me on my mother's work-worn knees. . . ."

A woman delegate shouted, "Right on, Samuel!" He saw some men passing a whiskey bottle and drinking. *God, how I could use a fast shot.* He shouted, "America is a one for all and all for one nation," and sensed they were beginning to listen. He shook his fists, promising them that militant dissidents would be dealt with as traitorous criminals. He felt charged, he felt power. Groups of men stood up and began applauding. He pounded the lectern. He felt like a crusading warrior.

". . . our time is now, and we will not let it pass. We either assert our greatness or sink into a morass of mediocrity. Nuclear disarmament is no longer a feasible political stand, not while. . . ."

Do this as many times as it is necessary to get the five political promises in. Use this scene not only to reveal his speech, but to explore his character—to remind the reader of the pressurized situation he is in. It is during these expository sections that the writer can create dramatic effects. He can describe the audience, the people on the dais, the reactions of the speaker's opponents, even the assassin who has been hired to kill him on his last promise. All this is happening while the character is still speaking.

When the speech is used with the articulation of human behavior, with the unfolding of situation, the intensifying of relationships, the heightening of conflict, then speech is incorporate with the total action of the scene.

Waiting for a Publisher's Response

A most maddening time in a writer's life is when he has sent off his novel and is waiting for a publisher's response. The depressions and anxieties are rusted nails being hammered into his consciousness. It is also a time when the writer's imagination and invention harass him.

The writer conceives of multitudinous reasons why his novel will be rejected. If there is no response for a month, he is obsessed with the belief that "My manuscript was lost in the mail." He makes hysterical inquiries. If he's assured that the novel was received, he creates other lunatic reasons. "It is a bad novel and they don't want to hurt me." "Someone heard a remark I made, and the publishers have blacklisted me." "The novel is ahead of its time." "The novel is behind its time." "I used invisible ink and the pages are now blank."

For some reason the writer never thinks that the novel is so stupendous that the publisher is passing it around proudly as "the latest literary find" while deciding on what amount to advance the writer.

There is only one effective way to avoid such depressions and anxieties while waiting: Begin another novel immediately. Become so involved in what you are writing that you absorb your concern for what is happening to what you have already written.

The profession of writing is not in the first novel you write. The writer is engaged in a life-long career. Just as he studies the craft he has chosen for his career, so must he study his own life, his concealed depths. He must know that imaginary fears are always more frightening than fears that are real. There is no way a writer can know what is happening to his novel once it has been sent off in hopes of publication.

The writer should not postpone his next novel until he hears about the one he has just finished. It may take months. Don't waste those months in depressions and anxieties. Spend them writing another novel.

Advantage of Multiple Viewpoint over Single Viewpoint

An advantage that *multiple viewpoint* (the viewpoint of many characters) has over the *first-person-viewpoint* (the single "I") is in the mobility of the writer's focus. In first person, all that can be known about other characters must come from the knowledge and assumptions of the narrator. He can reveal what is happening within his own vision; but can only assume what is happening to others beyond his vision.

The multiple viewpoint can explore more characters through their own responses. The characters can be viewed in different places at the same time. The story can develop greater variety through the array of other fully developed characters.

First person I had only 23 more forms to fill. Then home, in 43 minutes. I leaned back and smiled. Bernice was probably before the television set, waiting for me. She needed me so much. She was my slave.

Third person Bernice yawned and glanced at the night table clock. She crimped her mouth in annoyance. Harvey would be home in exactly 32 minutes. She turned to her side and pushed Wayne's bare shoulder. "Darling, it's time for you to leave." Wayne snored contentedly.

The first-person narrator can reveal only his own thoughts and feelings, and assume or guess the responses of another character. The multiple viewpoint allows the writer to explore the consciousness of several people within the same scene. The focus is mobile, it can shift.

First person She stood before me in sheer silk. She was hesitant, afraid my lusty embrace would crush her. I reached to her, lovingly.
Third person She stood before him, hesitant. *Can he see the gun strapped to my thigh?* He held his arms out. He did not know why she was hesitating. Was it because of the dark bulge on her thigh? Yes. She has a deformity and is ashamed. He reached to her, lovingly. She smiled.

First-person viewpoint is more intimate, more intense in focus, but multiple viewpoint moves with more versatility and into a greater range of character consciousness. Place is not a limitation in the multiple viewpoint.

Flashback vs. Recollection

A flashback is a full scene that returns the character into the past of his life. A recollection is a fleet fragment of the past brought back to the consciousness of the character. A flashback withdraws the character completely from the present. A recollection returns the character to the past for a few moments, but does not remove him from the present. The reader will remember a flashback scene, but a recollection is over too quickly to make a permanent impression in the reader's mind. The sustained content in a flashback has a lasting impact on a reader's memory. A recollection merely brushes across the reader's memory.

Story A woman gospel singer tours the nation. She meets a gambler, succumbs to his seductions, and becomes his mistress. She gives up the tour but she is constantly tormented by her conscience.
Flashing back The gospel singer is alone while her lover is gambling. The writer flashes her back to a time before she left on the tour. She is in the minister's office. He warns her "Men will try to cultivate your person for unscrupulous and wanton intentions." She denies the possibility. The writer returns her to the present. She knows her pride caused her to fall.
Recollection She is morose about being the mistress of a gambler. She recalls her father warning her about charming men who gamble.
Skip ahead nine chapters, about forty or fifty pages. The gambler has become abusive and cruel. The gospel singer wants to leave him.

If the writer decides to have the singer leave the gambler because of the recollected content of her father's warning, she will not be adequately motivated. The information in the recollection passed too quickly to be remembered clearly by the reader. It was over too soon to be sufficiently re-recalled. If the singer recollects the flashback, the flashback scene remained on the pages long enough to be remembered by the reader. The reader was there, in the past, when the singer relived the scene in the minister's office. The writer can even re-use some of the content that existed in the flashback. A flashback is a full scene. A recollection is more like an aside.

Necessary Introspection

Introspection is the deliberate implanting of thought into a character's mind to reveal his mental response to an event. If what a character thinks is not revealed, the reader has no clear way of understanding the effect events have on the character's life.

While the *physical action* a character takes in response to an event tells you something, what he thinks about the event *as it happens,* tells you more.

Example (without introspection) The Secretary of State pointed at John Stanley and denounced him as a spy. The other officers at the conference table were astonished. John Stanley stared at the wall. The Secretary of State waved a sheaf of papers, shouting, "Here is proof positive of your treachery." John clasped his hands on the oak table top. The men on each side of him shifted away.

If the writer omits the thought of the accused man at the moment of accusation, immediate insight into the character is lost. If the writer delays the accused man's thoughts about the accusation for use later on, the immediate impact of the accusation is diminished by the delay.

Example (with introspection) The Secretary of State pointed at John Stanley and denounced him as a spy. John tensed. He knew his wife had betrayed him. He made himself relax. *I'll take care of her later.* The other officers at the conference table were astonished. . . .

Introspection is supplementary information that lets the reader know the exact reaction of a character's responses to circumstance. The amount of introspection to be used depends upon the importance of the information contained in the introspection. It should be kept brief so the flow of the dramatic moment is not hindered.

Details of Setting

Details of setting can be troublesome. Often they are either used excessively, or not used at all. Used mechanically or ineffectively, they cause a separation between character and place. Details of setting should be incorporated into the activity of a character. When details are put down separately from the character, they either intrude, slow the pace, or take the focus away from the character.

Example (ineffective details) Jenny was bored. She wandered aimlessly about the kitchen. There were soiled dishes in the sink. A creased apron hung over a chair. The refrigerator door was slightly ajar.

You tell what Jenny feels like. Then you fix her in a particular place. A messy kitchen. But you have taken the focus off of Jenny to describe the kitchen. The messy kitchen has nothing to do with Jenny's boredom. It is just there. It doesn't emphasize Jenny's boredom. Bringing them together makes the description stronger. The details are then vital.

Example Jenny felt like the creased apron hanging over the chair. Aimlessly, she closed the slightly opened refrigerator door. She wished the telephone would ring. She watched some water drip onto the soiled dishes in the sink. She was bored.

You have never left your focus on Jenny and still have gotten in the details of the kitchen. Now Jenny and the kitchen are together.

All writing is composed of details employed to create and reveal the physical, intellectual, and emotional reality of the people you are writing about.

Professional writers use these details so skillfully that the reader sees them as inherent items of content—not as individual details set apart from the content.

Overuse of Adverbs and Qualifiers

It is generally assumed that overwriting means a repetition of scenes, an excessive use of description, narration, documentation, and dialogue. This is true. Yet there is an indirect, subtle form of overwriting that consists of an improper use of adverbs and useless qualifiers.

If an adverb does not enhance the meaning of a verb, do not use it. Unnecessary adverbs provide clutter.

Examples "He clenched his fist tightly," or "Swiftly, he raced across the street."

When someone *clenches* his fist, the word clench implies tightness. Fists cannot be clenched loosely. Anyone who *races* across the street must do it swiftly. Speed is intrinsic to the word race. If verbs like *clenched* and *raced* are used effectively, they do not need added emphasis. Additional emphasis will alter the exactness of expression the writer seeks.

Valueless qualifiers do not provide prose values.

Examples "She was rather beautiful," or "He was perhaps a bit too vain," or "The morning dawned in a kind of rosy glow."

Competent prose is assertive. The meanings conveyed through these "communicative symbols" should never be misunderstood or vague. *"Rather"* beautiful is not beautiful. It is either *almost* beautiful or *not quite* beautiful; therefore another adjective should be used. *Competent prose is persuasive.* It is the only visible tool the writer has in the practice of his craft. If he uses emphasis where emphasis is not needed: if he affixes verbiage onto the pages where vagaries are established, he is OVERWRITING.

Writers without the confidence garnered from experience in writing often use adverbs and qualifiers to emphasize what they do not believe they have written effectively. Do not burden the reader with your personal problems; overwhelm the reader with your competence.

Progressive and Inverted Resolution of Conflict

In a general sense, a novel is an orderly sequence of scenes that gradually accumulate into a complicated conclusion. Character conflicts that arise from these scenes *should be resolved in an orderly manner.* The reader should not be aware of this methodically crafted structure.

It is through the resolution of conflicts that characters are seen to be experiencing change. There are two general structures to use as a guide for resolving these conflicts: the progressive and the inverted.

Story A chemist has discovered a serum that will arrest the advance of leukemia. If he releases the formula to the public he will receive the Nobel Prize. If he patents it and sells it to private industry he will become a billionaire but gain no recognition. He is held in a critical decision.

Conflicts: in the order of their appearance in the novel
(1) Loathes anonymity and craves celebrity. (2) Is not respected by his family. (3) Is socially inept. (4) Colleagues are promoted over him. (5) Was physically abused by his parents. (6) Wants money to assert himself; to have power. (7) Has a fervent desire to travel.

Progressive resolution of conflicts When the last conflict is established, the novel is directed toward its conclusion. Start resolving the *first* conflict (loathes anonymity). Then resolve the second conflict (no respect from family), and so on. Until the last conflict (desire to travel) is resolved. When all conflicts are resolved the novel ends.

Inverted resolution of conflicts When the final conflict has been established, the writer directs all material to its conclusion. Resolve the last conflict (desire to travel) when it appears. Use that resolution to reach the conflict just preceding it (wants money/power). Then work back, in an orderly fashion, until the original conflict (loathes anonymity) is finally resolved, and the novel is ended.

Though the events which press against the lives of the characters may appear to happen in a chaotic, disorderly manner, that is the impression the writer wants to create. But it is the *internal order,* imperceptible to the reader, that makes the novel readable.

Blatant Foreshadowing

Blatant foreshadowing is a direct statement of a specific event that will happen *later on* in the story. The statement is outside of the text of the scene and is established by the writer.

The general purpose of foreshadowing is to clue the reader in to the possibility of future scenes, to prevent a sense of surprise when the scenes appear. This surprise can startle the reader out of his involvement with the story. Foreshadowing can also set up the future of relationships, scenes, changes in character, and events.

Yet some scenes which must be used offer no opportunity for subtle foreshadowing. These simplistic scenes are used to establish only one level of conflict, one alteration of character.

Example An engineer has lost his position with an airplane firm because of a canceled Air Force contract. He is in an employment agency, filling out an application. To acquire the position he will be forced to lie about his experience. He despises the idea of living a lie.

The scene is written only to get the character to face the crisis of having to lie. If he does not lie, his family will starve. Nothing unique or notable in the way of *action* happens. The content of the scene is static. There is no opportunity for using a conventional foreshadowing moment to reveal that the lie he places onto the application will, three years from now, cause someone's death.

It is an opportune time for *blatant* foreshadowing.

Example Franklin steadied his hand and wrote "Eleven years" in the Experience column. He shrugged. The company would never investigate. He could not know that his lie would set into motion events that would cause someone to die. He signed his name to the application.

This blatant, audacious intrusion of the writer is acceptable because the startling information jolts the reader yet involves him more deeply. How can a common lie cause someone's death?

Linking Episodes

To achieve greater unity and suspense in the episodic novel, use the *linking episode* technique.

Linking episodes are not to be confused with episodes that occur one right after another—butted against each other in a close relationship of place, time, and situation.

To link two episodes simply means to begin a new episode before the previous episode has been completely resolved.

Example A husband and wife are in a car. The wife tells her husband she has an appointment at her hairdresser's. She says, "Pull over there. I'll walk the rest of the way." She leaves the car. He speeds off. Two paragraphs later a tire suddenly blows out and the car plunges off the cliff. End of episode. The next episode deals with the woman whose lover is the hairdresser, and begins at a point in time within the last episode, when the wife gets out of the car. Her episode begins at that time and continues long enough for her husband's body to be discovered.

The unity in this episodic structure is strengthened because each episode is tightly linked to the episodes directly before and after. There may be a space break between the episodes, but there is no separation in the situation. As the reader moves from one linked episode to the next, there is no separation in the continuity of the situations. For a few paragraphs (moments) the reader is always a tiny step ahead of the character.

Example When the woman is seen leaving the car she goes to her lover's apartment. The phone rings. The lover answers it and is shocked. "It's the police, for you. How'd they know you were here?" As she takes the phone, she looks at her wrist watch. 11:00 p.m. The scene is ended.

The next episode begins at the car wreck, 15 MINUTES EARLIER than the ending of the previous episode. The dashboard clock shows the time to be 10:45 p.m. A detective is reading a note taken from the dead husband's wallet. "If I am found dead in a car wreck, my wife murdered me. You'll find her at her lover's apartment. 643 Smith Ave. Phone: 978-5762." The detective dispatches two cars to the address, then makes the phone call which has already been answered in the previous episode. The phone conversation is repeated, and the episode continues until the arrest is made. The two episodes are tightly linked through the phone call.

Writers' Groups

It is vital that an inexperienced writer find a group of writers who are working to become professionals. Whatever is written should either be heard or read. Within a group of inexperienced writers there is always a diverse assortment of capabilities, backgrounds, employments, and interests. Someone will always be able to contribute to what you have written. Whatever you offer another writer, critically, becomes a critical insight you can use.

Inexperienced writers must not become professional "sensitives." Vanity, conceit, and egotism hinder the writer's learning progress. It is an unrewarding sensitivity. If writers do not train themselves to become invulnerable to the pain of criticism of their writing, they will never cultivate an honesty about their own work. They will never become ruthless about determining defects in their own writing. They will see only the marvel, not the mud.

Writing groups also offer an inexperienced writer a sense of identity. It is a crushing experience to be alone in a desire or an ambition. Nonwriters may have disdain and disbelief for what you are working to achieve, and you begin to wonder "Is it all worth it? Why should I deliberately endure being a social oddity for some remote possibility of publication. Why don't I just shuck it all and marry wealth or bag groceries?"

This loss of "writing identity" is discouraging. Being among people who are writing to become professionals is an uplift, an encouragement. You are part of a living community *and not a private peculiarity.*

Every writer, regardless of his stance and protestation of humility, is an elitist. He knows he is the writer. Do not let this debilitating pride alienate you from the people you need and who need you. When you judge the other inexperienced writers as superficial and self-centered, you are standing before a life-sized mirror.

Don't Renege on Sex Scenes

Do not offer promises you cannot or do not intend to fulfill.

Readers experience disappointment when approaching the climax of a scene and the writer "breaks" and does not include the climactic scene.

Example A man and woman are brought together by the events of the story. A sexual set-up is instituted through the mechanics of a seduction scene. The couple is put through cunning ploys and tantalizing rituals until they must have each other—or just die.

(After four pages of sexual pursuit) They rushed to each other and embraced. The vibrance of her need jolted his senses. She felt faint from the urgency of his passion. He scooped her from the floor and carried her to the bedroom. They kissed with a craving that fused their souls. He kicked shut the door and raced to the bed.

The next morning she danced to where he slept and placed a rose upon his chest. She whispered, "Gaylord." He laughed, "Dear, dear, Dotty."

The writer has cheated the reader.

It is not that readers are lewd voyeurs who demand a charge every forty pages in a novel or else they will fling the book away. The writer has brought the man and woman together for developing the characters and the story. During the pressures of sex, many facets of character depth and plot line emerge. Don't tease the reader—*get the reader involved.*

Using a break to imply that the sexual act did happen, and then *later on* revealing what emotional changes took place between the people is giving passive information. It may be accepted, but the impact of emotion is lost.

If it is the writer's intention to avoid the sexual situation, then he must provide a substitute. Allow the rituals of seduction to reveal the character depth and plot effects that the sexual scene would have provided.

Show Emotional Changes

Readers are not as capable of understanding emotional changes in character as they believe they are. Most readers perceive the obvious and credit themselves with having grasped the subtle. If readers are not made privy to the emotional changes in the character, they will feel left out of the character's growth or deterioration.

Example Fifteen-year-old Ralph hates his father who is a drunk. One night the man confesses, "Ralphy, I lied to you. Your mom didn't die. She runned off with a Bavarian pickle peddler." The explanation, and lie, deepens Ralph's hatred for his father. He runs away from home.

The emotional changes that happen to a character over a passage of time should be noted by the reader. If the reader is not in on the small changes, then when the climactic emotional change happens, it will seem sudden, abrupt, and the new emotional condition of the character will not be accepted as credible. THE READER DID NOT SEE IT HAPPEN.

The writer decides that Ralph's role in the novel is to become like his father. It is done through a sequence of small emotional changes.

Example (a) Ralph, ever alert to find a highly moral woman, meets Pauline in church. He begins to love her although she always has three martinis before dinner. She claims her doctor prescribed the martinis for her gallbladder condition. Ralph believes her and, because he also has a gallbladder condition, begins drinking martinis. (b) Ralph marries her. They have a son, Gordy. Ralph is now always having martinis and is a drunk. Pauline is disgusted. (c) She runs away with a fried chicken franchise seller. Gordy is three years old. Ralph tells him his mother is dead. As Gordy gets older he starts hating his hopelessly drunken father.

The reader has been in on Ralph's emotional changes. The reader can now accept the result of these changes without being shocked. If Ralph does not become like his father, the reader is not disappointed.

Example Ralph, in an effort to regain his son's love, is about to tell Gordy that his mother is not dead, that she ran away with a fried chicken franchise peddler. Ralph suddenly has a flashback memory of how disastrous this truth was to him, when he was told the same thing by his father. In this emotional crisis Ralph gains the revelation that the only way to regain his son's love is to stop being a drunk. He joins A.A. and forgives his father.

This startling change in the character's destiny is unexpected, but acceptable, because the reader was involved in the "emotional changes" that happened to Ralph through a passage of time.

Rewriting

One of the many stages of writing that goes into completing a novel for publication is the effort of *rewriting*, an indispensable process.

When the writer completes a novel, he finally knows what it is *all* about. He has an intimate awareness of every element, phrase and subterranean level of the novel. Rereading the finished novel is the first stage in preparation for the task of rewriting.

As he reads, the writer immediately realizes he was remiss in *fore-shadowing*. This recognition must happen, and happens to every writer. He did not know *all* of his novel when he began to write; he knew only a general, over-all picture of it. He did not know every minute or minor part of it. He discovered the detailed remainder of it, while writing. He realized what the complete novel was all about when he completed the novel.

> **Example** The writer reads to page 47, when Henry Conner, an impor-
> tant secondary character appears. The writer knows now that later on, Henry
> Conner commits suicide—on page 165. But the suicide scene *was not
> foreshadowed.* The writer begins rewriting.

He starts with the scene on page 47 and develops a short circumstance or con-flict that will point to the act of suicide later on. The writer has no difficulty devising the foreshadowing interval because he knows his novel. He can devel-op this new material so it flows into and out of the scene: perfectly compatible with the tone of the writing, the dimension and temperament of the character, Henry.

It is in the effort of rewriting that the writer can apply his intellect, his ad-ministrative powers. He can appraise his work objectively, for the purpose of adding material or deleting material.

Until the novel is completed, the writer cannot actually do any permanent rewriting. An incomplete novel can only be worked on, until it is completed—enough to be rewritten.

Pace

Pace in writing is the rate of forward motion at which the characters, plot line, and relationships progress through the story. If the pace is not varied, then sharp climaxes are blunted, exciting moments are dulled, dramatic intervals become flat. The overall pace must be varied through the sequential arrangement of scenes. Pacing is done most effectively when rewriting.

> **Example (story)** A soldier goes AWOL to stop his wife from leaving
> him. The writer wants to postpone the meeting to reveal the soldier's charac-
> ter. (a) Plane ride to San Francisco. (b) In airport waiting for his wife. She is
> not there. (c) He rents a car and drives home. She is not there. (d) He drives
> to his mother's home. Wife is not there. (e) Drives to friend's home. She is
> not there. (f) He concludes she has left him. He mopes around, feeling en-
> raged. (g) Drive back to airport. (h) Plane ride back to camp.

It is almost impossible to vary the pace in this sequence of scenes. The soldier is merely driving around. There will be scenic descriptions, introspective memories, introspective speculations, but no opportunities for confrontation or dramatic action. Pace is founded on action. Pace is forced. Pace does not just happen. It is carefully devised by the writer.

To establish pace sequences, there can be no over-long dialogues, extended narrations, or prolonged descriptions. Avoid extraneous material such as spiraling excursions into the subconscious and penetrating soliloquies.

Example (same story) (scene sequence) (a) On plane to San Francisco. (b) Heavy fog diverts plane to Bakersfield. (c) Soldier rents car and picks up a hitchhiker who robs and tosses him from the car. (d) He loses memory and wanders. (e) Intuitively, he hitchhikes to San Francisco. The driver robs him, dumps him from the car; the concussion restores his memory. (f) He gets home to find his wife has left him. (g) Flies back to camp.

Although the end result is the same in both versions, the pace is not the same. It is advisable to assemble the pace sequence when rewriting. It is then that the writer has the novel within administrative control. He can pare down superfluous material, create new situations to heighten or slow the velocity of the plot, and tighten the prose to achieve compatibility with the pace of the scenes.

"Destiny" Novels

There are two basic structures possible in "destiny" novels. Though the story is the same, the plot lines and events will differ.

Story Six passengers board a stagecoach which must be driven through hostile Indian territory before reaching Laredo, the last stage stop.

In one structure, all characters are forced into each other's lives during the trip. When they reach the last stop, the novel ends and they separate. In the other structure, the coach reaches Laredo in the first chapter and the characters separate. The remainder of the novel reveals how destiny brings them together at the novel's conclusion.

Characters A pregnant woman, a prostitute, a drunken doctor, a consumptive gambler, a whiskey peddler, a bank embezzler. They pick up a gunfighter just escaped from prison. The Indians are on the warpath.

In this type of destiny novel, all action and events happen during the ride to the last stop. Suspense, anticipation, expectation, mystery are created by what happens ON THE WAY to Laredo. As each character is individually revealed and combinations of relationships occur, the situations intensify. As the action is heightened by events (breakdowns, hunger, thirst, panic, love, enmity, violence, etc.) more and more aspects of each character is revealed.

Plot line The drunken doctor befriends and protects the whiskey peddler as he drinks the man's samples. The consumptive gambler falls in love with the pregnant woman, who loves her soldier-husband. They vote to stop the ride because of the Indians, but the embezzler demands they continue. The doctor delivers the woman's baby, assisted by the prostitute, who now loves the gunfighter who is on a mission of revenge to kill the murderers of his father. The near-conclusion is a rapid, furious Indian chase. The gambler is killed. They arrive in Laredo. The mother and child reunite with the soldier-husband. Noticing the soldier's birthmark, the doctor realizes he is his son, whom he had abandoned. The gunfighter gets revenge and he and the prostitute ride off together. The embezzler is arrested. The others separate.

The drama in this destiny novel happens as the characters form relationships. Each individual problem is intensified and rendered critical during the coach ride. The unity must be tight; the end, a furious crescendo.

The other form of destiny novel uses the same cast of characters, but in this case the coach ride is uneventful. The characters, all strangers to each other, are described through the writer's narrative. He relates their individual interests and problems. The readers' expectation and curiosity is whetted. They have been brought together for a reason. The reader knows this. The characters do not. The ride ends in the first chapter. The writer follows the characters and tells their individual stories. Gradually, the stories converge.

Plot line The doctor begins practicing in the community. The embezzler rides on. The pregnant woman goes to her soldier-husband's fort. The gambler drifts. The gun fighter hunts the men who killed his father. The prostitute buys into a saloon. Toward the center of the novel, destiny in the form of events begins bringing them together. The same combination of relationships is formed as in the other destiny novel, and they meet at the fort. During a furious Indian attack their lives and relationships are resolved.

The gunfighter kills the murderers of his father, in the prostitute's saloon. The drunken doctor is called to deliver the baby at the fort. The gambler, in the prostitute's saloon, wins all the money from the embezzler who shoots him, then flees to the fort for sanctuary. The prostitute loads the wounded gunfighter into a buckboard and drives him to the fort for medical treatment. The doctor delivers the child and realizes the infant is his grandson. The soldier-husband is his son, whom he abandoned years ago. They both have the same birthmark on their wrists. The gunfighter and the prostitute find love, and they all fight off the Indians attacking the fort.

In the first structure, the characters are fixed in one area, and *one* external event (the coach ride) holds them together. In the other structure, the characters are dispersed and *many* separate events bring them together again. The purpose of both stories and structures are the same. Only the plot lines are different.

The Double Story—
Eliminating Flashbacks

If a writer cannot eliminate an abundance of material that occurred before the beginning of the present scene, he should not reveal this material through a constant use of flashbacks. It will become unwieldly and distracting. This past content should be developed into another on-going story *within the same novel*. This past story will run parallel to the present story. It should be concluded about the halfway point in the novel.

This is a complicated and somewhat deceptive structure. Deceptive, because from the beginning the reader is led to believe that the two full stories will not converge until the novel's conclusion. Complicated, because all the past events and relationships in the past story have a direct bearing on the present story and characters—yet it must remain a separate story until it merges with the present story.

Example (present story) Twin brothers, Brian and Leon, are campaigning to become the governor of Kansas. Their public rivalry is amiable and gentlemanly. Their only differences appear to be political.

(Past story) Starting at the age of 14, the brothers are seen in a malevolent, vicious competition. They connive and cheat to ruin each other. They both love Madeleine. This past story is followed until the day they are nominated by their parties. Leon has married Madeleine.

At the halfway point of the novel, when each brother has sworn to destroy the other, the past story stops. To reveal that now the present story will completely take over, the writer establishes a shocking crisis in the present. During a campaign speech, Brian is assassinated. Because the reader knows the past story, he believes Leon has had his brother killed.

The past story must be a complete story in itself. While they are being played out, both stories are given equal importance. The past story stops because it has caught up with the present. The reader must be misled into believing that Leon has killed his brother. This increases reader involvement. They are relieved to learn the murderer is Madeleine.

Guard Your Writing Time

Because a writer's "work" is not a conventional form of employment, people do not believe his "time is money." Writers must protect and constantly guard their "working time." Their working time is their career. They cannot allow themselves to be imposed upon or influenced by other people's limited understanding of their career. Even a writer who has not yet been published, must make people respect the time he uses for writing. Often, the respect he demands will be given to him when people realize the intensity of his commitment.

If people will respect someone who puts in a regular week of work at a job—plumber, bank clerk, engineer, advertising copy writer, welder, garage mechanic, etc.—they will respect the "regular working time" of a writer if he is assertive, positive, and his faith in his work is unmistakable. Writing is, in fact, a respectable profession.

Commitment is contagious. Family, parents, friends and children must not be allowed to impose upon or absorb the writer's "working time." People learn and understand through example. The writer who regards his working time as sacrosanct and vital will eventually infuse the same attitude into other people. The dedicated pursuit of a career will be respected as seriously as the achievement of that career. The world makes demands on the lives of people, and the writer is an undeniable part of the lives of people. He cannot isolate himself like some recluse who has abandoned the world. The writer is also nourished by the world and people, after he has put in his "time of writing."

This must become a principle in the attitude and vision of the writer, accepted as part of the total "writing commitment." A writer must not only want to work, he must be allowed to work. Parents, spouse, friends or children are not his adversaries or handicaps, they are the people in his life. They are as vital to his life as is his writing. But the writer must learn ways of helping them to appreciate his "writing time" and regard it as gainful employment. Writing is a conventional job, to the writer. Only the "time of writing" he chooses may be unconventional.

Freezing the Action

In fiction writing, an action that is started does not have to be completed immediately. The writer has the "poetic license" or option to use a *stop-time* technique.

Example An angry woman moves to slap a man's face. Between the motion and the connection of her palm to his cheek, there is an OPEN area of time which the writer can use for inserting other information. He STOPS TIME, holding the woman's hand and the man's face in a fixed moment to use the "in-between" interval.

The writer stops time for three reasons.

1. To include information through the viewpoint of the character who takes the action.
2. To establish the viewpoint of the character being acted against.
3. For a narrated overview of what the action means.

Example (woman) She raised her arm and swung at his face. *He'll never use me again for his crooked schemes—never.* Her hand jolted his head . . .
(Man) She raised her arm and swung at his face. He did not flinch. *She doesn't hate me. She hates herself for being tricked.* Pain flashed into his . . .
(Overview) She raised her arm and swung at his face. They would not forget this rage. These seconds of hatred would stay with them forever. Her palm cracked against his flesh and. . . .

A writer is always searching for opportunities to include information about character, conflict, relationship, and plot. The more unusual or interesting the moment he chooses to implant this information, the more emphatic this information becomes. It is information that might be overlooked if used in another area of the scene.

In real life, if a man topples out of a high window and is about to smash to death, he screams as he falls, and his flight does not take long. In fiction, the writer can use all sorts of revelations, realizations, plot line elements, recollections, regrets, and fear, before the character reaches his death. If the writer STOPS TIME to implant this information between the start and the end of an action, and the information is meaningful, the reader will accept the stopping of action.

The Deaths of Secondary Characters

When a secondary character dies, the writer should avoid lengthy dying, funeral, or gravesite scenes. The solemnity of the atmosphere drags the pace of the plot and the scene does not contribute enough information to justify its existence. A secondary character's death—the how and why he died—should contribute to the plot line development of the major character. The *content* of a secondary character's life, usually brought out in the dying/funeral/burial scene, is not as important as the death itself. The death contributes to the plot line, not the emotional or intellectual content of the deceased's character.

Example They listened to Uncle Fitzroy strain to breathe. Someone sobbed. The afternoon sun was warm against the shades. The priest's voice intoned, "You are forgiven, my son," as he performed the last rites. Aunt Agatha bit her lips. "Paddy, me dear Paddy," she moaned. She remembered him when he was thirty, standing on a hill, waving his rifle, bawling, "Cumm on, me lads, into the breech!" then charging into the gunfire of the British. Brave, brave Paddy. Now the dear hero was dying.

Such scenes, though appealing to the writer because of their melodrama, become areas in which overblown writing, superficial emotions, and synthetically profound thoughts are dumped. Grand and extensive intervals as dying/funeral/burial scenes should be reserved for the major character.

Let the secondary character's death happen quickly. His life and his death are utilities to provide more material for the plot line of the major character. The secondary character's presence in the novel is over. Only the *effects* of his life and death continue. If his death happens "on-stage," do not prolong it. Let his funeral and burial be referred to, *after the fact. "My, my, wasn't that a darlin' funeral." "Didn't Uncle Fitzroy have a peaceful death?"* Prolonged deaths and lengthy, dramatic funeral scenes belong to the hero.

Some Basic Devices

A writer must never become complacent about what he believes he knows about writing. There are seemingly *amateurish craft devices* that should be used even in ultrasophisticated forms of writing. There is no work so complex that it can do without the functional contribution gained from these basic devices, four of which should be present in every story or novel.

1. Identifying physical actions: (They quickly familiarize the reader with the character). Nail biting, nose scratching, nervous grinning, blinking, lip nibbling. Knuckle cracking, pencil tapping, pacing, hand gestures, etc.

2. Identifying verbal expressions: (used for economizing on the repeating of the character's name—or, tagging the speaker). "You know?" "So I said," "You hear me?" "Huh?" "Listen," "In my opinion," "Gotcha," "Who says so?" "Really?" "Really, now?" "My, my," etc.

3. Using character characteristics: (to provide a consistency of behavior that keeps the character believable). Gluttony, lechery, laziness, aloofness, cynicism, drunkenness, vanity, rudeness, timidity, inordinate propriety, verbosity, arrogance, etc.

4. Using physical appearances: (to eliminate repetitious descriptions and for quickly identifying the characters). Short, tall, fat, thin, muscular, bony, frail, slumpy, clumsy, graceful, militarily erect, sallow, ruddy, expressionless, stolid, etc.

The writer must be always alert not to use the *same* descriptions each time a character appears. If the characters are "walk ons" (incidental characters) who appear two or three times at most, a similar description can be used each time they appear. With major or secondary characters who require continuing development, the initial description is used as a *point of reference* for additional descriptions. The writer should then avail himself of the plethora of synonyms associated with the basic description and begin varying that description, to sustain its consistency rather than changing it.

Vanity Publishing

If you pay to have your novel published by a *vanity press,* it will quickly die, and no one will attend its funeral. While legitimate or known trade publishers do not always publish quality novels, they do advance the writer some money, rather than take it from him, as do the vanity presses.

Just because your life, or the lives of your parents, grandparents, other relatives, friends and associates are interesting, doesn't make you an interesting or competent writer. Writing is a profession that must be worked at. When your vanity or drive for some public recognition pushes you into an enterprise where you will be cheated, then your ambition is rendering you foolish. Publishers that require the writer to pay a subsidizing fee to have a novel published are to be avoided. They are always being sued by writers who feel they have been cheated.

The book you pay to have published will not be reviewed by any major or secondary publications. Your only reviews will be in the local newspaper or a church bulletin. Libraries do not purchase "vanity press" novels. Book stores do not stock them. The only autograph parties you will hold will be in your own living room. There is no distribution, no publicity, no promotion. If an advertisement does appear, it could fit in a spider's ear.

Still, if your vanity is more persuasive than your sense of reality, before spending from $2,500 to $5,000, try this precautionary test. Send the vanity press of your choice a synopsis of *a* novel. Make it as inane as you can. Phrase the writing in ridiculous grammar, and spell incorrectly any word with more than five letters. When the publisher responds, study the correspondence carefully. If they extol the splendor of your talent, the originality of your story, and are laudatory about your obvious writing skills—and that they will be proud to publish a work with such "potential"—with some financial subsidizing from the writer—suspect that they are more interested in your money than in launching you as the greatest literary find in American letters.

Flash Incidents

The writer should always be aware of how the novel is progressing. If there are intervals where it begins to drag, the writer should begin utilizing *flash incidents*.

A flash incident is an abrupt and unexpected intrusion into the plot that provides it with a spurt of energy. The flash incident seems to come from nowhere—like a flash flood—but it does have an origin.

Story The adventures of Brannie Brown and all that he encounters while traveling to frontier towns, peddling Brannie's Cosmic Tonic, which cures every ailment from galloping groans to wens. The year is 1843.

Flash incidents should have more to do with the character's profession than with his personal life. But the incident, caused by the activities in his career, should affect his personal life.

Example Brannie stood on the small platform on his wagon. He held up the bottle and shook the green liquid at the people. "Folks, this here elixer uv life cures coughs, rales, rasps an' room-ee-tizm. One swig'll turn ya snortin' an' rarin' tuh . . ." Someone suddenly roared, "Ya lyin' varmit, I'll git yer eyes!" People swung around to see a one-armed man wagging a gun. "I drunked sum-mer that 'lixer an' muh arm dropped offin me." Brannie leaped from the wagon and ran into the saloon.

This incident should not have been prepared for in detail. No foreshadowing or spoken forewarning. (*"There's a one-armed fella comin' for yuh, Brannie."*) The possibility of this incident happening should exist because of the character's profession. Without signals or signs, it comes out of the character's past, merely because he has a past. It is used as a catalyst to pick up the drag that happens in all novels. There should be no known cause for it—though its appearance should be viewed as reasonable. Once the *flash incident* is over, it disappears. The incident is used to revive the story. The result of the incident moves the story.

Summary Endings

Conclusions to novels can only be gratifying if they are clearly closed, if the reader retains no lingering curiosity about *"But what happened afterward?"* An interesting novel-ending technique is to produce *two endings*.

The first ending is the fictional conclusion in which all conflicts and relationships are finally resolved. The second ending is tacked on to the first ending and has the abrupt factual tone of nonfiction. It is a summary of what happens to the characters who have already played out their lives in the completed novel. This additional ending is also gratifying.

Story Four American pilots join the R.A.F. before America enters World War II. John becomes an ace, downing seventeen German planes. Paul is shot down and loses a leg. He marries an English girl and opens a tobacco shop. Bill is promoted to major. He becomes a military administrator. Lou is dishonorably discharged for black marketeering. The novel ends with a sentimental, humorous, bawdy, cathartic reunion. Each one then goes his own way to pursue the remainder of his life. The conclusion is final.

It is no longer important for the reader to be concerned with *"But what happened afterward?"* The story has all been resolved and concluded.

But the writer offers a bit more information to the reader. The characters are summed up in their "after-the-novel-is-over" life. The prose is factual, emotionless—the tone is that of a detached summary.

Example John tried to establish a new record for enemy kills. After his 99th, and against the advice of his flight commander, he tried for his hundredth. He was shot down over Portwill. His body was never found.

Lou increased his black market practices and rivaled the English Mafia until felled by a heart attack. In 1968 he became chief criminal advisor for Scotland Yard. He lives in Fellingdew and raises geese.

Bill was passed over for a promotion to general. He defected to Russia and began reorganizing the Russian air force. American agents were assigned to assassinate him. They succeeded.

Paul abandoned his wife for a Syrian belly dancer. She taught him how to do several types of one-legged ballroom dances. They became a famous night club act. They had three children. Paul retired happy.

The writer does this for all the principal characters and puts the final, irreversible cap on the wellspring of his novel. It is finally ended. Now everyone knows "what happened afterward."

Avoid a "Deus ex Machina" Conclusion

At the conclusion of a novel, avoid depending upon the use of the *"deus ex machina"* (God from a machine) character who suddenly appears to unravel an impossibly entangled situation. The contemporary reader will accept some unprepared-for surprises, a few unforeshadowed rescues, an unseemly coincidence, but the *deus ex machina* device is too clamorously obvious to accept. It is trite. It is an indication of amateurism.

This *deus ex machina* device originated in the ancient Greek theatre. Playwrights arranged for characters, at the end of the play, to become so enmeshed in unresolvable situations that they were doomed to go under. Then suddenly, a "machine" was lowered onto the stage and one of the many gods stepped out. With pomp and grandeur, and in his divine manner, he resolved what the weakling mortals could not. The Greeks cheered; contemporary readers will boo.

Example 1 An impoverished woman's husband is hospitalized and needs a costly operation, or he will die. She is on a park bench, weeping. An airplane is heard overhead. Suddenly, a bag of diamonds drops from the sky, into the opened purse from which she had drawn a hankie to wipe her eyes.

Example 2 During a family picnic on an English moor, an 11-month old child wanders to the edge of a cliff. She teeter-totters on the loose soil. The mother sees her and shrieks. The child falls. Suddenly a great eagle swoops down, snatches the child by the diapers and flies her back up to the picnic basket. Attached to the eagle's right leg is an identification tag, declaring in bold letters, "Child Rescue Eagle Corps."

In real life these miraculous interventions may be possible and acceptable. In fiction, *deus ex machina* events are caterwaulingly improbable. They are too sudden, too shocking. They jar the reader's reason; they yank the reader from the reading experience. Vital rescues and resolutions should be meticulously prepared for. An entire novel has been written just to reach the intense and dramatic conclusion. Don't disappoint with cheap tricks. Only in minor events can the *deus ex machina* be used. Before the reader has a chance to become annoyed, he should be into another dramatic situation that can absorb the folly of the *deus ex machina*.

Creating character and developing character are not the same. Creating character happens before the character is written. Developing character happens while the character is being written.

Don't Postpone Your Novel

How do novels ever get written? What kind of people write novels?

A realistic comparison can be drawn between a young married couple and the writer who has been delaying his decision to write a novel.

The young married working couple want children but the time is not right. They first desire economic security. There are so many parties coming up this year. In another year they will be promoted to higher paying positions. The year passes and they are promoted, but to have a child would force the wife to leave her job. The loss of income would be dreadful. There is just no sensible time for them to have a child.

The writer, who has been doing book reviews, short stories, some nonfiction, cannot find a practical time for starting a novel. It might take two or three years. He doesn't yet know enough about writing. He has never stayed so long on one project. Literary agents are not interested in new clients. The novel will be dumped into a publisher's "slush pile" and rejected. It's too risky to start a novel, now.

How, then, do so many first novels get issued in a publishing year?

They are done by writers who ignore the practicalities and assume the exceptional vision. They insulate themselves against the skepticism of parents, the ridicule of friends, the frightening stigma of a society that claims, "We have more writers than we need!" They believe in themselves, their talents, their skills, their character. They put their lives on the line because they are painfully dissatisfied with repressing their lives in the suffocating silence of conventions. They accept the brunt of this disdain as consciously as warriors know that lethal weapons will clash upon their shields. Yet in the depths of every unpublished writer there is hope that someone will understand and also believe in them. And if there is no one, they continue anyway. They are writers. And one day the world will read their novels and know they are writers.

Don't Use Flashbacks Immediately

Avoid the immediate use of a flashback at the opening of a novel. It is a deterrent. Unless the bulk of the novel takes place in the past, do not attempt even one flashback until the novel is truly launched into the present. You have not yet created a present circumstance that can provide excitement, suspense, or expectation. You cannot create a forward thrust into a character's life by immediately going backward.

Example (opening of the novel) Alvin flattened the creases in his black suit as he watched the pall bearers lift the bronze coffin into the hearse. His wife had died in a questionable accident. He remembered the day they met, fourteen years ago. It was raining. The library roof was leaking. . . .

Your opening has been stalled. You are reading about a stranger.

Some disadvantages of using a flashback too soon are:

1. The purpose of a flashback is to contribute material to the present that the present relationships and conflicts cannot provide. Backgrounds, insights, perceptions, motivations, failures, successes. Before this past content can contribute, A PRESENT MUST FIRST EXIST.

2. Until you know what the present character-conflict is, you have no reason to care about what happened in his past. WHO IS HE, REALLY?

3. Since the reader knows nothing about the characters in their present life, he cannot evaluate the consequence of an event in their pasts. There are no gauges for comparison. WHY AM I READING ABOUT THEM?

4. The present situation does not yet exist. After the flashback is over, what is there to return to? HEY, I CAN'T REMEMBER THE BEGINNING.

The purpose of the novel's opening is to get it started with vitality and drama *and excitement*. To let the reader care for the people as they unfold their lives in the "NOW" of their time. Only when the forward motion of the present is strong, should you risk leaving it for a little while, to return to the past.

First Person in the Short Story

An advantage of first person (subjective) over third person in the short story is how quickly the writer can move from the present into the past. There is no need for space devoted to devious mechanics. First person recollections seem more natural, more intimately true.

Example The street ahead was dark. The globes of three lamp posts were shattered. I could sense danger as I had sensed it when Jerry was attacked by four muggers. He was left in the gutter, bleeding to death. I drew my hands from my pockets and walked ahead.

Recollections flow from the first-person narrator as naturally as breathing. They are not mechanical as in third person. In third person, there can never be a complete break from the reader's awareness that the writer has selected the memories the character experiences. There is always the awareness that the "he" or the character's given name are being used in an alternating manner, so there is not a repetitive use of either "he" or the character's name.

Example The street ahead of him was dark. The globes of three lamp posts were shattered. He could sense it as he had sensed it when Jerry was attacked. . . . George drew his hands from his pockets and walked ahead.

Another advantage of first person is how easily the writer can use the character to reveal his past. Though there is a transition, no transition appears.

Example My sister Rosalie looked washed out. She was now like our mother who worked in the fish cannery fourteen hours a day and then had to raise us. When she was past thirty, Mom no longer moved as though she had reason to be alive. She shuffled and slumped like a woman too tired to find her own grave. The house we lived in was a dirt floor cabin. We were always cold and sniffly. Windows rattled and broke during storms.

The short story, unlike the novel, never lasts so long that the reader forgets that what he is reading was written by a writer. It is easier for the reader to flow into the "I" than the "He" or "She."

Breaking Up Narration

Pages and pages of pure narration can become tedious to read. The information about characters, the information about what has been happening, the information of cause and effect of this event and that conflict, are jammed together. The mass of information gradually blends together and the distinction between what is supporting material and what is *story material* is lost. While narration informs, it also must remain interesting.

It is also difficult to achieve a variety of *paces* within the body of a long narration. There are harmful visual effects when the reader must work through this extended narration. There is also the risk of seeming to be textbookish.

The writer should use some simple techniques to overcome the handicaps of prolonged narration: *break into it with dialogue and scenes.*

Story The novel takes place in the 12th century, when China was attempting to invade Korea and subject the Korean people to Chinese rule.

The writer begins to narrate the background of China and its many rulers, generals, and chieftains who have conspired over the centuries on how to conquer Korea. The narrations describe battles, intrigues, customs, moralities, prominent heroes, heroines, and rascals.

Example During some narration revealing that the peasants once re-volted against the oppressive conscriptions and taxes, *show* a scene in which the revolutionary leader is captured. Have the crowds mourn as he is dragged through the streets to where he will be decapitated.

Example After returning to the narration, which brings the reader to a time when opposing chieftains came together to merge their forces, bring in some of their dialogue, their plans.

Working these scenes and dialogue into the narrative will make the people real and the historical period "living." The number of break-ins into the narrative depends upon the length of the narration.

The Subjective and the Objective "I"

There are two pure forms of first-person writing: the *subjective "I"* and the *objective "I."* The writer should appraise the content and scope of the story and level of articulation he intends to give the "I" narrator.

A complicated plot with many characters will require a wide range and diverse analysis of people and situations. In this case, the objective "I" is more suitable. If the plot is simpler, with fewer characters, then the writer desires the impact of immediacy, personal depth, and emotional response, and the subjective "I" will work best.

The subjective "I" is intimately involved in all the relationships, conflicts, action, and events. Because he is limited by his physical nature, only some of what happens when he is not present can be told. He can only speculate or learn about what is happening elsewhere. The subjective "I" is the personification of now. Yet he can reveal his past or project his expectations, his anticipations. He talks to every reader, personally, with intimate explanations about himself, about other people, about situations.

The objective "I" is only cursorily involved in the story's relationships and events. He wants to tell the stories of the lives of the major characters, rather than the story of his own less interesting life. He narrates more stories and provides more insights about other characters than the subjective "I." He has mobility. He can manipulate time, moving backward and forward when necessary.

The subjective "I" tells about other people only when they contribute to his story. The objective "I" plays only a minor part in the major story. He is not the major character.

Example (subjective) I left my wife because she was boring and cold. I drifted for two years and became a waiter in New Orleans. I met Loretta:

passionate, interesting. I want to marry her but I'm afraid of bigamy.

Example (objective) I became friends with John Jays while he was a waiter in New Orleans. He was a quiet man, and lonely. He told me he left his first wife because she was boring, and cold. He bedded down with Loretta, a chubby blonde with varicose veins. She excited him. He wants to marry her but is afraid of going to jail for committing bigamy.

If the subjective "I" character is not articulate, the expanse and depth of the novel is diminished. While the "I" maintains immediacy, the story loses range because the narrator cannot legitimately explain what is going on around him. If the narrator is too articulate, he sacrifices intensity. He becomes over-explanatory. He strays from telling about what is happening to him in order to depict others not immediately involved in his conflict. It is what is happening in his present life that matters. The character is urging you to hear his story, to live his life.

Example I could not stop my affair with Loretta. She was fiery, she was sensual. She didn't care that my financial status was not enviable. She just craved me. My wife would never know about the affair because she was a cold, unloving squid. But she would not divorce me, and I didn't know why. I gave my all to Loretta, and none to my wife.

The objective "I" should be articulate, or else he will not be able to create others as he narrates their stories. He must be complex enough to be "all seeing," and analytical enough to be "all insightful." He must induce the reader into caring more about other characters than about himself. He must be able to provide information about the major characters that the subjective "I" could not know and is working to learn. The objective "I" is almost like the third person "He." Only some of the objective "I" 's story is told.

Example While John Jays continued his affair with Loretta, his wife hired three private detectives to find him, after learning that he was an heir to six million dollars. John was afraid Loretta would leave him. I was there the night he told Loretta he was married. "I hate her," he said. Loretta smirked in disbelief. He pleaded, "She'll never divorce me. All she cares about is her social reputation and her religion."

The objective "I" is not always required to explain his sources of information. Since he gathers material from so many places, the reader goes along with his deductions. Factually, the reader knows only what the subjective "I" knows, although he is free to evolve deductions from what the subjective "I" has revealed.

Interest and suspense are derived from the subjective "I"'s involvement with the conflicts and resolutions of the other characters. Interest and suspense through the objective "I" are gained by how fascinating he creates the people and tells their story.

Unspecific Adjectives

Presumptive, *unspecific* words are glib references to people, circumstance, or objects. They are *presumptive* in that the reader must fill in the details or images. They are *unspecific* because they carry no concrete image or direct detail.

Beautiful, handsome, lovely, ugly, evil, charming, good, darling, sophisticated, pretty, nice, delightful, unpleasant, etc. are imprecise generalities that should only be used in dialogue or introspection.

Example A lovely woman came into the fashionable room. She had long beautiful hair and pretty teeth. A tall and handsome man stepped to her and kissed her graceful cheek. They made a darling couple.

All that is actually known about this couple, from the detail used is that: a female with long hair and teeth came into a room. Her cheek was kissed by a tall man. All other adjectival details are unspecific or presumptive. The reader has to do the writing and the scene creating.

There is a workable guide to use when selecting your prose for the description of people, circumstance, or objects. If the same adjective can be used to describe the same sensation or surface, in five different ways, dismiss it as unspecific or presumptive.

Example *GOOD:* I had a good meal. I feel good. He's a good man. That's a good watch dog. This pipe is good. We had a good visit.
NICE: I had a nice meal. I feel nice. He's a nice man. That's a nice watch dog. This pipe is nice. We had a nice visit.
LOVELY: I had a lovely meal. I feel lovely. He's a lovely man. That's a lovely watch dog. This is a lovely pipe. We had a lovely visit.

Only the reader has the privilege of being general about language. The writer must always be specific. A scene, a character, a situation, is founded on specifics. Drama is based on precision and exactness of prose. Vague words render dramatic moments watery.

Be Inventive

Inventiveness is important at every level of writing. Without a sense of invention, a writer would soon deplete his store of perceptions about people and situations. He would become repetitious, and his work would be rendered static and predictable.

Inventiveness is that capability of being able to write outside of personal experience, writing about what never happened to the writer personally. This may appear to be a simple ability to develop, and professional writers will agree. The difficulty occurs when it is required of the writer to believe that what he has written is believable, and that if he himself does not believe what he has written, the work will be unpublishable.

There are five elements to an inventive story; if the writer can accomplish them, he is almost assured of publication and readership:

1. *Are you telling a fascinating story?*
2. *Are your characters interesting and loaded with conflicts?*
3. *Does the plot line razzle here and dazzle there?*
4. *Are you telling the reader what he already knows, in such a way that he does not believe he's read it before?*
5. *Does it make the reader feel and think and care about some of your characters?*

If the writer has those five elements throughout the novel, then the *writer* does not have to believe what he is writing. He needs only to write well enough to know that others will find what he has written believable.

A writer has some "guarantees" when beginning a novel. The literary agent or publisher who wants to garner money from what he is writing, the public that wants to read what he is writing—for the length of time it takes to read that novel, readers want to believe what the writer has written. Readers do not purchase novels to disbelieve them.

Notes on the Subjective "I"

Often, an inexperienced writer will choose the point of view of the subjective "I" because he believes it is easy to do. Just tell it the way it flows from the narrator who is revealing his story. But unless the writer understands some basic principles about the subjective "I" viewpoint, he will impair the value and power of the work.

A. The subjective "I" narrator is always the major character. He tells you about what has happened, or is happening to him. His attitude is intimate, his vocabulary should be compatible to his background. The tone is almost confessional.

Example I did a ten year jolt in Folsom prison for embezzling $4,000,000 from the Kansas lottery. I had blown it all on wild parties, on grade A opium, and blonde bar hookers. When I finished my stretch, big city life scared me. I signed on at the Open Heart Monastery in Utah and worked my knuckles bare planting bougainvillea bushes.

B. While the subjective "I" is concerned about the people he confronts, his major concern is with exploring and analyzing his own consciousness. When an emotional crisis causes him an "inner revelation" about himself, he explains what the revelation means, *after the fact*. He cannot explain how he is changing while he is changing, because he is too emotionally embroiled in the intense process of changing. These changes will seem sudden because there was no explanation while they were happening. After the specific change has been declared, the subject "I" should recount some of the stages of change that he experienced. This authenticates that a change did take place in him.

Example I left the monastery with a canvas sack of bougainvillea bush seeds. I would plant them throughout America. I looked at my hands and was again shocked. The cancerous looking wens and warts were gone. I should have known the bougainvillea bush leaves had curative powers when, three months ago, before Vespers, I was drinking some stolen Communion wine and noticed some wens and warts were gone. What was clearing my skin? I wondered. It couldn't be the Communion wine.

C. The subjective "I" narrator cannot feel and think at the same time. Feelings and thoughts are used for different purposes. Feeling causes the subjective "I" to respond with immediacy.

Example I smashed my shovel onto the pebbly earth. This rotten, cruddy soil couldn't grow midget cucumbers!

Thinking is what the subject "I" does when trying to assemble into meaning *what he has already felt*.

Example There was no reason for getting sore at the soil. Soil has no brains. It didn't deliberately make itself wrong for planting bougainvillea bushes. I had picked this spot because it was land the government didn't own. I should have known free land was just cruddy.

D. There is a taboo in the subjective "I" novel. The inexperienced writer is often tempted to bring the reader deeper into the novel by talking directly to the reader. This is a phony and intrusive device.

Example My mission to plant bougainvillea bushes throughout America was becoming futile. What would you do if you were bent over with arthritis? Would you go on working in the heat and the rain and the wind? Wouldn't you want to rest? Is it wrong to be a human being?

E. If the subjective "I" novel covers two or more years, the narrator should reveal the physical changes that have happened to him.

Example The sun was beginning to bleach my hair. I had lost at least thirty pounds walking from state to state carrying my bougainvillea bush bag. The bicep on my right arm was thicker than my left.

These references to physical changes makes the reality of time passing and change happening more believable.

Heroes Against Circumstance

The characters of heroes and heroines should include ingenuity and imagination. They must not depend upon other people or shifts of circumstance to snatch them from their crises. They are independent entities.

The goals or ambitions of heroes and heroines must never be fulfilled according to their original intentions. Novels thrive on conflict, handicaps, and impossibilities. Characters must go through their plot line like partially blind rats trapped in a maze—finding one open door leading to a sealed room that only a resourceful individual can open.

Story A trucking company cited for biased hiring practices hires its first woman driver, Velma, to transport a load of nitroglycerine to Montana. The explosives must be kept cool. It is a flaming summer.

If Velma merely gets to Montana the story is limp. Any woman can drive a truck. Velma's success must be fraught with hazard and handicaps: unforeseen and overwhelming. She needs conflict if the story is to become complex.

Example She should experience vehicle breakdowns, detours over pot-holed roads with steep inclines. The truck's brakes fail. She should stop to help some accident victims only to be grabbed by a hijacker who holds her hostage. After she does away with him, the truck should be stolen by larking teenagers who will be blown up on the first bump.

This is a story or novel in which the element of circumstance is the villain. If other *human* villains appear, they must be extensions of the realistic circumstances. Velma must deal with them only when they appear. She may be warned about them through foreshadowing, but she cannot expect them in the specific, or anticipate when they are set to arise.

   She must also experience fear, doubt, hopelessness. Heroism does not mean the absence of human frailties. Heroes and heroines are entities who, though special, contain all the defects of the "human condition." They are *special* because they will not ever be destroyed by these human imperfections. (Give Velma a need to prove herself.)

Ideas and Plots

An *idea* for a story or a novel is not a *plot*. An idea by itself is limited in content, but vast in possibilities.

   Example Mystery: The governor of Alabama is found dead in his bedroom. The windows are sealed. There are no secret exits. The air conditioning vents are too small for even a gnome to crawl through. The door had to be broken down. The only clue is the murder weapon, a whaling harpoon with an ornate handle still embedded in the governor's back.

This is an idea for a story or a novel. This idea can be developed into a hundred different plots. How to develop this idea into even a single plot depends upon the writer's skill at invention.

   Example When the writer introduces a detective who has a background in whaling history and determines that there were only four such harpoons ever made, *the plot begins*. The detective assigns a subordinate to find the four harpoon owners. The one who does not have his harpoon must be the killer. How was the killer able to sneak up on the governor? He must have been a friend. There is no blood in the bedroom, thus the detective concludes the governor was killed elsewhere and brought into the bedroom. *Aha, the plot thickens.*

While an idea may suggest a particular plot, the existence of plot can promote the development of new ideas, which can then promote secondary plot lines. The new plot lines depend upon how the writer used POINT OF VIEW.

Example The detective learns that all the harpoon owners have reported that their harpoons were stolen. He interviews them and concludes they all have motives for wanting the governor dead. The writer then picks up the viewpoint of the harpoon owners, and their stories are revealed through another set of plot lines.

Ideas do not contain particular stories, nor does a sequence of ideas compose a plot. If the writer does not work and exercise his ability to *invent,* great ideas will lie fallow. Plotting depends upon the writer's skill in probing the depths of an idea until the possibility of a plot or story is suggested.

"Writer's Blanks"

You are not experiencing a "writer's block" when you do not know what is going to happen next in your story. You are experiencing a *writer's blank.* Even a prepared outline, summary, or synopsis will not help you. You know what you are writing about, but you don't know what to write NOW. At such a bewildering time it is wise to assume the attitude stated in a colloquial adage: "Do something, even if it's wrong."

At whatever point of the story you are "blanked out" in, introduce a "starter" character.

Example She heard the window being opened. She turned and gaped, "Robbie, my God, I thought you were dead." He grinned, "So did a lot of other people."

This character may not have great significance now. But he has been introduced and must now be given a function. By the time you are ready to evaluate his function, you are also prepared to control him. He can be reduced, enlarged, or eliminated. He has "started" you filling in the blank areas. He exists, and thus can be manipulated.

OR, at the point of the story where you have "blanked out," use a break and begin at another place and time in the story. Eventually, the characters will be in that place and time. Get them there now. By the time that portion of the story is done, you will have found the material you need to return to that former place and time, to fill in the writer's blanks.

OR, shift the point of view to another character. Let that character take over the story for awhile. You may not be blank in his viewpoint. Seeing your plot through his vision may stir associations and resources that another character does not provoke from you. If, later on, you feel this character's viewpoint is intrusive or dominating, transpose the content into the first viewpoint you were using. The purpose is to gain the content you need to "write in the blanks."

OR, quickly, surprisingly, cause an unanticipated event to happen. Base the event on any of the material you have already used, or material you intend to use. It needs only a scant relationship to the total story. It is a scene you can write NOW. Your immediate concern is not the total story which, experience has proven, you will eventually finish. Your concern is to be writing: not to be blank.

OR, begin a sequence of "comic relief" accidents or mishaps which momentarily shift the plot line, or stall it for awhile.

Story The annual electronics company bowling tournament.
Example Pauline faced the long gleaming alley. The lone pin stood like a finger gesturing in vulgar defiance. She breathed deeply, imagining how the trophy would look on her bureau. Glorious. She raised the heavy ball and bent over. She heard a ripping sound. People started laughing. Warm air slithered along her panties. She swung around to cover herself. The ball dropped onto her toes. She yowled and hopped about the alley. Lanny rushed to her with a jacket. He stumbled over the ball, crashing into Pauline. They flopped along the alley. . . .

If this incident is continued for an amusing length of time, the writer's blank won't seem so expansively bare. Later on, if it is not useful, remove it.

OR, transpose already decided-upon scenes into other forms. If an area of the story is to be narrated, change the structure into a scene that is acted out. If there is a run of exposition used to provide background in a relationship, manipulate your characters into a dialogue where this information becomes an active part of their present relationship.

Use the known content of your story to create the still undiscovered content. Writing blanks are only temporary handicaps that must not be allowed to develop into writer's blocks.

It is through the many-faceted vision of the writer that content becomes manipulatable. A different application of technique can render static content dramatic. It is the same with a writer who has become static, or blank. Review your array of techniques, and when you reach a writing blank, use a technique to fill it.

Battle Scenes

Battle scenes, or any scenes that have scope and involve many people (including major and secondary characters), should be structured through the film technique of "four lenses": (1) *panoramic lens;* (2) *crowd lens;* (3) *close-up lens;* (4) *inner-lens.*

Example The Crusaders are battling the Saracens.

You focus the *panoramic lens* on the entire battle, sweeping the lens around to describe what the foot soldiers, archers, knights, and leaders are doing. Hold it long enough to establish the reality of the battle.

Change to a *crowd lens* and focus on many characters in more detail. Settle briefly on some secondary characters the reader is familiar with. A quick line of dialogue, a flash of point of view, will help.

Change to a *close-up lens* on the hero (or villain) showing him in a sharply detailed struggle. Hold on his physical actions, so his presence is fixed in the reader's mind. The panoramic and crowd lenses will have established the battle surrounding the hero (or villain).

Example: close-up lens Sir Milliam pointed his broadsword at Hamid Ahmed and spurred his mount. The Saracen's scimitar flashed at the knight's throat. Sir Milliam evaded the vicious cut and swung about, thrusting the heavy weapon into Ahmed's exposed back. The Saracen screamed. Sir Milliam jerked the horse to the side, searching for Gamil.

Now, drop the inner-lens into Sir Milliam and reveal his feelings, thoughts, plans. This will provide you with more material for sustaining the battle.

"Gamil," he shouted, "Where are you, you devil?" If the coward escaped, he thought, Lady Melathain was doomed to slavery.

Return to the crowd lens, involving familiar secondary characters, even dropping the inner-lens into them, to reveal bits of information for future scenes. Then use any of the four lenses you feel suitable for keeping the battle authentic, and ongoing.

Character Changes

Character changes cannot be referred to, they must be proven. All readers have the "show me" attitude. The proof of character change is in the demonstration of how the character's life is affected. There are three phases to a believable change in character:

1. A shocking awareness of a character fault.
2. A strong desire to change.
3. An action that proves changes have happened.

Example Travis, a former policeman, is now a drunk. His family despises him. He's in an alley when he hears a shot. A man bursts from a jewelry store, holding a woman hostage. She is Travis' wife. He tries to leave the alley to rescue her. He cannot. The robber shoots the woman. Travis collapses in tears. He realizes he's a helpless drunk.

The recognition of his character defect is brought to him with savage immediacy.

> **Example** At the funeral, he is desperate for a drink. His children curse him, "Filthy drunk. Why didn't you save Mom?" Travis desperately desires to change. He goes to Alcoholics Anonymous for help.

Attending Alcoholics Anonymous is *proof* of his desire to change. Show him in the trials of "drying out" and how ten months later he is utterly sober and working as a security guard for an ultra-posh hotel.

> **Example (demonstrations of change)** (a) Place Travis in a situation where it is impossible for him to refuse a drink, and have him refuse it. (b) Have his children need his help, and show how he helps them. (c) Let him perform a heroic act to make up for having failed his slain wife.

The event that forces this moment of recognition for a character change must be a shocking circumstance. The sense of inner understanding should be deeply *emotional*. The proof of change happens when the character performs in an emotional, mental, and physical manner he could not achieve before. *He is not the same: he is changed.*

Simplistic and Complicated Plots

If your plot moves in a straight line toward the conclusion, you develop a mechanical story. The reader easily guesses how the end is worked out. If the writer keeps the reader guessing about HOW the conclusion will happen, the story is interesting. If you produce many shifts and unexpected twists, the reader will not care how long you take to end.

> **Example (simple plot line)** The elderly chief of an Aborigine tribe, and Magumago, a warrior, desire the same woman. A "fight-to-the-death" ritual is required. The chief, too old to fight, has a surrogate warrior take his place. A ten-foot chain binds them together and they fight with spears. Magumago kills the chief's warrior and wins the woman.

Plot line depends upon character conflict. A simplistic conflict has limited alternatives for resolution. When that conflict is resolved, another is found, then another, to keep the story going. If the writer quickly establishes a complex conflict then the plot line has more alternatives and the conclusion is less predictable.

Example (complicated plot line) In an Aborigine village, Magumago, an elderly chief, is telling the people how he had once saved the tribe from extinction. Forty years ago there was a killing drought and the wealthy chief at the time, Poloppo, sent twelve warriors to find water. Magumago led the search party. He was married to the beautiful Undallum. Chief Poloppo, who desired Undallum, instructed the other warriors to kill Magumago. When they locate a hidden stream, the warriors attack Magumago. He kills three, then persuades the others that the chief is evil. Returning to their village they are attacked by a pride of lions. Only Magumago, heavily lacerated, is left alive. He gets to the village and tells about the hidden stream. Believing Magumago dead, wealthy chief Poloppo has made Undallum his concubine. He calls Magumago a liar.

Magumago leads the entire village to the hidden stream. They drink their fill, and return. In a ceremonial parade, they bring the chief and Undallum to the stream. Suddenly, one of the warriors believed to be dead staggers to the people and tells how the chief and Undallum had a secret cache of water and had conspired to kill Magumago. The people fling Poloppo and Undallum into the water and they drown. The story returns to the present with Magumago being applauded for saving his people.

Because of one great conflict, chief Poloppo's lust for Undallum, other conflicts are created. The plot line begins to develop complications which are not predictable. The story continues to be interesting even though the end is known at the beginning (Magumago is alive, and telling his story). Because the conclusion is obvious does not mean that the insides of the story should be uninteresting.

Famous Rejected Books

Writers must not be so tyrannized by their esteem for publishers or literary agents that they assume a rejection of their work is an irrevocable, dooming judgment. The history of books (fiction, nonfiction, poetry, biographies, etc.) that managed to become best sellers after having been rejected by many publishers, should be positive encouragement to the habitually depressed and unconfident writers.

A short list of books that have been turned down by publishers can become a long testimony to the blunted business acumen and jaded sensitivity of literary agents and publishers. Here are only a few.

Lust For Life, Dubliners, Peyton Place, Remembrance of Things Past, From Here To Eternity, The Lost Weekend, The Good Earth, War and Peace, To Kill a Mockingbird, The Tale of Peter Rabbit, The Sun Is My Undoing, The Joy of Cooking, The Rubaiyat of Omar Khayyam—some have been acclaimed as "great" books; others are fabulous best sellers.

Whether books become best sellers because of literary quality or through ruthless promotion is an interesting, and unanswerable question. Most publishers realize that many of the books they issue are "hack and nonsense." Too many are unaware of the literary works they reject.

If a writer has learned his craft, can make an objective, honest appraisal of his own work, and believes it merits publication, then he must persist in trying to get it published.

When anyone becomes a writer, he is endowed with an inheritance from men and women of courage and faith. If these men and women, fixed into the history of writing, had not had character and faith, many splendid books would never have been published. There is a "mystification" in writing that is beyond the publisher's control and, somehow—through an unexplainable *somehow*—good books are published, but only if the writer has the character and faith in self to persist.

Dialogue Shifts Viewpoint

Dialogue is a versatile component in the craft of writing. It is visible sound. Its presence in a scene is often used for more than just an exchange of on-scene information. It can serve several functions at the same time. It can intensify a moment between people, and point to future possibilities.

Example (A husband and wife are arguing about finances)
"Ella, stop hounding me about money. Do you want me to rob a liquor store? Hold up a gas station, maybe? I've just had some bad luck."

"You never do anything right. You're a loser. I don't care what you do. Just get food on the table, and pay the rent."

Besides revealing the antagonism in a marriage and some causes for that antagonism, you are also preparing the reader to accept the possibility that the husband might be driven to commit a crime. If it does happen, it will not be surprising. You have foreshadowed motivation for your character. If he does rob a liquor store his action will be believable.

Dialogue can be used to shift character viewpoint and vary the pace of the scene. You can also vary the tone of your prose.

Example Vicki is moody. Her prose is written in soft and slightly long sentences. Her mother is realistic, earthy. Her prose is done in short, abrupt sentences.

"Mom, I'm so lonely. I feel lost and wandering. Adrift, you know."

"Vicki, do your school work. It's getting late."

"How can you talk about school when my soul is crying out?"

Her mother slammed the dryer lid and strode from the room. *That child can wear me to a frazzle*, she thought. *When I was younger, I couldn't afford a soul.*

You have moved from Vicki's viewpoint to her mother's viewpoint. You have changed the pace from languid to sharp. You have also revealed character, attitudes, and a slight hint of the mother's past.

Melodramatic Writing

To a degree, in the first writing, it is essential to write melodramatically. Melodrama is an exaggeration of drama. It is overblown, almost a mutation of reality. Yet through this shrill enlargement of life, the writer finds the depths and subtleties of his story's content. Subtleties are elusive: depths are concealed. Often, they must be forced from content.

Example (melodrama) She hurled herself at him, shrieking, "You animal! You tore my virtue from me!" She beat and clawed at his face. He grasped her wrists. Confusion splashed through his brain. He heaved her across the room, roaring, "Harlot! *You* seduced me from the monastery!" She fell to the floor, screaming and shuddering, "Yes, yes, yes, yes."

The value of melodrama can be understood through a consideration of stage performers. While on stage the actors must exaggerate their gestures and facial expressions, if they are to project themselves to the far reaches of the theatre. When they begin acting in films, they cannot perform in this manner. The camera and microphones record every grimace, every nuance of sound. The actors look hammy. But once they adapt to the media of films, they become finer performers than those without stage experience.

This theatrical exaggeration is like melodramatic writing. Through the unavoidable process of rewriting, the writer finds in the excessive and magnified material what he needs to render the scene into a believable portrayal of life. Without the overblown exposure of melodrama, this material might remain hidden; the subtleties and nuances overlooked.

Example (re-written) Angrily, she sobbed, "You used me," and struck at his face. He grasped her wrists, confused. Abbot Clarry had warned him this would happen. He whispered, "No. I was content at the monastery." She huddled over, feeling the strength of his hands. It was finished. She had lost him. She suddenly clung to him, pleading, "I'm sorry, so sorry."

If the writer *edits* in his mind before committing the content into prose, many levels of creative resources are skimmed over. Content comes first; editing comes later.

Writing "In Between" History

To someone interested in writing historical novels, historical accuracy should not become a troublesome handicap. Historical facts are used to embellish literary invention. Professional historical novelists always write "in between" recorded history.

Example In 1724 Emperor Charles VI of Austria issued the Pragmatic Sanction to protect the succession of the royal family. The French and Spanish Bourbons objected to Charles' eldest daughter, Maria Theresa inheriting the Austrian dominions. In 1740, after Charles' death, the Bourbons attacked Austria, beginning the War of the Austrian Succession. The war continued for about eight years.

This is historical fact. There are records, diaries, and a plethora of other documents to authenticate these facts. These actualities can become a framework, rather than a handicap, for every category of the novel: adventure, mystery, fantasy, romance, war, etc.

Romance Maria Theresa's love affair with a cunning French duke who tries to persuade her to oppose the Emperor's fanatic drive to keep his progeny on the throne. She gives him up for the sake of the family name.
Adventure Emperor Charles is dying. Maria Theresa will succeed him. She loves Francis of Lorraine. French and Spanish assassins are sent to kill her. Francis, deeply in love with Maria, heroically stops them and they marry.

In historical novels, "facts" of history are used as a backdrop to authenticate the time and place. The writer's use of true history, as the public knows it, is more interpretative than actual. The historical novel is not dependent upon facts. The facts are used as identifying events *to support the story*. The only "absolutes" about history are the dates, type of events, and the names of people in those recorded times. The causes for the start, continuance, and conclusion of those events, are "relative." They are always subject to the writer's fictive interpretation.

Sacrificial Characters

The adventure thriller novel should contain two or more *sacrificial characters*. These characters are never given particular notice until they are ready to be killed off. Their positions are always subservient: chauffeurs, double agents, secretaries who are mistresses, aides to the villains, crooked cops, etc. Only at the point when they are killed is anything significant revealed about them.

> **Example** An intern has paid for his medical education by borrowing money from usurious shylocks. Instead of demanding their exorbitant interest, they force the intern to steal drugs from the hospital. He garners information about a drug ring which could have them all jailed. He is afraid.

The sacrificial character serves the plot, not the story. He is used as a proving ground for the hero or exists as a "weakness" in the formidable stature of the villain. He is killed when the hero attempts to get his information, or when the villain wants to quiet him. Some sacrificial characters should be skilled fighters or killers. When the hero defeats these characters, his prowess is verified. If the villain sets a sacrificial character against the hero and the sacrificial character is killed, this drives the villain into another facet of cunning—furthering the plot line.

Just before the sacrificial character's death scene, the writer should write the intern's short biography. The intern should be treated as important, just this one time—to give him some stature for a short interval. His struggle to become a doctor, his hope for position in society, his scheming to marry a rich woman. If the intern is a fighter/killer, write about his training history, his list of murders. Otherwise his death will not be accepted as a serious contribution to the hero's stature. A sacrificial character is important only one time in the novel—when it is his time to die.

The hero's stalking of the sacrificial character adds to the plot's suspense. Confronting and killing him becomes a "pivotal structure" on which the plot turns in a planned direction. If the hero gains information from the sacrificial character, the plot shifts in one direction. If the villain kills the sacrificial character before his information is revealed, the plot twists another direction. Sacrificial characters are utilities: they are important people only once.

Make Fiction a Reality

Don't let what *you* can't believe stop you from writing what others will believe. Fiction creates the *impression* of reality. It does not mirror or duplicate reality. If the reader wanted unadulterated reality, he would not read fiction. He would read financial statements.

Surely no one believes the Three Musketeers survived all those sword duels, that Perry Mason could never lose a court battle, that James Bond actually saved the world from total destruction. All fiction is "make-believe" and "once-upon-a-time." The fact that great fiction has influenced the morality and ideals of the world merely proves that readers take these fictive inventions seriously. Yet readers do not accept fictional characters and events as authentic or real.

The writer must not be restrained by his own sense of credulity. Believing what you write and believing *in* what you write, are not the same. You are not required to believe your own inventions—you are required to write them competently.

Example (unbelievable short novel) A group of different animals living on a farm engage in discourses about the condition of society and mankind. Some animals are humorous, some animals are serious.

That is the famous *Animal Farm* by George Orwell.

Example (a novel) A whaling captain has his leg bit off by a whale. He becomes obsessed with destroying the creature. In his pursuit of the animal he loses his ship, his crew, and his life.

That is the American classic *Moby-Dick* by Herman Melville.

Writing a novel or short story demands a "sense of invention." If you cannot "invent" scenes and situations, then *pretend* you can and invent your own "sense of invention."

Stream-of-Consciousness Narration

There are intervals in novels in which the writer is allowed to suspend the conventional methods and devices for implanting information. They are "suspended intervals." These are moments when characters are suspended in a condition that is not natural to their usual behavior, i.e., when they are drunk or affected by social or medical drugs, when they are feeling grief, fear, love, loathing, horror, dreams, madness, homicidal, etc.

In these unusual moments, the writer suspends the character in the plot and is able to free his consciousness. The character does nothing but express his consciousness. This suspended interval becomes a dumping bag for symbols, obscure motives, and a montage of information that cannot legitimately be revealed at other times. The character is freed.

Example (first-person dream) I was falling. The sun smashed into my face, scarring me. She was there, Mona, Mona, above me, feeding the flames. I screamed, "Don't leave me, I'll change!" Infinity snarled, "Free, free indeed." I was spun like a top. I plucked a wig from the air and shrieked, Mona. . . .

Extracted from the scene, this flow of stream of consciousness makes no sense. Yet within the texture of a scene it can have great importance.

Example (third person—drunkenness) Reeling, ruptured in soul, he suddenly laughed. Mary's face was on his face in the bar mirror. "Woman!" he shouted, shaking his beer glass at the gnarled image. He did not mean to kill her. He rocked on the stool. She knew. The scissor killed her. Hee, hee, hee, the scissor hated her. Snip, snip, hate, hate. He roared, "Bartender!"

These intervals are times of serious mental or emotional stress. They are chaotic, tumbled about with feeling and thought. Any information the writer needs planted into the plot is acceptable. It is human chaos. But these unusual moments must be crafted in an orderly fashion to *appear as disorder*. It is the disorder of the mind and emotion that makes them authentic and credible. The carefully planted information will not be understood unless this "impression of disorder" is meticulously crafted.

Writing Must Be Rewritten

Perhaps the calling to become a writer is sacred, but surely the writing itself is not. A writer who believes that all the writing he creates in his lifetime is worth only forty nickels had better watch his nickels. His range of expenditures will reach only to what he believes he is worth. Whenever he puts a nickel's worth of writing onto paper, he had better make certain it brings in bags full of gain. Being stingy, scrimping, and tight about his nickel material is understandable.

If the writer assumes his talents and skills are worth one million nickels, then he can become bold in conducting investments without fear of exhausting his resources. He can write, discard, and write more.

Writing should not be viewed as so personally precious that to tamper with its original arrangements causes the writer to believe he is being assaulted. WRITING MUST BE REWRITTEN. No writer alive should ever permit his work to be considered for publication with rewriting. Those legends in the history of literature who claim that there have been writers who were able to "write it the first time out" and have it published should be examined for veracity.

And if one or two such exceptions exist in the history of literature, a new rule is not established. They are freaks. They prove the verity and validity of the old rule. Fine, exceptional, or great writers must rewrite.

To write successfully the writer must view his work as a marketable commodity that has a public demand. It must be packaged presentably before being offered for publication. Believing that what you write is a perfection of prose and structure in its original form is amateurish. Rewriting does not mean that you are a grubby hack raping the virtue of "art." Respect for your profession demands that you achieve excellence. This excellence is gained through a ruthless comparison of what you have actually written with what you want to write. Remove what is excessive and rewrite what remains. You have an inexhaustible supply of "more writing." Only when you are famous are you allowed to become careless.

Avoid Excess Introspection

Every writer writes too much introspection. Don't continually use the character's mind as the main source of explanation. It becomes tedious. You must train yourself to stop this introspective gush.

Introspection is only a small part of an entire scene. If a character "overthinks," the pace of the scene can be impeded. A character must think *only enough* to bring clarity into the scene. Too much introspection can absorb a scene. An excellent exercise for training yourself on how to use introspection is to deliberately not write introspection.

Use half an hour of your writing day for composing scenes which require some introspection. Then write them, omitting all introspection.

Example Carol listened to John tell her they were finished. *I'll die*, she thought. *No—I'll kill myself*. John said, "I'm going back to my wife. She needs me." Carol felt obligated to commit suicide.

Without introspection, all you have is Carol listening to John say their affair was over. How can you reveal, *without introspection,* that Carol is going to commit suicide?

Example Carol listened to John tell her they were finished. She wound the telephone cord tightly around her wrist. "I'm going back to my wife. She needs me." Through her tears she saw her wrist swell and redden as the black cord strangled her flesh. John asked, "You won't think of hurting yourself, Carol, will you?" She looked at the full bottle of sleeping pills near her bedside.

Keep writing "non-introspective" scenes until the scene, in abject hunger, shrieks, "Introspect me!" Then place one introspective line into it. Be absolutely sure that that one introspective line adds an explanation to what could not be achieved through the overt description. Then get away from it.

Do this for one month and you will be astonished at how your scenes not only move, but explain themselves without ponderous and unstanchable cascades of introspection.

Humanizing Details

Not all details of character contribute to specific insights into character. Some mannerisms accorded to characters are used as *humanizers*. These small actions cast the character into a quick framework of "doing what human beings do" merely because they are human beings.

Example He felt nervous, and sniffled.

The sniffling merely emphasizes his nervousness, it is not necessarily a continuing trait. He can also be nervous and not sniffle. His sniffling when nervous does not reveal a penetrating psychological insight into his character or motivations. The character can be seen doing many other things—clicking fingernails, fidgeting, blinking. If he is nervous in a pressure situation, he is behaving within his character. If he sniffles, when nervous, his character is humanized.

These "humanizers" are not the same as indelible character traits, because the character does not *always* perform them. They are for the reader to speculate about when subliminally assembling the particulars of the character.

Example Joe annoyed the staff as he filed his fingernails during the sales conference./Eloise was seen wearing yellow plastic hair rollers as she shuffled to the mail box./Deep in thought, Jack plopped his ring of keys in his palm.

These trivial mannerisms focus more on the character's humanity as a person than on his behavior as a fictional character. They are like tassels on a lampshade. They do not alter the shape or function of the shade. They merely add to what already exists. While they are not vital, they are not padding, either. They are unobtrusive asides where the writer silently says, "Sniffling, when nervous, is just something a human being does. If you want to make more of the action, go ahead."

Writing, "Billy undressed," is not as interesting or as human as "Billy yanked off his shoes and tossed them into a corner." This may serve as a clue to *more* of what Billy is like as a boy, or it may be something any young boy does, because he is a young boy. He is a *humanized* young boy.

Dialogue to Give or Get Information

Dialogue must have a reason for being written. When a character speaks, it must be for more than just speech. Dialogue should be used:

1. To offer information.
2. To acquire information.

All offered and acquired information must be relevant to the scene's situation and to the relationships among the characters. It must not only sound natural as speech, it must also appear to be necessary.

Example (offering information) "I'm flying to Baltimore at noon."
Example (acquiring information) "Do you think the thunderstorm will affect my flight?"

Dialogue becomes more complicated when a character uses it to offer and to acquire information at the same time.

Example "I'm flying to Baltimore at noon. Do you think the thunderstorm will affect my flight?"

The character who responds to this offer of information and this bid to acquire information can confirm (or deny) this information, and then add more information.

Example "I heard the storm will blow over by eleven. But I don't think you should take the flight. I have a premonition of a disaster."

Characters should be directed to speak only when what they say contributes to the scene in "dialogue's" own unique function. Dialogue is a substitute or replacement for another writing technique that provides information.

When a character states *"I have a premonition of disaster,"* it can also be stated through narration rather than dialogue: *"He said he had a premonition of disaster."* But a narrated form of dialogue does not establish the intimate connection between characters that is gained through an exchange of dialogue. Narration is fixed on the page. Dialogue blurts outward. The reader does not hear narration as clearly or as dynamically as he hears dialogue. Narration can be mulched in or appear to be description or to offer background information, but dialogue never loses its individual characteristic. Dialogue is always speech.

Characters Can't Always Speak for Themselves

Fiction is not written for the writer to experience, or for the characters to experience. Fiction is written for the *reader* to experience. Writers should always be smarter and know more than the characters. If writers were not smarter than the characters they create, they would never be able to assist the characters when they need help.

A technique to use early in the novel (the first chapter, if possible) is to bring the major character to a critical moment where he perceives an insight into his own life, or the life of other characters, which he cannot articulate consciously. The perception may be so deeply insightful, that he either does not have the language or the conceptual sense to formulate the perception into an insight that advances his understanding. At such critical moments, the writer must take over.

Story An unhappily married couple decides that instead of divorcing, they will work at their marriage and render it a happy relationship.

The writer creates difficult situations for the purpose of bringing strong, surprising, or shocking perceptions to the characters.

Example The woman is standing over her husband with a knife. He suddenly awakens. "Oh God, she's trying to kill me, not because she has another lover, but because she thinks I'll pass on my latent albino genes to our children."

But characters are also developed with deliberately built-in limitations. If characters are all they will ever be when the novel opens, then they cannot be changed by the dramatic events the writer arranges for them. There are times when the writer deliberately limits the conscious understanding of the character (but does not leave the reader uninformed)—for two reasons:

1. If characters can perceive depths in themselves or in others that exceed their created limitations, they become unbelievable. (A garbage truck driver who never finished high school would not be able to advise a Federal judge on how to conduct a libel suit.) He would not be believed. If characters can always fully understand what they are perceiving, when they perceive it, there is a diminished level of suspense. Much of character conflict is based on *misunderstanding*. When understanding is reached, conflict is resolved.

2. Often, when a character is perceiving a deep emotional insight that might change his life, it comes to him in an intense and turbulent way. The writer can express it in a clearer and more orderly manner than the character could. The writer's focus is sharper, enabling the reader to understand more clearly.

Example Zeke snapped at Marge, "We'll be late for the party," and left the bedroom. He lit a cigarette to calm himself. Because he had never admitted even to himself that he loathed her cologned smell and shuddered with disgust at how her cosmetics made her appear to be wearing a death mask, he believed he still loved her. He did not understand that his constant anger was because he felt himself to be a compromising hypocrite.

The reader cannot understand what is not written.

If a character gains a significant perception during a critical moment, and the perception is not recorded because the character cannot articulate its meaning, THEN THE PERCEPTION DOES NOT EXIST. Later on, if the character's behavior is changed, his changed behavior is not understandable or believable. If the perception the change is based on has not been recorded, the reader does not understand the reason for the character's changed behavior.

If a character does not see his environment, that doesn't mean that the environment doesn't exist. Anything that the character does not see which is important to the scene must be described, because the reader must see it. Otherwise the reality surrounding the character will not exist for the reader. It is the same with perceptions characters cannot articulate, but which change them. The writer must explain the perceptions FOR THE READER'S UNDERSTANDING. Otherwise the character's changed behavior is not reasonable.

The writer should establish the technique of "articulating perceptions" for the character in the first chapter. As these "writer explanations" continue, the reader will welcome them as added knowledge of the character.

Pick Your Writing Group Carefully

Caution should be used when choosing a writing group. Incompetently conducted writing groups can be destructive or corrupting.

Writing groups should not be stroking centers where the writer goes for the uplift of flattery and all-out admiration for his writing talents. Being regarded with esteem without the foundation of accomplishment can lead to false self-appreciation. This false self-appreciation would collapse in an honest group.

Writing groups should not be aggressive psychological confrontation arenas, either, where every writer becomes a penny-ante psychoanalyst appraising the personality and character of the other writers. Only what is written matters. A critical analysis of the *writer* is a foolhardy endeavor that profits no one and deprives everyone of time, energy, and critical assistance.

Nor should writing groups become confessionals, where the writer brings his confusions, fears, rages, or social crusades. Such writing groups are not therapeutic or helpful. The reason for being there is to learn from each other. Not to become overflowing vats of woe you dump on each other.

Do not write for the approval of the other writers. After a few weeks in a writing group, you become familiar with each other's personal preferences and dislikes in reading and writing and know what kind of writing is likely to please other members of the group. Bids for approval from the group will not improve your writing. You are adopting a group of editors who are not yet expert in editorial critiques. Write only what contributes to your stories or novels. Regard what everyone says with moderate seriousness. Only the writer's own final judgment has meaning.

If the writing group is conducted by a semiprofessional writer (one who has had one or two stories published in a minor or local publication) or a professional writer (who has been writing a long time and has been nationally published with enviable frequency), be on guard against being led into viewing all writing through his personal vision. Do not let your special, unique, and highly talented self be *cloned*. Your "writing vision" is personal and exceptional. Keep it that way.

The "Split" Novel

There is an unconventional novel structure which, *if it can be adapted to the story,* can be very successful. There are only two major characters in the "split" novel. All other characters are functional, consistently minor. One major character begins the novel and, at a midpoint, the other major character takes over the remainder of the novel. The novel can be done either in the present, or be conducted through the past of the characters.

Story Two elderly sisters, Clara and Ethel, are in their nineties and live in the same home for the aged. The bulk of the novel consists of their memories, which reveal what they are really like as people.

The first half of the book is dominated by Clara's story, in which her sister plays a prominent part. They are seen growing up, graduating from school, marrying, bearing children. When they reach the age of 45, there is an abrupt, startling change in the story. Clara's viewpoint is stopped. Ethel's takes over.

Ethel's version of the story unfolds. Clara plays an important role in that story. The sisters' lives continue from the age 45 to their present. Their parents die, their children marry and provide grandchildren. Their husbands die, they grow old and are moved into a home for the aged.

Two excellently written novels developed through this structure are *The Collector* by John Fowles, and *One Hundred Dollar Misunderstanding* by Robert Grover.

The value of such a structure comes from gaining another viewpoint of the same story, just as the first viewpoint has about been exhausted. It is not that the first character has no more to say or do. It is that another viewpoint becomes a tonic. The same, continuing story is immediately refreshed. Some aspects of the story that were not covered by the first viewpoint are covered by the second viewpoint. Since each viewpoint has a different pace, a different rhythm of language, and a unique vision, there is great variety in insight, perception, and action.

Catastrophe and Response

If a character is seen running through the streets, screaming, "It wants to eat me up!" and people see a furry kitten chasing him, the character's intelligence and sanity will be doubted. Rather than being comforted, the character will be straitjacketed. In fiction, there must be a balance between the importance of an event and the magnitude of the character's response.

Scene The Chairman of the United Nations is hosting a garden party for ten ambassadors from ten different African nations. After the festivities there will be a conference to settle territorial disputes. The Chairman suddenly smacks his own neck, screams with pain, and begins rushing about the garden, shrieking, "I've been bitten by a rabid ladybug!"

The cause of his hysteria is trivial compared to the enormity of his response. His behavior is not compatible with his stature as a U.N. chairman. Later, when he conducts the United Nations conference, his credibility will be questioned.

The same principle *(action must be equal to cause)* can be applied to characters who underrespond to situations of genuine catastrophe.

Scene Four men are sailing a sloop around San Francisco Bay. A thick fog suddenly blankets the area. They hear boat whistles. Before they can maneuver the sloop, they smash into a battleship. The men are killed. Their bloated bodies are washed ashore. Later, their wives are seen staring at the dead men. The women shrug and, in unison, say, "Oh well, they never were much as sailors," and walk away to repair their smudged makeup.

There is an imbalance in the women's response to this disaster. The drama is diminished by their minimal display of feeling. The scene becomes unbelievable. Tragedy demands great character response, if the reader is expected to empathize with the characters. A minor event (like being bitten by a harmless bug) requires a casual response. The balance between reality and response often determines the credibility of the scene: it shades the drama shallow or strikes the drama deep.

Characterizing Details

Many inexperienced writers are troubled about describing characters. Physical descriptions are adequate, but not as effective as "characterizing descriptions." Give life to your characters, not just appearances.

Example (usual description) Charles stepped into the room. He was tall, with dark brown hair and deep-set eyes. A scar was on his left cheek. He said, "Hello, Laura." His deep voice drawled.

This establishes his physical reality, his appearance. But his character is still unknown. Adding a "characterizing" element can reveal more about him. If you describe and characterize at the same time you don't have to take time and space to do them separately. You can also sneak in a bit of his past.

Example (characterizing description) Charles stepped into the room and struck a shadow on the wall. He was tall and stood hunched forward as though ready to fight. His deep-set brown eyes held a menacing glare. A scar on his left cheek, gotten in a street brawl when he was fifteen, was a sharp hook. He said, "Hello, Laura." His voice was a threatening drawl.

You have created his physical specifics and the impression of his character. His appearance in the room is more informative, more dynamic. If you alter the imagery, he can be friendly rather than villainous.

Example The scar on his left cheek, gotten when rescuing a child from an onrushing truck, was a butterfly wing on his cheek.

You have placed information into the scene without being obvious. You have combined description and explanation and revealed his "type." You have made him interesting.

Critiquing Your Own Work

An important part of the writing experience is learning how to read your own writing. Inexperienced writers are too often overcritical of their own chapters. Not because the chapters are poorly done, but because they are criticized out of context of the entire novel.

A writer works on one scene, and then another scene, until the chapter is completed. A reader does not ponder over and examine every scene for the purpose of challenging the writer's skill. The reader reads each chapter *in context* of the entire novel. The reader wants entertainment, not instruction on how to become a writer. The reader reads a novel ALL AT ONCE, *a little bit at a time*.

The reader does not begin a novel on page 58, then skip to page 94, then flick back to page 17. But, on a writing day, the writer may start a scene that will eventually begin on page 61 and then skip directly to the novel's conclusion. When the scene is done, he rereads it to know if it is dramatic, believable—are the conflicts resolved to begin other conflicts, are characters consistent, etc.? The writer reads what he has just written, *out of context* to all that he has already written and to all that he will soon write.

Professional writers view their novels the way an artist studies an elephant he intends to paint. Stand too close and you see only texture without form. Stand too far away and you see shape without texture. The writer must be able to look at his own work from a point where he can criticize both its texture and form.

Many splendid chapters have been discarded because inexperienced writers have criticized their work out of context.

Be ruthless in the critical surgery of cutting away what is excessive and with repairing what is defective in each chapter. But be objective in determining how the chapter breathes through the *entire novel,* how each organ of a novel feeds the body-life of the entire novel.

Write for the Eye

Before writing is read, it is *seen*. The writer should compose his sentences for visual, as well as literary effect.

A large block of prose can force the reader to skim. The reader, faced with having to read a page-long paragraph, will quickly search that paragraph for its general meaning and ignore the shadows (subtle thoughts, inferred meanings, etc.).

It is the same when one character speaks a page-long block of dialogue. You are using the character to reveal important facts about the past, about the present, perhaps about the future but the *visual bulk* of writing causes the reader to think, "Do I have to read all that blather. What is the vital point he is making?"

Long blocks of descriptive passages will unquestionably establish the setting. But is this abundance of detail worth it? Does naming every flower in a garden create it as a "more garden"? What is the point where appropriate descriptions of setting become an excess of reality? When it slows down the motion of character and action, and when it forces the reader to not read.

Television and its takeover of the public's reading habits can be blamed to a degree. In television, the film and sound do almost all of the work for the viewer. Television moves quickly, it is social, and specializes in penetrating superficialities. It condenses human behavior, and the audience accepts this as empathetic participation. The public welcomes this synthetic experience. Why work at reading when you can relax at viewing—and believe you've gotten the same benefits?

The writer must write in his own time. This is the latter 1980s. In the middle 1990s the writer may produce his effects through one-line paragraphs. In the 2000s paragraphs may be reduced to phrases. But whatever lies ahead, the writer must write in the NOW of his time.

Incidental Characters

The writer's leanest, most selective use of details happens when dealing with *incidental characters*. They provide authenticity in setting. They offer mood images. Although they appear only once and are so minor they are not worth naming, they are necessary. You cannot have a full scene without them. They authenticate the political rally, the battle scene, the horse race, restaurants, church gatherings, weddings, and other such scenes. It is with the incidental characters, worth only one or two lines, that the writer learns how to use specifics and imagery.

Example To establish *setting:* An elderly woman with a hooked nose stood on the street. To establish *mood*: The screech of children scraped his nerves.

When incidental characters have only trivial actions to perform, do not name them. Writing "Gwenny came into the room and told her mother, 'Mom, you got a phone call,' " is not as effective as "A chubby girl with a runny nose called out, 'Mom, you got a phone call.' " Names of characters do not carry pictures. Naming unimportant characters is clutter. Images are more graphic, more realistic.

Incidental characters, though depicted individually, can be mulched together.

Example A gray-haired man lit a cigar. The woman beside him wrinkled her nose. The platform speaker's voice sounded like cracking wood. The humid air smelled of sweat. A skinny usher told a woman that drinking was not allowed during speeches. She capped the brown bottle and angrily shoved it into her floppy purse.

For establishing setting, the bulking together of incidental characters is more important than their individuality. Incidental characters must add to the scene, not distract from it. They cannot be written so vividly that they become more significant as characters than in their single purpose—*to authenticate setting or mood*. Though they are written with a selection of precise details, these details must be blurred in comparison to more important details or characters.

Additional Benefits of Good Writing Habits

Developing good writing habits does more for the writer than just getting him into the habit of daily, scheduled writing.

Every craft problem the writer solves brings him a conscious understanding of how to write more effectively. The writer uses these insights from the moment they are realized. He consciously applies them to whatever he is writing. Through a constant use of these insights the writer gradually *no longer thinks about them*. It becomes his habit to use these craft insights as part of his everyday habit of writing. He is freed to concentrate on resolving more complex problems. A writer always has writing problems. But the more he learns, the more he learns he has to learn more.

His knowledge of writing becomes as automatic to the writer as his knowledge of having teeth. He does not consciously think of his teeth while eating. He does not coax his teeth, "Go on, teeth, chew. There, that's a good loyal set of teeth." The only time anyone consciously considers his teeth is when they hurt. *When they cannot chew.*

The only time a writer becomes aware of his ignorance is when what he knows about writing no longer works for him. It is not enough for what he wants to accomplish. He must know more. *He begins hurting.*

There is no record in dental history that indicates anyone has been able to ignore a horribly abessed tooth for a year's time. The pain is unbearable. No writer who is serious about his profession can endure "ignorance of craft" for a long time. His progress is gradually crippled.

The writer's consciousness is like a well he empties through writing. When he has spilled all that he knows onto the pages, he must fill the well again, so he can again empty it. The daily habit of writing allows him to dip into all that he doesn't realize he already knows about writing to haul it up to his consciousness. As he has developed the habit of writing, so does he develop the habit of learning about writing.

The Option to Leave Situations Unresolved

Consider the technique of "optional plants." The creating of characters or situations which are to be further developed if you need them, or which can be left unresolved if they are no longer useful.

Example You are writing an intrigue or adventure novel. Your hero (or heroine) causes the capture and imprisonment of a maniacal, revengeful killer. Enraged, the killer swears revenge. The hero (or heroine) is given a long moment of concern. There is genuine cause for fear. The killer has always fulfilled his oath for gaining revenge. This maniacal killer is not the MAJOR KILLER OR VILLAIN. He is placed in the novel as a possible threat to the hero (or heroine)—so he can be used to intensify danger for a little while. He is just another handicap set against your hero (or heroine) if you need him.

This "optional plant character" can become a source of pressure that motivates the main character into an unusual action. Besides his quest to save the world from destruction, he has this added burden of being in constant danger from the maniacal killer. You can shift the scene by describing the killer's effort to escape confinement. (This change of viewpoint and scene can provide relief from the tedium of being in the consciousness of the main character for too long.) The hero can be placed in danger which he falsely attributes to the scheming of the killer. (This *legitimately* misleads the reader.) You are creating suspense and anticipation.

But the writer has the option of never using the killer again. The killer is a plant or red herring and need never again appear in the novel. After some events have transpired, and the main character becomes embroiled in other dangerous situations, the killer can be dropped—or killed. Or the writer reserves the option of having the killer released. The killer can be seen escaping confinement. He can then be used again.

In a novel, not all problems, situations, or conflicts have to be resolved. You can plant characters into the novel to create problems *for awhile*. These problems then cause primary or serious problems that must be resolved. But you do not have to resolve everything.

Deepening Character

Depth of character is achieved through a subtle, gradual, accumulation of insights and perceptions. It is an extension of the character's original concept. This extension moves both inward (through the character's innermost thoughts, emotions, beliefs) and outward (through the effects of external events)—sometimes simultaneously, sometimes alternately.

> **Example** Abraham Lincoln is ambitious. He wants to become a country lawyer. He leaves his rail-splitting job to study by candle and firelight.

If he fulfills his ambition, he is admirable, but not deeper. Depth will begin when outside events place pressure on his ambition, when his original intentions must be modified. He may experience discouragement, despair, or unexpectedly desire another goal. When Abe is forced *inward* to reach more personal resources to deal with his personal conflict, he becomes deeper and then reaches *outward*.

If a woman he loves demands, "I want you to give up the law and become a rail-splitter!" Abe Lincoln is forced into a sequence of conscious choices. The choice he makes must arise from within him, predicated on reasons that surprise him because they are based on motives he did not realize he had. By being forced to reach deeper into himself, he becomes a deeper character. Then his choice drives him outward.

Example Abe casts the woman aside and becomes a lawyer. He meets another woman. She encourages him to leave the law and pursue the presidency. A senator is shot in a duel. A political bloc approaches Abe to run for the senator's seat. He is overwhelmed. He is deeply troubled.

Again he must discover motives within himself for dealing with this rush of events. To contend with the "outside," he must plunge still deeper "inside." As he becomes deeper, he becomes larger. The reader observes these extensions of depth and size as "character changes." But he is not changed. He is only more of the original. When he is elected to the presidency, he is not another person, different from the one he was when he was a rail-splitter. He is a character who has extended outward while he was deepening.

The Aging of Characters Over Time

In a novel, the writer must establish the physical changes that happen to characters, or the passage of time will not be convincing.

Story The fortunes and fate of the Longstreet family begin in 1849, when Beauregard is sixteen. He is tall, muscular, and redheaded. The novel covers three generations. It ends when Beauregard dies, surrounded by the three generations.

If Beauregard, at 89, is seen in his plush bed as cherubic, still muscular, and with fiery red hair, the drama of the scene will be lost because of its inauthenticity. Time did not cause changes in Beauregard. Eighty-nine-year-old men are usually wrinkled, scrawny, and bald.

In writing, the aging process must not be neglected. It is filtered in like an almost invisible mist, never glaring, but somewhat noticeable. The writer does it sneakily, selectively. It can be narrated or demonstrated.

Example (narrated) Beauregard was beginning to feel his age. Fifty-three. He could no longer leap onto a horse and ride into town like thunder. He had to use his wife's carriage. Thick streaks of gray hair were crowding away the red. Crescents of flesh were puffed below his eyes. A thick flap of skin wagged under his chin when he talked. The townspeople were beginning to call him "turkey neck."

The physical changes of the characters should be described with periodic regularity. These changes offer verification of the characters' reality and their relationship to the passage of time. Sometimes you demonstrate the aging process by demonstrating the effect the aging has on the character.

Example (demonstrated) A chubby carpetbagger ogled Beauregard's daughter, then caressed her thigh. Beauregard pulled his hat from atop his graying hair and slapped it across the man's face. "Suh!" he shouted feebly, "You have dispahr-edged me doughta's honhar!" The chubby man shoved Beauregard aside, "Houta mah way, old man!" Beauregard lay in the muddy street, wiping mud from his wrinkled face.

Pivot Chapters

An average-sized novel (230 to 340 printed pages—about 350 to 450 typewritten pages) should contain at least five pivot chapters. A *pivot* chapter is any group of scenes that contains a crisis strong enough to change the direction of the novel. The change can be expected, or surprising.

Story Three men in an agency protecting natural resources investigate companies suspected of illegally dumping toxic wastes. One investigator loves the daughter of the Ecology Agency chairman.
The novel has reached the third chapter. There is a romance and racketeers who disregard agency rules and illegally dump toxic wastes for large companies. One of the investigators has been kidnapped by the racketeers. A township of 7,000 has become infected with maladies.

It is an average, workable plot line thus far. To heighten the action and suspense, a change, through a crisis, is needed.

Example (pivot chapter) A news conference is called by the chairman. He intends to reveal that 36 trucks are being loaded with deadly waste. They will be dumped in isolated areas of the country. The chairman has been warned by some industrial conglomerates not to reveal this information. If he does, his daughter will be killed. The chairman, a man of honor, won't be intimidated. The television cameras are ready to flash his statements to the nation. Suddenly someone screams and points to a lamp post. There is a dead man hanging from the lamp post arm. It is the agent who was kidnapped by the racketeers.

The novel now stands poised to pivot in a new direction. If the chairman keeps silent and is found out, he faces dishonor and conspiracy charges, but his daughter will live. If he tells, she will die. The two remaining agents must now avenge the murder of their associate. The novel can now *pivot* into any direction the writer wants.

Anticipation, Suspense, Surprise

There is a combination of three techniques that must be used in all forms of fiction: *anticipation, suspense,* and *surprise*. Without these, all fiction is either mechanical, monotonous, or reportorial. These three techniques must appear in order: You cannot have a surprising resolution, then build anticipation, then promote suspense. Anticipation must lead to suspense, which then allows for a surprising resolution.

Anticipation depends upon the reader's ability to predict the outcome of a situation. It is based on facts that the reader has been conditioned to accept as true or inevitable. (During the tornado season, for example, a tornado is expected. This expectation must be fulfilled.)

Example (newspaper item) The body of Thelma Winder, a known prostitute, was found in Whitechapel District. Her throat was severed. The instrument used was a surgical scalpel. This is the fourth such murder.

The reader knows that either Jack the Ripper, the son of Jack the Ripper, or a killer pretending to be Jack the Ripper, is on a killing rampage. It is in the hunt that suspense happens. *(How many prostitutes will be murdered before Jack is caught? Is he the one the Chief Inspector believes him to be?)* The writer blends his character/story/plot to the reader's "conditioned expectation." He delays, misleads, misdirects, and thus builds the factor of suspense.

Example There are actually three mentally disturbed doctors in the story. Will Jack be caught before he murders the Chief Inspector's daughter?

The surprise occurs in how the inevitable resolution is reached.

Example Jack is never apprehended, but the Chief Inspector's daughter is rescued in time. Jack turns out to be a woman, or the Chief Inspector himself.

In retrospect, all the facts, clues, and incidents are brought together to prove the resolution is logical. Though the reader predicted what would happen, the way the actual resolution unfolded did not conform to the reader's predictions. The reader is surprised, but not disappointed. The anticipation and suspense make the novel work and conclude satisfyingly.

The Series Novel

Completely developed characters who should not change are the *series* characters. (Sherlock Holmes, James Bond, Perry Mason, etc.) If series characters are changed by the demanding adventures they experience, their value as heroes or heroines is diminished. They become *credible* people and thus, unbelievable. Series characters must be vastly above average. Some general guides for creating series characters are:

1. They must stand for causes that are currently judged as *good*. Their personal deficiencies contribute to their completeness as characters. They can be drinkers, sexually active, dopers, former criminals, but they cannot be what is considered socially perverse (child abusers, wife beaters, etc.). It is their noble cause that redeems them as heroes.

2. Background motivation must be limited. The hero/heroine requires at most one tragedy in his/her past as an incentive to track down evildoers—such as the brutal murder of a family member or lover. One page of expository explanation in each novel should cover this background.

3. The locale is optional. Government heroes have great opportunities to travel. Private detectives may travel, but must always return home. Lawyers should have assistants who travel for them. Licensed policemen must always confront superiors for permission to leave, and must submit expense reports.

4. The novel must be conducted through three sections composed of defeats and victories: (a) four warm-up defeats to one taste of victory, (b) three serious defeats to one telling victory, (c) a final defeat which is impossible to overcome, and then the astonishing, tremendous overcoming of that defeat to a superlative victory.

Heroes and heroines in a series must never die or be drastically crippled. The public's preference in this matter has not changed over the centuries. Arthur Conan Doyle was forced to return superhero Sherlock Holmes from the dead because of a reading public's outrage. If a series character dies, the series ends. If the original writer passes away while the series is still popular, other writers will take over the series character.

Originality is Impossible

You should not strive to be original. You will be setting yourself against insurmountable odds. Everything that will be written has already been written.

As a writer you are the inheritor of a vast heritage of writings. For hundreds of years men and women have been creating works—literature—in every form and on every subject known. They have provided you with an inexhaustible supply of content, characters, situations and stories. It is not immoral or dishonest to use them. *Just don't lift them.* Use the material that appeals to you, in different combinations, other eras; switch sexes, blend the work of many writers.

Ideas, story lines, characters, situations, and techniques are in the public domain. You cannot copyright the abstract. If ideas could be copyrighted, there would be no publishers and television would be instantly defunct.

If you have nothing to write about, go to your local library. Browse through the stories and articles of the 1920 and 1930 issues of *Redbook, Saturday Evening Post, Colliers, Liberty, Cosmopolitan, The New Yorker,* and other popular publications. Study the digests of "famous novels," the condensed plots of operas—even the published summaries of old movies. This is not unethical. William Shakespeare, Henry Fielding, Henry James, George Bernard Shaw, and Honoré de Balzac all used ideas, stories, plots, characters and concepts that others had used in the past.

It is not stealing or plagiarizing. It is not even slyly adopting or adapting from other writers. You are drawing from your inheritance. In time, when you produce works, others will draw from the inheritance you leave.

Dialogue Creates Character

Dialogue is one of the most simultaneously obvious and subtle writing devices a writer can use. Dialogue proves that what the writer says about the characters is true. If, through expository narration, the writer tells the reader a character feels hatred for his university professor, it is opinion. If the character expresses his hatred in dialogue it is a convincing fact.

Example Randy huddled in his seat, hating Professor Holman for always making him feel stupid. The professor pointed to him and leered.
"Randy Cox, tell your peers the chemical content of lactonium."
"It's made up of—of—eh, I don't know it."
"You don't know much, do you?"
The students laughed. Randy yelled at the professor, "I know I hate your guts!" Some students gasped. Randy spit on the desk, "I hate you, yes!"

Dialogue offers simple and complex information.

Example (simple) "Your cooking is still lousy. I'm going downtown to relax and have a steak."

The character is not only telling his wife he has long been dissatisfied with her cooking. His dialogue also shows that he is aggressive, that their relationship is tense, he doesn't enjoy his home, he has some money, she cannot stop him from leaving.

Example (complex) "There was no point to my being a doctor. My taste was for big bucks and excitement. Arms smuggling, now there's adventure. Being against the law don't faze me."

The character has revealed a great deal about himself. He was once conventional, wanting a safe life. Economics stopped him. He chose a hard, risky lifestyle. He discovered concealed depths in himself. He is a criminal associating with other criminals. He makes a lot of money, likes the risks he takes, is not ashamed of how he lives, has disregard for conventions. He is a changed man.

Dialogue also offers the reader relief from reading. Narration is the "silent" imparting of information. Dialogue-prose is speech sound. If the writer defines the quality of the characters' voices (loud, shrill, hesitant, etc.) or their actions (haste, idleness, etc.) then the characters' voices become real as they speak sounds in the reader's mind.

Example (scene with dialogue) Harry's voice was hushed. "Honey, I love you." Angrily, Corrine pointed at his eyes, "You lie! You never loved me." He drew back, startled, confused. "I do love you—I mean it. I do." She suddenly punched his right eye, cursing, "Liar! You love me because I look like my sister. You love my sister!"

A. The writer has kept the dialogue in one paragraph to create proximity between people—rather than separating them by putting each speech in a separate paragraph.

B. The writer has first defined Harry's attitude of speech (hushed voice: intimate, intense).

C. He then defined Harry's emotional and physical response *before* Corrine's reply (anger, pointing at his eyes; then response, "You lie!"). The reader is now hearing two different voices and seeing the actions of two different people.

D. Harry reveals his attitude by how he reacts to Corrine's accusation (drawing back, startled, confused), and *then* he replies ("I do love you . . .")

E. Then Corrine's physical response reveals her emotional state and the tone of her spoken reply ("Liar! You love me because I look like my sister. You love my sister!"). In this emotionally charged interval, the writer has specifically defined what the people are doing and feeling while they are speaking—giving their speech volume, tone, and drama.

Dialogue changes the tempo of writing. Most dialogue is indented on the page, interrupting the sameness of the reading rhythm. At times, dialogue is more efficient than narration. The writer works to establish the "living" presence of the character, but until the character speaks, he is not convincingly alive.

Example The doctor jammed his hands onto Albert's chest, urging, "Breathe!" Mona wept, "Oh God, he's dead." The doctor heard a beep on the Spectroscam. "Now," he shouted, "He's alive!" Mona rushed to Albert, kissing his face. "Alive, you're alive—oh Albert, you've been given a miracle."

The writer can go on for pages, describing the recovery. He can have Albert do push-ups, jog two miles, eat six plates of spaghetti—but until he speaks, the reader is not absolutely convinced that Albert is alive.

Written dialogue should not contain all the verbiage real-live people use when they speak. The court-stenographer reporting of actual speech is windy, disorganized, without vitality. The charisma of the real-live speaker creates the dynamics in actual speech. In fiction, the writer creates the individual dynamics of the speaker through both description and speech. Fictional characters are not real people. It is the writer's skill that provides them with the presence of life.

Obvious vs. Hidden Clues

In crime or whodunit fiction, the writer must understand the function of clues. If the criminal is unknown, clues can lead to his discovery. If the criminal is known, clues can lead to his apprehension. There are two types of clues: (1) obvious clues and (2) hidden clues.

An *obvious* clue is visible. A gun near the crime, lipstick on a glass, a bloody handkerchief, a female's blond hair on a black tuxedo, etc. Such clues are offered in a manner that renders them either insignificant or ultrasignificant.

Example A man is found dead at his desk. There is a gun on the floor, a bullet hole in the wall. But the man was poisoned. The bullet in the wall is not the same caliber as the gun. A cobra is asleep in the bookshelf.

A *hidden* clue comes into existence through the actions of the characters. The characters carry or perceive the clues needed to solve the crime.

Example A woman is found dead from gas, an obvious suicide. The windows are sealed, the doorframe is stuffed with rags. Later, the hero re-members that the woman has a severe case of knee arthritis. He deduces that she could not have bent over to stuff rags at the bottom of the door.

Obvious clues lead to solutions by how the hero puts them together. *Hidden* clues lead to solutions by how the hero makes clever deductions.

The writer tricks the reader into overlooking clues in two primary ways.

1. *Distraction:* Just as the clue appears, the writer causes something im-portant to happen so the message in the clue is overlooked.

2. *Disguise:* The *real* clue is offered among many other possible clues, but its true value is not discerned. It is there, but hidden among the clutter.

Bringing the clues into the story after the crime has been solved is poor writing craft. The reader feels, "No wonder I didn't get it," or "The writer just figured out the clues himself." Through a clever distribution of clues before the solu-tion, the reader will declare, "I should have known," or "Sure, it was obvious all the time."

When the quality of prose is common, mundane, conversational, or general, the reader can un-knowingly finish the writer's sentences without reading them. This causes a loss of reader involve-ment; it urges the readers to skim. They just want to get on with it, to get it over with.

When a Recollection is Not Enough

Sometimes a writer will be tempted to avoid using a flashback in fear of inter-rupting the present story. The writer includes a brief recollection instead, but this device is not always sufficient.

Example Four shipwrecked sailors are afloat in a rubber raft. There is enough water for only one man for three days. One man decides to kill the others. His desire to live is extraordinary. He has a terrible secret buried in his past.

If the writer uses a short, introspective recollection to reveal this information, the depth of the character and the drama of his intentions will be lost.

Example I must stay alive, he thought. He visualized the large bag of diamonds he had hidden in the raft. Until enlisting in the Navy he had lived in savage ghettos. He would not give up his one last chance for the good life. He had killed before.

This recollective information is too hastily planted. When a character kills *en masse,* he should be clearly motivated; the past should be starkly demonstrated, at length, to qualify this motivation. A flashback into the murderer's past is more effective.

Example He pretended to sleep, though he watched the other men. He would kill the scrawny one first. Should he plan it, as he had planned the other murders he had committed? He breathed slowly, remembering eleven years ago. He was only sixteen then. He was playing poker. He knew the older men were cheating him. The light above the table was bright. He tossed cards into the pile, saying, "I'll take three." The chubby dealer nodded. "Three cards for the kid, comin' up." Before this deal was over he would work out a plan to kill them all. He studied his cards.

You show him performing one past murder. When he is returned to the rubber raft, and he kills, his actions are motivated and believable.

The Horror Novel

There are general guidelines for writing the *horror novel*. These guidelines are elastic. They merely indicate what the horror novel should contain. How they are used depends upon the writer's skill and vision.

The core of the horror novel is based on the fear present in the major character, and the existence of a supernatural entity outside the character. This fear need not be rational. It can contain psychological overtones and implications, but the *cause* of the fear must go beyond psychological analysis, or it is explainable and can be dealt with through human resources. Horror novels should contain mysteries that have no solutions in the realm of reality. The supernatural entity originates from any inventive source the writer can make believable.

The central character can be either a child or an adult. The supernatural entity must be sinister, arcane, and potentially lethal. Its origin can be in legend, folklore, superstition, or the occult. At the novel's opening it should be intangible, incorporeal, invisible. It appears at first to have been created by the character himself. As the novel progresses, it should gradually become tangible, visible. No matter what shape it takes, it must be terrifying. Its power must be unquestionably supernatural.

The people involved with the central character must be unbelieving at first. They fear for the character's sanity. Whatever happens as the result of the supernatural entity's work should be credited to coincidence or acceptable oddity at first. Only later on—after a strange disaster, an injury, or a death—do the other people begin to believe in the possibility of its existence. They must now fear the central character even as they try to help him. They are helpless. Only a "good" power can help him. There should always be the promise of a "good" power intervening.

Example The child's fear should be recurrent. It may affect the child internally or externally, or both. He should have positive evidence of this supernatural entity's existence such as nightmares, delusions, object distortions, or exaggerations of his five natural senses. The child seeks help but his evidence is discounted by the adults as imaginative. He is then forced by the supernatural entity to do something that makes the adults believe in the existence of the evil supernatural force after all. The supernatural entity *wants* to be known to exist. It delights in causing fear.

The character must begin as a "good person." He is not evil in himself. He is a hapless victim of an overpowering evil.

Example (adult) His fear should be dominating and beyond his control. It may be phobic or based on a childhood experience. Through an event he gains evidence that his fear is valid. A car wreck where everyone is killed. A burning building from which only he escapes. He must begin doubting his own sanity. He should be alienated from family and friends. He must blame himself for all disasters or deaths caused by the supernatural entity. He must try to fight it, scheme to destroy it.

Example (child) His fear should begin during a "strange" interval in his life: A high fever hallucination, being locked into a dark closet by a vicious parent, etc. During that time a "creature" should be present to help him in his terror, his estrangement from reality. It shows him ways to get back at the vicious parent: It calms him during his burning fever. They become friends. The creature is visible only to the child. Its supernatural reality is so appealing and loving to the child, he should care less and less for the real world. Eventually the creature manifests into a terrible form and is seen by others.

The child or adult should suddenly develop unusual powers and capabilities. They must undergo some physical and character changes. They do not have to become ghouls, zombies, or werewolves, but the changes must be obvious to other people. At first, they must be reluctant to harm others; then they are taken over and do it willingly.

If a "good" power is to be used, it should be called upon by someone who loves the victim. It should originate in the *supernatural*, the *religious* or the *divine*. The redemption or damnation of the victims depends upon the writer's vision.

Intention vs. Reality

What the writer intends to do in his novel offers no value to the reader. The reader does not know or care about the writer. The writer is an amorphous creature fixed in some distant orbit of the cosmic order. The only consequence the writer has to the reader is how he creates a "work" that entertains or provides a gratifying reading experience. It is what is read that is judged—not what the writer intends his writing to mean.

The writer must not underestimate or overestimate the intelligence and depth of the reader. The most experienced writers do not judge the reader at all. They are concerned only with what they are writing. The novel can only be believable, dramatic, and interesting if it is immediately clear. The reader cannot strain to enjoy and actually enjoy at the same time.

Readers are not exceptionally dumb or astonishingly intelligent. Fixing value judgments upon their minds and sensitivities is a disastrous guessing game. You can't write down for the dumb and write up for the smart. An unchanging achievement the writer must direct himself toward accomplishing is to always be clear in what he is writing.

The writer must not assume that he will be read by a public who is skilled in the interpretation of hidden allegories, incremental repetitions, leitmotifs, or *explications de texte*. If a writer is compelled to include such content it should be considered as subterranean material to be gained after the original intention is stated with clarity.

A one-to-one, intimate relationship is established, not between the writer and reader, but between the reader and the novel. The writer is appreciated and offered accolades only after the novel is read. Grandiosities of meaning intended to be understood only by the esoteric intelligentsia are "literary affectations." Write a fascinating story and reveal the myriad depths of human character unfolding clear writing and you will create a winner.

Four Simple Transitions

Developing skill in writing transitions can eliminate overwriting, increase pace, aid in viewpoint changes, and create many other effects.

Some common transitions:

1. Young Ralph Miller is worried about being liked by Mary Lowe, the high school beauty. You end the scene with Ralph pacing the school corridors, worrying that Mary will not date him. You break to the next scene (an inch space between scenes constitutes a space break) which begins: *Ralph huddled against the car door, annoyed that Mary would not stop trying to kiss him.* You have shifted from one place to another. You have resolved Ralph's former problem and created another. You have advanced time and also revealed a change in attitudes.

2. Paraphrases of *"meanwhile, back at the ranch"* and *"two hours later"* are excellent transitional devices. But try disguising them.

3. Holding a reader to portions of a scene that do not contribute to drama or character can be avoided through time transitions within the scene. *Bill watched the people passing by the art museum entrance. He hoped his wife would not be late. Fourteen cigarettes and three bags of popcorn later, he still waited for her.* You have avoided trivial introspections, eliminated a marathon of unnecessary descriptions of people who go in and out of the museum.

4. Let a character, through dialogue, provide a viewpoint transition.

Example Melanie was afraid the swarthy-looking man standing across the street was planning to burglarize her home. She called to her mother, "Mom, why do you think that man is watching our house?" Her mother stroked Melanie's hair, shushing her. "He's the new minister who moved into town." Her mother knew Melanie needed psychological counseling for a low threshold of hysteria.

No transition, simple or complete, is mysterious. The writer diligently goes about learning how to achieve them.

Environmental Details

The details of environment serve several functions. They establish the authenticity of the time. They serve as a visible reality in which characters play out their story. They allow the writer to create a larger world outside of the characters' limited interests. And people are defined through those details.

Story A writer has left the business of the city for an area where he can be isolated and regain contact with his spiritual resources.

In the dry plains of Arizona He walked the dusty road, hands pushed into his pockets, trying to conceive of a first chapter. A squat cactus was a gangrenous growth in the sand. The novel he wanted to write was like that coarse stump, deep within him. Hurting, ugly, scabrous. He shuddered, feeling as dry as the earth below the cactus.

Lazing in the greenery of Vermont He sat with his back pressed against the coarse tree trunk. He could feel ants crawling up his ankles. They were like the ideas beginning to nibble in his soul. Tiny, irritating. He breathed deeply and looked up to the tree. Clumps of leaves hung heavily on the branches. I'll bloom too, he thought. Ideas would soon burst from him and spread as thickly as the leaves.

At an Oregon seaside He listened to the squawk of sea gulls. They skimmed the air like thick feathers in an idle breeze. He reached up, wanting to grasp one as he was grasping for an idea, a story line. Suddenly, he shouted, "Stop! Settle down. Let me touch you!" His voice caused some birds to leap into flight. The novel he wanted to write had become like the sea gulls. Beautiful, but always out of his reach.

If the writer knows how to use the details of environment, they become useful for more than mere background description. The writer does not have to force his imagery. The details create it for him. The writer blends the character into the environment by using the details as part of the character's sensations and thoughts.

The Investigation Novel

The investigation novel is a complicated and versatile structure in which two individual stories and two separate plot lines unfold. One story and plot line move back into time—the other story and plot line move forward. Though the stories are separate, the plot lines begin to converge on each other. There is a mystery in the past which also poses a danger in the present. Characters in the present are also characters in the past. Both the present and the past hold part of the answer to the total mystery. The "investigator" does not (generally) have an active relationship to the past, but he must fit all the pieces together *in the present*. The narrator begins in first person: subjective, then evolves into first person: objective.

Story 1988. Some youngsters discover a skeleton in Fresno. It is the body of the vice president, who disappeared in 1930. An investigation is started but dead-ended by time. An investigative reporter whose mother was once engaged to the vice president, gets a list of suspects the police do not know about. He begins interviewing the people who were involved. His search puts him in danger. The murderer or murderers are still alive. He continues with the investigation.

The present story (the investigation) begins in first-person, subjective viewpoint. The reporter becomes deeply interested in learning the truth. At the point where he is placed in danger, the reporter's viewpoint becomes more objective, to allow for analysis and explanation of the mystery. He must bring the fragments to a whole solution.

The investigator interviews the people on the list. When the people respond, the writer shifts into spoken flashbacks, which are written from a third-person point of view. The character relives the time he is relating. The interviewer can never be on scene in that past story, because he was not yet born. The vice president is revived in the past. He becomes the major character in the past, while the investigator is the major character in the present. Both the vice president and the reporter have their own story and plot. The vice president's role is in the past. The narrator's role moves forward in the present.

The dead in the past become as alive as the living in the present. The vice president is re-created as he was, through the stories the other characters tell about him. He becomes a fully developed character. Generous, lusty, corrupt, a family man, forthright, ambitious, honest. His fullness is developed as the fragments are brought together.

Example (the V.P.'s best friend, now eighty years old, is interviewed)

"Oh yes, Jethro was never one to let a crook get to him. I was in his office the night Barry Crimps came in with an attaché case of bribe money and tossed it onto the desk. Jethro drummed his fingers on the desk and waited for Barry to offer the bribe."

(The scene of the attempted bribe is played out in flashback.)

The next interview can be with Barry Crimps.

Both characters, the vice president and the reporter, must experience critical pressure in their time. The vice president is going to be killed, the investigative reporter is in danger of being killed. Suspense, in the past, is created as the reader wonders which character killed the vice president. Suspense in the present depends upon the intensity of danger placed upon the reporter.

The investigator should have a love interest, someone who is indirectly involved in the present story. (A grandchild of the V.P. or one of the people being interviewed.) When the reporter learns the truth, he should experience resistance in having it believed.

Example (solution to mystery) The murderer (still alive and trying to kill the reporter) is the son of the former president of the United States. The former president's son doesn't want the reporter to reveal that his father

(now living in retirement) murdered the vice president to keep him from revealing that the Chief Executive was a Nazi agent planning to lead the country into siding with Adolf Hitler.

The past story stops when the murder is discovered, and the present story takes over. The remainder of the novel deals with the investigator and the decision he makes—whether to risk his life by exposing the murderer, and gain the Pulitzer Prize by exposing this fifty-year-old crime.

Two-Page-Long Sentences

There are writers who are still in the "potential" phase of writing because they cannot overcome the rule-making restraints of the formalists. They cannot see beyond the rules to learn the techniques. Unless they overcome their intense concern with proper sentence structure and grammatical propriety, they will never write with the freedom their talents and skills demand.

There is an exercise which will release the writer from the restraints of tradition. *Begin writing one-page-long sentences*, incorporating as many writing techniques as you can (*dialogues, details, research, character analysis, action, situation*, etc.). Then extend this into a two-page-long sentence.

Example Greg Helman quit the University of Wisconsin to work as a Jacquard twine winder because he wanted to know the feel of the finest-grade linen thread, to lovingly dip skeins into deep starch barrels and know the joy of spreading the skeins on the rollers of a polishing machine, though his fiancée, Maureen, told him, "I will not have my husband a Jacquard twine winder, what will people say?" and her outrage smashed his dreams though he had always known she was an ambitious woman who wanted him to become dean of the university and write books about the madcap adventures of bringing retarded students into brilliance, but he decided to give up Maureen rather than sacrifice his career, and he left her and tears of grief so blurred his vision that when he entered the bank to withdraw his savings he did not see the people laying on the floor while four burly men wearing ski masks were robbing the bank, and one robber, thinking Greg was a cop, shot him in his Jacquard twine-winding hand and Greg wept in horror for who would hire a. . . ."

After accomplishing a two-page-long sentence, without losing clarity, situation, or continuity, and maintaining the flow and sweep of the scene, work on a three-page-long sentence, and upon accomplishing that you will have overcome the tight, formalistic restraints that have hindered your "freedom of self-expression" and you can then go on to doing a four-page-long sentence. . . .

Necessary Delusions

Writers are not usual people: their inner life is not average.

Unless a writer lives with a periodic *delusion* of his greatness, he will not continue writing. He must believe, against all reason and evidence, that the public will experience a catastrophic loss if he does not complete his novel. The public is just clamoring to give him his fame.

The writer who is still unpublished is beset by all manner of unreasonable and undeserved handicaps. No one really trusts, believes, or respects him. He is unpublished. You are not a writer until you are published. His family is appalled by his ambitions in so precarious and eccentric a profession. He works as hard, and often as long, as any laborer or executive, without pay, no fringe benefits, no union protection, without hope of social security. His career is a continual speculation.

If he does not delude himself into an almost fanatic belief in himself, he will never withstand the profession's hazards and discouragements. He must work at his writing, believing that this first novel, when accepted by a publisher, will gain him a $1,000,000 advance, that it will be selected by major book clubs, be translated into a dozen languages, and earn him the National Book Award and Pulitzer Prize. A writer cannot indulge himself in nickel-and-dime, penny-ante, niggardly delusions.

The writer must also be angrily critical of other writers, even if he admires their work. "Garbage!" "Tripe!" "How did this junk ever see the light of print?" He must know that he can produce a better work even if he wrote with one hand behind his back, and partially blindfolded.

While he writes, a slender vein of daydreaming should be pulsing through his consciousness. He must see himself speaking in crowded auditoriums, attending ultra-posh parties where he is lionized. This delusion must be part of the writer's bloodstream.

It is the "healthy madness" that keeps him sane, and writing.

When to Digress

Within the body of a novel, there is room for many inventive structures. These structures should be used only after the writer feels the reader is so firmly held by the novel that an inventive departure from the usual form will not interrupt the reading.

There are times when the writer believes a little digression from the immediate moment will contribute to the scene.

Scene The year is 65 A.D. Two Roman senators are strolling near a hill in Golgotha. One senator points south, "It was upon that very mound I witnessed the death of—what was that zealot's name? I have forgotten." The other senator replies, "He was called Jesus. A poor carpenter. He was made to carry the very wood upon which he died."

It is at this moment the writer can digress and bring in a narrated history that will interest the reader, and because it is part of the scene.

Example There was no record of the type of cross upon which Jesus was crucified. Was the shape that of a T or a + sign? It was believed when God ordered Ezekiel to mark the foreheads of the men in Jerusalem with the tau, the Greek T, it was a prediction revealing the type of cross to be used. To construct such a cross, the *titulus* was placed onto the *patibulum* and affixed by hammering four nails into the wood.

This fragment of history contributes to that portion of the scene; it does not intrude. By the use of Latin terms, it also authenticates the time and the flavor of the speech.

This technique can also be used in dealing with character analysis.

Example Melanie blurted out her feelings. "I love you, Sidney, but I just don't trust you." He turned away, too enraged to speak.

He was a descendant of the pirate Stripebeard who roamed the seas, hunting unarmed galleons. Sidney believed crime was in his blood. At the age of fifteen he had entered a monastery to purge his soul of any genetic traces of that infamous pirate. He had not succeeded.

This technique should be used with selectivity and discreet timing.

Intertwining Three Stories

In a novel, when three separate stories are developed, in a parallel motion forward the stories should appear to be happening simultaneously. Otherwise a staggered effect is created with each story waiting its turn to happen.

Stories Three brothers begin a used car business. Charlie is a drunk. Ernie believes in humanity. Gary is crooked. Each brother has his personal story *outside* the dealership. A serious conflict among the brothers involves the type of business practice to institute.

Imagine three large, rapidly growing plants on the same table. As the leaves grow upward, long tendrils are growing outward. The tendrils begin curling about each other, while the leaves grow. The plants are still individual entities, but they are no longer separate. They are connected by tendrils and appear to be growing together.

A novel with three (or five) separate stories, must grow in the same manner. Each story brought together while still unfolding separately. These tendril connections happen when each brother brings the other brothers into his life through thoughts and feelings, when they are not together. When the brothers are together in a scene, the influence and impact that each has upon the others' lives is obvious.

Example While Ernie's story is unfolding, he must think about his brothers and their effect on his life—when they are not with him. By doing this, he brings their story life into his own. Charlie and Gary must do the same with Ernie. Bring him into their lives.

That the brothers think about each other when they are not together *proves* the impact the three lives have on each other. They are tightly connected, not only because they are brothers in the same novel but because their lives reach out and influence each other.

They are still three separate lives, but not three separate stories. Their story lives are connected and appear to be happening simultaneously.

How to Avoid Stereotypes

All characters are, at first, *stereotypes* in their own environment. A queen in her realm, a surgeon in a hospital, a missionary in a jungle, a schoolteacher before her class. Every character on earth has already been written about. Unless a character has three ears and an eye in the crook of his elbow the character is recognizable. The reader is somewhat familiar with him.

The two general ways of avoiding this condition of stereotype are (1) by immediately exploring the innerness of the character, (2) by placing the character immediately in a unique situation.

Example Jim Masters was a bricklayer with heavy muscles. He enjoyed the envy he stirred in smaller men. He was becoming bald and tried to hide it under a buttery blond toupee. His hobby was flinging stray cats into the river, then diving in to rescue them.

The first line of description brings the character into existence. The second sentence reveals an "inner" fact about him. In the third, he is described further, in an odd way. In the fourth the reader is startled by his peculiar form of pleasure. He is no longer a stereotype.

> **Example** The world-renowned tightrope walker balanced himself on the high building ledge. He was not afraid of the harsh, eccentric winds. He feared the knowledge that his wife was at the other end with a hacksaw. Fifty stories was a long fall.

The tightrope walker is seen about to perform an action common to his profession. This common situation is made critical by the wind. The third sentence defines an uncommon, murderous possibility. Now, while the reader's concern is for *what will happen,* the writer can go on to explore the uniqueness of the character further.

Establishing immediate reader interest in the character or the situation gives the writer an edge over stereotyping.

Spoken Flashbacks

Spoken flashbacks, which are developed from the actual speech of a character, offer a good alternative to flashbacks that occur only in the character's consciousness. Even when the flashback is important to the story line, overlong stretches of dialogue can be tedious to read. The story may be interesting, but the "speaking" of it will lack intensity and drama.

> **Story** A soldier on trial for treason is asked to tell the court where he was Monday night. The soldier begins "speaking" his testimony.

If the writer allows the soldier to speak the full story, the scene's pace and theatrics are diminished. The "natural" dialogue becomes wordy. There is no gesture, no facial expression, no bodily motion. He is just offering information through natural, verbose dialogue. The "told" story is never as graphic as the "shown" story.

If the soldier tells the story the way it would be written by a writer, it would be too organized, too precise. The dialogue would sound unnatural. It would sound written rather than spoken.

To avoid runs of tedious, wordy dialogue, the writer should WRITE the story after the soldier begins speaking. The story is converted into a sequence of acted-out scenes within the present scene, the trial. It becomes, in essence, a SPOKEN FLASHBACK. The transition is simple:

Example (soldier's testimony) "Well, on that night, I was in my barracks, shinin' up my boots, when this captain comes in, you know. He was pure spit 'n polish. I jumped like a jack rabbit, scared, you know. . . ."

The officer strode to him, then grinned. "At ease, son." The soldier felt sweaty. The captain drew an envelope from his pocket. "There's $19,000 in here, son. It's yours for an hour of duty at the. . . ."

The depicted story continues until the scene is fully developed. The acted-out scene is stopped a line or two before the end, when the writer returns to the courtroom where the soldier is finishing the story in his own words.

Introspective Transitions

Introspection can be used for more than conveying a character's thoughts. It also has value as a transition device. Introspection can serve as a span across which the writer moves from the mental focus to the emotional or physical focus of a character. It can be used for the shifting of viewpoints. Introspection can bridge space and change from one character's viewpoint to another character's viewpoint, in another place.

From mental to physical The fake diamonds in the statue's eyes glittered at Tom. *What a mean mockery of art and antiquity.* He suddenly grabbed a hammer and smashed its head.

From mental to emotional Dolly studied the cold, uncaring attitude in Gordon's eyes. *He never really loved me. He was only using me.* Her mouth trembled. *How I wish I could hate him. Hate him, till I was free.*

For changing viewpoints Charlie slumped against the lamp post. *I'll never make it home. I'll die in the streets.* Sidney grabbed his shoulders and shook him. "Can't take it, can you?" he snickered, then shrugged. *If he can't hold his liquor, why'd the fool come out to drink?*

From one place to another place Millicent crushed the letter in her trembling hands. She hated Ralph for not including her in his will. *He knows I need the money.* While she fought back tears, Ralph waited in his office, staring at the vicious black gun laying on his will. He would show them. *I'll make them sorry for only wanting my money and not my dear soul.*

Introspective transitions serve two purposes:

1. To link two objective sentences in a tighter unity. "He walked in the park. ↔ *I like walking in the park.* ↔ The clear air invigorated him."

2. To separate two objective sentences subtly. "She watched the moon drift behind some clouds. (↔) *Is there really a man in the moon?* (↔) She jumped when she heard a shot.

Before using an introspective transition, decide if you want it to bring two sentences closer together or if you want it to separate some sentences. All introspective transitions should be immediately associated with the sentences that precede them. If the association is not immediate, the connection will be broken and the introspection will appear to be a "deliberately planted" thought.

Perception and Insight

In writing, there is a marked difference between *perception* and *insight*. Though both responses are so closely related they have become interchangeable in life, they remain separate in writing.

A perception is a character's sudden emotionally-charged realization of the true significance of the event that is occurring before his eyes. Perceptions are always related to on-scene actions and characters.

> **Example (perception)** Peggy heard her small son laughing. She snuck to his room. She gasped at how he methodically stabbed a Raggedy-Ann doll. *My God, how he hates his sister.* She turned away, listening to his laughter.

An *insight* is an intellectual glimpse into the nature of the human condition. It is formulated through associations, recollections, and comparisons. It is a realization that occurs *after the fact* of action. It is new information based on old information. Insights, always based on events that have already happened, can be thought into existence—after a while.

> **Example (insight)** The leader of a guerrilla group is organizing the capture of an ammunition train. He knows Seraphina is pregnant. While issuing tasks and strategies he considers that Seraphina would be overly cautious during the fighting, to protect her pregnancy. He assigns her to gathering the horses once the men have boarded the train.

Insight can be delayed. It is the result of a character's reflection. Information upon which it is based, sometimes collected from different sources, has already been absorbed by the character. As the character assembles the information into an insight, the reader follows his logic.

Perception happens in an emotional instant. Though it may be based on what has happened before, the meaning of the events that bring it about never occurred to the character until the moment it is expressed.

A perception should be short, succinct. An insight can be longer, more detailed. Both are used for providing information at different times and with different intensities.

To "Show" or To "Tell"

There are times when action that is *"shown"* would be more interesting if it were *"told."* At other times, the content of what is being "told" would be more dramatic if it were "shown." It is important to develop an awareness of what type of writing, at what particular time, the reader will accept as most dramatic.

The reader is always grasping for proof that characters are not only real, but that the events that happen in their lives are important. This is proved by the way characters react and respond to what happens to them. This also includes what has already happened to them. Every act a character commits should be important to the *reader*.

Example Aunt Louise set a bowl of oatmeal before Oliver. He disliked the cereal. When he was a child in boarding school, it had been slopped into a bowl, lukewarm. He ignored the oatmeal and reached for some toast.

This is "told" dislike for oatmeal. Though it may be an interesting fact in Oliver's background, it has no emotional significance. Because it is cited as information only in passing, *it can be told*. Or, if the reader skims and the information is not noted, the loss is not a disaster.

Tell is intellectual, distant. Show is emotional, intimate.

The "show" aspect enters when what the character feels comes into the scene. Feelings are triggers snapping the characters into responses.

Example Oliver wrinkled his mouth at the bowl of oatmeal. He did not breathe, afraid the odor would make him dizzy. He stood up, mumbling, "Gotta go to the bathroom," and hurried from the kitchen.

When an item of information is just another detail in a list of information, tell it. If Oliver leaves the table without emphatic response to oatmeal, then it is not that important. If he reacts emphatically, it is important and will cause other reactions.

At what moment the reader should be SHOWN, or be TOLD, depends, not on the rule of "Show, Don't Tell"—but upon what the writer judges as dramatic and interesting for the reader.

How to Be Interviewed

If you are closing in on your first novel and believe it is a winner: a testimony to the creative or commercial genius of this generation, it is wise to begin practicing how to be interviewed. Popular writers have been forced to become public images. What you say will be widely read and become literary canon to still unpublished writers.

You must overcome your natural personality and emerge as colorful. Concoct your life into a fiction. Find some minor events that momentarily intruded into your usually banal life, and exaggerate them into uncommon adventures. Gun running in Africa, a few years as a bordello madam, some time in a raw criminal institution, horrifying abuse as an orphan, periodic sex changes, etc. Be intense, be grim, extol the benefits of suffering.

Make it impossible for the next generation of writers by claiming you work 14 hours a day, and rewrite everything a minimum of 74 times. Confess you have sacrificed family and friends to take long moonlight walks to commune with your creative muse, accompanied only by your loyal dog or parakeet. Research some obscure but scholarly European and Asian writers and claim they influenced your career.

Rehearse a skill for blurting out spontaneous epigrams. They need not be relevant to the subject being discussed, or make much sense. It is the way writers are supposed to speak. "No one can be graceful walking down hill." "Parents are mills grinding out neurotics." "Only in the dream does one behold reality." "Democracy is not a concept, it is a vibrant cosmos." "Motorcycling is a launch into the universe of mankind."

You are almost a genuine novelist. You have earned admission into a cult of national and international deceivers. The uniform is either attire so meticulously current you obviously employ a cadre of designers, or so disorderly that "rag-bag" is your fashion statement. You are a novelist—the public stands in anticipation of your illustrious presence. Do not disappoint them by appearing to be ordinary.

Gothic Heroines

Writers of gothic novels should avoid creating heroines of such gross naiveté that they are almost stupid. Innocence does not connote retardation. A foolish female will be pitied, but not loved. When a hero loves a fool, how intelligent can he be? Heroines are also thinking humans.

Example Fredrick, the master of Moormont, comes to love Charity, a beautiful female brought to his manor to tutor his small son. Fredrick's second wife is jealous of Charity. At one time she tries to poison her. Another time she tries to push her from a high window. One morning she lures her into a forest populated with killer boars and leaves her there. Charity also realizes that the woman is trying to kill Fredrick's son.

Unless the writer gives Charity a reason for remaining in a residence where her life is endangered, she must have enough intelligence to leave. Otherwise she will not be sympathetic or believable. Whatever superb action she takes to wrest the son, or Fredrick, from the villainess will not be credible. If she remains, she should be given intelligent, emotional motives for remaining. She loves Fredrick and knows his wife will murder him to inherit the vast estate. She loves his son and wants to save the boy.

If the heroine puts her life on the line, it must be done for a cause or person she believes is more important than her own life. She begins as an ordinary female, but love, and danger to those she loves, render her capable of extraordinary courage and sacrifice. She is then recognized as a woman of noble qualities. A dumb martyr is rarely credited with dying for an intelligent cause. Intelligence must be part of her character. Readers care about heroines who are able to set evil and corruption aright through their character and intelligence.

If the hero is strong, inherently good and intelligent, he has no reason to fall in love with a dumb woman. No matter how beautiful and virtuous she is, if she is dumb, and he loves her, his heroic stature is lessened, and his intelligence is questionable.

Delayed Character Changes

The *delayed character change* is an excellent technique to use when trying to develop character complexity and plot complication. Through the intense pressure of a critical situation, the character realizes something about himself that he never understood before. This inner revelation causes a change in the character. But it may be inconvenient to the plot line for the character to recognize the change in himself during that critical situation. The pressure passes and he goes on to other scenes.

If the character is not allowed to recognize that he has changed, then as far as he himself is concerned, he has not changed. Yet, even if the character does not know he has changed, the change still exists. The character's recognition of the change is delayed, held in abeyance for another critical interval.

Story Clara needs money to pay off her mortgage. She goes to the town banker, who is a known lecher. She hopes he will not try to seduce her. She will refuse him, and lose the loan. He makes a pass at her, and, instead of immediately rejecting his attentions, she allows him to trifle with her. She plans to tease him until she gets the loan, then refuse him. But, unexpectedly, she is gripped in the passion of the moment and, to stop herself from submitting to his lust and her own desires, she flees.

No appreciable change in her character seems to have happened. For a fleeting moment her virtue was endangered when she was tempted to succumb to her own passion. But she fled, morality intact. At best, her take-home lesson would be "Don't play with fire or you might be burned." Clara continues moving through the novel, seemingly unchanged by her experience.

In Clara's own consciousness, she was not changed by the experience. Circumstance cast her into a dreadful situation, but she emerged unscathed. But the reader is presented with a view of Clara's character that was not known before. Within the staid woman is a passionate depth. It frightens her.

Story continued Seven scenes later, Clara's fiancé, Marvin, is given leave from the army. They are alone in her parlor and Marvin, an ultramoral young man, suddenly confesses that he has had several bouts with "women of the town." Clara is outraged and about to dismiss him. Then she recollects her scene with the lecherous banker and her unexpected passion and temptation. At that critical moment, Clara realizes that Marvin is only human, like herself—though he was not strong enough to resist the call of the flesh. She is forgiving.

It is in that pressuring situation, seven scenes later, that the change in her character (which was deliberately postponed) emerges in her consciousness as an inner revelation. The character change has happened.

A *delayed character change* creates a perceivable continuity with scenes of the past. It provides a new function for a scene that has already taken place. It offers either a shift or an addition to the plot line. It alters relationships, establishes new conflicts, and creates suspense.

A recounting When Clara does not submit to the banker, she is true to her characterization. She is not changed, merely uncomfortable. The restraint she shows confirms the consistency of her character. Seven scenes later, when Marvin confesses his infidelity to their vows of premarital celibacy, and Clara is forgiving, the writer has:

1. brought a delayed character change into existence through Clara's realization of her heretofore unsuspected sexual passions,

2. brought a past scene which has already served its purpose (Clara and the banker) to the present and given it an additional function, providing Clara with an inner revelation she did not experience at the time,

3. recalled the near-disastrous time with the banker to establish a continuity with the past.

Knowing what she now knows about herself changes Clara's relationship with Marvin, and alters her own self-image. Her near "fall from virtue" has given the banker a knowledge of the passion beneath her respectability, which he may use against her. Another conflict appears.

Delayed and immediate character changes are equally dramatic. The choice of which to use depends upon when and how the change in character affects the character relationships, conflicts, and plot line.

Moral Pressure on Heroes and Villains

A major character cannot be sympathetically heroic or despicably villainous until his "moral fiber" has been tried under "moral" pressure.

Example (usual heroic act) A four-year-old boy runs across an ice-covered pond. The ice cracks and he falls in. He screams. The major character is strolling in the park and hears the scream. He shucks off his coat as he runs to the pond, dives in, and quickly rescues the boy.

The writer has revealed the major character's courage. Such bravery is expected of him. In the novel he performs several such acts in different forms. The hero gains admiration, not necessarily love.

Example (usual villainous act) During a high-stakes poker game a businessman holds four aces. He bets $10,000. The villain sees him and shows a royal flush. He is accused of cheating. The villain kills the businessman.

The villainy of killing is not despicable. This is what villains *do*. If he does not kill the businessman, he is without honor, without pride. It is in the "moral realm" that heroism or villainy is determined as true.

Example The hero has just had a coronary bypass. Excessive activity will kill him. A four-year-old boy falls into an ice-covered pond. The hero hears the screams. He hesitates. Saving the boy might kill him. Another scream is heard. The hero chooses. He races to the pond and saves the boy.

Now the *character* is heroic, not only the act. His act is one of morality, not only bravery. HE CONSCIOUSLY MADE A MORAL, HEROIC CHOICE. He is loved.

Example In the high-stakes poker game the businessman reveals he is trying to win money for his mother's operation. The villain's own mother has just died of cancer. The businessman shows his four aces, reaches for the pot, saying, "This will save my dear mother's life." The villain thinks of his dead mother and the grief he felt. He knows how desperately the businessman needs the money. The villain sneeringly lays down the winning hand. Because he cannot save his mother, the businessman draws a small pistol from his pocket and kills himself at the table.

The villain is truly villainous because HE CONSCIOUSLY MADE A DESPICABLE MORAL CHOICE. He is a self-made villain, worthy of hatred.

Ongoing Identifying Characteristics

The general, the identifying traits a writer uses to describe his characters must be continued throughout the story. The traits may be modified or intensified by the situations and events, but never dropped. They must also be constantly proven. *Referring* to a character as witty, brilliant, vicious, generous, slothful, or morose does not create a character of that particular stature.

It is unlikely that a cynical, always-depressed character who is also a miser would happily volunteer to play Santa Claus at the local department store— handing out ten-dollar bills from his personal treasure. A scientist is not portrayed believably if he acts dumb and never does anything scientific. Providing him with a gray goatee and thick glasses does not make him a convincing scientist. People (even in stories) do and say what they are. Their identities are solidified by their actions, interests, and dialogue.

Example Brenda is a nationally syndicated gossip columnist who writes about film and television personalities. She is reputed to be a brilliant woman with a cutting wit. She is at a lavish party where luminaries of the profession are gathered. A film star, no longer famous, believes her career was ruined by Brenda. She begins calling Brenda slanderous names.

If Brenda replies, "I'll not dignify your comments with an answer," the writer has not proven the identity given to Brenda. If Brenda replies, "How unfortunate your mother didn't have children," then she is believably sustained.

This trait of a cutting wit must be part of Brenda's continuing personality. To be a full and dramatic person there must be many other facets to her personality, but her identifying characteristic should always be present. It is the quick and certain way the reader recognizes Brenda, and remains familiar with her, never questioning Brenda's identity.

Recounted Narration

A recounted narrative is one in which, at the beginning of a new chapter, you recount what happened a few days ago, in the previous chapter. It is a time-saving and pace-quickening device.

Example (chapter) The war is over. Steven is shipped back to England. His wife will meet him at the dock. He bids his buddies goodbye, then takes a long train ride to LeHavre. He is poor, but happy.

The writer wants to get Steven back to his wife, quickly. But before he does, one vital event must happen. A man offers Steven a thousand pounds to deliver a small box to an address in London. While the incident is vital, it may take seven static pages of a train ride before it happens. Omit the total train ride. Pick up the story in the next chaper, *three days later,* when Steven is at the boat railing, waving to his wife. Then, *recount,* in narrative form, what happened on the train.

Example (next chapter) Steven waved his hat at Louise. He could barely see her amid the crowd. She held their son high to show how Milburn had grown. Steven made himself laugh to conceal his fear. The small box in his pocket was hot against his thigh. There might be police waiting for him. *God, don't let them catch me.* He kept waving, but he did not feel happy as he thought of small, sneaky Mr. Alexander.
    They met while he was seated at the train window, staring at the scenery. Mr. Alexander sat beside him and whispered, "I need a favor." He had held out a glossy green box slightly smaller than his palm. "I must have this delivered to my brother in London. It contains our mother's ashes, Lord rest her soul." Steven knew it was a lie, but with a thousand pounds he could purchase a flat. The box was small enough to. . . .

You have overcome a three day lapse of time. You have extracted the vital event from the past and avoided static material. You have complicated the present chapter by placing another problem into it.

Reading to Your Friends

There is a built-in compulsion that accompanies the act of writing. Every writer needs approval (constantly), admiration (continually), encouragement (unendingly). Your friends are there to give you all this when they read your writing. But they have scant knowledge of what writing is all about. They will not lie to you, but they do not have the critical knowledge and insight that you need. Their critical appraisals will be superficial.

Enjoy the flattery, the stroking and esteem they offer. But do not regard their criticism seriously, even when it is exactly what you want them to say. They are your friends. They may point out aspects of your work that they dislike but honesty without knowledge will not help you. Many inexperienced writers have been misled into believing their work was great when it was still mediocre. Good intentions are not competent criticisms.

Allowing your work to be read by enemies will not bring greater critical rewards. Your enemies are out to discourage you. They are cynics, deriders, people who do not want you to obtain your career as a professional writer. Enemies are not any more knowledgeable than friends.

There is no ideal or exact social realm to search for qualified, writing-oriented people to read your writing. The highest level of critical guidance you can hope for is to be misled, misunderstood, and confused. Yet finding an environment where other writers congregate for the purpose of discussion and debate about writing is probably the most beneficial environment. THEY HAVE THE EXPERIENCE OF ACTUAL WRITING.

Writing, like any art form is a deeply personal act. Expecting to be understood by anyone outside of that experience is angering and futile. But writing traditions and history reveal that a writer cannot stop himself from reading his work to people. It is the unexplainable drive to be known that prevails over reason. And there is only one protection. Expect to be misled, misunderstood, and confused, and continue writing until you can do it all by yourself. Only the writer really knows what the writer must know. It just takes time to learn all that you must know, but the knowledge is there to be learned.

Character Motivation

If character motivation is not clear and recognizable, then the character performs actions that are either unexplainable or unbelievable. Character motivation originates from two basic sources: (1) from the inner nature of the character as it has been established before the novel begins; (2) from a series of external events which move him toward particular needs and expectations after the novel has begun.

Example Vern is a good man, and humble. His farmland is about to be reclaimed by the bank. Though the farm is fertile and the seasons have been fair, Vern is failing because he is afraid of success. (*Motivation*) Vern's father, who began as a squatter, became a land baron in ten years. When poor, he was a loving man, but success turned him vicious and greedy. Vern is afraid that if he succeeds at farming, his personality will begin to resemble his father's.

This motivation to fail is intrinsic to all of Vern's behavior and enterprise. It has been with him long before he became a character in a novel. Only if he is shocked into a recognition that he fears becoming a replica of his father, can Vern change. The realization that this is causing his failure is brought to the reader as the story unfolds.

External, circumstantial motivation can be derived from an event, a person, or from both. It happens after the story has been started. An unexpected, surprise event is always effective.

Example Vern is a farmer whose land is about to be auctioned by the bank. (*External motivation*) His wife is stricken with a disease that only a great deal of money can cure. (a) Vern robs a bank to pay for her treatments or (b) Vern begins growing marijuana or making whiskey.

Motivation becomes a visible, tangible aspect of character when the reader begins to understand why the character feels, thinks, and does what he does. Motivation is proven by the actions of the character who is motivated to act.

Motivating Superheroes

In the adventure/thriller/espionage novel, heroes and heroines must be created in "larger than life" dimensions, and their character motives should not be analyzed too clinically. Psychological exploration into the essence of heroism (in fiction) reduces the remarkable to the average.

Character background in writing, and character-psychiatry in real life are not the same. It is acceptable for Superman to have been born on another planet and to have dedicated his unearthly powers to righting the wrongs of the world. That explains his background and why he does what he does. But if Superman is psychoanalyzed through childhood traumas and nervous tics, he becomes Clark Kent in a ridiculous costume.

Readers do not identify with *realism* in superheroes and heroines. Readers gladly participate in their outrageous exploits, but their identification is with the "fantasy concept" of such incredible characters.

Readers know that they themselves can never achieve the extraordinary capabilities that heroes and heroines display through the superlative deeds. If they were capable of heroic marvels, they would not be reading for escape, they would be living the violence of great adventures.

An average person who has overcome psychosis and physical handicap to find fame and fortune is uncommon, but not a *superperson*. Readers do not want to believe their heroes and heroines are real. If they were "true-to-life," they would be a constant source of mockery to the average person. Thus, in an adventure/thriller/espionage novel, it is wiser to provide glib motives for heroes and heroines. Glib motives are quickly covered and absorbed by fabulous deeds, while deep motives that explain the reason for the deed, are examined and inspected by the reader, and reduce the great deed to a form of human behavior.

Create Authentic Dialogue

Creating authentic dialogue does not mean reporting speech as it is actually spoken. Few people are direct or instantly clear in stating what they mean.

Example (usual speech) "I want to tell you something that's been on my mind a long time. Not a short time, a long time, you know. You know the clothes you wear? I mean the clothes you always wear, you know what I mean? Well, I want to tell you something about them, all right? I mean, it's important, so I want you to hear it, all right?" etc.

This is wordy. It requires much space. Read the court transcript of any trial and you will find hundreds of pages of loose, rambling dialogue, verbosity that stops only when the trial finally ends.

A writer selects from the disorderly outpouring of actual speech only those lines that are directed to stating what must be said. The writer then rewrites it into language that sounds like someone actually speaking.

Example (written dialogue) "For a long time now I've wanted to tell you about the clothes you wear. They're just awful."

Turn of the century writers tried to recreate the sounds of ethnic speech, to achieve literal authenticity. *Dutch:* "A laty coom in de udder tay to puy a pair've garters und I ask her vat kind did she vant." *Yiddish:* "So, dis laidy the udder day kums hin for puyhink some gardders, you hearist me, nuh?"

Such idiomatic imitation is no longer necessary. To create the impression of authentic ethnic speech, merely alter the verbal meter and arrange it into an interesting grammatical pattern. Make it *read* right. *Dutch:* "To buy a pair of garters, the other day, comes in a lady . . ." *Yiddish:* "So for a pair of garters, this lady comes in, so I ask her . . ."

The Yiddish can be switched to Dutch, the Dutch to Yiddish. The reader will believe it. It is an *impression,* not a *duplication* of reality.

Opening Scenes

The opening scene of a novel should show a character involved in a conflict, or in a situational crisis. A character who is not under some pressure appears inert, and the situation remains static.

A prince strolling about his palace is not an unusual person in an unusual environment. If he is strolling to the scaffold where his wife is about to be hung, then the prince's actions are no longer passive nor is the circumstance static. A surgeon in an operating theatre is not a peculiar person in an exotic environment. He belongs there. But if he is operating on someone and cannot tell the difference between a lung and a liver, he is unique, and the circumstance becomes a critical situation. Without the pressure of a critical event, the character has no credible reason for revealing anything unusual about himself, and the circumstance stays static.

Example (circumstance) During a political convention, a pickpocket steals a man's wallet. He takes it to the men's room and is surprised to see a list of names among the bills. Four names have been crossed out. They are the names of prominent men who have recently been assassinated. The pickpocket is frightened. The next name is the leading delegate of the convention.

A political convention with masses of people is not an unusual environment in a political novel. For a pickpocket to ply his craft in such places is not an unusual occurrence. Opening a novel in this manner is using unimportant scene-setting activity. Nothing yet has happened. Only when the pickpocket realizes he has stolen the wallet of an assassin who is at the convention to kill does the situational crisis occur. The writer can open with a focus on the assassin or the pickpocket who is now afraid of what he has discovered.

It doesn't matter if the character of the pickpocket or the assassin has only a minor relationship to the entire novel. Some aspect of the novel has been started. The purpose of the opening scene is to compel the reader to want to read more. Scene-setting is a bland promise of more. A critical situation is a dramatic interval that *is the novel*.

When you open with a major character in conflict with his circumstance, his conflict changes the static circumstance into a critical situation.

Character novel Morgan Ankers, a minister, is being tempted by the "flesh." A female parishioner is trying to seduce him. His wife is a closet drunk. His son is a car thief. His faith is wavering.

Because readers did not have the distractions existent today, a writer in the 1930's could open with a leisurely landscape of Morgan's rural town. Then a household scene. Morgan writing a sermon, his wife drinking in her room, the son repainting a stolen car. Seven or eight pages would pass before a significant moment happened.

Yet *this* novel will be written and read in the 1980s where speed, intensity, and impact are required. The writer does not sacrifice the integrity of his craft by opening with strong drama. He is flowing into the tempo of his time, without the loss of quality or integrity. The 1980s writer should begin with Morgan in a critical situation that reveals what this character novel will be all about. The life of Morgan Ankers.

Example Morgan Ankers drove through the dark night. He kept glancing in the rear-view mirror, worried about the headlights behind him. *I have no cause for guilt*, he assured himself. *I am a minister*. He was meeting Cornelia Haas, to console her on the death of her husband. Not to become her lover. He touched the Bible beside him, then pulled his hand back as if burned.

Creating a novel in the 1980s can be compared to the situation of a writer who has not eaten in five days. He has just panhandled some coins and bought a ham sandwich. Before taking the first bite, he receives a telegram. "Your novel accepted. $100,000 advance. You must sign contract at exactly 12:00 PM, today. If not exactly on time, contract is canceled." It is 11:45 AM. He has no carfare. He must walk three miles. He is weak and will die of exertion. He is starving. The food will give him energy. But there is no time to eat. How can he get to the publishers to sign the contract? And live? *He eats the sandwich on the way.* When writing a novel in the 1980s, the characters are fattening with content WHILE the story is unfolding. Speed, intensity, impact, quick drama, conflict, situation—at the very opening.

Describing the Indescribable

Every mother, at one time, has heard her child ask, "What's the mashed pota-toes taste like?" Trying to describe the taste of any food is like using sign lan-guage to decribe the sound of music to a deaf person. You can define the texture of food (creamy, thick, watery, etc.) or the color (green, pink, orange, etc.) and its shape (flat, round, lumpy, etc.) but you cannot describe its taste in such a way that the listener can taste it, without needing to taste it. Trying to describe "hot" or "cold" forces you into the realm of statistics. The degree of tempera-ture establishes the state it is in, but does not communicate the food's sensory condition. If then, the indescribable cannot be described, do not make the at-tempt. The only way a writer can prove the authenticity of a sensory condition and communicate its meaning is to DOCUMENT ITS EFFECT.

Example (heat of the day) Long strips of sweat stained the back of his shirt. He shielded his eyes from the sun. He tore open his tight collar and staggered to the spread of shade beneath the leafy tree.

Ten sentences describing a cold day will not be as convincing as a single sen-tence documenting the effect of the day's cold. *"A heavy wind beat against the tree, rattling the branches laden with icicles."*

Language is impression, not substance. Prose merely identifies an as-semblage of what exists in and around us. The ultimate success the writer can achieve is an allusion to what the sensory responses actually absorb. In the reader's sense-impression, "blistering hot" is not any hotter than "scalding hot." The senses of the reader can only be provoked if he can be made to identi-fy with the effects that the climate has on the character. The climate itself is in-describable. An effective allusion to climate (or any of the sensorial responses) can be achieved through the use of inanimate objects. *"He cracked two eggs on the hot sidewalk and watched the yolks smoke and sizzle."*

Stop Your Self-Pity

Oh how dreary it is to be constantly negative. No guests ever rush to attend a "self-pity party." Give up that futile, energy-wasting attitude. The only reward it offers is helplessness. The work still to be done on your novel cannot be seen through tears wept for yourself.

Your self-pity for all your failures in writing is probably the strongest common connection you have with Faulkner, Hemingway, Tolstoy, Chaucer,

Shakespeare, Joyce, Camus, Hawthorne, and a slew of other notable writers who are still being read with envy and jealousy by other writers. Their negatives were as grim and gross to them as your negatives are to you. They worried, they cried, they hated themselves. The first scribe who ever hacked words into a stone felt incompetent and constantly unworthy.

Scene (Gustave Flaubert's writing room) The inkpot is filled, the quill pen is sharpened, the writing paper is blank. He is pacing, he is gnashing his teeth, pulling his hair, rubbing tears of despair from his eyes. Suddenly, he kicks the desk and shouts, "I am no good, and everyone knows it!" He rubs his bruised toes, moaning, "I am without talent," and flings the inkpot against the wall, shreds the paper and shrieks, "I will never write *Madame Bovary*—I have no talent!" then rushes to the opened window and leaps out to crash on the villa stones. He lies there, his shattered bones soaking in his blood—a dead man.

Happily, the history of Flaubert makes a lie of the above scene. His pity parties always ended quickly. Yet merely scan the records of literary history and learn of the great writers who have destroyed themselves. Some of the causes were because they did not believe in themselves even while they were creating great works. Their pity parties went on for too long.

Be realistic! You chose to become a professional writer because you believe you can and because it is a good life. Why interfere with your growth? Self-pity turns you into a bore. According to standards of social acceptability it is always better to be a struggling writer than to be a bore.

Blending Dialogue and Narration

Dialogue bare of all description (other than some "he saids" or "she saids") is useful for changing pace and inserting quick information. It is most effective when only two people are in the scene. The speakers are easily identified by naming them before they speak.

Example Fred put his arm across Jack's shoulder. "Let's go to the Pelican for some drinks."
"My ulcer's acting up," Jack said.
"I really need a drink bad."
"I can't. My ulcer's acting up."

With three speakers, this bareness of description slows the pace.

Example Fred put his arm across Jack's shoulder and nodded to Phil. "Let's go to the Pelican for some drinks."
Phil said, "My wife'll kill me."
"My ulcer's acting up," Jack said.
Fred insisted, "I really need a drink bad."
"I can't take the chance," Phil said.
Jack said, "I can't. My ulcer's acting up."

This dialogue is busy, busy. A more competent technique for a *crowd* dialogue is to blend the spoken word with described speech.

Example Fred put his arm across Jack's shoulder and nodded to Phil. "Let's go to the Pelican for some drinks." Phil said he was afraid his wife would kill him when he got home. Jack said, "My ulcer's acting up." Fred began insisting that he really needed a drink, but Phil shrugged, "I can't take the chance." Jack sighed, "I can't. My ulcer's acting up."

Blending the dialogue into a paragraph of narration mixed with speech creates a flow from one character to another. The impression that the men are together and talking to one another is achieved. They are not just separate voices.

Flashbacks and Recollections Revisited

The difference between a *recollection* and a *flashback* is not only in length but in completeness. A recollection is a fragment of a larger past scene. A flashback is a full scene. While a flashback is usually longer than a recollection, it need not be lengthy. To be a full scene, it simply has to be a complete, individual entity.

Story A priest is performing the ritual of becoming a bishop. While prone before the altar, he is tense, remembering the time when he was young and killed his twin brother who had seduced his fiancée.

Example (recollection) . . . and his prayers were shaken as he saw his hands jamming into his brother's back, shoving Kenny through the window. Now, prone before the altar, he wept with sorrow. He was so ashamed.

Long before the recollection appears, the writer has informed the reader that the priest killed his brother. The recollection is used to reveal the priest's continuing distress, his guilt.

Example (flashback) . . . and his prayers were shaken as his depths cried to him, "Hypocrite. There is blood on your hands!" He clenched his body to stop from shuddering. He was seventeen again, jogging along the edge of the forest. He was happy. In four days he would marry Carol. Her sensuality would stop him from becoming homosexual and . . .

The priest takes the reader back to the past, describing how he hears laughter in the forest and jogs toward the voices. He thinks of how Carol's money will support them while he attends medical school to become a surgeon. He enters the forest and sees his naked brother leading a nude Carol to a blanket. In rage, he smashes his hands against a tree, breaking many bones. The sequence then changes to an apartment building. His brother is wearing dark glasses and tapping with a white cane. He is pushed to the window and shoved out. The entire scene unfolds as it once happened.

In the recollection the priest recalls the act of killing his brother. In the flashback he relives the entire experience of killing his brother. In the recollection, all that is brought to the reader is knowledge that his act of murder is still troubling him, *an act the reader already knows he committed.* In the flashback, additional information is given the reader. It is learned why the priest never became a doctor. He had shattered the bones in his hands against the tree. He believed a heterosexual marriage would cure him of homosexual desires. The reader did not know that Carol planned to support him through medical school. The reader did not know that his brother was blind.

A recollection is functional only after the character's motivation or the cause of the event being recollected has been revealed. A recollection recalls what has already been revealed. This recalling of the past does not alter the motivation or reveal more about the event. It is a quick remembrance of what is already known.

Because a flashback is a complete scene, it needs only the character's thoughts about the past event to provoke its existence. The character journeys into an on-scene reliving of the past to provide heretofore unrevealed motivation or insights into the event that were not known before.

In a recollection, when the writer returns to the present, the priest has not changed. He is still troubled by the memory and knowledge that he is a murderer. There is not time to probe his character or the event. Recollections happen quickly—they are fleet.

When the writer leaves the flashback to return to the present, the priest is changed. The reader knows more about him; more about the event.

A recollection is used to bring forth a fragment of the past *without appreciably altering the pace of present events.* A flashback is used to bring forth a complete scene from the past, *to deliberately vary the pace.* There is not enough material in the recollection to do more than support the tempo and motion of the present. Because there is a fullness of content in the flashback, the past scene achieves its own pace.

Mood and Situation

The tone of the prose should always be compatible with the situation it describes. If the "mood" of writing is not blended with the activity in the circumstance, then the drama is diminished. The situation creates the action—the prose creates the drama.

Story One of the three little pigs sees the wolf loping to his straw home. The pig is frightened. The wolf knocks on the door.

This is a situation of fear and impending violence. The writer must create tension. He must obey the fundamental grammatical tenet "the verb takes action." He cannot use passive, dawdling, slow verbs.

Example The wolf elevated his paw and touched the door. "Are you in there, little pig?" The pig was so upset, he sneezed. The unusual sound reached the wolf's hearing. He pressed his torso against the straw barrier and exerted maximum strength until eventually it collapsed. He observed the porcine shape ashudder beside the beige wall.

This is descriptive of what is happening, but it is not exciting. The verbs (elevated, touched, reached, exerted, etc.) are too bland, without vitality. Their tone sets them apart from the situation.

Example The wolf banged on the door. Straw splattered. "Hey, pig, lemme in." Fright made Joey sneeze. The wolf tensed. He jammed his shoulder against the door. It shattered. He saw the pig shivering against the wall.

The wolf is anxious for his dinner. He will not approach his prey in a disposition of slow-motion consideration. He wants it right now.

In the second example the wolf becomes part of the action. He is depicted through aggressive, charged verbs: *banged, splattered, tensed, jammed, shat-*

tered, saw, shivering. The scene also becomes aggressive, charged.

When the prose is not compatible with the situation, the reader becomes uncomfortable. While the scene may be believable, it has not been written at a high level of competence.

Avoid Repetitious Settings

When rewriting, be alert for a repetition of setting. This repetition quickly reveals that the writer has been lax in his use of invention or is uninformed about the time in which the characters are living. To avoid this, list the settings you have already used and determine how often you have used them.

Example

Modern	Historical	Cowboy
Apartments	Mansions	Cabins; ranches
Offices	Dens; libraries	Gunrooms; dens
Automobiles	Coaches	Stagecoaches
Trains	Trains; caravans	Wagon trains
Airplanes	Merchant ships	Cattle drives
Bars; cafes	Taverns; inns	Saloons

When the settings become repetitious, it indicates that the writer is rushing, getting down his information and moving the story through plot sequences just to reach the conclusion quickly.

In the first draft of a novel, it is reasonable for the writer to repeat settings. He is not being careless or indifferent; he is working to complete the book. The time to be meticulous about weeding out repetitious settings is when rewriting, after the novel is completed.

The repetition of setting tends to limit the scope of the novel. All dramatic moments seem to happen in expected and familiar places. The remainder of the world or environment is either blurred or nonexistent. The writer is also wasting the rich texture of his research.

If this repetition of setting exists in your novel, return to your research and employ your sense of invention to rewrite the setting. Compose a list of possible settings that have not been used and relocate your scenes. Be certain to check out all past references that indicate a scene will happen in the setting you have already used, and change them to refer to the new setting.

Shifting Tenses

Every writing structure allows for *special effects*.

An immediate advantage that the first person viewpoint has over the third person point of view is in the level of intimacy that is reached between the characters and the reader. The first person is right there, openly responding, telling you, *in person*, what is happening. The third person *is being written* by someone who is telling you what is happening to someone else, from a distance.

A technique for creating an even tighter sense of intimacy in the first-person form is to shift from past to present tense and modify the meter.

Example (first person writing) Matilda did not know I was watching her. When the counter clerk turned to another customer, she quickly sneaked a vial of perfume into her purse. She was the fastest shoplifter I had ever seen. I would have to arrest her.

The narrator, though directly involved in the action of the shoplifter, is still distant from her. He is an observer. To establish a more intimate connection between them, the writer shifts from the "I watched . . ." to the "I watch . . ." This changes the tone of the particular interval of narration. Through difference, it provides emphasis.

Example I watch Matilda. She waits for the clerk to serve another customer. I see her sneak a vial of perfume into her purse. She is quick. She shoplifts expertly. I walk to her, ready to arrest.

In this first person form, the distance between the observer and Matilda has been decreased. The shift of grammatical tense and the use of short, abrupt sentences brings attention to that portion of the action. It is separated from the other prose, by special emphasis, making it more important.

This short interval of writing change is more stylized. It offers a variation of prose and a variance of pace. It is more immediate and quickens the tension. The purpose of a special effect is to single out what is being treated in a special manner.

Fictional Children

Children between the ages of four and nine are among the most difficult characters to create. The image of what a real-live child is is always hampered by the children the writer has, has had, wants to have, has known, has read about. All children between those ages are indefinable. They are mercuric of temperament, quixotic in disposition, always changeable.

They are deep, shallow, bright, dumb, sickly, healthy, hostile, noisy, hateful, pouty, bawling, mute, spiteful, cuddly, a curse at times and at other times a blessing. Mean, generous, jealous, loving, unreasonably helpful or confusingly uncooperative. Meticulous, slothful, etc. Anyone, regardless of profession, who states he "knows what children are like between the ages of four and nine" is indulging in a conceit or an inane fantasy. They may have some workable rules for understanding them, for awhile—but they do not have a stable set of insights.

If you intend to use a child in the four to nine age range as an important character in a novel, do not use a real-live child for a model. The characterization will appear warped or unbelievable. Invent, make up, design the child you will use. Find the particular characteristics you need and assemble them together as a "representative child" and allow the plot, the relationships, the circumstances, to fit the creature into the novel.

The unalterable characteristic of a child's "changeability" should be used as a source of surprising behavior AFTER the credibility of the child has been established. But first find the traditional and acceptable "universals" shared by all children, which are recognizable by readers. Create a believable image through these universals. Then gradually inculcate individual particulars into the characterization to render the child unique. If you try writing about children from a premise of what they are actually like IN REALITY, you will be giving your control away. To make children between the ages four to nine believable, they have to be completely made up.

Four Ways to Open a Story or Novel

There are four interesting ways to open a short story or novel: 1. an exciting character, 2. a dramatic situation, 3. an interesting background, 4. a combination of all three, *in one paragraph.*

Example 1 He stood in the hallway like a boulder ready to fall. His mouth was a scar under a thick nose. His eyes were moldy green, and glazed. He said, "I've come back," and his voice scraped on the walls. He laughed, "No grave can hold me." He laughed and mud shook from his suit.

Example 2 The saloon owner struck the bar, silencing the patrons. "We got a play-off tuh get started." They looked to the two pool players holding their cue sticks. They sneered at each other. The bartender said, "When I call three, it starts." The players tensed. "One." They leaned over the table. "Two." They gripped their sticks. The men began shouting bets. "Three!" The players leaped onto the pool table and began clubbing each other.

Example 3 A chain was bolted across the garage doors. A scrawny cat slept on a crumpled newspaper. A splotch of blood had dried on the concrete. The black wreath in the window was withered and cracked.

Example 4 The tugboat rocked in the rough water. Jake stood on the deck, waiting for Gippy to lift the diving helmet. A slat of black rubber was taped to the patch on his right eye. Four years ago the eye had been gouged from his face by a shark. Jake looked at Gippy and asked, "You fix the air hose?" Gippy said, "All fixed." The cold wind suddenly chilled him. Could he trust Gippy? If the body below was Gippy's father, Gippy would go crazy and tear up the air hoses. Jake started to pray.

It is the opening paragraph that convinces the reader to finish the page. If you have sustained the reader's interest in the dramatics and the intrigue, he will read the next page too. In fact, novels and stories should be written so that every page leads the reader on to the next one.

Immediate Foreshadowing

Immediate foreshadowing is a technique for using prose as a warning of something that will soon happen *within the same scene*. For this type of foreshadowing to work, the writer should develop skill in the uses of prose. Ordinary surfaces must be changed into images.

The cinema constantly uses this technique through changes in the background music.

Movie scene Three cowboys are riding to a fort. The landscape is lush, the sky is clear. The background music is a serene run of sound. Suddenly, the music changes to a sharper, throbbing run of sounds. The cowboys are still riding at a casual pace. *They do not hear the music.* But through the tom-tom beat and rapid rhythm, the movie viewer knows that Indians are nearby, ready to attack the cowboys.

This same technique should be used in writing, through prose. Prose becomes the music. Ordinary objects become tailored images.

Example Ethel walked down her sister's basement steps. There were long strands of cobwebs dangling from the ceiling. She saw lines in the dusty floor. They crossed over large foot prints.

This describes Ethel descending into a messy basement. She does not know someone is about to club her. Neither does the reader. But alter the prose to a more imagistic description and the reader is clued in.

Example Ethel walked slowly down the basement stairs. The shadowy air hummed. Long thin lines trailed on the dusty cement floor. She stood still. Mice? Or rats? Cobwebs near her face were trembling fingers reaching to her throat. A shadow bulged near the wall. She shivered.

A change in the disposition of the prose—from functional to descriptive— prods the reader into suspecting that more exists in the scene than is being observed. There is not only a warning, there is suspense. The character is unsuspecting, but the reader knows something will happen—but what, and when? It is the tone that foreshadows, not the specifics. Yet the scene is specifically clear.

Avoid Opening with a Dream

Avoid opening your novel with a dream being experienced by the major character. Opening dreams can be misunderstood for two reasons.

1. The reader has no idea who is doing the dreaming. There is no way of knowing where, when, or why the dream is happening. Since the dream is an unreality, the circumstances of the present have been delayed. If the dream is done realistically, the reader might misunderstand the dream as being the reality. Readers who are fooled, easily become annoyed readers.

Example He stood on the window ledge forty stories above the city. Wind whipped his clothes, making him sway. Behind him, voices pleaded, "Don't jump, Alfie. They'll find a cure for your disease!" He pressed against the building. Long sweaty hands reached to him. (The dream continues for a page, then:) The alarm clock rang. Alfie awoke.

2. The writer may believe he is foreshadowing an inevitable event—but since no story yet exists, it is retarding the beginning. First begin the novel with a situation, then let him have his dream.

Example Tendrils, as ghostly limbs, entwined through his consciousness. A moon elongated into a serrated sphere, undulating amid screams solidified into spears piercing the elasticity of his being. Shuddering, convulsing, he tumbled into endless chasms of glutinous dark, shrieking, shrieking "AAAlll-fff-iiieee," wailed the goblin shadows . . . (the dream continues, then:) The alarm clock rang. Alfie awoke.

There are symbols, obscure meanings, hidden references, none of which are yet significant to the reader. There are more speculative interpretations to a mystical dream than there is actual content. The opening paragraph should contain a situation dynamic enough to bring the reader into other paragraphs. When possible, always open with an immediate sense of the novel. Do not delay.

Clichés

The only valid reason to use clichés is in the speech of a character. "I could *hardly believe my eyes.*" "I got home *drenched to the skin.*" "Such tasty chickens are *few and far between.*" But in the use of any other form of prose—narration, description, exposition, documentation—clichés are ruinous.

A cliché is a phrase, sentence, or short expression that was once original but has now been used so constantly that its former value has been spent and its present value is zero.

There are three basic areas of language from which clichés are derived. The *idiomatic*—a form of expression that stems from an ethnic, professional, or social-class group. "He felt *fit as a fiddle.*" "They huddled together, *thick as thieves.*" "He did not want *to lead a dog's life.*"

The *hackneyed*: too frequently used phrases. "She was his *better half.*" "He went on *an errand of mercy.*" "They were *kindred spirits.*"

Foreign language phrases: "He was given *carte blanche.*" "His policy was *caveat emptor.*" "She spoke *sotto voce.*"

Clichés are indications of sloppy writing. The writer does not respect the scene he is trying to dramatize enough to fashion it through precise prose and imaginative imagery. Clichés are often the production of hasty writing—or of indifference to the language of the craft.

When the reader can finish a sentence for the writer (because the writer's language is so familiar), then he is not creating a new impression. He is merely reminding the reader of what the reader already knows.

Clichés are also the result of writers who are not too diligent about reading. They are not familiar with the multivaried heritage of language and phrase that has already been used—or interested in developing prose from the diverse heritage of prose combinations that have not yet been overused.

Action

In action scenes, the writer must give the *impression* that the characters are engaged in true-to-life behavior. All that happens during a fight, a chase, a hunt, a war scene cannot be included. The scene would drag and collapse under its own bulk. The writer selects only those details that reveal what is happening and guides the reader into filling in the remainder. The *impression* becomes the full reality.

> **Example** Flame exploded through the closed window. A child cried. His mother screamed, "Help!"

You do not tally the glass bits flying in the air, the paint bubbling on the window frame, the intense heat. You do not explain that the infant is afraid, that the mother is terrified and unable to save her child. The experience and imagination of the reader fill that in.

Inside the burning room, you do not impede the action with descriptions of the bed, bureau, toys, color of walls, design of carpet. Such details diminish the intensity of the crescendo towards which you are building. Sneak them in while describing the furious motion.

> **Example** The child flopped near a patch of burning carpet. The mother snatched him up. She crushed toys in her rush to the bolted door. Through the crackle of flames she heard a screeching siren. She pounded on the oak wood, pleading, "Help us. Oh God, hurry!"

An action is a single event, deliberately isolated and held in a tight focus. The prose must be clear, precise. There is little room for imagery, little time for introspection or contemplation, and no room for erudite explanation. The reader projects himself into the scene through similar or imagined experiences. The reader provides the emotional and mental explanations you have left out to sustain the pace.

Multiple First-Person Viewpoint

There is a novel form which allows the writer to reveal expertise in dialogue, first-person narration, plot complication, and perceptions from all types of characters. It is the *multiple first-person* novel. It must be crafted with precision, or it will tax or possibly confuse the reader.

Story and plot A wealthy man's will has just been read. His four sons are each left a quarter part of a map that leads to a treasure worth fifty million dollars. They must search together, or they will not gain the fortune. The plot line deals with how they pursue the treasure.

The writer then uses the first-person viewpoint, alternating chapters or scenes for each brother. Each brother relates the story of what he is doing and what is happening. The alliances and enmities. The greed, courage, loyalty, betrayal, ambition, and violence. The viewpoints always alternate.

This is a difficult form, but if accomplished, it can make for fascinating reading. While one "viewpoint" is being narrated, some or all of the other principals should be on scene. The plot, relationships, and action are revealed from that character's viewpoint. Then the next character's viewpoint appears and the same plot and relationships are revealed—but not in the same way. The story now emerges from a narrator with different standards, morals, feelings, and intentions. Then the third viewpoint is explored. The same situations, the same relationships are there. But now the reader sees differences that not even the characters are aware of. *The reader knows more than the characters* but still not more than the writer. Nor does the reader know how the plot will all be worked out.

Included among the individual stories are secondary character stories. Each brother has his own story, apart from the story involved with the map and treasure. This introduces the lives and interests of other characters—and their tertiary stories.

The novel can be the "small novel" in which an intense focus is placed on the four lives or it can be the sprawling saga that encompasses four lives engaged in the sweeping events of an extravagant time in history.

Completing Impossible Scenes

The time to be relentless in completing a scene is when you are absolutely certain you cannot accomplish it. If a writer works only through his 'known' skills, he is using only what he already knows. What the writer knows now is never enough. It is that impossible scene, when completed, that teaches the writer more about writing.

Long before he begins as a writer, he has unknowingly absorbed hundreds of writing techniques from his reading experience.

The writer must constantly work to discover more material and methods. Insight, form, perception, technique, intuition. These discoveries cannot be gained by a writer's casual perusal of his memories. The writer does not know what he knows. You must remain with a difficult scene for as long as it takes to dig deeply into yourself and discover more of what you know. You not only complete the scene, but add to your store of writing skills.

A writer works through veils—always uncovering his material, his knowledge. Behind one veil hangs another, and another behind that one. Perhaps, if the writer is ever able to remove all the veils masking his knowledge, his insight, his intuition, he will stand and behold himself.

As you dig for one possibility in a scene and realize it is not useful, you are, by association, given other possibilities. Another beginning, a different pace, another viewpoint, an insight you overlooked, a device another writer used. The possibilities suggested to you from the depths you have reached become your solution to the impossible scene. It is also admittance into the "writer's classroom" in which you are not only the student, but also the teacher.

The "short breath" writer is facile and easily discouraged. When he exhausts what he knows, he rearranges and never learns anything new. He repeats and re-repeats. The "long breath" writer plunges deeply until he finds what he needs. He emerges from the depths of "self" with new material, new techniques. He learns from himself.

Double Foreshadowing

Double foreshadowing within the same scene can save writing and quicken pace. It is accomplished through the use of the *"dual"* viewpoint structure.

Scene A young murderer is brought into a prison. His father is the warden. They loathe each other. The only dialogue between them is the warden's instructions. The young murderer remains silent.

To foreshadow a later scene from the son's viewpoint, you break into the warden's indoctrination speech and flash into the son's mind.

Example ". . . and the least infraction of rules gains you a month in solitary and . . ." Joey pretended to listen, though he was troubled. Would Teresa send the coded letter telling him how to find the central sewage system? His father's voice droned. He stood in sham obedience. Teresa swore she would send it. He would never get out if she didn't.

This foreshadowing is continued long enough to describe Joey's future plans emphatically. An escape is in the offing.

Example (father's foreshadowing) Before the son leaves, the desk phone rings. The warden picks it up and nods to his son. "It's your mother. You have one minute." While Joey talked with his mother, the warden edged his hand over the receipt for a four-carat diamond ring he had just given his mistress. He glanced at his son's smooth face. If the boy learned of the affair he would tell his mother. He crumpled the receipt. If he could provoke his son into trying an escape, he could have the nasty bugger shot down. He grinned as the boy kept talking.

There is now no need for individual scenes to set up a possible escape by the son or to describe how the father plans to do away with his son. When these scenes are ready to appear, the writer just starts them *from a point of action*. The reader has already been prepared to accept them. Double foreshadowing has set them up. The material (escape and murder plan) are disguised because they are part of the story.

Emotional Facts vs. Impersonal Facts

An organized assembly of real facts establishes a setting, an environment, a historical background. But it is the personal, emotional facts that make this impersonal reality believable.

Example (real, impersonal facts) Algeria is in north Africa. Natives are of mixed Berber and Arab stock. / Greek soldiers wore bronze helmets. The crest was made of horsehair. / In Kincardine-on-Firth, Scotland, there is a Swing Bridge. It is in disrepair.

Example (emotional, personal facts) He hated oranges grown in Algeria. The Greek soldier's bronze helmet irritated his ears. Aggie stood under the old Swing Bridge and watched it sway. She ran, afraid it would fall on her.

Letting characters play out their lives in a setting that is authentic begins the process of convincing the reader. When these accurately established facts become part of the characters' lives, they become emotional facts. An emotional fact need not be read as separate, to then be coupled to a response, and then become an emotional fact. Emotional facts can be intrinsic to the setting.

Example The elderly woman stroked the rocking chair arm and smiled at the photograph of her dead husband. "I sure do miss you, Sam."

The hard facts are the rocking chair and the photograph. They are instantly emotional when she strokes the chair and talks to the photograph.

Whatever fact a character uses becomes personal, emotional. In war scenes, put creases, fingerprints, beer stains on battle-site maps. In gothic romances let the heroine sneeze because the oriental carpets are dusty.

Real, impersonal fact The sunset was like a spill of peacock feathers drifting beyond the mountain crest.
Emotional personal fact She gasped at the marvel of the sunset, which was like a spill of peacock feathers drifting beyond the mountain crest. Emotion gives life and intensity to a bland, lifeless fact.

Pivot Character Changes

Just as there are *pivot chapters,* during which a crisis alters the direction of the story, so are there *pivot character changes.*

Characters cannot be the same at the end of a story or novel as they were at the beginning. If the internal nature of characters is not changed, they are either not worth writing about, or the writer has not effectively used the events in his plot line. *Major characters must change.*

Example A lowly construction worker aspires to become a contractor. A. He achieves his goal. B. He fails to achieve his goal.
A. If he succeeds, his inner self is changed by the handicaps he overcame. He goes from doubt to confidence. Timidity to arrogance. Doubt to hope.
B. If he fails, his character must change because of the events and inner defects that stopped him. Hope to doom. Love to hate.

When these changes occur in the major character, the direction of his story *pivots* (turns, shifts, moves in a new direction). When the major character's story line changes, the overall story line is changed. An absence of change indicates an immobilized, motionless story. A series of *recognizable* character changes proves the dramatic effects and mobility of the story. A changing story is an interesting and complicated story.

A change cannot happen in a character unless a startling inner revelation occurs. This startling revelation cannot happen unless a crisis of event causes it. When this event, which causes characters to experience change, takes place, *the story line can no longer remain the same.* A major character's change must cause a story change.

Example A child, blind from birth, is raised in an all-blind community. Ten years later his parents are forced to move to a city. Suddenly he is changed. He realizes he is different from other boys—he is blind. His life and his story must now pivot into another direction.

Three Fundamental Story Lines

There are three fundamental story lines upon which all novels are based. Each story line is large enough to accept all structures, all known writing techniques. They are easily identifiable: Man against himself; man against man; man against nature.

Man against himself: a serious physical, emotional, or mental problem that stops the major character from achieving happiness, success, love: He is a child molester and enjoys setting churches on fire.

Example A man buys a map to find pirate treasure buried somewhere on the African Gold Coast. He takes along his wife, although he knows she will try to kill him, and that the treasure probably never existed.

Man against man: unrequited love, an enemy, a miserable marriage, a business tyrant, a dictator, being hunted by a maniacal murderer.

Example Two brothers and a sister live in a country ruled by a lunatic dictator. They escape the country to make their fortune. They will buy armaments and raise an army to free their oppressed people.

Man against nature: storms, earthquakes, power failures, plagues, droughts, wild animals, a sudden dropping of stars or planets.

Example A strange, killing disease has overcome an obscure aborigine tribe in Africa. Medical missionaries are dispatched to provide help until a serum can be developed to inoculate the people.

The overall story of each of these individual novels is large enough to incorporate the other two plot lines. By using a combination of two, or all three, the writer will never lack opportunities for developing relationships or inventing situations. All manner of devices and skills can be used.

If two overall stories are used (man against man, man against nature) the writer should alternate them, letting each story be equally dominant.

Example The brothers and sister encounter wild beasts as they are hounded by government troops. They escape by sea and join the family hunting for buried treasure. During a storm at sea, one brother falls in love with the treasure hunter's wife. They learn that there is a disease in the area of the buried treasure. They land the boat and meet the medical missionaries. They are asked to help innoculate the natives. To keep his wife away from the brother who loves her, the treasure hunter takes his family to live with the missionaries. The brothers and sister hunt for the buried treasure.

By allowing the "man against man" story to dominate the plot, then letting the "man against nature" story dominate the plot, the writer can use the elements of nature to keep the characters in action. By returning to the "man against man" story, the writer shows the effects of stress and danger on the individuals and their relationships.

If a combination of all three overall stories is used, the writer should alternate, allowing one to dominate and the other two to become subordinate. When the dominating story line reaches a point of exhaustion, bring up one of the subordinate story lines and let it dominate.

Example The fortune hunter is an unrevealed coward trying to gain courage. His wife is a cold woman who is trying to overcome her inability to love. One brother is greedy and a womanizer who wants to steal the treasure. The other brother is a rabid patriot who craves to become the next dictator. The sister is a lesbian who tries working out her sexual problem with one of the medical missionaries. The fortune hunter's young son is a dreadfully obese boy unable to control his gluttony.

By bringing all three story lines into one novel and alternating between character plot, a sequence of natural disasters, and a plot of conflicting relationships, the writer never needs to worry about having enough material for the observation of human nature or the invention of situation.

Throw in an asthmatic pet puppy always being chased by a lion and only the illiterate will not read the novel.

Don't Justify Bad Writing

There is a curious rebellion that arises when the unpublished writer completes a novel and begins rewriting. He refuses to correct three elemental defects that always exist in a first writing.

1. Dialogue that tells content which should be depicted in a scene.

2. Scenes that are overlong and carry only one dramatic effect or point, which could best be related through narration or dialogue.

3. Overlong introspections with an inclusion of polemics.

With ruthless objectivity, the writer begins eliminating and amending. At first he is willing, though grudgingly, to make these changes. As he continues appraising what must be changed, he becomes reluctant to make the changes. Then he becomes canny and, with ferret-like desperation, begins developing justifications for why the defects can remain. The immediate and ever present "truthful justification" is this:

(Writer's justification) "Maybe the craft standards I'm imposing on myself are just too demanding. I've read best sellers that have worse writing and more defects in them than I've produced. I could list a hundred novels to back up that statement."

The unpublished writer is not overstating his justification. The three listed writing defects appear in many past and current best sellers. This sloppy, inept writing can be explained. Most publishers are no longer concerned with the quality of fiction. Their interest is commerce, *not art*. This is not an absolute. There are some publishers who still care about fiction. The list is not inspiringly long.

The unpublished writer should not use "defective writing" which is published as his example of what is acceptable writing. He must establish craft standards that are universally excellent and sustain them regardless of what he sees published and how much money and fame mediocre work might bring the best selling writer.

Finding a Writing Instructor

When searching for an effective writing instructor there are five fundamental personal traits to consider before letting him instruct you.

1. Be certain his ego, vanity, or pride is not so domineering that he eliminates your own. You are to be instructed, not tyrannized.

2. Avoid any instructor who cannot be objective and evaluates all writing through his own preferences or interests. Your instructor should be able to suggest methods of writing that will aid you in what YOU want to write, through the criteria of your own creative vision. The instructor's personal tastes are of no value to you. His critical insights must be unbiased and sensitive to your vision, whether he approves of it or not.

3. Avoid any instructor who is derisive, humiliating, or discouraging. Or who is flattering, excessively admiring, or constantly enthralled with what you write. You can't be that bad and you surely are not that good, yet. Either type is ineffective or misleading. There is a median level at which the instructor can be objectively truthful without debasing the efforts of the student, and without puffing the student into believing in a delusion.

4. The instructor should be a professional writer who has been paid for various forms of writing for publication or production. The craft involved in doing many different forms of writing will help the instructor evaluate the work of students who write in different styles.

5. Avoid any instructor who "gives it away for free." He is either on an ego trip, needs some elevating adoration, or is foolishly generous. Students should make sacrifices for their instruction. They listen more attentively and work harder when it costs money.

It is not necessary to like or love your instructor. You are required only to regard him with some esteem—otherwise you will not learn.

Don't Overcomplicate Your Characters

An effectively developed major character is depicted within personal boundaries which he never oversteps. Once the character's realm or "dimension" is established, it should remain fixed. Adding more complexities will not make the character more interesting. Unnecessary character complexities distract the reader. They offer misleading motives and promise situations that never appear.

> **Story** Dana is a deep-sea diver who hires himself out for the locating of sunken treasure. He has an international reputation for honesty, reliability, and expertise. His services have been contracted by Spain to locate a treasure-laden galleon sunk off the coast of Portugal in 1535.

The writer may include various types of relationships, intrigue, and adventure within this general story. But the plot should remain within the limits of the concerns and capabilities with which the major character was first developed.

> **Scene** Dana is now 300 feet under water. It is his last job. He has a heart condition that might kill him if he becomes unduly excited. He has just killed a giant octopus and the water is black with the creature's ink. There are man-eating sharks swimming toward him. A team of murdering treasure hunters have threatened to kill him before he locates the galleon. A typhoon is about to ravage the area.

Dana should be involved only with the present sequence of problems. His feelings, analysis, and speculations should remain focused only on his circumstance and the range of material within his characterization.

Dana does not need religious doubts at this time, nor an obsession with dieting, symbolic fears that harass him when underwater, or distressing extra-sensory perception. This is "fringe" material that does not benefit him at this time.

Within the original range of characterization, the writer can develop many directions of thought, feeling, and interest. There is no need to go "outward" to make Dana more complex. The writer need only dig deeper *into the content that already exists* to find more material.

Cumulative and Immediate Characters

In a novel, the writer must create many types of characters to be used for a variety of reasons. There are: 1) characters who are developed cumulatively; 2) immediate or obvious characters; 3) characters who are both cumulative and immediate.

Major characters are always *cumulative*. They must grow continually until, at the end of the novel, they are fully complete.

Example A Conrad is a bank clerk actually working for the I.R.S., trying to discover corrupt banking practices. As the novel progresses he is seen as a man with a family, who yearns to be in the field to avoid his wife. He is supporting three children he's had by other women.

Immediate characters play only one role. Whenever they appear, they are always the same. They are recognizable by their semi-stereotyped parts. The family butler, the local minister, a lawyer entrusted with a will, the governor of a state, a traffic cop.

Example B Conrad visits each of the women who have his illegitimate children several times, but the women always remain the same. They do not change from scene to scene. Nothing new is ever learned about them. Their function is simple. They are obvious.

Secondary characters can be both *immediate and cumulative*. They have specific roles which support the major character, yet have independent stories of their own. When they appear, they are immediately recognizable by their function— but as they function, more can be added to them. Their development occurs in proportion to their contribution to the major character's story and to their own independent story.

Example C Conrad's wife is a religious woman. She believes his work for the I.R.S. is immoral and evil. Believing she will convert him, she will not divorce him. *That is her obvious role.* To develop her further, let her learn about the three children he is supporting. Have her take some action to separate him from those relationships which she considers irreligious.

Psychological Case Histories

When writers use a psychoanalytical focus to detail a character, they risk losing the characterization and replacing it with a psychological case history. A created fictional characterization is open-ended, can be probed within many dimensions of human behavior, and still be dramatic and credible (the passing years, virtues and evils, successes and failures, family and friends, etc.). There is always more to be written about the major character.

Psychological case histories are dead-end characterizations. Once the case-history framework is established, the major character is locked into that frame and cannot get out. If he does, then his behavior is unnatural to his psychological portrait, and he becomes unbelievable.

Example (a composite screen treatment of a hundred already-produced television and cinema films) A mild-looking young man picks up a dreary looking B-girl. Before getting to her room, he strangles her with a nylon stocking. A red heart is embroidered on its heel. He kills six more B-girls. The city is in terror. The police are desperate. They cannot find any store that sells stockings with red hearts embroidered on the heel.

The film viewer is guaranteed that two particular scenes will be shown. The hero-detective chats with the police psychologist who explains the killings in psychological terminology, all related to the current trend in mother fixations. Three more women are strangled. The next guaranteed scene is the young killer in his room, embroidering a heart onto the heel of a stocking. Behind him is a photo of women dancing in a chorus line. One of the dancers is circled. She is high-kicking. On the heel of her stocking is a blazing red heart. When the youth finishes the stocking, he turns to the picture and cries in gut-wrenching sobs, "You, you whore—my mother, a whore!" He twists the stocking in rage. He is readying for another kill.

Psychological case-histories in fiction are usually facile. They are umbrella insights into human nature which are glibly applicable to most people. Fiction is a precise focus on the individual. Case-history characters are predictable. Once the clinically detailed motivation of the major character is known, he can no longer cause surprise. He is obvious.

Unless the plot line motivates the character in the present, the plot line cannot become complicated. The writer may hoke up the plot with a slew of secondary plots which engage the secondary characters, but the major plot line remains simplistic, because the major character's motivation is simplistic. The youth who strangles women with a heart-embroidered stocking has no present. He is closed into his past. His mother had an assembly of lovers that he wants to replace. He could not become his mother's lover, so he hated her. He is now killing women who symbolize his mother. That is his case history. That is the core of his focus. There is no more to him than that.

The purpose of a plot line in a novel is to force the character to grow enough to change. In fiction, a case-history detailing of characterization brings the character to a dead end. He cannot become more of what he was when he began. A fictional character must always be more than the sum of all his background parts. When the character is introduced, only some of his "dramatic persona" should be known. As he is put through the events in the plot line more and still more is revealed about him. He is constantly "becoming" until the novel is done.

Tension and drama in character are derived from what the unknown factors of the character's personality will cause him to do when he confronts crisis and conflict in the present. If he is a statistical compilation of known factors that relate only to his past, the reader can predict exactly how he will behave and why.

Psychological insights should not be omitted entirely, because they are unavoidable. But a psychological motivation should only be a portion of the characterization. When this psychological motivation is infused into the major character's characterization, it should be disguised.

Intermediate Characters

There are two general types of intermediate characters. (1) Any individual who appears only once but is vital enough to cause changes in relationships and story lines of the major characters. (2) Any individual who is carried throughout the novel, appearing at strategic times to change the lives and stories of the major characters.

An intermediate character is not, in his own right, important. His background need not be developed. His purpose is only to affect the major characters. When using a type 1 intermediate character, focus all his feeling and thought and function on the major characters and their situations.

Example During a wedding ceremony there is a woman (intermediate character) waiting to announce that she is the groom's (major character) undeclared wife. Her revelation will drastically affect his story.

The writer need not elaborate on the intermediate character's history. Her story is small, important only enough to give credibility to the writer's purpose. After she ruins the wedding, she is dealt with, and disappears.

In the use of type 2, the intermediate character *should have his own story* which is involved with the major characters. Though he may appear only a few times, his story line must be strong enough to be remembered. His story is important enough to affect important lives.

Example When Everett went into the priesthood, his brother (intermediate character) went into crime. While Everett advances in the church, his brother advances in crime. Everett's position in the church is now threatened by the notoriety of his brother's criminal activities.

The type 2 intermediate character must have his own story, so when he appears, now and then, his story does not seem unrelated to the overall plot line. If the character is always turning up and the reader knows nothing about him, the reader wonders what he is doing in the novel. He is more of a writing gimmick, a convenience, than a genuine person.

Real Speech vs. Written Dialogue

Dialogue spoken by a character is immediate. Dialogue that is narrated by the writer is always an instant behind the action. In real life, much dialogue is idle, cluttered with hems, haws, and repetitions. In writing, dialogue must be precise, selective. A character is given dialogue to speak because dialogue is the strongest, most interesting, and most relevant method for establishing certain information. If the situation demands immediate response from a character because it is vital that the character express himself at that moment, then he should speak. If what he says is trivial or not immediately related to what is happening, then the verbal exchange should either be narrated, or deleted.

The difference between "*I feel marvelous,*" and *He felt marvelous,* is not in the quality of the feeling, but in the intensity. "*I feel marvelous*" is an on-scene "you-are-there" recreation of a character's actual feeling. *He felt marvelous* is detached, a less personal recounting of what the character *has* felt. There is a distance and a passage of time (though only an instant), and this diminishes intensity. Although the thoughts are the same, the language they are expressed in is not the same.

> **Example** *Spoken feeling*: "I feel down today. Lower than a snake's belly."
> *Narrated speech*: Today he felt depressed. He was without self-esteem.
> *Spoken thought*: "I feel lousy today on a'counta I felt lousy yestuhday!"
> *Narrated thought*: He believed that the depression he was feeling today was related to the low he felt yesterday.

GENERAL GUIDE: When a character's feelings and thoughts must come into the reader's hearing with immediacy, use dialogue. It is authentic and irretractable. Narrated speech is not a direct statement by the character. It is the related observation of the writer.

Youth Odyssey Novels

There is no reason for any writer to be without a novel to write. There is one novel that can always be written and its freshness and universality is inexhaustible. It is the youth odyssey novel, the story of the adventures of young men or women who leave home and wander the land in search of self, of Truth, of God, of personal identity.

The youth odyssey novel has been written thousands of times and in hundreds of forms. Someone, right now, is writing another. And today, another one has just been published. It might be read by a small populace or become a best seller. Perhaps the one that is published tomorrow will be yours. Everyone has lived through an odyssey.

There is no need to develop bizarre plots to fit inside weird story lines. The locale need not be exotic. Europe, Asia, Timbuktu. There is no need for constant murder, outrageous sex, continual national disasters, nuclear submarines carrying bombs set by intergalactic terrorists.

The soul of humankind will never become uninteresting.

Superb novels have been written in this genre: *Look Homeward, Angel, Crime and Punishment, The Red Badge of Courage, On the Road, Tom Jones, Jude the Obscure, David Copperfield, An American Tragedy, The Magic Mountain*, etc.

All different structures, different characters, different eras—yet all sharing a universal theme that has captured readers and changed their lives. They have scratched the superficial face of societies and left their distinguished marks. These youth odyssey novels are the truly important novels. Your own life contains your own odyssey. It is the autobiographical novel—the living experiences you have accumulated, which are translated and reinterpreted into a work of superb fiction.

The great American novel is still waiting to be written, again.

Settings In Mysteries

Writers of mystery novels who understand how to use details of setting become cleverer and gain more admiration from readers than do writers who depend upon the brilliance of the sleuth to solve the mystery. When the sleuth, through observation, contemplation, and analysis does all the solving, the reader becomes a patient bystander, rather than a participant. By using properly placed and seemingly unconnected "setting details," the mystery writer feeds the reader several absolutely correct solutions to the crime—though only one can be the correct solution. Yet the reader is happy to be fooled and misled—as long as he or she can do some sleuthing.

> **Example** The maid had just cleaned the den. Elton lay sprawled on the oriental rug. A blurred powder burn circled the bullet hole in his forehead. A large .45 Colt was near his long nicotine stained fingers. The windows were tightly shut. Precisely handwritten pages of Elton's latest novel were neatly arranged on the desk. A small pile of ashes and four crushed cigarettes were in the amber ash tray. A chessboard with ivory pieces was beside the black leather lounging chair. The white king was set down.

Without making exposition necessary, the setting details offer information. The victim was shot. He was well-to-do and neat. He smoked cigarettes while he wrote. He played chess. Just commonplace details. But there is more. No suicide note. The pile of ashes amid the cigarettes indicates that someone who smoked a pipe entered the room after the maid had cleaned. The white king being set down implies a checkmate—a killer with a sense of irony.

One mystery-writing technique is to demonstrate first how the sleuth deduces meaning (finds clues) from commonplace details of setting. Then wean the reader from the sleuth's work and allow the reader to observe details and analyze them on his own. Before the novel ends, the reader should have guessed the truth about several suspicious characters, but not have been able to solve the entire problem. When the mystery is finally solved, the solution is both believable and surprising. The setting details that gave the reader clues to the solution actually misled him—but they also served to get him to participate.

"Sudden Scare" Scenes

Some brutal, shocking scenes should happen suddenly, *without foreshadowing*. They should be unexpected, startling. After the scene is read, the reader will accept the surprising event as logical. The scenes that follow will prove the unexpectedly shocking scene necessary.

Example The parents of a college student are driving to his graduation. Suddenly, an out-of-control semi hurtles toward them. The father panics and stalls the car. The truck smashes into them, dragging them to a cliff. They are flung over the cliff to crash and burst into flames.

At first, there seems to be no justification for the violent scene. The reader does not know that the writer needs this scene to motivate the college graduate, who in the next scene is steeped in grief and rage. His life is changed. He swears vengeance on the company that owns the truck. The reader is now drawn into the graduate's story. The writer is forgiven.

Example A missionary doctor has established an infirmary in a backward African village. He is inoculating an elderly native. Suddenly there are shrieks and roars. The village is attacked by warriors. The villagers stand by while the doctor is being slaughtered, and his body searched.

The reader is surprised by this sudden event. There was no preparation for its appearance. Reader annoyance is about to set in. But, the next scene distracts the reader from this annoyance. The leader of the warriors flings open a medicine box and shows that the doctor had been poisoning the villagers in order to steal their diamonds.

The use of sudden shocking scenes is an efficient method for getting into your plot quickly. But such scenes are not effective in the opening chapter. They create a headlong pace that is difficult to sustain. Nor should they be used too frequently. Their effect will be deadened. The reader will begin to expect the unexpected.

The Family Novel

The family novel has been around for centuries, but its traditional plot has not been rendered hackneyed. It has endured for so long because of its freshness and appeal to every generation of readers. One interesting type of family novel deals with a young person who, because of an unexpected circumstance, is forced to learn about the hidden, arcane, extraordinary stories of the lives of his family. If diverse techniques and an interesting array of characters are used, the novel can combine the intimacy of the first-person narrator and the mobility of the third-person multiple viewpoint.

Story A young man gains leave from his job as a hotel manager to attend the funeral and the reading of a will left by his wealthy Aunt Greta. During the pre-funeral and burial ceremonies he talks with the other relatives who have collected together for this solemn occasion.

For this novel to be successful, there should be at least ten prominent characters. The narrator should have a serious conflict in his own life: a hidden crime, a sexual predicament, a need for revenge, debts accrued from a gambling compulsion, etc. As he becomes involved with his relatives, he should begin learning about them, and about himself.

Example I did not know that Uncle Edwin had once been a feared mobster. He was a mild man who wore thick bifocals. He enjoyed building ships inside of bottles. When cousin Tina told me, "Never cross Uncle Edwin. He still has mob connections," I wanted to laugh. Then I saw him standing in the kitchen, swatting flies. He would pick one up from the sink counter and smile as he slowly squashed its tiny head.

The narrator then tells the story of Uncle Edwin. When the story reaches a critical interval, an impactful crisis, decision on the use of technique must be made by the writer.

A. The narrator can finish Uncle Edwin's story and then begin another character's story.

B. The narrator leaves the first person narration and allows the character to play out his own story *through the third person.*

Example B (first person) I visualized Uncle Edwin as he was tied to the wall. How he watched the three killers pick from a deck of cards. Gunsel drew the ace. He aimed a gun at Uncle Edwin's heart and fired. Uncle Edwin slumped. They laughed and drove away.

(now third person) Edwin listened to the car drive off. He remained slumped. The bullet had struck the thick diary he always kept above his heart. He chuckled. Even when faced with death, Mom was still saving his life.

C. There can be a mixture of first person and third person viewpoints, using an alternating structure. Some of the novel is told; some of it is played out.

The inexperienced writer should not be misled into believing that the family novel structure is simplistic. A skillful control must be used at all times. There are five aspects to the family novel that the writer needs to know.

1. The conflict the narrator brings into the novel must be worked out through what he learns about his family. This information becomes experience which forces his life (ambitions, emotions, etc.) to change.

2. When the "other" people are being revealed, they must become major characters for the time they are featured. The awareness of the first-person narrator must be absorbed and not be present for the reader.

3. Each featured character must be involved with the next (or several) characters who will be featured. Each member should have a significant role in the life story of other members. It is a "bound" family.

4. The past is almost as vital as the present. There has to be a constant shifting from past to present. The past material is "chosen" by the writer because it has a clear bearing on what the relatives are like in the present. They are bound together in the past and the present.

5. It is important that the writer create an articulate, analytical, imaginative, and sensitive narrator. A clod is an uninteresting story teller. His depth is limited, his vision is narrow.

Redundancies

Redundancies are watery phrases used by careless or negligent writers. Why not use *but* instead of *on the other hand*? *He said he would personally testify* should be *he would testify* since personally refers to the character himself and he cannot testify without himself doing it.

Redundancies are also conversational phrases which have been accepted into the language of speech as convenient identifiers of meaning, but they are superficial and should not be used in the "language of writing."

Using *few and far between* instead of *few* does not add anything to a sentence. *The car was completely destroyed or, to put it another way, it was totally demolished,* instead of *The car was destroyed,* wastes eleven words which do not provide emphasis or additional information. The word *demolished* cannot destroy the car more and, if the writer says he is going to "put it another way" he should actually do it.

Redundancies are blurry expressions that provoke misunderstanding because they befog clarity. *Surrounded on all sides* fails to stress the condition of being *surrounded.* You cannot be surrounded on only three sides. Or perhaps the object being surrounded is circular in shape and has no sides. *At the present time I am feeling dreary* wastes four words—*at the present time.* If you are feeling dreary, you imply *now* (at the present time is *now*).

Redundancies impede the flow and purity of expression. The purpose of writing is to communicate and persuade. When a reader is forced to reread a sentence for its true meaning, the writer has tampered with the purity of content in that sentence. The reader is being put to work in areas where he should be entertained.

It is excusable if a writer overlooks the use of a redundancy. It is inexcusable if an editor allows it to remain. ("The difference between the right word and the almost right word is the difference between lightning and the lightning bug."—Mark Twain)

Polemics and Sermons

A writer should be able to speak his mind in his work. Yet why doesn't sermonizing, polemic, or expository oration work in writing?

1. The reader may not agree with what is obviously the writer's opinion or attitude. The section will create unnecessary dissension. Antagonism of this type alienates the reader from deeper involvement with the book.

2. It is an intrusion. It hinders the flow of the story, the scenes, the action. It forces the reader to think about content that does not emerge from the novel's inherent content.

Story An auto mechanic's wife is involved in women's liberation. She is harassing him to hire a sitter-housekeeper so she can work. The illiterate mechanic is in angry opposition to such an arrangement. They have four children.

Example (polemic) Vinny stood over the engine and imagined it to be his wife. He wagged a wrench, bawling, "Why'nt you jus' bug off, huh? Jus' lemme be, huh!" and looked away to study the motor. Silently he told her this assertion of women into the sacrosanct province of men was becoming an outrage to reason. It was not economically rational to open the ranks of business to women. They would be depriving men of employment while neglecting the home for which God created them to attend. Vinny tightened the wrench onto a hexagonal nut and imagined it was his wife's neck.

Regardless of the subject matter of the polemic, it is an obvious set of statements issuing from the writer, not from the character. While this may be the character's attitude, it is clear the writer is ignoring the character to impose his own views, in his own language, into the story. Vinny would shake the wrench at the motor and scowl, "Stop breakin' my ears with that women's lib jazz. Just say home an' raise the kids, see."

It is not that the writer's attitudes or beliefs have no place in the novel. The writer's responsibility to his craft obligates him to develop characters who convey the writer's beliefs, in their own language, in their own time, through their own situations, based on their own solid characterizations. The writer must remain where he belongs—in the background, writing.

Scrud

Part of an editor's job is to attend the publisher's demand for leaner novels because of high publishing costs. This forces the editor to become a cunning surgeon who cuts down a writer's novel. A protective device the professional writer uses is *scrud*.

Scrud is purple prose, minor characters who are unnecessary, verbose dialogue, subtle and metaphysical character motives that do not provide depth, rambling streams of consciousness, excessive background material, flashbacks that can be reduced to recollections, etc.

The writer uses all his expertise to find areas where scrud will not damage the novel. He makes this scrud obvious enough for the editor to find. The scrud device is based on a "two-for-one" principle. The writer should plant two portions of scrud before those portions of quality writing he anticipates the editor will also want to delete.

The practice of editing was instituted to help the writer bring his novel to a state of excellence. Depending upon the personalities involved, the relationship can be amicable or hostile. Contemporary editing conferences are more often just "bargaining sessions."

The editor reaches the first scrud portion and begins deleting. The writer objects, then grudgingly agrees. The second scrud is found. The writer's objection is stronger, but he agrees. When the editor reaches the quality writing and wants to delete, the writer refuses. "Look, be fair. You had two—let me have one." Aware of the writer's previous cooperation, the editor agrees. This haggling continues until the novel is edited. It is one of the many ways a writer can prevent an insensitive aggressive editor from destroying his novel.

All-Good or All-Evil Characters

All civilized societies, in the general sense, are sentimental. In every recorded age there is the standard belief that "no human being is either all good or all evil." In fiction, the completely good or the completely evil character can exist (believably) only if he is not a major character. Secondary characters can assume the all-good, all-evil status because their function is limited, not over-whelmingly complex.

Major characters must be motivated by complex impulses and reasons. The more complex the character is, the more likely he is to be awarded motives the writer did not intend. Readers bring their personal experiences and senti-mentalities into their reading. Given the latitudes present in complex charac-ters, the reader can attribute good to some actions of the major villain, and evil to the actions of the major hero. Only in the simplistic behavior are there abso-lutes. Secondary characters are more simplistic than major characters.

Example (villain) He has been methodically poisoning his wife. She is now dying. A priest is providing last rites. Her beloved canary is beside her bed. While the priest is reciting, the canary begins singing shrilly. The priest is distracted. The villain silently reaches into the cage and snaps the canary's neck. He stands at the bed in pious solemnity.

The reader wonders if the husband has killed the canary because he enjoys kill-ing, or to be sentimentally considerate and not let his wife's last moments be disturbed. Was it to show the woman his utter contempt for her, or to lovingly stop the bird from grieving, or to reveal to the priest his cynicism about God? The writer's choice is that he enjoys killing. Anything that causes him displea-sure, he kills.

He is the major villain. Whatever he does is significant. His actions must not be misunderstood, misconstrued, or misinterpreted. The more the reader knows about the major character, the more the reader can understand what does not belong in that characterization. The reader will not accept as believable a major character who is all good or all evil. But the reader does not invest that much concern in the secondary characters.

Let the wife-and-canary killer be a secondary villain.

The Secondary Story

There are several techniques for introducing a secondary story. One method in-troduces it immediately, along with the major story. If the secondary story is in-troduced immediately, it should have a direct bearing on the major story.

Example (major story) Three convicts conduct a prison break. They all have passports to Uruguay where they cannot be extradited and returned to the United States. In Uruguay they buy a ranch and start a neo-Nazi party.

(Secondary story) During the break-out the warden's brother, the chief guard, is killed. The warden vows to travel to Uruguay to kill all the escaped prisoners and anyone belonging to the neo-Nazi party.

Another technique allows the major story to unfold for a substantial length of time, then unsuspectedly, introduces the secondary story. The secondary story is introduced either through some unexpected circumstance or as the result of a personal relationship in the major character's background.

Example (circumstance) A Russian submarine commander is dispatched to a destination where he is to wait for a message to launch some bombs on New York. About seventy pages later, he learns that one of his officers is an American agent who has notified his agency.
(Secondary story) One hundred pages into the book, the American navy sends out a submarine to find and destroy the Russian sub. Aboard the American sub there is a Russian spy who begins committing sabotage.

Example (personal relationship) A scientist is working to raise funds to develop a new rocket fuel. The government won't make the expenditure. People are trying to steal the formula.
(Secondary story) The scientist's former mistress has gone insane and kidnaps his son. She believes he is really her child. She has homicidal tendencies.

The secondary story that appears later need not have a direct or immediate connection to the major story. Only a slight connection with the major story is needed. But as the major and secondary stories continue, they must begin converging, until they become deeply interwoven. The secondary story then becomes absorbed into the major story—complicating and giving it greater excitement.

When to Let the Reader Fill in Details

Because creating a story or novel is not a collaboration between the reader and writer, rarely should the writer presume that the reader knows exactly what the writer means. Yet there are times when the writer must assume the reader knows what he is saying, or else the story or novel will become excessively long or heavily overwritten.

Scenic values, cliché characters, and *some action* can be presumed to be a part of most readers' experience. But vital mental and emotional responses should always be detailed, to mean exactly what the writer wants.

Example (scenic) The shingled roof sagged from dry rot. Weeds, like goblin fingers, crawled up the split siding. Clumps of mud wasp hives clung to the door jamb. A teenager sprawled in the yard, sunbathing.

Example (cliché character) The elderly man hunched over the pile of coins, rubbing his hands. With loving patience he began counting.

It is reasonable for the reader to presume the house is occupied by negligent owners and that the elderly man is a miser and loves money. The writer wants the reader to *presume* this circumstance and attitude—so additional writing will not be necessary.

In the case of particular and individual character responses, the reader's presumptive abilities and experience may be shallow, naive, incomplete, or careless.

Example Wally called his son a drunken fool and slammed him across the face, tumbling him to the wall. Robbie slumped to the floor and covered his eyes. Wally strode to him and shook his fist, "You're no better than a filthy street punk, you hear?" Robbie sniffled.

What the father feels is obvious. What the son feels in the specific is not known. What he feels and thinks at that tense moment must not be left to the reader to fill in through presumption. The son's response is too important, too individual to be presumed. It must be exact, to further the values of the scene and the meaning of the dramatics.

Tape Recorders

Do not use a tape recorder and transcribe the spoken word onto paper and, with a few changes in the text and the inclusion of punctuation, assume you now have the written word. Although spoken language and written language use the same words, they are not the same language.

Speaking is a literal expression of the writer's consciousness. There is no time to pause and scoop exactly what you want to express from the depths. You cannot phrase, construct, or visualize the appearance of the spoken word into the form as effective as the written word. The insights and perceptions, the ideas and techniques contained in the consciousness of the writer are minimal compared to what is contained in his depths. The consciousness is glib, facile. A writer's depths are intuitive, dramatic.

The writer uses three basic levels of language. 1.) *The conversational:*

general, clichéd, unselect, circuitous, limited and superficial in vocabulary. 2.) *The silent:* the language of reading. Definitions are more accurate, tightly associated to the meanings they express. The vocabulary is extensive. 3.) *The written:* precise, selective, personal, particularly in fiction. It is connotative and denotative. It brings words and sentences into an organization to create specific impressions. The writer's language is the dramatic language. It can be rewritten to become fastidious.

The tape recorder should be used for recording ideas and for noting down techniques and writing structures that might be forgotten. It should be used for making cursory outlines of scenes or chapters; for insights about plot, speculations on story, perceptions about character and relationships; for possible material and craft the writer is too inconvenienced or lazy to write down.

The written word is the most difficult for the writer to find. The writer must probe into his deepest resources. The general language spoken into the tape recorder is quickly used up. When the full expenditure of conscious language is reached, the speaking writer begins repeating himself. When transcribed into print, spoken language looks amateurish.

When to Stop Foreshadowing

After the three-quarter point in the novel is reached, do not *foreshadow*. The remainder of the novel should become linear, moving at a direct, uncomplicated pace. Foreshadowing is unnecessary because whatever happens after the three-quarter point should already have been prepared for. There is no need for adding information on the characters, their backgrounds, relationships or story line. It is now time to surprise, startle, and even astonish the reader.

Story line (to three-quarter point) Archaeologists Ralph and Jennifer have located the ancient tomb of Ramasenthentut, the twin brother of King Tut. Kranshaw, a mercenary archaeologist, has tried to stop them so he can steal the treasure. There has been murder, intrigue, governmental interference. At the three-quarter point in the novel, the tomb has been unearthed, and now the archaeologists must gain entry. It is dangerous, for there are deadly traps.

The purposes and relationships of the important characters have already been revealed. Additional story twists or new characters will interfere. If any unsuspected complexities of character arise in the principals, they will have to be foreshadowed to be accepted. This would slow the action. The surprising story complications should come from *external* sources. They should be unexpected but credible.

Last part of story The hero and heroine gain entry into the tomb without being killed. The villain is crushed when the ghost of Ramasenthentut drops a boulder on him. The discovery gains world renown.

Any surprises that happen during this portion of the novel should be circumstantial *and not prepared for.* Sudden cave-ins. A laborer who had been featured earlier is really a cultic high priest who doesn't want the tomb desecrated. Earth tremors (spooky or natural) that reveal still another tomb, that of Ramasenthentut's cousin. The heroine realizes she's pregnant and is afraid the child will be cursed.

At the closing of the novel, keep the reader busy with events.

Incredible Deeds

Characters who perform incredible deeds should be created through conditions that are credible. They should not suddenly, unexpectedly, become infused with superhuman powers. (Exceptions exist in fable, fantasy, horror and science fiction.) When this remarkable event happens, it should occur because of a believably developed crisis or emergency.

The reading public has been conditioned to accept extraordinary acts of heroism, physical power, and self-sacrifice, but only under extreme or unusual conditions of peril, fear, or love.

Example Everyone has heard of how an ordinary man once lifted the rear end of a heavy truck so his wife could be pulled from under the wheel that was crushing her. He did not undergo a sudden physical transformation from simp to Samson as do the movie werewolves. The mysterious powers infused in him arose from the crisis, the emergency.

While the man's action was incredible, the man remains believable because he performed it with ordinary attributes (hands, feet, legs, etc.) which reverted back to a common state when the crisis was over. It was only during that critical interval that he became extraordinary.

Example An 83-year-old farmer paralyzed with arthritis and rheumatism cannot be shown leaping from his mule to rescue his great-granddaughter from the rabid jaws of a berserk grizzly bear. While his act of self-sacrifice and heroism is believable, the way he rescues her is not. His age and physical condition must be considered. If he hurries to stand before his great-granddaughter and faces the crazy grizzly bear and shouts, "Stand fast, you berserk beast!" and in the fascinating tradition of great hypnotists, stops the bear by the unearthly power emanating from his eyes, the beginning of an incredible moment is happening. Then, if still emitting power, the aged man talks to the bear, "You are a cuddly kitten, come and cuddle us!" and the bear drops to the ground and begins purring, his action is believable because such hypnotic power is capable of coming through him, whereas enormous physical power bursting through an ancient, rickety body, is not too believable.

Though the elderly man's stopping the great bear is incredible, his fantastic deed is believable because he did not suddenly grow muscles and employ black-belt karate. His great love for his great-granddaughter and her peril, evoked from him superhuman power ONLY FOR A LITTLE WHILE. When they leave the area of the bear, the 83-year-old man does not go onto the theatrical circuit as a "great hypnotist." When he and the child are in a place of safety, he reverts back to an elderly man. The superhuman power lasts only as long as there is a need for it.

No Perfect First Chapters

In the vast and various realm of "how-to-write guides" there is no law, canon, edict, ukase, tenet or rule that declares the writer must begin at the beginning of the novel he wants to write. The only fully functional rule that exists is one that states, *any handicap or barrier that prevents you from beginning your novel must be overcome.*

Yes, the writer needs a strong, interesting, believable, dramatic and reader-hooking opening chapter. It is essential. But what if he hasn't found it yet? Is the remainder of the novel to stand poised in some musty, suffocating corridor, waiting to be launched into existence? You must not be stopped. Procrastination is the thief of time.

While the first chapter is probably the most important in the novel, it is not the entire novel. If you cannot find the "perfect" opening chapter, then ignore it. Begin your novel at any point in the story or plot line that you feel capable of writing, *right now.*

The traditional guides in the "how-to-write" realm are valueless if they stop you from writing. Begin *anywhere* in the novel and in time, as you write, you will acquire the perfect first chapter.

Searching for the perfect first chapter can become the most justifiable excuse for not writing your novel. It is a superbly reasonable postponement. But there is an interesting insight about first chapters that must be seriously considered. A startling percentage of first novels published, are not published with their original "perfect" first chapters.

The writers stewed and dallied until they arrived at their perfect first chapter. As they progressed into the novel and discovered more of what they were writing about, the gloss of their perfect first chapter became scarred and pitted. At the end of the novel they realized it was all wrong. It is the total novel, in its completed form, that determines the perfection of the first chapter. Down with perfect first chapters. Full speed ahead!

Closet Novels

Closet novels are those in which the writer does not include the effects of the world on the characters. Not all novels need be historical epics like *War and Peace* or *Gone With the Wind*, but they should take into account events outside the lives of the main characters and their immediate personal concerns.

Example A family of four living on a ranch in Montana. The father is a weak man, the children are unruly, the mother is the dominant figure. The story is about how this conflict-ridden family learns to live with each other in harmony, how the father becomes resolute.

If the writer excludes the world (town, the nearby railroad, etc.) and deals only with the familial problems, the novel becomes closeted, limited. It also becomes *inauthentic*. People (whether in fiction or real life) are shaped and motivated by the conflicts within their relationships and by the events outside their lives.

If the father leaves the ranch to buy provisions, the action should not be a shadowy two lines: *Basil allowed little Ruth to accompany him to town for supplies. The trip home was uneventful.* There should be a stony-hearted banker holding the mortgage who wants the ranch. Religiously righteous townsfolk should harass the parents to bring their children to church. The town strumpet should be interested in tempting the husband from his chores. Threaten the cattle with an impending tornado.

The pressure within the relationships and the pressures coming from the world drive human resources from the people that cannot be forced out of them when just confined to family difficulties. If the conflicts remain only in the cloistered privacy of their lives, the novel takes on the impression of being "esoteric"—separate from the similarity of lives that other people lead—people like readers.

Short Story vs. The Novel

The difference between a short story and a novel is not only in their length, but also in the complexity and complication of its content. A true short story cannot be turned into a novel, although the idea for a short story can be developed into a novel. A short story deals with an event in which there are several incidents. The novel deals with many events, and the incidents are compounded in number as the plot continues. A short story usually deals with a few characters. A novel usually deals with many characters.

The characters in a short story are engaged in one interval of experience in their lives. They are changed by the impact of this experience. In a novel, the characters are engaged in many intervals of experience and undergo many changes as a result of these events. When the characters in a short story are changed, the story usually ends. The characters in a novel are constantly changing as the plot continues.

A short story has a single plot line that moves in a linear direction. All suspense and expectation is directed to climax at the end. In the lives of the many characters in a novel there are many levels of suspense and expectations. A short story opens on a single point and moves with undeviating progress until the point is reached. There may be secondary incidents that create undercurrents in the action—but not a separate, individual plot. The single plot line in a novel serves like a great aorta with outbranching arteries (other plot lines). Though associated with the opening plot line, the other plot lines are individual and separate plots.

Example A child wanders from her yard. A child molester is in the area. Many people search for her. The molester grabs her. She is rescued.

This idea can be developed into an excellent short story, but not a novel. To work the "story idea" of a lost child who is taken by a molester and is rescued into a novel, the stories of other lives and their plot lines must be explored. The short story does not have the expanse or variety of backgrounds that exist in the novel.

Example (short story opening) Jenny is seen sneaking through the backyard gate and wandering off. A respectable, middle-aged man is seen near her.

(Opening of episodic novel) A man is angry at his wife for not loving his seven-year-old daughter. The wife complains that the child does not love her. (break) The child wanders from the backyard. (break) Another woman is seen carrying her bruised and violated child to a hospital. (break) The child molester is a respectable-looking man strolling past the day care center playground, watching the children. (break) Jenny's parents notice she is not in the backyard, skipping rope. (break) Neighbors begin searching for her.

The short story plot must start immediately and progress forward. Events in a novel must also happen immediately. But a novel with several plot lines will have several "starts" that branch outward as they all move forward.

A short story should cover a short span of time. It might be an interval of hours or two days. Extending the time span into months would demand too many transitions, breaks, and changes in viewpoint. This could be harmful to the intensity and unity of the story. A novel can and should cover many weeks, months, years and eras. The many transitions, changes in viewpoint and place, and backgrounds provide structural variety. A short story should not be cluttered with many characters—a novel should have many characters.

Only one aspect of the historical influence of an era can serve as the backdrop for the short story. Any more would force the unit into an uncomfortable length. If there is a greater range of historical influence on the character, it must be implicit. The reader's knowledge provides it. If the reader does not have this knowledge then it does not exist. If a novel does not have many historical influences, on the other hand, it appears skimpy. The plot lines are too limited, the complexity of character is diminished.

The intensity and forward thrust of a short story is sustained (generally) for fifteen to twenty typewritten pages. In a novel, the same intensity and forward thrust must be sustained for (at least) 350 typewritten pages.

Copy Editing

When first novelists sign their first contract they must learn to protect their writing against the work of copy editors. Where an editor deals with the total novel (story, organization, characterizations, logic, etc.), the copy editor deals with the language, punctuation, grammar, and spelling of the actual text. They check the accuracy of facts, are alert for libelous statements or plagiarism, and typographical inconveniences. Copy editors do not necessarily have a talent for language or creative sentence structure. Their concerns are clarity through grammatical propriety. A writer can protect himself against this unwelcome assistance by learning how to copy edit his own work *when rewriting.*

Incorrect spelling is simple to overcome. When you see a word which seems questionably spelled, look it up in a dictionary—then correct it.

The writer must be able to develop his individual manner of writing within a framework of acceptable grammar, or the copy editor will begin tampering with his prose. Academic language will be substituted for creative prose. General terminology will be used for an imagistic, dramatic vocabulary. There is no blame to be directed at copy editors. They are paid to amend what the writer has overlooked. They are copy editors, not writers.

There is a latitude given the novelist that is not offered to television and screen writers. Once a script has been accepted, it is up for grabs. Anyone with influence in the production can mangle it to suit his particular preferences. Actors who have to be helped to sign their own names may change carefully wrought dialogue. Directors, advertising agency personnel, producers, all have the right to tamper with what was written. The novelist must not give away this control he has over his novel by being negligent, careless, or sloppy. Give a copy editor license with your verbs and he'll grab your verbs, adjectives, and fricatives.

When you reread a sentence that is longer than you can handle, break it down into smaller sentences. Simple sentences do not have grammatical problems. If you use a word in a manner that is not conventional, make a note of the word and the section in which it appears. When you receive the printed galleys or whatever form of printed matter the publisher issues the writer for approval, return what the copy editor has removed.

Mixing Tenses

Grammatical tenses, in writing, should almost always be consistent. If past and present tenses are mixed, the reader is usually annoyed rather than appreciative of unusual or dramatic effects. But when using the third-person present tense, the writer can sometimes make an exception that allows for the additional inclusion of the past tense.

Example (third-person present) Martin is walking along the street, watching the pigeons clutter the park benches. He sees Francine. She is caressing the cheek of a handsome man who is reading the Sunday comics.

Martin tenses. *She abandoned me for this clod.* Martin sees the man pick a wet wad of gum from the bench and plop it into his mouth. Francine watches him form an enormous bubble. She smiles.

Third-person present tense has the feel of first person. It places the character on the scene and in the mind of the character, although the observations are actually being offered by the writer through the viewpoint of the character. Within the confines of the third-person present tense the writer can often subtly include the third-person past tense as well. He should do this only during scenes where a lot of action occurs. Without this use of the third-person past tense during action scenes, the writing seems awkward, phony.

Example The mugger punches Martin in the nose, which begins to bleed. Martin falls to the ground, his head hitting the hard concrete. He is afraid to speak. He passes into unconsciousness.

Too many sentences like this make the scene sound forced and inauthentic. This scene needs the distance effected by use of the past tense. In this instance, the writer should use a blend of past and present.

Example Martin moaned as the fist hit his nose. He feels blood splatter his cheek. The mugger jumped back and laughed. Martin tried to focus his eyes. The mugger puts the wallet in his pocket and walks away. Martin closed his eyes and saw no more.

A blend of both tenses, at the right time, becomes a contribution to the writing and helps the reader better understand the character. It offers both realities: the immediacy of the character's experiences, and the immediate circumstances outside the character.

A Character's Decisions

There are two basic types of *character-decisions:* the *contemplative* and the *sudden.* The believability of these decisions rests on how they are developed. One development happens while the decision is being reached; the other development takes place long before the situation arises.

Contemplative decision A young woman is harassed by her parents to marry a wealthy man she does not love. Her family is desperate for his money.

Sudden decision A house suddenly catches on fire. A man's wife and brother are inside. He can only save one. He charges in and saves his brother.

In the contemplative decision, because there is time to choose, the writer follows the evolution of why she elects to accept or reject the wealthy suitor. There is no need to detail the quality of the young woman's character and background to prove why she reaches that decision. That material should already have existed through previous situations and conflicts. Nor does that prior material need to have a direct connection to the present decision she must make. It is only characterizing material which qualifies the decision she does reach. The writer deals only with the *now* of why she decides what she decides. The material she contemplates while reaching the decision should be new information.

In the *sudden decision*, there is no time for contemplation. The character must act now. Going into the reasons why he saves his brother and not his wife would slow the pace, diminish the drama and excitement. Yet to authenticate his decision as an action compatible with his characterization, the writer must set up the material for the sudden decision, *long before the possibility of the residential fire comes into existence*. There should be no hint that a fire will happen, that such a dilemma will arise.

Earlier in the story, the reader must be informed that the man knows his brother is having an affair with his wife (which urges him to let his brother die) but that his wife has a $1,000,000 life insurance policy which is assigned to her husband if she dies. Thus, while his decision to save his brother and not his wife seems sudden, it has long been prepared for.

The Major Character's "Size"

There are two general types of *major characters:* 1.) Those who are created through a concept of size (not physical) and increase or diminish through emotional/mental experience and adventure. 2.) Those who are "average people" and are unexpectedly plunged into serious personal conflict and adventure. Depending upon their nature, they either grow in stature or become less than what they were when they were introduced.

Dramatic stature in major characters is gained by the magnitude of their ambitions, goals, purposes. They are cast into immediate complexity. Characters who are given trivial aspirations are difficult to develop into complex characters. They do not begin engaged in expansive, complicated enterprises.

Example Shoe clerks are rarely kidnapped and held for a $1,000,000 ransom. Eighty-year-old parish priests are infrequently seduced by Russian agents to reveal secrets about the Catholic Church. A postman who aspires to an "indoor" promotion because damp weather aggravates his bursitis is not as compelling to read about as is a young attorney who connives and murders in his effort to become the governor of Georgia.

Fiction is the magnification of the dramatic and the minimization of the mundane. A large-sized character provides greater opportunities for a grand-scale story and complicated plot line. He either draws events to himself because of what he is—or because his position causes these events to happen.

Example A Texas rancher, who acquired his vast spread by defeating Indians, chasing land grabbers, and fighting crooked government officials, cannot avoid social, economic, or political pressures./A prince, because of his status in the kingdom, is always in some national or international difficulty.

"Average-people" major characters gain their dramatic stature accumulatively. They must first be caught up in the excitement of events before they become exciting.

Example A single woman who is a grade school teacher wants to adopt a child, but her marital status blocks her. She begins campaigning and petitioning to change the law./A shoe clerk discovers that all the size ten, EE shoes in the store are being used to smuggle diamonds. The smuggling ring tries to kill him before he reports the crime.

The myth of the "average person" is that he is average because he leads an anonymous, unvarying life-style. If he was able to provoke large events he would not be average. To achieve "complexity of character," the writer sees an *external focus of pressure*. Society is gradually or suddenly pushed upon him, forcing him into an inordinate action. The moment he achieves an "inner revelation" or an alteration of his condition, he begins becoming complex. He has no desire to change his life; he is forced to change his life.

The career of a writer can be regarded as a marathon effort. You cannot conduct a marathon if you believe you haven't the stamina, the power, or the character to endure. Your collapse is inevitable.

Example He is struck by a car. When he recovers, his memory is gone. He inherits a fortune and after he's given the money, it is learned that he is the wrong heir./He is seventy-three years old and on their 50th anniversary he impregnates his wife.

The moment the "average person" becomes complex, the plot-line can become complicated.

If the major character is one of "size" his complexity already exists and he opens the novel already involved in a plot-line. The magnitude of his goals, ambitions, and pursuits, infer diverse experience and notable expectations. The *focus of pressure* imposed upon him is *internal*.

Example The mayor of a metropolis wants more power than his office offers./He is dissatisfied with his wealth and how it has corrupted his children./He is afraid someone has been paid to assassinate him./He believes someone who tells him, "Beware of St. Patrick's Day."

There is no certain method for judging the stature of the major character. Some writers find their story and use its concept for judging the stamina of their major character, and what he can assume. Some writers first develop their major character and tailor the story to fit his stature.

Contradictions in Character

If heroes and villains are always heroic or villainous, they will develop a predictability that eventually leads the reader to tedium. What they do will be expected. People without problems are uninteresting. Absolutes in character flatten the dimensions of that character. Contradictions within the character can create complexity and eliminate this predictability. Complex characters can be surprising.

The hero should have some evil in him; the villain, some virtue. Not because popular morality or religion proposes that no one is all good or all evil, but because writers have to develop complex characters.

The evil in the hero and the virtue in the villain should exist *within* the character. The pressure of events on the lives of the characters finally brings out a handicapping characteristic that has always been present.

Example A liberal senator who is always fighting for reforms within the criminal justice system is a compulsive shoplifter. His political career is now threatened by his inability to stop stealing.

The head of a foreign government's "Department of Torture" is an adoring father. His reputation for being the "beast of the bureau" is threatened because his love for his daughter is lessening the amounts of information he is getting from prisoners he no longer enjoys torturing.

These character contradictions give dimension (and complexity) to people who might, in time, become predictable. The good will always be doing good; the evil always doing evil. Contradictions in character also create suspense: a reader is not always sure of what they will do. These "other" conflicts also develop the story more interestingly. They offer additional reader identification, since all readers can recognize the contradictions in themselves.

When a Character Doesn't Realize He's Changed

When the shock of experience causes a character to reach an inner revelation about himself, and he acts upon it, then genuine change is proven. Yet there are portions of a story in which the character, though changed, should remain unaware of it. *Only the reader and other characters must know that a change has taken place.* This odd condition can be achieved through the observation and response of another character.

The technique of dialogue can be used to bring this about. Not through a direct statement like, "My, my, Lonny, how you have changed!" This is glib and not too believable. It is based on another character's opinion, without qualifying proof. The proof is developed through the other character's *inner dialogue.*

Example A shoe salesman has just returned from a weekend convention. He's having breakfast with his wife. She is cheerful.
"Did anything interesting happen at the convention, darling?"
"No. Just the usual jibber-jabber. Hours of talk and sales hype."
"Now, Lonny, surely there must have been something interesting."
He slammed his hand onto the table, shouting, "Nothing, I said, nothing at all." She frowned at him. He's falling apart. She wished she could comfort him about his father's death. Lonny tore a slice of toast in half and jabbed the pieces at her. "What were you doing while I was away?, and I want the truth." She stirred her coffee. His father had been a suspicious man, and vicious. Lonny was slowly becoming his father.

The change in her husband is revealed through the wife's inner dialogue. It is *his* action that provokes the revelation in her. Without the wife's inner dialogue expressing her inner revelation, Lonny's disinterest in conversation, his slamming of the table, and his accusation would merely portray him as a grouch. It is through the wife's expressed revelation of the reality of Lonny's change that it is explained and accepted as a true change in character.

When to Avoid Blatant Foreshadowing

A consideration to be studied in the use of *blatant foreshadowing* is to evaluate the information it contains, then appraise the effectiveness of its function.

Blatant foreshadowing (a writer's direct statement within a scene, about an event that will occur later on) can cause unanticipated damage to the scene if used improperly.

In a life-and-death scene, the action must move with an uninterrupted velocity. Life-and-death struggles or conflicts are created to keep the reader either edgy or in suspense. The focus has to be tight, intense, undeviating. Only after the first crisis of excitement ends and there is a momentary lapse in the action, can you occupy this area with a "forecasting" moment.

Example (foreshadowing within a chase scene between angry Indians and five children) The children did not know their mother was watching them being chased by the Indians. They could not hear her hysterical screams.

Then continue with the chase.

Do not use blatant foreshadowing to predict what will happen *within* the chapter that you are writing. Do not end the chapter before it ends for the reader.

If you are observing someone you love in a life-and-death situation, you will become horrified at the possibility of her death. If someone you care for is in danger of being killed and you *know* she will be rescued, then you are impatiently biding time until she is rescued. There is no horror, no fear, no suspense.

The purpose of a life-and-death scene is to create an exciting discomfort in the reader. Do not deprive the reader of that discomfort.

Use blatant foreshadowing in a life-and-death scene only when it forecasts what is going to happen in a much later scene, to someone not involved in the present action.

Hack vs. Artist

A writer conducts his career as a craftsman engaged in the profession of writing. He ends his career as a craftsman who has left a body of professional writing. During his lifetime, he may be judged as a "commercial hack" or an "artist." The writers of today, and of the future, who are serious about their craft will achieve a state of emotional and spiritual tranquility if they ignore these arrogant judgments. They are spurious, and impermanent.

The definitions of "artist" or "commercial hack" contain no absolutes. They are as immutably fixed as a lone bowling pin in the path of a powerfully launched boulder. They are transient evaluations established by a minor populace of critics and historians jamming academic criteria through a sieve of personal tastes. They offer *razzle-dazzle* assumptions, but the case is still in the public courts.

Because the writer consciously uses techniques and forms for the purpose of achieving deliberate effects does not mean he is a commercial hack whose public fame is doomed to be forgotten after his last novel is remaindered. Waiting on infrequent gushes of inspiration is for amateurs. Writing is a "worked-at" craft.

Nor should writers purposefully try to create art or commercial junk. There is no unchangeable public taste. There are only public trends. Much of what is appraised as art, is cunningly promoted junk. And a great deal of writing that was once intended as junk, has later been judged as art.

Dostoevski worked to pay off his gambling debts by writing for newspapers. Rushed, harassed, careless. His commercialism became art.

A writer must never impose upon his own work the stigma of "commercial hack work" merely because he is writing to earn money or wishes to acquire celebrity.

Too Many Sex Scenes

Be careful of how many *sex scenes* are used in a novel, and the type of sex scenes you allow the characters to experience.

Limiting contemporary writers to one or two vivid sex scenes would seem to be the extreme of censorship or catering to priggish preferences. Yet the issue is not one of morality, but one of "craft and function." Merely because publishers and public permission supports sexual license in writing, there is no reason to use what is not useful in a novel.

The purpose of a sex scene is to change lives and relationships, to cause or resolve conflicts, to reveal depths in character that cannot be revealed in any other type of circumstance. It is a situation of physical and emotional/intellectual pressure. Though the reader may not become bored by many sex scenes, they can become repetitive. Unless the writer strains to put the characters through remarkable erotic logistics, what they are doing is only a repetition of what they have done before.

There is another practical reason for limiting the number of sex scenes in a novel, but most books on writing craft omit it. Readers will happily participate in the adventure, heroics, romance, ambitions, successes and failures of the characters—but when sex scenes emerge, the reader-character relationship changes. The writer is now touching the intimate, the actual, the real life of the reader.

If the sex life of the reader is marvelous, then watching the characters perform is merely a curious spectacle. If the reader's sex life is miserable, then the pleasure the characters are having causes resentment which interrupts the reading experience. If the sexual activity of the characters is ugly, the reader is annoyed either because it mirrors his own sex life or because it is unpleasant to watch people struggle to perform what is meant to be a natural function. If the characters become extreme and indulge in muscle straining calisthenics, the readers will become annoyed because they cannot find someone to join them in an emulation, or because they cannot duplicate the gymnastics themselves, and the serious purpose of the scene is dominated by the sex partners' exertions. If the sex is bland and without graphic emphasis, it is functional and the reader thinks, "So they made it, so what?"

Readers purchase novels, not for the number of sex scenes, but for what the sex scenes portray. The conquest of one character by another during the sexual interval. The exploitation of character through sexual guile and prowess. Sexual humiliations and brutality that cause changes in plot and relationship. Discovery of character through previously unrealized or unadmitted sexual difference or aberration. The writer should use the odd intimacies of sexual action to bring the reader into the character.

Use the purpose of the sexual encounter as the major point of the scene and the sexual activity as a secondary interest. Limit the number of sex scenes, and make those you use important. After the first momentous sex scene, allow the others to become references to having sex. Then, when the plot line calls for another important sexual interval, use the scene as a resolver to start, end, or prove the permanence of a relationship.

Blink Lines

A writer should not sacrifice his content for the sake of brevity or starkness. Do not throw away significant lines by writing them so short or mutely that if the reader *blinks,* your material is not read. Hold your focus tight and give body to the writing, so the feeling or intention or action of your character is remembered.

Example John looked through the kitchen window. The sun was swaddled in clouds. He thought about killing the governor. A bright red bird perched on a branch. He leaned to the window and squinted. He was certain the creature was a robin. He had never seen one before.

The line "He thought about killing the governor," can be missed IF THE READER BLINKS ON THAT SENTENCE. The line is also too fleet and hidden in common detail. You are not being subtle or underwriting. You are offering inadequate information. If, in a later scene, John prepares to kill the governor, the reader is startled by his intention. When did he decide to kill the governor?

When a significant action, thought, feeling, or motive is part of the situation or plot line, WRITE IT. Don't allude to it, imply it, be hushed about it. At times it is vital to be heavy-handed. You can always caress lightly when dealing with less vital material.

Example John gripped the kitchen table edge and studied the sharp bread knife. He would use that if he decided to kill the governor. He would sneak into the governor's private bathroom and wait. The man was always washing guilt from his hands. When the governor bent over and rubbed soap into his hands, he would bury the knife into his back. He would hold it there long enough to whistle the national anthem, then withdraw it and run.

The focus of this intention cannot be blinked away. Every line is tightly connected in context to every other line. If the reader misses one line, the next line will hold his attention and keep him within the content of the story.

Use All Five Senses

Do not narrow the range of your descriptions by using only one of the five senses—sight. Feelings and thoughts are provoked in a character by more than sight responses. *"She was beautiful." "He was handsome." "A squat white house was set in the dark valley like a chunk of snow."* Characters respond to reality WITH ALL THEIR SENSES. *"He stepped back from Frank, who smelled like an old orange." "She listened to the wind slash through the trees." "The boy's hair felt clogged with grime and insects." "Her kiss tasted of wine and cheap cigars."*

The writer should also use all five senses when creating the physical world outside of the character. Focusing descriptions through all five senses alters the condition of "place" from a facet to a dimension. A facet is a surface with area. A dimension has many facets, plus depth.

Through a use of the five senses, the descriptions of characters broaden and they are rendered more interesting and on-going. A major character may be tall and muscular and, of course, he remains tall and muscular. But a constant reference to his height and muscularity whenever it is necessary to describe him becomes repetitious, and tedious. When describing a character through the five senses, the writer can also characterize.

Example The elderly woman sat at the oak library desk, using a magnifying glass to read Lincoln's biography. Her veiny hands trembled as she touched the words. She smelled of lavender talcum powder. She kept licking her dark, berry-flavored lipstick. She began giggling. "Oh dear, what a scandal old Abe was." Her voice was a skitter of mice nails across slate.

Because readers are not aware of how continually they use all five senses (their dependence is upon the *visual*), the writer brings a richer, fuller quality of reality to their reading lives.

Block Descriptions vs. Strung-Out Descriptions

When introducing an important character in a novel, do not depend upon *block descriptions* to make permanent impressions on the reader. Readers are not memory banks retaining and storing the impressions of character that they read. But block descriptions are always more effective than *strung-out* descriptions.

A block description is one where comprehensive amounts of information about a character (physical, attitudinal, age, background, profession, etc.) appear in one uninterrupted chunk.

Example Harvey was a big man with sloping shoulders. He was thirty-three years old and becoming depressed about his political career. High school records revealed that his I.Q. was 78. Gray hair was beginning to shade the long black waves. Thin red veins spattered his nose and cheeks. He hated to eat in public because strings of meat always stuck in the crevices of his teeth. He always carried a packet of toothpicks.

The inexperienced writer has the tendency to assume this one-time block description will be fixed in the reader's memory throughout the novel. In reality, the reader's first impression of a character, though it is vivid, begins to fade in about twenty pages. If the vivid impression of the character is to remain with the reader, his description must be periodically revived through additional descriptions.

A strung-out description is one where the writer will peck in a sentence of information about a character. "Harvey was a big man with sloping shoulders." The scene will continue for about a page, then the writer will poke in, "Harvey was thirty-three years old and becoming depressed about his political career." Then, six paragraphs later, "High school records revealed that his I.Q. was 78." And so on, until the description is all put down, over about four pages.

Readers do not take the time to collect all the fragments of description together to create one vivid person. The reader just reads on, without ever gaining a solid reality about the strung-out character.

Imagery to Enhance and Economize

Imagery is an important contribution to writing. Some writers use metaphors and similes as naturally as a kitten licks its paw. Other writers must plan them with skillful deliberation. Too many writers ignore the value of images. Imagery is used to replace a set of dull, mechanical details. It is an enhancing and efficient use of language. There are two general levels of imagery: The "physical-character" image. The "overall, tone-setting" image.

Example (physical-character image) He leaped from the bed like a suddenly uncoiled spring. (simile) OR He was a coiled spring leaping from a bed. (metaphor)

In each instance the simile or metaphor replaces the details of arms, legs, or torso as the character leaves the bed. The image also defines the general mood of the character. He leaves the bed quickly.

Example (overall, tone-setting image) Jeff felt naked and trapped in a celebration of lunatics. The masquerade party was a blast of noise, a blare of color. He had forgotten which costume Laurie said she would wear. A clown leaped before him and shrieked some giggles. He squinted at the garish cosmetics to know if it was Laurie. Feathers scraped his face . . .

The opening images set the tone and type of party; the attitude of the participants. Not every costume and action need be detailed. The writer can focus on the principal characters and the initial situation. Now and then other images may be used to revive the "sense" or "impression" of the party. The images, quick and fleet, replace the plodding details of specific descriptions. The images are as colorful as the costumes.

An image should be easily recognizable. If it is strained or over-elaborate, the reader must work to gain both the enhancement and the details the image replaces. An over-long image dominates the action or characteristic it is meant to define. An overly-artistic image stands out and seems to be imposed upon the prose, or appears exhibitionistic. The image must flow along with the prose, contributing rather than detracting.

Fiction vs. Nonfiction

Every category of writing presents its own defense as to why it is more difficult to accomplish than every other category of writing.

Nonfiction (biographies, histories, literary criticism, etc.) is simpler to write because you merely arrange information. In fiction (novels, short stories, novellas, etc.) you must dramatize reality.

In nonfiction, recorded history establishes the credibility of people and events. The readership, interested in that particular person, time, and event, does not question the authenticity of what they are reading. If they are dissatisfied, they can find other books written about the same people, time, or events. In fiction, the characters are not real, the setting has only some fact in it, the events are merely references from which the writer invents a reality. He must bring into literary history what has never happened: give real life to people who never existed.

In nonfiction, the emotionality of the writer is a distraction, a bias. In fiction, emotion is the writer's foundation. Without emotion, the highest level of drama the writer can achieve is to be merely interesting. Nonfiction places pressure on the writer's intellect. That stress is rarely demolishing. He can always research and learn more. When the fiction writer exhausts his feelings, he is blocked. He either waits to fill again, or he digs deeper into himself to find more.

Nonfiction writers are considered "aristocratic reporters." Fiction writers are often called "creative artists."

The fiction writer is obliged, by reason of his integrity and dedication, to believe that writing nonfiction is casual compared to the difficulty of writing fiction. The only time this meticulously developed prejudice changes is when the fiction writer tries to write nonfiction. He is then quickly astonished at its difficulty.

Take Care of Your Body

Writers should protect their writing time by remaining healthy. It is difficult to write when bedridden or beset by continual physical illness. Rather than isolating the function of the body from the function of mental and emotional attributes, recognize that each part of the human being must operate smoothly, SIMULTANEOUSLY. Writers should achieve an understanding with their bodies—its temperaments, allergies, physical limitations and capabilities and demands—and keep the body healthy.

Fatigue not only decreases the writing output, it also dulls the sharpness of sensibilities, intuitions, and the precision with which the writer reaches his concealed resources. Emotional distemper always encroaches on the inner serenity a writer needs for remaining concentrated on the selective development of character relationship scenes. Mental agitation is ruinous to the intellectual procedure of organizing and arranging content into an efficient dramatic stature. Illness of any kind requires attention, energy, and time away from writing. If this unproductive expenditure of time can be avoided, learn how to avoid it.

The writer should study his body as he would any academic course planned to provide him with helpful knowledge. What foods, regardless of their appetizing qualities, disturb the body, by causing feelings of bloat, acidity, diarrhea, headaches, hemorrhoids, gastronomic eruptions, gingivitis, or drowsiness, etc.? What types of soap, clothes, or climate activate allergies. If sex before writing drains you of vital energy, wait until you have done your work, then have at it. If you need eight hours sleep, don't settle for six or five.

A writer is always sitting. Legs become flabby, buttocks flaccid, vertebrae misaligned, shoulders slump, arms lose strength, neck muscles develop unevenly, an unwieldly paunch sags heavily. Mild, but regular exercise is essential. There is no need to turn your physical concerns into an obsession, a fetish, but for the writer, a touch of hypochondria can be a healthy neurosis.

Beginning the Historical Novel

When writing a *historical novel,* characters and events must be immediately convincing and credible. The historical event and the nature of the characters are alien to the contemporary reader. In the novel of contemporary times, the reader presumes familiarity with the time, assumes a mutual relationship with the contemporary characters. In the historical novel the reader must be offered an immediate identification through the opening situation. Only morality and mores change, not the people.

Example In 1785, in Salem, Mass., four children suddenly fall to the floor of a church and begin writhing. They scream, "Belinda bewitched us, she cast a spell on us!" A terrified woman is dragged from the church, given a quick trial, prayed over, then raised to a tree and hanged.

This event is alien to the contemporary reader. How could children be so cruel? Belinda was a fool for not "plea bargaining." Because it could not happen today, the reader has difficulty believing that it did happen two hundred years ago. To establish the credibility of such unfamiliar circumstance, the writer must render his opening situation believable.

The use of artifacts, historical documents, speech and customs, is not enough, or effective. The opening situation must be directly and humanly related to a situation familiar to this time. The writer must find a universal connection that links the past with the present.

Examples (1) The children who fall to the church floor are being encouraged by a townsman who wants Belinda hanged so he can appropriate her property. (2) The local minister was having an affair with Belinda. She is pregnant. She has threatened to expose his lechery unless he marries her.

Only through a situational, human connection between the past and the present can the writer render the opening of the historical novel believable. The reader must think, "Yes, that could happen to me, today!"

Outlining

The ideal time for developing an *outline* for your novel is *after* your novel is finished. Outlining is a conscious effort to bring the events you will be writing about into existence and order. An outline is a directive, a guide. Yet for every professional writer who treats an outline as seriously as the novel itself, there is a professional writer who believes an outline is a waste of time.

Some outlines are cursory and brief; others are thoroughly detailed and lengthy. Some writers will outline the overall story, and then begin the writing. Others will outline only the plot line, or merely outline scenes just before they begin writing them. There are writers who cannot begin their writing day without consulting their outline. Other writers commit their outlines to memory, just through the act of sketching them in, and then ignore the transcribed form.

There are writers who dictate their ideas into a tape recorder and refer to the tapes when they are held up in the writing. Some writers use a four foot square of cork board above their desk and tack on notes, reminders, and abridged scenes. There are writers who design large maps bearing characters, relationships, dates, events, secondary characters, etc., and like warring generals, study each day's strategy of attack. There are thousands of outlining systems and practices because there are thousands of writers with different academic backgrounds, working habits and mental capabilities. The option to outline and the method used is always an individual choice.

An *advantage* gained from using an outline is in never having to search for something to write about. The entire novel is before you. You can "spot write"—writing out of context or continuity. You write what you feel like writing. A *disadvantage* in using an outline is that it can become limiting. Your novel, in outline, is held into a static form. It is established and fixed. It tends to remain in a rigid state, discouraging the inclusion of new material, in fear that an imbalance will be created and there will be a need to change the outline.

A traditional and thorough outline is the break down outline. It can be used for all novel forms. The overall story and plot line are broken down into chapters. Each chapter is outlined and broken down into individual scenes, which are also outlined. Each character is broken down for analysis of his origin, relationships, characteristics, conflicts, temperaments, goals, fears, hates, importance, etc. The background of the novel is broken down into the history of the time: the settings into details of costuming, authenticating mores, customs, beliefs, diverse mechanical equipment, medical practices, etc. This type of outline often requires from sixty to eighty pages. It may be kept in folders or on index cards. Outlining of this caliber is a specialized craft in its own right. It may take months to complete.

Outlines contain only what the writer consciously knows. They do not contain content the writer must still discover. The *dramatic sense* that is the source of all talent is not present in the outline. In an outline, a scene may be used to reveal a character's effect on others. When the scene is actually written, the writer may realize that the scene would actually reveal *how the character is affected by others*. The act of writing is an intuitional connection to content, which is alive in the subterranean strata of the writer's depths. It has no order. It must be discovered and given order as it applies to the total novel.

In the writer's fantasy, and in his outline, the novel is a symphony choired by angels. When the work is brought into the "reality of writing" it becomes a pipey ditty jangling with flat notes.

After the first draft of a novel is completed, it is ready to be "professionalized" through rewriting. If the novel is outlined *then* instead of before the novel is even begun, the writer is working with an existing reality. The outline puts a refined order onto what already exists. It contains almost all of what will be discovered about the novel. It can now be arranged into the order the writer requires. There is no longer a need to change it, only to improve it.

To outline, or not to outline, that is the question—and the answer is always the choice of the individual writer.

All Novels Use the Same Techniques

The same writing techniques are used for all novels, regardless of their general category: only the effects and appearances are different.

Examples of beginnings (Fantasy) Calimnar was totally destroyed during the reign of Monarch Endelvin. Only his grandson, Elizer, survived. He was given shelter by the Wizards of Bartimmon. They taught him their wizardry and how to use the Gem of Gaylandia, that he might avenge himself upon the barbarous Zeldenans, in the Kingdom of Zeldenia.

(Romance) I was nine years old when my small village was leveled by German tanks and troops. I was given shelter by the Kopek family, in Vatikville. They risked their lives to hide me. The instant I saw their daughter, Sonja, I loved her. She did not laugh at my torn clothes, the smell of the sewers still clinging to me. She kissed my cheek and whispered, "Welcome to our home, little David."

(Science fiction) He guided the Voltrek to drift above Planet M-ZII and through his Spectromislem, watched it disintegrate. The warring ships of Octavia Seven hovered in the misty atmosphere, unwilling to leave until all was demolished and diffused into galactic iotadits. He covered the prismatic dimension scan and sobbed. Faltena had gone to M-ZII to visit her mother. Now she was dead.

The overall story and inner plot lines are crafted in the same manner. The behavior, motivation, and conflicts of the major characters in all novels are the same. They must have the same emotional and mental capacities, or else a reader will have no relationship with them. The writer will not, otherwise, be able to create sympathy for his characters. The reader will not be able to *identify* with them.

Only the places, times, armaments, conveniences, artifacts, costuming and names are different. In realistic fiction you write, "He walked across the street." In fantasy fiction you write, "He walked across the clammy mist."

Chapter Summary Headings

In the eighteenth and nineteenth centuries, chapters in novels by writers like Stendhal, Dostoevski, Dickens, etc., appeared with summary headings of what the chapter would contain. The reader was told what he would be reading.

Example Chapter 9: "In which is decided and ended the stupendous battle between the gallant Biscayan and the valiant Manchegan." (Cervantes, *Don Quixote*)

Summary headings are not part of the chapter. They are placed above the opening of the chapter below the chapter title, usually in a different typeface than the text of the chapter. Some summaries are short poems (Kipling used his own poetry). Some are quotations from other writers (Walter Pater used those). Some are in Latin or other languages.

The concept of summary headings can be adapted for use by contemporary writers. Briefly clue the reader into some of what will happen in the chapter. By not telling all, you will create suspense.

Story An Alaskan cannery worker is smuggling pearls to his family in Brooklyn. The family sells them to a Swiss exporter, who uses them as payment for drugs bought from the Chicago Mafia. The Alaskan smuggler drops the pearls into cans of diced haddock. He is afraid the haddock inspector is a federal agent and is watching him too closely.

Example (summary heading on Chapter 9) Nanook Drops Eleven Pearls Into Six Marked Haddock Tins. The Haddock Inspector Is Watching Him.
(Beginning of chapter) The machines thunked around Nanook. He watched the inspector from the edge of his vision. The eleven pearls were already in the six haddock tins. He would wait for the inspector to take his toilet break before sealing and marking the tins so his mother-in-law would know which ones to steal from the Brooklyn grocery.

This technique can serve as a chapter connector. If a chapter ends with a suspended conclusion, the writer can carry that crisis over into the next chapter, avoiding tedious details by simply telling how the crisis was resolved through the summary heading the next chapter.

Story (thus far) Chapter 9 ends with Nanook sneaking the six cans into his locker and, as he shuts the door the haddock inspector shouts, "Nanook, you pearl smuggler, stand where you are!"

Example (Chapter 10's summary heading) After Bribing The Haddock Inspector With A Pearl, Nanook Gets Drunk And Meets Chinny-She.
(Beginning of Chapter 10) In the crowded and smoky igloo where the tin canners met for their drinking, Nanook drank high-proof seal beer and watched chubby Chinny-She do a belly dance in her shimmering penguin-skin skirt. He knew he loved her.

Use this device sparingly. If it is used too often the reader will expect it and begin guessing—not reading—the remainder of the chapter.

Keep Writer and Character Separate

Many inexperienced writers are discouraged about writing novels with major characters who are not the same gender they are. They believe that creating a character to appear like its gender depends upon how effectively they use the "masculine" and "feminine" words in the language. But the American language is androgynous. They are being discouraged by a myth.

Many splendid novels have been written about characters who were not the same gender as the writer. *Lady Chatterley's Lover* (D. H. Lawrence), *Alice in Wonderland* (Lewis Carroll), *Jerome: A Poor Man* (Mary E. Wilkins-Freeman), *Jacob's Room* (Virginia Woolf), *Tess of the D'Urbervilles* (Thomas Hardy), etc.

This separation between writer and character is a persistent difficulty, particularly in first person writing. Creating a believable first-person narrator begins with a use of traditional details (general details usually attributed to a gender).

Example Females do not usually roll up their pants legs and flex their calf muscles in the men's locker room; men do not usually check to be certain their panty hose are not wrinkled.

There are also traditional "what is seen and how it is expressed" details that create the impression of gender, regardless of who is writing the first-person narration.

Example *(Male writer using first-person female narrator, wrongly: Contessa Giraldi is telling of the time she prepared dinner for Baron Rispotalli.)* I dumped the dish of hot spaghetti by the baron's side and tossed him a lace napkin so he didn't mess up that monkey-looking beard around his chunky chops.

The tone is too masculine. The impression of speech is male. Contessas are traditionally refined, cultured, utterly female.

Example *(a more believable rendition)* I placed the dish of steaming spaghetti before the baron. The aroma was pungent. I held a lace napkin before him. His manner of eating was not notably elegant. Caked within his dark brown beard were traces of this afternoon's lunch.

The impression this writing creates is that of a believable female.

Accept Quick Success

Be wary of professional writers and writing instructors who tell you, "Quick success in writing can be harmful." The statement is a sly adage dragged out of a long-dead philosophy. The greatest encouragement any writer can experience is instant success.

Given the choice between quick success which is supposed to harm, and the constant failure that is known to destroy, the choice is obvious. Too many thousands of writers have shunned the haunting of the "literary ghost" because their prolonged anonymity and unrewarded efforts became intolerable.

The writer will always be beset with personal and career problems. Life is not a "peaceable kingdom" with everyone living la-la-la-la in Eden. Grab success when you can. Buffer your problems with fame and wealth. Not one of these professional writers or instructors would ever dare tell a realtor who opens an office, "Be careful of doing great business and making great profits. It will spoil you."

The profession of writing is hectic with uncertainties. Worthy writers are overlooked while schlocky, untalented writers are turned into celebrated idols. Even while publishers are searching for best sellers, they are rejecting the novels that will earn millions. But OPPORTUNITY DOES NOT KNOCK ONLY ONCE. Opportunity knocks on the doors of writers a thousand times a day. But they are often away, in the company of professional writers and instructors who are advising them against accepting or working for quick success.

If your first novel might earn you a million dollar advance, can be serialized in six major magazines, might be chosen as a main selection for several book clubs, could be translated into seventeen languages, with a promise to be made into a motion picture, you must force yourself to accept these opportunities, against the advice of your professional elders.

Extraneous Material

Extraneous material is any portion of writing that does not belong in the story or novel. In fiction, extraneous material is often imposed into a character's thoughts. It is not the overburdening *amount* of thought that is extraneous, but rather it is the *content* of the thoughts themselves that does not belong in the character's consciousness during a particular situation.

> **Example** Walter saw the shadow beside him. It was not his shadow. He stood still in the semilighted alleyway. The shadow moved. It was not his brother's shadow. Carl was larger. It was not his mother's shadow. She was a stout woman. His sister's shadow would be be taller, leaner. If it was not his shadow, it had to somebody's shadow.

This is too much thought for a single point. The writer should have Walter think: *No one in my family would cast such a shadow.* He turned to see who was behind him.

This introspection is excessive, but not extraneous. All the thought is fixed onto the same point. It belongs. Extraneous material comes from without—foreign material that is not related to the matter at hand. It is not germane.

> **Example** In the semilit alleyway, Walter saw a shadow beside him. It was not his shadow. No one in his family would cast such a shadow. Tomorrow afternoon he would buy some insect repellent for Sunday's picnic. He was outraged that the bank would charge such high interest rates on his electronic toaster. He thought it was unfair of the circus to graft horns onto goats and foist them off as unicorns. He walked along the alley, still wondering whose shadow it was. He turned to see.

Extraneous material has no direct relationship to the point being thought about. It distracts from the significance of the intended content. It creates possibilities that do not belong in the immediate situation. The unrelated material directs the reader away from the material the character should be thinking about.

When Is Lengthy Introspection Okay?

Question: When is it permissible for characters to "introspect" for a length of time that would be excessive or dull in other situations?

Answer: When the scene following this interval of introspection promises to bring into existence an event of great importance. And while the characters are waiting for this significant event to take place.

Example (a) A murderer is in his cell waiting for the governor's decision to let him die or to commute his sentence to life. (b) During her pregnancy, a woman ingested drugs known to cause defective births. She is in the delivery room. Her husband is outside, pacing the corridor, both dreading and hoping.

This is an interval for deepening and complicating character. Introspection is expected. The writer can use the interval as his "collection bag" for vital, but ordinarily undramatic information. The power of the excitement that precedes the interval, and the power of the excitement that will follow the interval are strong enough to make this introspection *active*. It is an interval of internal character pressure. It is a fertile interval that must be carefully nurtured.

What was not known about the character can now be revealed. What was known but not understood can be explained. The interval can be electric with emotion or informative with "thinking." But be careful.

There are three general areas where the writer might misuse this legitimate opportunity for lengthy introspection. 1.) Producing mental meandering or trivia. Exploring only what the character is obviously experiencing. (*Will the governor commute the death sentence? Will the baby be born with horrible defects?*) The writer should reveal what has never been known or understood about the character. 2.) The writer might *not* use the content of this introspection for creating the promise of future scenes. 3.) The writer might believe this is his chance to reveal his "artistry" with splendiferous prose so purple that the reader becomes livid with boredom.

Cameo Characterizations

Cameo characterizations are descriptive summaries of incidental characters who always remain the same. Their function is limited. Only the material they contain is important. The details within their characterization can establish the era of the setting, create atmosphere, provide necessary information. They are created externally. They are never given introspection or dialogue that causes the reader to examine their characterization.

Example The coachman was a warty-faced man with a reputation for loyalty to the duke. His sons were in the duke's employ as gamekeepers.

Only he was allowed to drive the duke home from the tavern. He carried two pistols in his tunic. The duke had once beaten him for stealing.

The coachman always remains within that characterization. The slight summary of him offers information about customs of the era. Whatever he does (driving the coach, helping the drunken duke, etc.) contributes detail to the scene. The coachman is a "human detail" of setting. Nothing more.

Example (authenticating the community feeling in a small town)
Pastor Milson watched a lean man wearing rimless glasses and violet shorts jog by. He smiled sentimentally. Gilly Stone. A faithful churchgoer whose fetish was picking the parishioners' pockets. After the service Gilly always brought the wallets to the pastor's office and piled them on the desk. At 2 PM the parishioners would come to collect their wallets. They did not report Gilly to the sheriff. He never stole money. As long as he was allowed to pick pockets on Sunday, he did not go berserk and kill. Gilly was a dear soul.

The cameo characterization defines Gilly, uses him to tell about the parishioners, the sense of community in town, and an insight into the pastor's attitudes. There is foreshadowing that may or may not be used.

Cameo characterizations can be used for comic relief, for easing or intensifying pace, for providing knowledge of the era's history, etc.

Example The coachman had seen the duke plotting with the Loyalists. If the duke was apprehended by the Royalists, he would not betray his friends.

Cameo characterizations are useful and can be used many times.

Conflict Springs from Environment

When searching for a cause of conflict, look to the environment in which the major character functions. The major character, as the novel opens, has a particular amount of prestige in a specific environment. Change the conditions in either his prestige or his environment, and conflict is the immediate result.

Story Della Smotts is mayor of Oakland. She begins a crusade against bookstores and movie houses that traffic in pornography. Her stand is accepted by the constituents. There is a heavy police crackdown.

Example (change in prestige) Della's husband, a stockbroker, has embezzled $500,000 from his firm to pay for Della's political campaign. If the crime is exposed she will be impeached. The brokerage is owned by a wealthy man who also owns a string of bookstores and movie houses that traffic in pornography. If Della calls off her crusade he will not prosecute.

The mayor is fixed into a conflict by this change in her prestige. The conflict may arise from an external or an internal source.

    A. *External:* She feels no moral distress about her campaign being paid for by embezzled money. She just wants the crime kept secret. She calls off the crusade.
    B. *Internal:* She feels ashamed by her husband's crime. She wants to remain on as mayor but she loathes merchants of pornography.

Change the environment Della has been re-elected to a second term, but with an entirely new board of supervisors. They are, en masse, opposed to her crusade against the proliferation of bookstores and movie houses that traffic in pornography. Such places draw many tourists and provide much revenue. If Della opposes what the board of supervisors favor, they will work to have her impeached for incompetence. Della is in conflict.

Neither type of sudden change—in character prestige or in place—that causes conflict in the major character need be prepared for (foreshadowed). These incidents are out of the character's control and awareness. The intensity of the conflict, the gamut of alternatives, and the drama of the situations will render them believable. Without preparation, the reader, like the major character, is startled by the change.

Write Visually

Do not lose visual contact with the physical reality you have worked so hard to create. Continue to write visually. The *visual* aspect of storytelling is indispensable to the continuing authenticity of the novel.
    After first establishing the realistic details of environment, writers become negligent and tend to believe that because they see the scene in their "mind's eye," they have also transposed it onto the pages for the reader to see. The visual reality must continue throughout the novel.

Example (historical romance) Harlech Castle crested the long hill, its tall circular towers almost concealing the sky. Guards lazily patroled the pitted walls, their halberds tilted against their shoulders. The wide moat was spanned by a heavy wooden ramp. The grimy water was low.

As the novel continues and the castle becomes a focal point for a sizable portion of the action, the writer drifts into a level of "referential writing." The castle loses its physical reality and becomes a reference associated with a former, but now dimmed, reality. The castle is gone.

Example The troop of cuirassiers galloped into the castle. The captain dismounted and hastened to Sir Elroy's chambers.

Without a continuing use of visual facets and dimensions the reality of the scene disappears and the reader has the chore of creating the physical scene WHILE READING. The reader should not be forced to remember.

Readers are withdrawn from the reading experience if they are compelled to create while reading. They cannot respond to the action, passion, and character conflicts and relationships if they are also expected to constantly construct the physicality of scenes in which the drama happens. KEEP THE SCENES VISUAL. When necessary, the same places should be described more than once, but differently each time. If done skillfully, visual details do not intrude upon the action and emotion of characters.

The visual reality of scenes should not be realized only by the writer within himself. He must keep bringing it out, into the entire work. The writer's visual sense causes the reader to see, as well as read.

A True Story

This is a true story. It happened in New York City, in the spring of 1955. If the same event occurred today, the literary criteria and writing standards prevalent in the book publishing business would change the ending. But there is a moral to the story that transcends the posturing, dissembling, and pharisaism current in publishing today.

Maximillian left Paris for New York, carrying a thick manuscript. He was a cultured, erudite, flamboyant Russian. His wife, a once famous model who had posed for Matisse, Rouault, Picasso, Modigliani, and Utrillo, was dead. Maximillian had produced films in Europe and America. A severe condition of rheumatoid arthritis had crippled him. Gradually, his fortune had waned, his "contacts" lost interest in what he could offer. His only important possession was the manuscript. He had one hope left.

He approached a young writer whom he had once helped in Europe. The writer had acquired celebrity in America. They met in the Russian Tea Room. Now in his sixties, Maximillian was so bent over he appeared hunchbacked. "I have this manuscript I want you to bring to your publisher. It is unpublished stories by Tolstoy, Dostoevski, Gogol, Balzac, Chekhov." The young writer was astounded. "Are you serious? You don't need me. Any publisher would pay a fortune for this material. Hire yourself some bodyguards."

"You will do this for me, yes? I have nothing left, but this."

The young writer brought the manuscript to his publisher who could not believe his good fortune. He spoke of an enormous advance, book club editions, foreign translations. Four days later the publisher summoned the young writer to his office. He seemed comatose with sorrow.

"I can't use this collection. Believe me, it hurts, but I can't use it."

"Are you crazy? How can you reject such great writers—*great* writers."

"Because I have never read such rank amateurism, such tripe, in my life. No one would believe they were written by Tolstoy, Dostoevski, or the others. No one in Europe would publish it either, believe me."

Great writers are not withdrawn from the womb, pen and paper in hand, squawling with impatience to do their great works. They work at their profession. The road to "literary acclaim" is littered with the discarded pages of failure.

Make Stories Important

The dramatic "size" of a short story depends upon the depth of the writer's vision. Trivial incidents, kept trivial, will not interest the reader. Writing about a favorite uncle who caused irremedial trauma to his little nephew because a severe case of heartburn made him behave grumpily is not the basis for a dramatic story.

If the writer does not create his stories with a sense of dramatic importance, the skillful use of techniques, the excellence of prose, or the dazzle of plotting will never get that story published.

Readers will not become vicariously involved in fictional trivia: they have enough trivia in their own lives.

A basic difference between the writer and the reader lies in "dramatic vision." The reader sees only common meaning in common events. The writer sees the dramatic in the array of the usual, and writes of it.

To the reader, a scrap of carbon paper is a scrap to be discarded. To the writer, a scrap of carbon paper contains part of a last will that was stolen: it is proof of a corrupt secretary's selling of company designs; it holds the impression of a murderer's fingerprints.

Example (trivial story) A girl who is shy is given a surprise party by her friends. She is overjoyed and begins to lose her shyness.

(Story of size) A girl who is shy is given a surprise party by her friends. She suddenly begins screaming and chasing them from the house. They do not know she has been told she has leukemia and will live only three months more. When she recovers from the shock, she decides to give a party for her friends, as her apology for terrible behavior.

Life, death, love, hate, hope—these are the elements of a story of size. Affection, sentimentality, spite, peevishness—are the "asides" of human behavior. They are mildly interesting, but lack *passion*. They do not have the lasting content needed for drama.

Innuendo and Implication

Beginning writers often deliberately haze or blur a scene, believing the specifics are a deterrent to achieving *innuendo* and *implication*. They consider the "surface action" as a necessary mundanity leading to the richer, uniquer content below. The scene that is read is only a pin tip of information compared to what the scene implies. This kind of writing ends up in confusing obscurity.

Example A mother slaps a teen-age daughter for carelessly spilling catsup on her grandfather's photograph. The girl calls the mother a filthy name, swears to run away from home, and rushes from the room.

The scene is used to disrupt the mother-daughter relationship and force the girl into the streets to become a drug user. If the scene is meant to contain more information, the writer must not depend upon the reader to provide it. The writer must maintain total control over his material. Implication/innuendo content is mercuric, unstable. Unless it is clearly directed by the writer, it can be missed or misunderstood.

If readers are forced to strain to understand the characters, their emotional absorption is diminished by their intellectual efforts. They are reading about "human beings flopping about in the eddies of human experience," not decoding cryptographic puzzles. If the reader is to gain these deeper insights from the surface action, he should be led into those depths through intention and craft.

The scene of a mother striking her daughter, designed to drive her from the home, can include more content than just that, but only if the writer crafts it into the scene. Otherwise the varied backgrounds and personal experiences of readers will provoke varied interpretations from the secondary content: teenage rebellion against authority, homicidal desires against the grandfather (with catsup symbolizing blood), the manifestation of latent myopia or epilepsy. Without the writer's direction, this secondary content becomes a "grab-bag" of speculations—none of them dependable.

Of the many myths shrouding the profession of writing, one is: "Don't tell the reader everything. Allow him to do some work. Don't limit the reader by being obvious." The principle is theoretical, not realistic. All writing is founded on specifics.

A reader must be led into contact with the implied content if it is to reveal a direct relationship to the surface content. Every action performed by the characters, and every implication derived from those actions, should be written by the writer. This "subterranean dimension" of content should reach the reader in the exact way the writer wants the reader to be reached. Meaning on any level is not haphazard or vague.

If the writer wants to reveal the daughter's rebellion against authority, her desire to kill her grandfather, and a latent case of epilepsy, the writer uses the craft of writing to bring this "under material" in.

Before the striking incident occurs, the writer plants the information of the daughter's rebellion, that she has fantasized her grandfather's death, and has occasional fainting spells. Then, when the striking incident occurs, ALL readers will see the scene as cause for the daughter leaving home. Many will gain the implication of rebellion and homicidal desires against the grandfather. Some will suspect epilepsy. This "subterranean content" is there to be found IF THE READER CHOOSES TO FIND IT.

There is a "gray area" in writing where the reader is allowed to interpret meaning that extends beyond the direction of the writer. After they have attained all the writer wants them to reach, they can then impose nuances, shades of personal experience onto the writer's content. They do not change the content—they add to the content.

Deliberately hazy, blurred, or vague writing is risky. The reader may not be able to bring this undirected implied content into a focus of meaning. If, later on, the writer bases other scenes on this implied content that was missed by the reader, the later scenes are either misunderstood or appear baseless.

Exposition

Writers should not drop *exposition* into a scene as casually as a baker drops raisins onto a cupcake. Exposition (a device for introducing characters, to provide setting, for creating tone, to explain ideas, to analyze background, etc.) should be immediately related to the event that causes its presence.

Example An archaeologist finds the first evidence that the riches of Pharoah Tumtishmava are present at the digs. He is elated.

The writer should not go into an expository flow about why whales have never been discovered inhabitating a Florida swamp. This subject is not relevant to the circumstance, or the scene. Exposition is not to be used merely because the writer has an abundance of research he must dump somewhere, or because the material in itself is interesting. Exposition of any kind, if it is not immediately relevant to the event that is being read about, is a distraction that does not contribute.

Example A woman is about to swim the English Channel. Spectators watch her walk along the pier to the place from which she will dive.

The writer may use this opportunity for an expository excursion into the history of other attempts to swim the channel. He may tell of how many swimmers have drowned trying the feat. Or about how many swimmers have succeeded and how long it took them. He can bring in swimming statistics, training practices, the benefits of international acclaim. He can bring in odd subjects pertinent to the situation. The tricky and dangerous underwater currents, bizarre fish who have distracted swimmers, how the swimmers grease their bodies, the aides who follow in a boat feeding them vitamins and hot liquids, the hectic betting that transpires. He may use some of this exposition to create suspense. (*The swimmer's mother knows she has a heart condition. The supervisor of a water carnival is rushing to the pier to tell them that a shark has escaped from a zoo and is in the channel.*) But when the exposition is completed, the writer must return to the woman as she is walking along the pier to reach her diving platform.

Wide and Narrow Openings

There are two "classic" openings for the novel: (a) *Wide*: An important event has already happened, which drastically affects the lives of a set of characters. The event has happened *outside* of their lives. The characters were not responsible for its appearance. (b) *Narrow*: A set of characters has committed an act which has caused an event to occur. They portray their roles in the novel through the incidents caused by this event, which is intimately associated with their lives.

If the writer begins the novel with an event "outside" the characters and then the characters appear, the focus is wide because the ingredients of the event—its place in the history of its time—happen first. First there is the world, then there are the people. The view then gradually *narrows* as the important characters appear and begin to act out their lives.

Example A retired missile expert, now the happy owner of a fishing retreat for vacationers, is suddenly called back into the service of his country. He is an agent specializing in protecting the missile secrets of the nation. He is commanded to track down one more spy.

If the novel opens with a set of characters who cause an event to happen, the focus is narrow because the characters then have to move outward to incorporate their lives into the event and its place in the history of the time. First there are people, then they go out into the world. The view gradually *widens* as the full meaning of the event emerges through their lives.

Example A retired missile expert who owns a fishing retreat for vacationers is bored and restless. He contacts the chief of security of the agency he once worked for and asks for "some excitement." He is given a task vital to his nation's security.

Both these openings, narrow and wide, can be modified, varied, and combined. The size and expanse of the full novel are not affected by either type of opening. They are models, and flexible.

Wide: Begin with two separate events, affecting two separate sets of characters whose only relationship is that they were in the same place in that time of history. Let the events bring them together to start their stories and plot lines in the novel.

Narrow should begin with two separate sets of characters whose existence causes the occurrence of an event. Let their stories and plot lines be brought together through their purposes incorporate within the event.

Example 1) A retired missile expert is restless to leave retirement. He asks for a field assignment. He is directed to find and kill an enemy agent who has stolen detailed maps of secret missile sites. 2) An enemy agent with detailed maps of secret missile sites wants to bring the maps back to his country personally. He wants credit for the job, and to be with his family.

The chief of espionage in his nation commands him to remain where he is until the maps are picked up. He is in danger, he is hunted.

The choice of the focus—*wide* or *narrow*—depends upon what the writer wants to establish at the novel's opening.

By opening *wide,* with an external event bringing characters into existence, the writer creates the feeling of expanse and worldliness while gradually narrowing into character-intensity. The event opening implies the presence of many characters and a "drama of plots."

By opening *narrow*, with characters causing an event, the writer creates the feeling of character-intensity which will gradually widen into a sense of expanse and worldliness. The character opening implies the "drama of character" caught up in plots.

An "alternating focus" can also be used. First *wide*, then *narrow*, then *wide*, then *narrow*—the variations and combinations serve to create suspense, expectation, and surprise.

Extending Recollections

There are two levels of recollections used for returning the reader to the past of a character: 1.) a new reference to a past incident, and 2.) the furthering of a repeated reference to an incident in the character's past.

A new reference to the past through a recollection brings into existence an incident that has never been cited before. Because it is recalled for a reason, this new content adds to the character's present existence. The reader understands more of him.

Story A doctor has lost his license to practice medicine because he was drunk while operating on a patient. The patient died. He travels to Brazil and opens a clinic to treat the poor. He wants to redeem himself.

The reader knows of this drunken incident in the doctor's life. If, during an operation on a Brazilian native, he recalls a time before (or after) the drunken incident that caused him to lose his license, the information is new. It adds to his character.

Example Stupid, stupid, I was so stupid to use a quart of vodka to ease my toothache and not be so distracted by the pain.

He recollects this now, while he is operating.

If, while operating on the Brazilian native, the doctor recalls the drunken incident of the past as it was originally written, it is a repetitious recollection. The reader has already read of it. If the writer needs that recollection to appear again, he should probe deeper into its content and come up with additional material.

Example When I saw my fingers tremble I should have stopped and let Wilson take over. But I was too vain.

The writer justifies referring to a familiar incident by furthering its meaning through the addition of new material (an insight, a perception, the extension of the circumstance, etc.). The writer can refer to the same incident many times, but only if he keeps adding new material. It is the addition of unfamiliar material infused into a repeated recollection that deepens and intensifies its meaning and justifies its re-use.

Discipline and Character

There is a phrase that all writers—professional and inexperienced—have used when appraising the amount of writing they do. If they are not writing enough hours, they complain of a lack of discipline. Their insight into the problem is misguided.

Discipline is related to the writer's ability to remain focused on his writing without being victimized by writing distractions. A slightly exaggerated example is when a writer begins a story and halfway through, abandons that story for a better story—then leaves that story half finished to work on an even better story. At the end of the year, he has thirty splendid half-finished stories. He "lacks the discipline" to keep focused on what he is writing until he finishes it. He is "undisciplined," without control of his concentration. Discipline *keeps* you writing what you are writing.

If, while writing a story, you are inspired to write a "better" story, do not stop what you are writing. Make a note of this "better" story. It will wait to be written. And when you get to it, you'll be a better writer because of what you learned from the story you just finished.

It is the *character* of the writer that brings him to the desk and keeps him there for many hours. Because he has the desire to write, he can train himself to become disciplined. But it is from the depths of his "faith in self" that he gains his character.

Commitment, ambition, desperation, a passion for creating, a willingness to sacrifice average gratifications and expectations are all part of the writer's character. Having all this in your character will still not get you to your desk every day, and keep you there. FAITH IN SELF MUST DOMINATE IT ALL. Believe that your writing is important to the world and your faith has begun. Publication awards you the recognition of being a writer. Faith in self gives you the writer's character. Writing through all adversity, depression and rejection is proof that your self-faith is well-founded. Publication is erratic, transient. CHARACTER IS CONSTANT.

Editors Can Be Helpful

The inexperienced writer with a still-unpublished novel can avoid many depressions by not comparing what he is still writing to what another more professional writer has just had published. The comparison will damage the inexperienced writer's self-esteem. The published novel has had an advantage not available to the writer who does not have a novel that is "being published"— *the services of the professional editor.*

The professional editor usually has a background in the reading of contemporary writing. She can relate to a writer's sense of drama and can set aside personal preferences in writing to regard the writer's work objectively, and without bias. She has some knowledge of how a novel is brought together by a writer, and what is acceptable by the publishing company in which she is employed.

With this editorial expertise, she can find clumsily written passages, intervals where characters or events are unbelievable, when dialogue is phony, stilted, or rambling, where supposedly subtle shifts in relationships are written in a vague or blurred manner, etc.

The editor's function (in part) is to find these, and other faulty areas (if they exist) in the novel, and refer them to the writer. If the editor is mature and insulated against the writer's immediate response (passionate resentment and smoking rage at the crass intrusion of commerce into the realms of art), she will offer suggestions on how to rectify the questionable areas. Happily, because editors, like writers, are human, it has been realized that editors are not infallible, and the writer has the option of trying to persuade the editor that she is wrong. If temperaments can be held in abeyance, editorial sessions can be a time of congenial negotiation.

To avoid unnecessary depressions and times of grim discouragement, the inexperienced writer should not compare his unfinished novel to the recently published novel. It is a disadvantaging comparison. Before the recently published novel was given editorial help, it was probably not as professional as it appears to be when it is published.

Repeating Dialogue

A subtle misuse of dialogue, barely noticeable at first, becomes obvious when it occurs too frequently.

This is telling the reader what the characters will say—and then having them speak the same information—or else having the characters speak to each other and then telling the reader what it is they just said.

> **Example** "Are you going to Fred's to see his expensive fish tank?"
> "Yes. I also want to see his gun collection."
> He wanted to see the elaborate fish tank Fred owned, then look at his gun collection.

Using the same information in another technique does not provide additional information or advance the story or relationships.

If this same information, placed through another technique, is used for the purpose of a transition—from speech to thought—it is sensible to add more information so your story is advanced.

> **Example** He wanted to see Fred's fish tank and gun collection. When Fred was not looking, he would sneak a rifle from the rack and shoot the fish.

Advance, advance, continually advance the story and relationships.

> **Example** After Reverend Wilcox preached on the sins of drink and chewing tobacco, the congregation sat in condemned silence. Abner leaned to Matilda, whispering, "He preached agin drinkin' an' chawin'." Matilda nodded. "I heer'd."

The reader already knows what the Reverend preached on—so does Matilda. If repetition is necessary, use it to establish an attitude through added information.

> **Example** Abner whispered, "Matillie, he drinks worse'n me, an' chaws more."

If this misuse of dialogue is caught in rewriting, either remove it or substitute added information through character analysis or a narrative interpretation of what was already said.

Difficult Types of Thrillers

Two types of novels have immediate disadvantages which are difficult to overcome: the *first-person thriller* and the *historical thriller*. The writer must be cunning in how he develops them.

Example This first-person (subjective) narrator is telling the story of what happened when he was searching for the Lost Dutchman gold mine—that he was hunted by killer gangs through forty different states.

Only a fair degree of suspense can be gained from the narrator's plight. The reader already knows that no matter how terrifying and dangerous is the first person's experience, he will live. Had he been killed by the killer gangs, someone else would be telling the story about him.

In some historical thrillers a disadvantage to overcome is that right at the opening, historical fact reveals the novel's conclusion. Facts diminish the credibility of fictional events.

Story examples a) Fifty aristocrats devise plans for assassinating Napoleon. b) The plot to kill Abraham Lincoln is discovered by a Kansas senator. He must get to Washington to warn the president. The plotters take chase to stop him. c) American agents learn of Japan's war intentions. The agents plan to kidnap the Japanese emperor before the order is issued.

The reader cannot be entranced by these stories. The monstrous intentions of the villains are rendered pointless. Napoleon was not assassinated. Lincoln's assassination was not thwarted. Japan did start a war with the United States. Historical records remove the mystery, the suspense.

An effective method for overcoming these disadvantages is through developing complicated plot lines and character problems that are tense and fascinating. You fool the reader into believing that the first person narrator might actually be killed. You diminish the value of history by creating spellbinding events of fiction. The reader must be made to believe that what is being read is the true but heretofore untold background of known and recorded history.

In both types of novel, the writer uses the plot line and character problems to distract the reader from the awareness that the story is all make-believe. Situation and pace control the entire novel.

In the first-person thriller, concentrate on how other important characters are trying to kill the narrator. The writer must be thorough in integrating the story lines of these *other* characters into the plot and the narrator's struggle for survival. Several people dear to the narrator should be killed. The more he grieves about them, the more the reader believes the narrator will again rush into peril to achieve his goal and to avenge the deaths of his loved ones. The motives of his pursuers must be as vital as the narrator's. Everyone's commitment must be absolute. The closer he comes to death the less the reader remembers that he is really alive.

In the historical thriller, create authentic bureaucratic and police procedures, and discuss the political issues of the time for greater credibility. Use actual, though minor, historical events as a backdrop for the villains and heroes. This validates the possibility that the fictional events did happen. Both villains and heroes should be Machiavellian, resourceful, fanatically dedicated to fulfilling missions. Use the "episodic" structure and many viewpoints. Think of water bugs on the calm surface of a pond. Suddenly a branch drops into the water. The bugs skitter away. Keep characters skittering and follow each one's flight. The main character is the "adventure of events." Characters merely carry out the many plot lines.

In the first-person thriller, toward the end the situations should change. The focus is on how the narrator defeats his enemies and stays alive. Readers accept this as confirmation of what they suspected at the opening—the first person did not die. In the historical thriller, you distract the reader from the conclusion until the conclusion is reached. Then all the fictional facts confirm the historical facts. Make-believe has come true. History proves it. The reader was not fooled after all.

Free Association

Writer's block, writer's block, oh, if I could only think of a novel to write and shatter my paralyzing writer's block. Listen! A deep problem always contains its own inherent solution. The technique of free association is neither passé nor dead. Conceive a character and let him offer a plot.

Example *(Matthew Grant. What does the name suggest?)* Thirty-one years old, born in 1853, a former frontier sheriff, wants to live a conventional life. Rugged, good looking, lusty, enjoys hard work, has some experience with women. Shrewd, a quick judge of character, has a grade school education. Parents were killed in an Indian raid—his younger brother was taken by the Indians and is presumed dead. Now working as a ranch hand for a cattleman who has twin red-headed daughters. Both flirt with Matthew. Jennifer is evil. Melanie is good. He can't tell them apart. Land squatters begin encroaching on the cattleman's land. Matthew is sent to chase them. They beat him viciously, crushing his gun hand. The twins nurse him. An Indian takes one of the twins. The Indian looks like his younger brother.

If you cannot turn that into a novel, study engineering.

Example *(Benica Armstrong. What does the name suggest?)* Twenty-two years old, the daughter of wealthy parents. A graduate of Barnard College. Snobbish, aloof, vain, sexy and sensual. After graduation she works in one of her father's publishing houses. Clever, quick, ambitious. During the office Christmas party she drinks a drugged drink. She awakens aboard an oil tanker, naked and bound to a bed. Three other girls are also bound to beds. They learn the captain is a "white slaver" for a Chinese potentate who enjoys Caucasian females. When he is done with them he gives them to his soldiers to use. Benica vows to escape.

Two novels, unplanned, spontaneous, flowing from the free association suggested by two names that carry individual impressions. Writing blocks are the fictions—writers are the realities. Reach into yourself—in your depths is all you want. It has cost you all your life to amass this vibrant, living, useful content. And now it is free.

Secondary Characters and Plot

In the adventure/thriller/spy novel, the events which unfold the story come through the major plot line. Yet all the excitement and suspense that keeps the novel moving from critical interval to critical interval comes from the secondary characters and their portion of the overall plot. Without the portions of plot given to these secondary characters, the major plot line would be simplistic and obvious.

Example A Russian spy, carrying stolen plans that reveal America's complete security system, is killed as he is about to board an airplane. A West German spy takes the plans. He is choked by an East German spy who takes the plans. He is stabbed by a French agent who is then killed by an English agent, who is killed by the American agent assigned to find the plans and return them from where they were taken.

The *story* is how America's security system is kept from being handed over to a hostile nation. The major *plot line* is the direct effort of the American agent to retrieve the security plans. This overall plot line never disappears from the story. Right up to the conclusion of the novel the American agent is always working to regain the plans. But it is the series of secondary plot lines and characters (what the other foreign agents are doing to get and keep the plans) that provide the obstacles, handicaps, hazards, and twists and turns to keep the novel moving. Without the secondary characters and their secondary plots contributing to the major plot line, the agent would quickly retrieve the plans and the novel would be over. There is only one major plot line, but there are many secondary plot lines, through the secondary characters.

Example The West German spy has the security plans. Just as the American agent is about to get them, the spy is killed by the East German spy and the American agent, so close to success, must now go after him.

Without an abundant supply of secondary characters carrying secondary plot lines to complicate the major plot line, all that is being written is a long short story or a simplistic novella.

Reduce a Scene to a Poetic Form

An excellent exercise for training yourself to cut down on "excessive writing" is to reduce any scene over eight pages long, to a seventeen word (or less) free-verse abridgment *poem*.

Not the theme of the scene, but the *plot* of the scene. Themes are simple to abridge. Thousands already exist as adages, relative truths, and traditional verities. "Crime does not pay." "Infidelity leads to divorce." "The road to hell is paved with good intentions." Any one of these can be transposed into a story. The exercise of abridging your scene into a free-verse poem is to make you realize the amount of writing you do not need.

Example (scene excerpted from a novel) A patrol of seven American soldiers is in the Vietnam jungle. They are alert, but frightened. The enemy is nearby. Suddenly, the leader of the patrol is shot and killed. The others fall to the ground. They crawl into the bushes. Twenty Vietcong charge from their cover and kill the soldiers. They loot and butcher the bodies.

A scene of this type opens opportunities for the writer to let loose with description, dialogue, action, exposition, flashbacks, lyrical introspection. The writer must train himself to avoid such opportunities. There will be many other opportunities later on. (Try avoiding them, too.)

Example (free-verse abridgment)
Soldiers on patrol. Jungle dense. Leader shot.
Soldiers hide. Guerrillas attack. Soldiers killed.
Bodies slaughtered. Brutal butchery.

There is no need for details. Break the scene down to the naked minimum. Then, using the free-verse abridgement, reconstruct the scene with all inessential, excessive writing removed. You are not training yourself to become a free-verse poet. You are training yourself to avoid the traditional habit of excessive writing.

Drugs and Alcohol

Drugs and alcohol are lethal to the writer. They cause irreparable damage to the body. They warp the sensibilities, intuitions, perceptions, and memory. Do not be tricked by historical public relation promotions. Although there have been writers who drank continually or were drug addicts, and still wrote well, they were rare exceptions. Even they did not do the bulk of their writing "under the influence" or while on a "high," a "low" or an "out." Consider how much more and greater they would have written had they written when without drugs or sober.

The "public mind" is not rational. Foolishly, it mythologizes the drug addict and alcoholic writer. To the public mind, the writer is an alien. They love the legend and shun the fact. While drunk or drugged the writing feels like some symphonic swing that bursts to the heavens. But when the music stops and you reread the work in the silence and stark of the day, it is without melody, and it jars.

Alcohol and/or drugs are destructive additions to the writer's life. Any critical biographies that *exalt* the uniqueness of writers who wrote while drunk or doped are biographies not worth reading. The biographer is either superficial, unthorough, naive, or an academic innocent enthralled by notoriety and ignorant of truth.

Any "celebrity" writer who publicly reveals that he needs booze or his sniff, or a shot, before he can get into writing, has either already slipped into personal ruin or has become threateningly stupid. If a writer is to protect his works, he must first protect his life.

For undeniable proof that there is no control over the effects of drugs or alcohol while using them, investigate the factual history of past writers. You will read of suicides, of insane asylums, of "drying out" or "kicking it out" institutions, of groveling back-alley bums, burnt-out whores, and wandering zombies. Do not admire or emulate these writers. Cry for them, and grieve for what they might have written.

Long-Standing and Immediate Motivation

Motivation is brought to the reader from two dimensions of character: *the long-standing* and *the immediate*.

Motivation is the core of character. Motivation is the recognizable explanation for why a character feels, thinks, says, and acts as he does. It is why he endures all he must experience if he is to succeed, or fail. The reader should be able to quickly understand what is motivating the major characters. The major characters need not ever know or they can eventually recognize their own motivations.

Long-standing motivation originates at the beginning of the novel.

Example (1) To gain the approval of his peers, a youth born with a deformed leg trains with fanatic concentration to win a school race.

(2) A Roman centurion, appalled by the corruption of the empire, deserts the army to find a moral, religious meaning for his life.

These long-standing motivations affect the character's behavior throughout the novel. All problems, conflicts, hopes and energies used in achieving intentions are directed from the core of the character's motivation.

Immediate motivations are actions of the character that deal with immediate circumstances. They need not have a relationship to the deeper motivation. They are reasonable responses of the character.

Example (1) To return a favor to a friend, a municipal judge finds an excuse to dismiss his drunk driving charges.

(2) A prima donna ballet dancer slaps the face of a man who says her tutu is beginning to bulge.

The effects of the youth's deformed leg will be with him all his life. The Roman centurion will continue his search for meaning. The ballerina feels insulted but can go on a diet or buy a new tutu. The municipal judge has paid off his favor and need never warp the rules of his office again.

Explaining Character Changes After the Fact

An interesting method for introducing vital changes in a character is to first demonstrate the change, then explain how it happened *later on*. The writer uses the past for qualifying the character changes.

Story (family novel—1878) Gilbert, nineteen years old and the only son of a shipping tycoon, is a pampered softie. One day he disappears. A year-long search is started. He is not found. His parents assume he is dead. Two years later he reappears. He is hardened, shrewd, ambitious. His parents are astonished. His father never liked Gilbert.

If the writer does not explain how and why Gilbert has changed, the changes may seem false, a pretense. Before the changes are explained, Gilbert must first do something to prove the changes are authentic, permanent. Gilbert's actions must also be useful in helping the present story progress.

> **Example** Gilbert tells his father he is going to start his own shipping line. Angrily, the father strikes at him. Gilbert easily blocks the blow and forces his father to sit. The father claims, "You have no money of your own." Gilbert draws a bag from his pocket. He pours out thirty rare black pearls. "This will get me started. I'm going to ruin you."

At this point the writer brings forth the explanation. He reveals that Gilbert was taken by a press gang and forced to serve as a cook's helper aboard a whaling ship. After a year he jumped ship and drifted through the Solomon Islands. He went pearl diving; had a child by a native girl. He left her to make his fortune, promising to return.

The writer has two options on how to write this past information. If Gilbert's past can be used for some area of the present (the native wife tries to find him) then portions of the past should be played out in scenes. If the writer merely wants an explanation of how the changes happened, none of Gilbert's past need be shown in the present story. It can be easily narrated. Then the reader knows that whatever Gilbert does in the present is justified by the explanation.

An added benefit for the writer is that the reader knows more about Gilbert than the other characters know about him. They have not read the explanation.

Continuity

While there are many craft principles vital to the creation of a novel, none is more important than the element of *continuity*. Without continuity a novel becomes a structure of scenes, one following another, but early portions of the novel either appear to have been dropped or to have been forgotten. The tenth chapter will have a relationship to the first chapter only because it is about the same people, in the same locale, in the same calendar time—but there will be no intimate connection between them.

Continuity is that "hidden structure" in the novel that relates all of the novel to the novel's beginning. It is the unifying essence, the congealing element, the invisible network of veins spreading throughout the body, feeding it a life-giving fluid. All of the novel, either by implication or statement, should be contained in the early portions. It is from the early portions of the novel that the entire novel unfolds.

The opening of the novel should contain at least three types of crisis: 1.) *character crisis;* 2.) *situation crisis;* and 3.) *relationship crisis.*

Story A European family of four—mother, father, teenage daughter and son—migrate to America in the early 1900s. They want a new life.

Character crisis: The father takes a job running numbers for small-time racketeers to earn money. He is arrested and sent to jail.

Situation crisis: The family is evicted from their tenement residence and forced to move in with relatives. Fourteen people are crowded into two small rooms. The bathroom does not work. The son becomes ill with polio and is crippled.

Relationship crisis: To keep a lecherous uncle from seducing the daughter, her mother becomes his mistress. The aunt, a seamstress, gets the daughter a job in a clothing factory. She is harassed by the foreman who demands she have an affair with him or lose her job. The girl is terrified.

If all this can happen within twenty-five to thirty-five pages, the writer has created a novel with a high potential for continuity.

Continuity, in action, is an ongoing accumulation of events that become references and recollections after the events are completed and the reader has gone forward to the reading of other events.

Example On page twenty-two the immigrant son is playing on a dock above the East River. Some rough kids toss him into the dirty, polluted water. When, on page thirty-nine the boy becomes gravely ill and develops polio, the scenes are connected—though separated by the interspersion of other events and scenes. The polio scene is continuity to the being tossed into the river scene. When the boy is confined to a wheelchair, that is a continuation of the polio scene. The only times the polio and river-dumping scenes are used again are in the character's references or recollections.

In every opening situation there should be a secondary-level crisis, a crisis that is less intense and which happens before the major crisis at the scene's end. The father's vow to gain vengeance against the criminals who set him up, or a threat to his wife to remain faithful. Any of these secondary-level crises contains material for later situations and chapters. The moment one of these secondary-level crises becomes another plot-line situation, continuity has begun. The beginning is now extending forward.

Before the mother becomes the mistress of her husband's brother, there should be a secondary-level crisis.

Example The wife of the philanderer goes to the prison to inform the numbers runner that his wife has become involved with his brother. This secondary-level crisis (the husband's hatred of marital infidelity) now becomes the basis for another crisis situation. When these OTHER situations take place, additional continuity is established. All other later material is connected to the beginning.

Continuity never allows the reader to forget earlier content. Early content is always present through references to it in the character's consciousness. A man hates, loves, kills, flees, becomes heroic or villainous in his present because of what happened in his past.

A reader recognizes and believes in changes in character and relationships because he realizes where it all came from. Continuity carries the reader along.

Landscape the Setting

When landscaping a town, province, or village for the purpose of *setting,* use those features of the locale that will function prominently in the story or novel. Select them carefully for *function.*

Story A frontier town in 1854. The beloved sheriff is shot in the back by a stranger. The townspeople are enraged. They apprehend the killer, drag him to the limb of a tree located toward the end of town. Their intention is to hang him.

When you first create your setting, describe the wide dirt street with a large oak tree. The tree is used as a marker separating the virtuous part of town from the notorious. Show some rope dangling from the thickest limb. Add some powerful horses tied to a rail in front of the sheriff's office. Detail cowboys swaggering into a saloon.

As the story begins to unfold, you may bring in other associative details of description indigenous to such a locale.

The function of a descriptive setting is not simply to *invoice* all the properties of the frontier town for authenticity. Mere setting is not enough. It is a superficial use of description. It is not interesting.

Example DryHole was a narrow stretch of wooden buildings thirty miles south of Abilene. A wide, crooked trail was worn in the rich earth leading to the railroad stockyards. The land was flat. The nearest ranch was six miles north of town. There was no church. On the north side of town there were thirteen saloons, two barber shops, and a dry goods store. On the south side was a two-story bank, an assay office, a blacksmith, and a dentist. The farm area, three miles west of the tannery, grew corn, milo, and some wheat.

This is more statistical than evocative. The details of setting are meant to create *expectation* as well as place. If violence is going to happen, use the symbols associated with violence. A sheriff's office, holstered guns, a tree limb with rope from a former hanging dangling from the limb. The reader intuitively arranges these symbols into a subtle pattern that suggests eventual violence.

Let the Reader Fill In Information

The writer cannot demonstrate, relate, and reveal all that a story or a novel requires. The number of pages would be too cumbersome to read. The writer uses many techniques to elicit the reader's collaboration. A technique, *in description,* is "tacit presumption" on the reader's part.

The writer focuses on a select combination of sense impressions, arranges them in a pattern, and the reader fills the spaces with images (references) from his own personal experiences.

Example An abandoned ferry boat wallowed in the brackish water. Clumps of moss hung from the huge wheel. The thick smokestack was cracked.

The writer did not include the river bank, the trees, the sky, etc. The reader puts them there. The writer has used only the sense of sight. Without urging, the reader fills in the area through silent presumption by quickly visualizing what you have shown him, and through the accompanying objects you have not shown him.

The writer must be studiously selective about what he includes in a scene. If he is careless, he opens opportunities for the reader to imagine alien details that do not belong in the scene. The scene then becomes the reader's creation, not the writer's.

The fullness and expanse of the description depends upon the number of senses you allow the reader to project into the scene.

Example An abandoned ferry boat wallowed in the mucky water. An alligator yawned loudly, then scrambled after a fish. The water rippled, causing the cracked smokestack to creak. Behind a tree an aged Cajun sang as he stirred the fire below a pot of peppery beans.

The area is larger now. Not because it has more objects, but because the reader can now tacitly fill in *sound* and *smell*. The added sense impression has drawn more from the reader's personal experience. The writer does this deliberately, not by some mysterious happenstance.

"How-to-Write" Books

The writer, working to become a professional, should read as many "how-to-write" books as he can, but never regard them as being important to his career. The writer is always his own manual of methods.

"How-to-write" books will reveal techniques for developing scenes, creating character and plot lines and relationships tight with conflicts. They will advise the writer on where to get his material, how to rig up dramatic sequences: to motivate, sustain, and deepen character and complicate story. The writers of these books will reveal their own experiences, attitudes, methods, explaining personal resources they have used for overcoming whatever writers must overcome. These books offer the hopeful writer hope. They are often informative, inspiring.

At best, however, these manuals of technique will be more interesting than truly helpful. Before the writer can adapt and employ what they contain, the writer must first have the problems the "how-to-write" books solve. There must be a *compatibility of timing*. Having hundreds of solutions to problems you do not yet have is as useful as having hundreds of problems for which you have not yet found solutions.

The writer will learn, in time, that when he can recognize the writing problem, he will also realize he already knows the solution. Every individual problem contains its own inherent solution.

The importance of "how-to-write" books is in their suggestive value. The writer often comes upon personal writing solutions through how he disagrees with other writers. There are many solutions held between how professional writers contradict each other. They provide evocative associations to bring forth what the writer already knows. Their value is not in "how it is done" but in the evidence that "it has already been done." The writer is encouraged. "How-to-write" books are not Bibles containing "divine absolutes"—not even this book on writing.

Include the End in the Beginning

There are two parts of the novel that should be known by the writer before he starts writing: the *beginning* and the *end*. Everything in between is discovery.

Somewhere in the opening of the novel the writer should include a suggestion of the conclusion. Readers will not recognize the "end-in-the-beginning." How can they? But when they reach the novel's conclusion—no matter how many side journeys you have led them along—they will feel a sense of completion to the novel. The "end-in-the-beginning" provides the reader with two indispensable aids.

1. All that is read infiltrates the subterranean grasp of the readers, as they are reading. They will know what the end is, but not consciously. Then, when the end is reached and they recognize what they have known all along (without knowing it), they will not feel disappointment.

2. When the end is reached, no matter how unique or startling it is, the reader will accept it. They already knew the end.

Story Four men and three women, all professional divers, are in search of a Spanish galleon that was sunk in 1574. It was carrying gold. At the end, one man and woman will be dead, one man and woman will have abandoned the search. The remaining two men will vie for the love of the remaining woman.

In the opening chapter, while setting the scene, developing the plot and relationships, the writer carefully fixes signs and implications into the action, *through the characterizations. Brad kept himself cheerful so the others did not know he believed he would die before locating the galleon.* The reader accepts this as part of the opening characterization. It is not realized as foreshadowing for that character's future. *Zelda ignored Aaron's stare, though she knew that he desired her. Gil studied the creased map he had stolen from the drunken captain. Idly, he scraped a spot of dried blood from the corner.* The writer has begun setting up the conclusion.

If you do not know the conclusion of the novel, begin writing anyway. When you reach the end you can include some of it in the opening by rewriting. The end is already there, but it all starts from the beginning.

Sustaining Lengthy Scenes

A positive sign of growth from inexperience to professionalism is in the writer's ability to dramatically sustain lengthy scenes.

There is a constant need for short scenes (one to four typewritten pages) to quicken pace, to conduct rapid transitions, to set content into a sense of *immediacy.* Yet if too many short scenes are placed one after another, a staccato quality is introduced into the pace. The reader is not given space to become absorbed into the full picture. There is no time for the reader to reach a deeper connection with the "unstated content."

Unstated content comprises those elements of motivation and feeling that are *implied* in the behavior of characters. It is also the hidden essences within relationships that can only be sensed through lingering with the scene. The *total* scene must be experienced, not just the action.

Story A police captain's child is kidnapped. Unless he allows a prisoner to escape, the child will be killed. The captain goes into action.

(Scene sequence) a) Eliminating possible suspects. b) Harassing stool pigeons for information. c) Grilling prisoner for kidnapper's name. d) An anonymous phone call reveals criminal's identity. e) The chase. f) The gun battle. g) The captain's heroic freeing of his child.

The pace is rapid, charged with excitement. But the speed conceals many nuances and insights into the captain's character. What is he feeling in his depths? The element of human terror is missing. Professionalism in writing is often determined by how the writer assembles these fast scenes into one longer scene without drastically diminishing the pace, and by including the "human" factor.

To avoid a jerky structure, the professional will narrate the elimination of suspects, describe the harassment of stool pigeons for information, then lead into a brutal action scene of grilling the prisoner. Interwoven in this graphic material will be the feelings of the police captain, his choice between civic integrity and his child's life. Without a break in the scene the captain will act on the anonymous phone call, take part in the shoot-out and risk his life to rescue his daughter. The professional can sustain one scene for one hundred pages, if necessary.

Character Descriptions

A technique in writing that holds some appeal for inexperienced writers (the appeal passes when they gain writing experience) is to believe that the physical descriptions of characters are unnecessary—that they limit the readers' imagination and stop them from creating the characters for themselves.

This technique is unrealistic. How dreadfully diminished many great characters in literature would be if other writers accepted this belief. Emma Bovary, the Karamazov family, Ahab, Don Quixote, Quasimodo. People know these characters better than they do relatives.

Physically described characters should not require filling in by the reader. The writer does not collaborate with the reader. He always directs what the reader sees. Writing, *She was a lovely woman whose manner hinted of an aristocratic background,* is vague. If she doesn't have a long slender neck and syrupy brown hair, no one will see her. *He was short and his thick stomach pushed out his shirt tails,* is a physical description that is visible. Physical attributes create the reality of the character.

It is difficult to follow the life and times of a shadow throughout a novel. Incomplete physical descriptions of characters will not encourage readers to complete them. Readers do not have the imagination or patience that book reviewers or literary critics accord them.

The compelling nature of a story or novel does not hinge on the detailed physical appearance of characters. The story or novel is read because it holds the reader to the lives, conflicts, relationships and story line the characters live through. Command the reader's participation and you can have chartreuse monkeys taking over Wall Street, and it will be believed. But you will still have to describe them.

"Bulk" Descriptions

Bulk descriptions (seven solid sentences or more) should be created through the logic of the average eye. When first meeting a person or stepping into a setting in real life, the human "visual sense" operates first from a wide range. It registers an area or a shape, then a collection of details, then the specifics of what the viewer is interested in seeing. The writer, though possessing the "universal and personal sense," cannot know what *every reader will see and then look for.* If he is using a "writer's viewpoint" (omniscient vision) he should show what he himself looks for and determine its suitability for what he is writing. If he is using a character's viewpoint, then depending upon the characterization and interest of the character, show what he would first see. In either instance, description should be created through a "visual logic" (first things first).

Character introduction: Begin with size, structure, appearance or stance. "He was a short man, slovenly dressed in overalls, standing like a discarded store window mannequin." Then bring his face into focus. The general shape: oval, square, long, lopsided, etc. Then the hair, brow, eyes, nose, mouth, then chin. Unless one feature is outstanding. "His broken nose was like a wad of chewing gum between his crossed eyes," description is a progressive assemblage of the details of character or setting.

Setting: area or size—spacious, narrow, circular, etc. Then dominant colors and the "mood" of the room. Then furniture, fixtures, windows, etc., unless the writer needs to focus on a particular object. "The rear door was a massive slab of solid wood. There was caked blood on the brass handle." When he is being omniscient, the writer should use his own sense of setting, and trust it. When describing through a character's vision, describe what the character needs to see (for the scene) or what he must reveal for the reader to see (for the reality of the scene). In both instances the descriptions should be compatible with the mood of the scene or of the characters occupying the scene. When describing, the writer becomes a camera's "eye," creating detailed pictures for the reader.

Details of Setting that Interfere

Avoid using a setting whose descriptions require almost as much activity as the scene. The setting of a scene is used to support the action. When the setting must be as graphically described as the action in the scene, it becomes an interference. Change the setting. It is the scene that matters.

Example The president of an advertising agency is a pregnant woman who expects to deliver in about five days. She is promoting a fund raising drive and must fly to a conference at a mountain resort in Arizona. The success of the fund drive and her agency hinges on her presence there.

The "cliché event" is to have the airplane suddenly assaulted by headwinds that batter its structure, causing the woman to go into labor. It is not the *cliché* that defeats the scene. It is the onrush of external descriptions that must be included.

The demands of the setting diminish the dynamics of the woman's labor. The furiously shaking plane, the panic and actions of other passengers, the busyness of the setting distracts from the intensity of the woman's harrowing experience. If the setting is not described, the scene is unreal.

Only if it is a multi-character scene—a montage of lives—where many people are being dealt with, should the "labor incident" be used. Then her delivery at that melodramatic time, *is part of the setting*. Her delivery is not an isolated incident. The intensity of focus is concentrated on many people and on the plight of the airplane.

The plot purpose is to bring the woman into labor when it is inconvenient and threatening to her conference. Use the dreadful airplane ride. The reader will expect the labor to happen then. It is a "cliché event." Surprise the reader. Let the plane land safely. Get her into a limousine, racing to the conference. *Then get her into labor on the way*. The setting will not interfere. There is only the limousine, the curving mountain roads, the chauffeur (who is just as good at delivering as an airplane pilot) and the woman. The setting is not exceptionally active. The delivery is.

Writing as Therapy

Is writing a form of personal therapy? Can it be used for therapy?

Any form of self-expression is therapeutic. Every consistent effort to achieve an emotional/intellectual catharsis will help someone who needs periodic or continual "purgings of self" to gain a peaceful state of living. But the writer is not to believe that this outpour is professional writing. After years of writing, experience indicates that writers often use their work as a means of emotional release—as a pressure valve through which they gain some personal ablution. But this release from tension or the psychological manifestation of "inner-self" *is always removed in the rewriting.*

If any of this laxative expression does remain in the writing, it remains because it is part of the story or novel, because it contributes intellectual insight and emotional perception into the characters, relationships, and conflicts. If the writer is compelled to burst forth with his own tormented self and allows it to affect the work, there may be little he can do about it at that given time. But when he rewrites to organize, refine, eliminate, intensify and dramatize the work, he must absolutely remove that turbulent, purgative discharge.

It is self-serving and intrusive. The reader is not interested in the writer's subjective vomitive revelations when they offer no contribution to the story or novel. If these deeply revealing and profoundly moving revelations do happen in the writer, while he is writing, and they actually edify his personal life, he should feel blessed. But he should be professional enough to avoid turning a blessing into a handicap.

The most therapeutically satisfying experience a writer gains from his work is to realize that he has acquitted himself with professional competence and integrity. A constant and reassuring benefit achieved from excellence in writing is publication, enormous sales, and world-wide recognition. This acclaim has the power to diminish feelings of insecurity and provide the writer with a sense of being loved.

Predetermining a Scene's Length

A scene is written for the function it serves. The number of pages it requires is part of that function. Predetermining how many pages a scene *must* have, before it is written, can be harmful and disappointing. Writers must allow for the "discovery" of new material *while writing.*

Story A young sailor has not yet proven himself to his mates. They enter a bar in Australia and are rowdy. They do not know that in the rear room the bartender-owner's father is dying. Suddenly a fight starts.

The writer intended this "ritual of masculinity" to happen in four pages. As he writes, he discovers he should give the character a quality of "complexity"—from which he can draw other scenes, later on.

Complex masculinity The youth is battling the bartender and notices the man is crying. Before smashing him with a bottle, he asks, "Why are you crying?" The man sniffles. "Me futher, he's dyin'." The youth drops the bottle, helps the man up. They go into the rear to attend the solemn death interval. The youth has proven his masculinity and also revealed a sensitivity to human sorrow.

To achieve this "character complexity" required *two extra pages*.

Perhaps the writer decides "heroics" are better than complexity.

Heroic masculinity During the fight the youth sees an enemy sailor draw a knife to stab a friend. He yells, "Zeke, watch out!" He lunges between friend and enemy and is stabbed. The fight is stopped. The youth is carried back to the ship and treated. He is the hero.

The scene ended *a page less* than was originally anticipated.

The writer must allow for imponderables within his own consciousness and undiscovered personal resources to bring content into his writing. A preconceived concept (an abstraction) of the number of pages a scene requires is not always compatible with the material that will emerge during the actual writing. Outlining a scene merely guides the planned material—it cannot predict the number of pages that will be required.

Single-Purpose Scenes

Within the structure of an episodic novel it is important that a writer use many short, *single-purpose* "connector" scenes. They heighten the pace without complicating the already ongoing story.

A single-purpose scene is a short, abrupt interval that has only one purpose: *to make one immediate point*. It serves as a short span of action fixed between two longer episodes.

Example (the story thus far) A boat race is happening. The hero has a torn sail, a drunken crew, and the anchor is loose. He's at the helm, trying to control the boat. He desperately needs the $10,000 prize.

The writer ends that episode on the hero's struggle to keep the boat afloat. The scene shifts. His wife and her mother are watching.

Example Bernice grasped her mother's arm, whining, "Mom, I'm worried. He's in trouble." The chubby woman adjusted her binoculars.
"What did I say the day you married him? He's just a loser."
"Stop that, Mom. I love him. He's doing this for me."
"If you knew him like I do, you'd really worry about him."
"What do you know about him that I don't?"
"Your husband, *the idiot*—he can't swim."
Bernice gasped and pressed the binoculars closer to her eyes.

This quick, single-purpose scene reveals only one immediate point. The hero is in danger in the ocean and can't swim. The writer shifts back to the hero in the boat. The sail collapses, the mast snaps, one of the crew falls overboard. This is a longer, more complicated episode.

Sandwiched between the longer, more complicated episodes, the single-purpose scene is an abrupt, quickening change of pace. There is no beginning to the scene, there is no end to the scene. *The scene begins in its center.* Its beginning exists in the scene before it. Its ending exists in the scene that follows it.

Complications

Complications in fiction occur when events and the interests of characters are set into opposition. These clashes of interest create troublesome entanglements from which the characters seek resolutions that will disengage them. The complications that beleaguer and harass the characters should be the results of a careful intermingling of plot (the unfolding of the story) and events (what happens in the lives of the characters).

Like a forest stream, complications (simple and complex) should flow throughout the novel with a smoothness and variousness of motion. Readers should not realize that the writer is creating these complications. Readers should never become so involved in the writing process that they stop reading to wonder: "Which came first, the unexpected event that caused a shift in the plot line—or was it an unexpected shift in the plot line that brought the characters into the event?" The reader should be so engrossed in what they are reading that

HOW the dramatic events and plot line happened doesn't reach their interest at all.

> **Story** An unemployed young man and a wealthy young woman are in love and desire to marry. Her family objects to his low economic status and believes he's a fortune hunter. They will stop all her finances if she marries him. His family objects to the young woman's lack of religious concerns. They believe she is wanton. If he marries her they will assume the ancient and traditional attitude of committing him to the already dead.

There are two basic forms of complication in a novel. The simple and the complex. The simple complication is quickly resolvable and final. The complex complication is continuing and open-ended. The simple complication provokes a few incidents, and ends. The complex complication continues for awhile and, before it ends, provokes the existence of another complex complication. The simple and the complex complication have different effects on the character relationships and the plot line. There are three reliable gauges for determining if a complication is simple or complex.

1. The importance of the gain or loss resulting from the resolution.
2. The type of character changes resulting from the resolution.
3. The discovery of unexpected alternative resolutions to the problem.

This traditional story of the young couple from different backgrounds is one of several story lines in the novel. The effect their relationship has on the lives of the other people, in the total novel, depends upon the "type of complications" that beset them and what the resolutions provoke.

> **1.) Simple complication: gain and loss:** The young couple marries, certain their families will not sustain their promise to cut them off. They are correct. The families were just testing them. They gain happiness.
> **Complex complication:** They accept the rejection from their families and marry. Their families continue to hound them. Their loyalties to their families cause rifts in their marriage. Their problems are not resolved.
> **2.) Simple complication: character changes:** They marry, are accepted by their families and are happy. He spends her money, she converts to his religion. The families become fast friends. Their characters are slightly changed.
> **Complex complication:** They marry, are exiled from their families and begin angry confrontations because of money and religion. She is forced to work and believes in birth control. He decides to become a religious writer and get her pregnant. Their character changes are significant, drastic.
> **3.) Simple complication: alternatives:** They decide to postpone the

marriage until their families accept the relationship. They live together. She becomes pregnant. Both families want grandchildren. They insist on a marriage. That plot sequence is concluded. There are no alternatives.

Complex complication: They decide to postpone the marriage. They live together. She becomes pregnant. The families become more hostile. Economic and religious differences between the couple start separating them. She gives birth to twins. They separate, each taking a child. There are many alternatives.

All major characters should have several complex complications and many simple complications. To render the simple complications quickly soluble, they should come from *outside* the characters—from external circumstance. To keep the complex complications ongoing and open-ended, they should occur from *within* the characters—from their existing inner conflicts.

Overheard Scenes

There is a type of scene which has fallen from favor and is not much used in contemporary writing. It is the "overheard scene." Information is overheard that is detrimental or beneficial to the listener. Or it may be harmful or helpful to someone else. It is information that the listener was not meant to hear, or not hear at that particular time. This scene device always furthers the plot line and changes character relationships quickly, economically.

This type of scene was used frequently in the early days of mass publishing when the hyperbolic emotion and melodramatic action was prevalent. But in the early 1900s readers were becoming more sophisticated, and realistic. The gimmicks of melodrama became unbelievable caricatures, the amplification and extravaganza of emotion became preposterous puffery and bombast. The overheard scene drifted out of style because it was either a blatant coincidence or an obvious device.

This is not a valid reason for not using it today. Is there any scene more hackneyed, cliché, or cornball than a love scene, a sex scene, a chase scene, a murder scene?

Example A butler who needs money to open his own catering business overhears a conversation between his master and mistress. He eavesdrops.

"But Jeffrey, I saw you kill him. I watched you hide the gun in the flowerpot by the fireplace. Your fingerprints are still on the weapon."

The butler now has a source of income. The murderer has been revealed

Overheard scenes are particularly effective when probing the relationship between parents and children. There should always be a scene in which a child overhears something about himself that is hurtful, or complimentary, which he misunderstands as slanderous. It is a splendid source of "child trauma."

All scene devices have been used before. Never dismiss the use of a scene device because other writers have used it. *A scene device is only a cliché when you execute it unskillfully.* Only then does the reader become aware of the device you are using.

A guide the writer has against being discovered is to not use a corny scene device in the beginning of the novel. Wait. A cliché scene device should be used only when the reader is so absorbed in the characters and the plot line that they suspend their usual cynicism. The writer is not writing for literary critics—he is writing for people.

Jot Down Ideas

The computer is quicker than the human mind, but the machine is not selective on its own. The computer can retain more and for longer periods of time than can the mind. It cannot bring together all the information it contains and, like the sensitive imagination of the human mind, develop a unique perception. A human presses the computer's buttons to make it think and respond. It is still not known what makes a human think, what is the total texture of a thought, or what starts the human heart beating. Build it properly, and a computer is reliable. A computer *is*—but a writer is always *becoming*. A machine must be fed—*a writer needs a notebook.*

While tight with concentration on what is being written, the writer has a thought, an insight, a partially articulate concept. The natural response is to think, "I can't stop what I'm writing. I'll remember the idea," and continue writing. The writer is wrong. *He will not remember it.* The thought, the insight, the concept will disappear. It may return, but you will not need it then, or recall when it might have been appropriate.

Insights and perceptions pass through the mind like fleet fireflies. Lit for an instant, then gone back into the dark. They are precious, irreplaceable. Stop what you are writing and write them into a notebook, onto a napkin, a scrap of paper. ANYWHERE. They are more important than what you are writing now. What you are writing now is there. It is visible, tangible. You will not lose the mood, the flow, the roll.

Tradition promotes the legend that writers are strange, rude, egomaniacal. Be wise—use the license society issues the writer. When it is your turn at the plate during the annual office ballgame and you are touched with a perception, drop the bat, rush to the locker room, and write it down. A writer is continually a writer. When the novel is published, containing all the splendid content derived from what you impolitely "jotted down," society will forgive and applaud your eccentricity. Proprieties of behavior and average social considerations change. Important "work" remains. Go for the Big One—the WORK.

Choosing a Viewpoint

When choosing the viewpoint for the story you want to write, it is wise to review some limitations and advantages of the first- and third-person points of view.

In first person there is a simultaneity that must be established. While the narrator is engaged in an action, he must reveal his reaction.

Example While I kissed her, I despised her. It took all my will to remain relaxed. I wanted my hands to choke rather than caress.

Third-person descriptions can be broader. The characters, though separate from each other, are brought together through their inter-reactions.

Example He kissed her gently, caressing his fingers along her slender neck. She shuddered, her breasts pressed against his chest. He willed himself to ignore the hatred he felt. Softly, he touched her neck, wishing he could choke her. She whispered, "I'm so happy you love me."

While the first-person narrator is acting and reacting, he must also include the actions and reactions of the other characters to achieve this simultaneity. Otherwise the narrator may be crackling with excitement but the other characters will appear blurred or wooden.

Example While I kissed her she did not know I hated her. She was a clod, depending only on her five senses, never her intuitions. I wanted to choke rather than caress. She whispered, "I'm so happy you love me."

This need for depicting other characters' responses can diminish the intensity of the first-person narrator. From a third-person point of view, the scene may not be as intense, but the insights and responses can be more detailed and deeper.

Example As he kissed her he willed himself to ignore the hatred he felt. She throbbed with the passions she had feared all her life. He loved her, she knew. Love was a taste on his mouth, the gentle way he held her. He pressed against her, keeping his hands from her neck.

The choice of *viewpoint* depends upon the intention of effects. Each viewpoint is equally dramatic, but not in the same way. It is wise to let the story content dictate the viewpoint to be used.

The "first-person spoken story" has to be meticulously developed through "colloquial dialogue." The articulation and erudition are concealed beneath the deliberately ungrammatical "colorfulisms" and the excitement of the story being told. The writer should carefully research the locale and environment of the fictional speaker. The entire story should be created as though being related in a musty general store, around a warm potbellied stove.

Proximity vs. Togetherness

Dramatic intensity is lost when characters are placed in the same scene, but are not together. Proximity does not guarantee togetherness. Unless the writer uses an "intertwining" technique during scenes of intimacy, a condition of separation remains. The moment may be interesting, but it will not be intense.

Scene (a dual viewpoint sexual moment) This intimate act is used by the writer to reveal facets of character that cannot be revealed in any other form of intimate behavior. It is essential that a quality of "togetherness" be achieved. One participant provoking the resources of the other. A tight blending of selves.

Example His caresses were gentle, steady. His breath soon became harsh, warming her neck. He pressed against her, his strong arms holding her still. She placed her hands against his chest. Perspiration filmed her forehead. She whispered, "Will you respect me in the morning?"

The writer had placed a man and woman in the same scene, doing something together. Yet they are separated by the method of description. First focusing on him, then focusing on her. The separation occurs through this "first him, next her" use of focus. First his action is treated, then her action. While they are locked in the proximity of a scene, they are not together. Each one is waiting for a turn to appear to the reader.

To achieve togetherness the scene should reveal an intertwining motion. The writer skillfully shares the focus equally.

Example His caresses were gentle, steady. She placed her hands against his chest. His breath soon became harsh, warming her neck. Perspiration filmed her forehead. He pressed against her, his strong arms holding her still. She whispered, "Will you respect me in the. . . ."

Through an alternating focus, the motion of the scene is created. The characters are brought *together* in an intimate unity.

The Dynasty Novel

In the *dynasty novel*, major characters eventually become secondary characters, and secondary characters gradually become major characters. Two or more generations of a family are covered. The story is sprawling and general: what happens to a particular family through several generations. The plot line is precise and specific. It unfolds through the perpetuity of the major characters' lineage. Included among the complex dimensions of the major characters there must be three outstanding characteristics: 1.) average needs that are emphasized into becoming extraordinary (love, hate, loyalty, pleasure, greed, revenge, etc.); 2.) a drive for power and 3.) a desire for immortality through their accomplishments and children.

Story A Civil War deserter joins Quantrill's Raiders and they sack Lawrence, Kansas. During the looting the soldier finds a hidden cache of gold and jewels. He deserts the Raiders and travels east to begin a dry-goods store which, in three years, becomes a large department store. He marries wealth, has three children, makes enemies, then becomes ill. He trains his children to take over what has now become a multimillion dollar empire. When he dies, the children take over (a few may rebel and lead independent lives, but they are usually brought back into the fold). The children form alliances and enmities. They are innocent, saintly, innovative. They increase the extent and the influence of their empire. They marry and have children who are trained to take over the empire. In every generation some children are good, some are evil. The grandchildren are good, and some are evil. The novel ends when there are great-grandchildren, some of whom are evil, and others good. What they ALL do changes the world.

No matter how many generations the novel covers, each major character in each generation must have an onus, a tragic burden. It should deal with the family or society, or both: 1.) The murder, betrayal, or ruin of the mother by the father, or vice versa; 2.) A physical, sexual, or emotional disability that alienates him/her from the average society; or 3.) A crime he/she committed which remains as a potential source of destruction.

The major character or characters who open the dynasty novel should have obscure beginnings. It could be one character, two brothers, brother and sister, step-brother and sister—any combination that is suitable to the story and plot. They must be complex, become richer, more powerful, more evil or more humane, philanthropic or power-mad, and have children or adopt them. The men should have mistresses; the women, lovers.

While the opening generation are playing out their plot, their children are dealt with cursorily. They are to be overlooked. The only attention given them is to cite their dominant characteristics. A minor incident is used to provide proof that this is what they are really like. They are the "held-in-reserve" characters foreshadowing what the next generation will be like. All they are doing in the novel, at that time, is growing up. Occasionally, they are mentioned and seen, but only in regard to their specific temperament and character. Their later characters will be based on the characteristics they reveal.

When the first-generation characters begin to age, the force of their story wanes and the children begin gaining prominence. When they begin taking over the plot, their full character emerges. They are elaborations of what they were when first introduced as children. The opening major characters gradually become secondary characters as the children take over the story and plot, to become major characters. The pattern is repeated for developing the next generation—the grandchildren are "waiting in the wings," secondary characters biding time until they become major characters.

The family empire is created as though a bloated placenta with many umbilical cords. Some second- and third-generation children may try to leave its influence and hold, but there is always a connection pulling them back. The events that alter the character of the family and the individual lives come from two sources: the dynamics in the society which aid or oppose them as a family and empire, and the specific ingredients within each individual in the family. There is no happy or tragic ending. There is only the promise of another generation waiting to be born.

Making Characters Credible

Not all fiction writing is based on personal experience. The creating of fiction also depends upon the writer's ability to invent and write about human behavior that he has not personally experienced.

Inexperienced writers must be careful about including their own personal attributes and preferences in fictional characters, if these traits and tastes are not compatible with what the created character is like. Fictional characters and writers of fiction should be kept apart in the writing. Otherwise the fictional characters will become inconsistent.

Example Bosco Gans, an illiterate prizefighter, attends an art showing of paintings by Masaccio and the Carmelite monk, Fra Filippo Lippi. As Bosco hunkers through the gallery, he turns to his trainer. "You discern, of course, that Fra Lippi preferred to work on frescos and do panel pictures of Madonnas, whereas Masaccio is celebrated for his ability to establish volume of objects in their relationship to space." The trainer picks food from his two gold front teeth and nods, "Yeah."

It is obvious that the writer, not Bosco, is the aficionado of art. The writer has attributed interests to Bosco that are not indigenous to his background, his concerns, or his ability to express them.

Another way of executing the same defect is through a use of narration.

Example Bosco Gans, an illiterate prizefighter, attended an exhibit of paintings by Masaccio and Fra Filippo Lippi. He stood before the scene of *Madonna Doing Her Beads* and understood why Fra Lippi was so great. His ability to establish the volume of objects in their relationship to space was phenomenal.

Projecting incompatible characteristics into a character, which makes him unbelievable—and projecting the personal characteristics of the writer into the character, which makes him unbelievable—is not the same defect in characterization. The difference is slight, but both defects are detrimental to creating a believable fictional character.

Don't Marry Another Writer

It is not advisable for one writer to marry another writer. What promises to become a stimulating, exciting life, with mutual interest in each other's work, usually becomes a ritual of daily torment. Although there have been some compatible marriages between writers, they are phenomenal exceptions and cannot be used as stable criteria or models.

Every writer, possessing the character of an authentic writer, knows that he or she is one of the finest writers in the literary community. Some of this attitude is delusional, some of it is vanity, and the remainder is an objective appraisal founded on subjective faith. But perfection becomes a monstrous burden when two perfect people live together in sustained proximity, *while writing*.

The self-centeredness of the writer is unalterable. The obligation of writers who are married to attend to each other's needs is constant. While you express appreciation, admiration, and esteem, you are soliciting the same for yourself. This ever-present demand for confirmation of greatness eventually becomes tiresome, synthetic and cynical. The effort to be so continually "sensitive to each other" is exhausting and affects your work. No matter how thoroughly a writer is understood, he/she is never understood deeply enough or is thoroughly understood at the wrong time, or is unkindly exposed by that understanding. The genuine writer's focus is always on being hopelessly misunderstood. Then a phase of competition begins nibbling into the marriage. All natural appetites are affected. A tacit push to surpass each other in writing achievement, sales, and stature, is the next stage. It is when "I'm sorry, Dear, I haven't time to listen to your writing, now," begins to happen, that the marriage is storming into mutual misery. The common interest which brought them together has become the irritant and rage that is destroying their relationship.

Only the naive reading public views the marriage of two writers as idyllic. They are founding reality on romantic assumptions that collapse under the weight of reality. Writers should marry people, not other writers.

Characters with Inner Contradictions

Major characters with *inner contradictory conflicts* are more interesting and complex than characters who are void of these inner contradictions. Inner contradictory conflicts that cause ambivalence in character are not the same as "good" characters who contain some evil, and "evil" characters who contain some good. "Ambivalence: Simultaneous attraction toward and repulsion from an object, person, or action." (*Webster's New Collegiate Dictionary*).

When a character contains both good and evil, that is not a contradiction of character. It is merely a condition of character. A contradiction of character is when a person is drawn to two opposing or antagonistic desires, values, actions, relationships, *at the same time*.

Example 1) A woman is making love to her husband whom she dislikes and is desiring another man she loves. 2) A surgeon is operating on a patient who, in a drunken spree, killed the surgeon's father. He has a chance to kill the patient without being discovered, yet while operating, he is reciting his oath to preserve life. He wants to kill, but cannot.

Inner character contradictions give characters a great potential for unpredictability. While deeply involved in one pursuit or feeling, the reader does not know if the character will suddenly shift into a different pursuit or change his feelings. Opportunities are opened for pivoting the plot line in another direction. While readers will become deeply involved in the character's life, they will not completely know or understand the character. Enigmatic people are always more interesting than people who do just what you expect them to do.

Ambivalence in characters does not render them incompletely developed. *After* creating the major character in an almost unchangeable status, it is wise for the writer to instill character puzzles through contradictions. The reader constantly learns more about the character as the novel progresses. Only at the conclusion of the novel should all be known about the major character. Then, the contradictions become oneness.

Plot Line Determines Major Character

When the time arises for you to decide upon who will be your major character, search the plot line, not the story.

The *story* covers the overall idea of what is going to happen to the people in your novel. It contains the main theme and some of the general events that occur before the conclusion. The story is flexible and unoriginal. Many different novels and plays are based on the same story.

The story of *Romeo and Juliet*, three centuries later was rewritten into the musical *West Side Story.* The *story* of *Tom Jones* (Henry Fielding), *Tess of the D'Urbervilles* (Thomas Hardy) and of Pip, in *Great Expectations* (Charles Dickens), are all the story of young people growing up in their particular place and time. Their stories are unoriginal.

It is the plot line that gives the story its uniqueness. Tom Jones, Tess, and Pip do not work out their destinies in the same manner, through the same adventures. They do not share the same motives.

Example (the story of a play) Petruchio, a cavalier seeking a wealthy wife, comes to Padua and learns that Baptista, a rich merchant, is willing to bestow a fortune upon the man who can tame and marry his unmanageable daughter, Katharina.

226

This is the story of *The Taming of the Shrew* (Shakespeare). In the description of the story, there is no mention of how Petruchio manages to tame Katharina. The methods he uses to tame her are part of the plot line. There is no mention of other characters and how their stories contribute to the overall STORY.

Example When describing the *story* of the play *The Taming of the Shrew*, you do not cite that Baptista wants Katharina married because she is the eldest of his two daughters and the younger, Bianca, who has many suitors, cannot be married until Katharina is married.

Added example No mention (when relating the general story) is made of the fact that the entire play is actually part of a practical joke played by a nobleman on a drunken tinker, Christopher Sly. Everyone pretends that Sly has just recovered from a fifteen-year bout with insanity and to cheer him up and stop him from going insane, a company of players puts on a comedy they call *The Taming of the Shrew*. That is part of the plot line.

The plot, which unravels like a ball of string (i.e., plot *line*) is the page-after-page sequence of events and relationships through which the story evolves and concludes. The story is told through the plot line.

Within the plot line there are three factors that will aid the writer in deciding upon who should be the major character: 1.) *Which character is closest to the bulk of drama?* 2.) *Which character carries the brunt of the action?* 3.) *Which character provides the most conflict?*

Story Petruchio, a cavalier seeking a wealthy wife, comes to Padua and learns that Baptista, a rich merchant, is willing to bestow a fortune upon the man who can tame and marry his unmanageable daughter, Katharina.

If Katharina's manner of resisting Petruchio's efforts to tame her is more interesting than his attempts to tame her, then *she* becomes the major character. She is closest to the bulk of drama; she carries the brunt of the action; she provides the most conflict.

Although the story is about Petruchio and Katharina, the plot line need not be focused on them if the life of someone else is more dramatically affected by the activities of Petruchio and Katharina.

Example *Bianca,* the younger sister who is being pursued by so many wooers.

Bianca's concerns about which one of her many suitors to choose and their zany and comedic attempts to win her might be more interesting, dramatic, and appealing than the shenanigans of Petruchio and Katharina. Thus, while the overall story is about the bizarre courtship of Petruchio and Katharina, the major character can be Bianca. She is closest to the bulk of drama, she carries the brunt of the action, she provides most of the conflict.

Uses of Dialogue

Although love, hate, friendship, partnership, marriage, etc., are realistic fictional events, characters must still speak with each other before their relationship can actually happen for the reader. Through the use of dialogue, the writer causes relationships to begin officially. The writer uses dialogue to indicate that relationships are beginning, are deepening, are being confirmed, reaffirmed, continued, or concluded.

> **Example** *Beginning:* "You look familiar to me. We know each other, don't we?"
> "Yes. We met at the shoe salesperson's convention, three years ago."
> *Deepening:* "I can't remember how I lived before meeting you."
> "The same for me. You've changed my life into a long, long dream."
> *Confirming:* "I love you as much as I love life."
> *Reaffirming:* "After all these long years I still love you."
> *Continuing:* "We need a child to be really fulfilled. Agreed?"
> "Yes, darling, agreed. Why don't we start working at it tonight?"
> *Concluding:* "You've become a grim bore. I want out." "And you've begun to bore me to death. I want out, too."

When dialogue is used for the starting, the building, or the ending of a relationship, it can carry explanations without wearing the reader down with the prosy grind of exposition.

> **Example** They lay below a burst of cedar tree branches. Fredrick kept picking ants from his nostrils while thinking of how he had just told Gabriella that he loved her because she was beautiful, passionate, and the sole controller of her insane father's fabulous fortune. Gabriella was not shocked at his honesty, because she was just as honest. She had lit the cigarette in her diamond encrusted ivory holder and blew smoke at a hummingbird nibbling on a leaf, then told him that she loved him because he was muscular, astonishingly virile, and still had all his hair. He wiggled in the grass and almost purred at her truthfulness. She brushed some ants from his ears and continued, revealing that he knew how to make a woman feel alive and that she did not care that he was after her money and knew that he would soon rob the three safes she had in her bedroom, because money could be replaced, but love, once gone, was lost.

A more direct method for establishing the beginning of the love relationship would be through dialogue.

> **Example** Fredrick: "I love you because you are beautiful, passionate, and control your crazy father's fabulous fortune."
> Gabriella: "I love you because you are muscular, virile, and still have your hair. You know how to make a woman feel alive. Although I know you will rob the three safes in my bedroom, I do not care. Money can always be replaced—but love, once gone, is lost."

Important material, facts, or details contained in the exposition can be included in the content that follows—after you establish the relationship through opening dialogue.

Splitting "One-Event" Scenes

In an episodic novel, a source of reader agitation comes from splitting a one-event scene into several parts.

The crisis of a one-event scene comes at the end. Splitting the scene into sections annoys the reader because only the last part of the scene is satisfactory. The earlier parts which have no crisis in them, become preparation for the crisis, forcing the reader to wait until the final part appears.

> **Story** Two teenagers explore an abandoned lighthouse. Legend warns that a vampire haunts the structure. The writer's intention is to bring the teenagers to the top floor where the vampire is waiting for them.

In the episodic novel, which usually contains several viewpoints and other plot lines, the inexperienced writer will use this method:

> **Example (sequence of scenes)** (a) Teenagers enter lighthouse and explore a little. (b) Parents of teenagers aboard a cruiser, enjoying themselves. (c) Police searching for a murderer who drains women of blood. (d) Teenagers on third story of lighthouse, getting scared. (e) An unsuspecting woman is asleep. The window opens. She screams. (f) Teenagers finally get to the last door, and open it. Grinning at them is the vampire.

Splitting the scene into three portions, interspersed with the situation and viewpoints of other characters, prolongs the scene. There is no suspense—only a realization of the inevitable—they will meet the vampire or there will be no vampire. The scene is a strung-out stall.

To keep the full scene from being fragmented, the writer should provide each fragment with its own crisis. Then the fragments become short, individual scenes. The crisis in the first two portions should be less intense compared to the final crisis. The writer then gains suspense.

Example (first part) Someone suddenly charges past them, screaming, "He's there, it's alive!" The teenagers want to stop, but won't. (Second part) A portion of the stairs collapses, almost killing them. Now they must continue up. (Third Part) They finally find the vampire. Terror, horror.

Each portion is now connected not only by locale and circumstance—each fragment is a complete scene, all leading to a strong climax.

Too Many Two-Character Scenes

Writers who have decided to break from the short story form to write a novel should be alerted to a common defect present in first novels. Because the short story form is limited in scope and complication, there is a tendency to develop the novel through too many two-character scenes. The short story writer, from long experience, becomes dependent upon two-character scenes.

Story (novel) A guerrilla band is assigned to taking a fortress where high-ranking generals are plotting the overthrow of Argentina.

If this, and many other novel types are written through a bulk of two-character scenes, the novel will become overlong and ponderous.

Example (two-character scene sequence) 1.) Generals studying a map and chatting. 2.) Guerrilla officers checking equipment. 3.) Sentries talking about pending attack. 4.) A pilot and mechanic checking an airplane. 5.) Guerrilla major kneeling in church and confessing to a priest.

By relying on this uncomplicated form, the writer restricts the novel, which should be continually expanding. After a long run of two character scenes, the pace becomes static. The repetition of similarly structured scenes lessens expectation and increases predictability. The fictional world fades.

Scenes are composed of story points that must be made. Points of plot, points of relationship, points of character changes, etc. If the plot line is well integrated, several points can be developed in one scene that contains several people. This is not "mulching material" together to shorten the novel. "Group scenes" are used to develop more content in more interesting structures. The author can use a greater array of his skills.

Two-character scenes depend greatly upon dialogue, introspection, and narration. They do not encourage historical documentation, expansive setting, or background. They confine the novel to a narrow path, and the reader is always waiting to get to the next scene—not because suspense is high—but because they must push through unnecessary writing to get to that scene.

Moving a Future Scene into the Present

At select times in a story or novel, the writer can extract a scene from a future situation before the situation arises. For a reason.

Story A meat cutter is due to lose his job. He can't stop from removing too much bone and fat from the cuts of meat. While he's working he imagines the confrontation he will have with his boss.

Example Herman kept sawing the thigh bone of a steer. He imagined himself standing before Mr. Wekman who was shaking his fist. "You take off too much fat and bone from the cuts. People pay by weight. The less weight, the less money I make. So, Herman, I'm firing you, right now!"
Herman stopped cutting the steer's thigh bone, and sniffled. What a time to be fired. Two weeks from Christmas. He sliced away more fat.

This imagined scene has not yet happened. It is a projection into the future. The story can shift to another place, through another viewpoint. Herman's wife preparing for a lavish Christmas. When that scene is concluded, the writer returns to Herman's situation. He is in the meat factory, cleaning out his locker because he's just been discharged.

You do not have to write the discharge scene. It has already been written through the imagination of the character. Merely refer to it.

Example Herman angrily yanked open his locker door. "After five years of loyal work," he muttered aloud. "He fires me before Christmas." He pulled work clothes from the hooks and stuffed them into a bag.

A benefit gained in using this technique is that if the projected scene happens during a time of conflict, it adds to the conflict. It contributes to the scene's complication. It allows the writer to avoid writing an additional scene.

This technique should not be used too frequently. The writer risks infusing the characteristics of mystic or psychic into the character, who should not possess such supernatural powers.

Practice Your Public Image

There you are—finally—a best-selling writer. Your presence will now be solicited for diverse occasions. Book-signing events, lectures, posh parties, dress-up affairs, etc. Your opinions, insights, ideas about life and critical estimation of other writers will be demanded.

But there is another reality to face. Most writers do not have "public charisma." They are not exceptionally interesting or spell-bindingly articulate. Few are exciting personalities, and too many are lumpen. To achieve this public acclaim they had to overcome decimating depressions and discouragements or have turned reclusive and somewhat eccentric. Becoming a literary success without establishing a fascinating "public image" is like scaling the Alps nude and with foam rubber ropes.

Public speaking is an *avocation* for the professional writer. It pays well. You must practice. Your ability to persuade audiences that you are a provocative person will bolster your book sales. Begin with your friends.

No longer have casual conversations. *Conduct orations.* Not with passive platitudinous ponderosities, but with dynamics and charm. Use the body language of a shadow-boxing pugilist. Develop cunning facial expressions. Grimace as though pained with profundity. Wink, pout, sigh, crack your knuckles in contemplation. Use a repertoire of snappy jokes employed by any popular dentist. Be direct, outspoken, bold. Do not become subtle or ethereal with implication. Audiences are not talented at grasping existentialist innuendo. *Rehearse being extemporaneous.*

An itinerary of speaking engagements will be prepared for you, with suitable material. Adapt this general material to your individual manner. *Improvise.* There are four essentials for achieving a successful "public image": 1.) Tell odd stories about other writers; 2.) Develop a flexible political attitude that agrees with everyone; 3.) Bring a supply of your books. Arrange to have them displayed for sales. State that you will autograph each one purchased; 4.) Memorize the name of the city you are in.

Go—you best selling writer—you are now adequately prepared.

Characters in Reserve

There is a *reserve character* who is essential to adventure novels in which the conclusion hinges on a last-minute, desperate rescue.

> **Story** The president of the U.S. has been kidnapped and taken to a monastery in Tibet. It is invulnerable to attack. The kidnappers want $5,000,000,000. They have already killed the secretary of state to prove their sincerity.

If an obscure lama pops up to give the rescue teams a map of secret tunnels under the monastery, it is an acceptable "solution through coincidence," but not satisfactory, or believable. Not even if, earlier in the novel, there had been mention of secret tunnels and an existing map. It is a spurious form of foreshadowing. *It tells how the writer will use it.*

"Solutions through coincidence" are effective only in the central portions of the novel. The forward thrust of the remainder of the novel can cover over this glib coincidence. But used at the conclusion, nothing comes after to absorb the coincidence. The satisfaction and excitement of the rescue is seriously damaged. *The "gimmick" prematurely reveals the solution.*

The writer should create a reserve character earlier in the novel. In relationship to the entire novel, he is an incidental character. Yet when he appears he must be given space. He should be developed as an "inside vignette" to provide comic relief. A bit bizarre, sleazy, amusing. The rescuing heroes need something that he has, but his offering has no connection to the end of the novel. He is never seen again. When he appears at the conclusion, he is remembered because of the space devoted to him. His appearance is surprising. When he produces the map detailing the hidden tunnels, it is astounding. But his offering is believable. He is real.

The use of a reserve character is more effective than a blatant coincidence because the "credibility of his person" in the early part of the novel overcomes the "incredibility of his contribution" in the conclusion. Because in his initial appearance he has no direct connection to the latter rescue, he is not a foreshadowing device. He is created, then "held in reserve" for the one vital contribution he can offer.

Character, Plot, and Story

Which comes first, the person or the plot? Neither. They happen together. One cannot exist without the other. The only time a plot does not exist in a character's life is when he is living in a vacuum. A plot cannot exist unless it has a character to reveal it. Though inextricably bound together, character and plot are individual entities contained in the greater framework, *the story.*

Characters have conflicts because they are people. Plot deals with the sequence of events that occurs in a character's life. The plot may appear first, or the character. Though separate, they are always together.

> **Example (plot first)** An earthquake happens, then people appear.
> **(Character first)** People are suddenly caught in an earthquake.

Characters unfold through events that cause conflicts to happen in them. A conflict is any external or internal pressure that prevents a character from having what he desires, needs, or must achieve. Without conflicts characters are merely suspended in time. They are not involved with life. The way in which the characters resolve their conflicts is the plot. When you have several characters with interwoven lives which affect each other, *you have a story.*

> **Example (character)** Peter is a prince whose father, the king, is dying. He is second in line to inherit the throne. He is a schemer.
> **(Plot)** Peter is hindered from becoming king because Rudolph, his older brother, is first in line. Peter plans to kill his brother.
> **(Story)** Rudolph does not want to be king. He wants to abdicate to marry a commoner, Elizabeth. Peter doesn't believe Rudolph will abdicate. King Bernard, a widower, is the lover of Princess Milicent, who is infatuated with Rudolph. She is pregnant by the dying king and wants her child to be recognized. She wants the king to banish Elizabeth so she can pursue and win Rudolph. Peter is negotiating to incorporate the small kingdom with another nation so he can gain more power.

Each character carries his or her own conflict and plot. All the character conflicts and plot lines brought together within one framework *is the story.* The story is always larger than its parts.

Complexity comes through character. Complication comes from plot.

The *complication* of a novel depends upon how many character conflicts and plot lines intermingle. If characters do not affect other relationships, they are simplistic and the novel is not particularly complicated. If there are only a few events that create pressure on the characters, the novel is not complicated and is in danger of becoming mechanical.

The *complexity* of the novel depends upon the nature of the characters. The more conflicts the characters have, the more dimensions of their persona are revealed. The more effect they have on each others lives, the more conflicts and events arise.

A complicated novel with complex characters is always interesting. There is a constant unfolding of drama, suspense, and reader involvement.

Example The king is given a steamy, exotic potion which quickly cures his lethal illness. He must take rule again. He knows Milicent is pregnant. He never much liked his sons. He believes they are weak.

At other times the writer can choose to allow the existing conflicts to cause events. Some can be surprising; others can be unexpected.

Example Evil Peter begins flirting with his older brother's lover, Elizabeth. He wants to provoke the brother into a duel and kill him.

An always workable novel structure is when the writer selectively alternates his choices. Character conflicts cause events that affect the lives of other people who, because they are under pressure, cause events which act upon other characters, causing them other conflicts, then the plot thickens and the story eddies and swirls interestingly.

Overlapping vs. Compartmental Structures

A technique for creating suspense through character problems is in the use of an "overlapping" structure.

Example (overlapping) Mary Wilson, a government clerk, must acquire $20,000 or her father will be jailed for embezzlement. She is offered $20,000 by a foreign agent to photograph a highly classified document. She commits the traitorous act. While giving the microfilm to the agent, she is observed by the supervisor of her department. She gives the money to her father who is released. Mary is then called to the supervisor's office. Four government agents are ready to grill her.

The "overlapping" element is in Mary being observed by her supervisor before she saves her father. Thus, another problem is building for Mary just as the present problem is being resolved.

The "overlapping" technique is more economical and suspenseful than the "compartmental" structure.

Example (compartmental) Mary withdraws the $20,000 from her savings. She gives it to her father. He is rescued. Mary is THEN approached by the foreign agent. To replace her savings, she commits treason. When she gives him the microfilm she is observed by her supervisor. She is called into his office to be interrogated.

In the overlapping structure, there are no lapses in the character's problem. Resolving one problem creates an even greater problem *in the same scene*. There is suspense and danger.

In the compartmental structure, the writer creates a problem, resolves it, then must create another problem, resolve that one, then create another problem. There is always a slight lapse between the creating of one problem and the building of the crisis that resolves it. In the "overlapping" structure there is a pending problem being created while the *present* problem is being solved. There is no "slowing lapse." You are also writing economically.

Writing is a Window

There is a constant irony present in the writer's life. For many years he studies the use of prose and writing techniques only so he can employ them so skillfully *that they are not noticed by the reader.*

If readers become aware of how marvelously "prosed" and ingeniously crafted the novel is, they are not truly involved in the story the writer has created. They may be awed by the academic expertise of the writer, but they are not participating in the substance. The writer has diminished his writing and worked at exhibiting himself.

Example The sun was an annoying flame on Judd's face when he entered the office to repair the computers. He completed his work and was relieved to feel the evening breeze ruffle his hair when he left.

If the reader stops reading to comment, "Aha, the writer used the weather as his transition from afternoon to evening. How clever. A less skilled writer would have used an obvious wall clock. Bravo!," the writer has failed.

Prose and writing techniques serve the function of a window. A window is not to be seen, *but looked through.*

Example A horticulturist has grown a remarkable garden on his lawn. He enjoys sitting in his living room, staring out at his lush garden.

If he first looks at the *window,* the garden behind it becomes a meaningless blur of color. *He is seeing the window.* If he looks *through* the window, he sees the garden and is able to enjoy each clearly defined, individual flower. The window also frames the garden, emphasizes it.

Periodically, all professional writers want to let loose with some flamboyant artistic threatrics. *They* want to be seen by the public. But experience and writing failure teach them to sacrifice their vanity. Purple prose soon fades and blatant techniques become tawdry gimmicks when they dominate the living content. Prose and technique should be admired—*after the work is read.*

Exaggerating Minor Incidents

Any *minor incident* that causes a shift in the plot line or begins a change in a character, a conflict, or a relationship should be given an exaggeration not provided other minor incidents. While the minor incident should not be blown up into the proportions of a major event, it is to be given a noticeable distinction. The content of the incident should be equal in appearance to the other common incidents, but the drama and character response to its appearance should be more emphatic.

Story Brazo Corday, a former gunfighter, has married a minister's daughter and purchased a small ranch. He is being harassed by the prominent land and cattle owner of the territory to sell out. Brazo refuses. The land owner begins a series of harassments. Fences are torn down, a barn is burned, water rights are taken away, he is boycotted from buying supplies and must ride thirty-seven miles to another town. A violent clash seems inevitable. One morning he rides to the grazing range and finds fifty of his steers brutally slaughtered.

This harassment is a routine event in the old days of the old West. But the writer's object is to find ways of pressuring the gunfighter into retaliating—though Brazo has sworn to shun the life of violence. To force Brazo to break his oath, the writer exaggerates the meaning of one of the harassing incidents common to frontier life. The choice the writer makes depends upon what is most meaningful to Brazo.

Example When Brazo rides to the slaughtered cattle, he sees it, not only as a brutal deed to animals, but as a threat to his family. Anyone who will kill cattle so indiscriminately will kill people.

Example Brazo can tolerate a lot of abuse, but when his water rights are stopped, he is furious. His cattle will die, his wife's garden will dry, his children can't play in the pond. Now Brazo will surely fight.

The incident that is used to spur Brazo into fighting should be exaggerated only enough to prompt him into fighting. It is not to become the total, overall reason for why he fights. (He fights to maintain his land, not to gain revenge for having his cattle slaughtered or his water rights stopped.)

When to Leave Your Writing Group

Avoid becoming a writing group *devotee*. What begins as a benefit to your career can turn into a destructive habit. For a given length of time, writing groups are helpful. Other writers contribute their critical faculties to your work. But a time comes when the benefits begin to diminish. If you continue attending long after you should leave the group, you lose personal initiative and the reliance upon your own resources.

The length of a writer's career often depends upon how isolated and independent he remains. All ideas, concepts, learning of craft, and energy must come from his own ambition. He must not rely on anyone for help, encouragement, or the revitalization of flagging energies. Everyone will disappoint him, fail him. When he begins writing he needs the support, assurances, and critical feedback other writers can offer him. He needs to identify with other writers to *feel* like a writer. But if he is progressing into his career, there is a time when he can no longer learn from other writers and must begin learning from himself.

It is the writer's sensitivity and intelligence that limits the value of a writing group. Intuitively, and often unknowingly, writers accurately analyze each other. They learn the general preferences and personal appreciations of the group. Coupled with the writer's human weakness—*a constant need for acceptance and congratulation*—the writer becomes his own victim. He modifies and tampers with his writing to achieve group approval. When this begins to happen, the writer must leave the group.

A writer cannot be burdened with a need for this specialized approval. Other writers comprise only a minimal amount of the reading public. A sensible writer writes to be read by the vast public. He is not concerned about what other writers or critics think about his work. He writes for the millions, not the chosen few.

When the writer has taken all he can from what others have to offer, he must leave them. Otherwise, he is deliberately living a repetition because he is afraid to assume his individuality, his uniqueness.

Ballad as Dialogue

A dialogue form rarely used in contemporary novels, and too infrequently in the historical novel, is the *ballad dialogue*.

Any historical novel *could* employ the story teller. A minstrel, a soothsayer, town crier, wandering troubador, religious prophet, a cowboy hunkered near a camp fire. Someone who tells the history of a city, the fable of a legendary relationship or great battle, about an old castle.

Example In the 14th century King Philip the Fair attempts to destroy the Knights of Templar. He wants their wealth and property. The Templars are scattered. A stray band is hidden in the forest. An aging knight begins telling about their leader, Sir MacEsque the Blade.

> We will sing his glories throughout time,
> His steed was champion, breathing fumes of power.
> Though loved he Lady Agatha of Wen he yet forsook
> Her to scatter the armies of craven Philip the Fair.
> His Lady was taken to the befouled dungeons of
> The royal beast to bring Sir MacEsque to kneel.

This traditional device is still serviceable. It is a ballad, but it is also dialogue. *Someone is speaking*. This form can recount portions of the past the reader has not seen happen. It can forecast events soon to happen. It fills in backgrounds of people—prepares for characters who will eventually appear. It can become a substitute for the writer's explanation and analysis of what really happened.

It is a flexible device. It can be broken into at any time—to let the scene the balladeer is reciting begin happening *as an actual scene*—then back to the ballad. It can be broken into many times.

The ballad dialogue should be considered seriously by writers of historical novels. It is a spurt of energy and dynamics at a static time.

Keep Writing!

There are several methods for overcoming the legendary "writer's block." One method is to keep writing, even if it is nonsense you will never use. The act of writing begets writing. You can never outwait a writer's block. It will not break apart and dissolve by itself. The longer it remains the more calcified it becomes.

If you are stopped on a story or a novel, then rewrite in a semisummary form a story or novel you have read and remember. Begin with fables or fairy tales. The story of Cinderella contains excellent elements of story, conflict, events, relationships, and a plot line.

Example Underprivileged and abused girl. Ambitious mother. Vain, shallow sisters with evil characters. Cinderella's daydreams. The arrival of the fairy godmother. The mystery of transforming objects. The suspense of deception. A royal affair. Flight. Jealousy. Pursuit. Etc.

Ideas come from other ideas, and compound themselves as they reach the consciousness of the writer. Feeling gives you the content; intellect directs the content into an order. It is the initial effort of stepping against that writer's block that begins to shake it.

Try "The Three Little Pigs" if your inclinations are to violence. "Jack and the Beanstalk" if you are writing adventure. "Beauty and the Beast" for a classic romance. "Hansel and Gretel" for the horror story.

Write into the stories and novels you already know and let them provoke associations related to your own work. One technique another writer has used can prod your skills into either duplicating or adapting that device.

A writer's block is often an indication that you are reaching new depths and drama in yourself through the writing you have already accomplished. Growth is always a painful process everyone resists, not only writers. A professional writer is never permanently blocked; he has merely lost contact with his deeper, personal resources.

Balancing Plot and Character

If only the plot of a short story is remembered, the writer has failed in creating a character. If only the character is remembered, the writer has failed to create a competent story. Neither character nor plot should assume prominence over the other. Their prominence must alternate in an unobserved rhythm. They must not be in contention, or contest for attention.

A short story is a structure of writing that is long enough to provide a full reading experience, and (generally) brief enough to be read in one sitting. The story is about something happening to someone.

Story The pastor of a church, adjacent to the community ball park, is warned by the town council to cancel the Sunday morning choir. Their singing is distracting and has caused a lowering of batting averages. The township is predominantly atheistic and prone to violence. The pastor is afraid they will burn his church—but singing is part of the service.

If the writer concentrates on the complex character of the pastor (his relationship to the parishioners and to God, etc.), the physical threat to his welfare and church becomes obscured. He is so involved in the experience that the reader loses sight of the actual danger. The plot is dimmed by the glare of a man agonizing over a momentous decision.

If the writer's main focus is on plot, then the character is flattened by the preponderance of events pushed against him. The space limits of the "short story form" will not allow for a deep characterization. The human dynamics of body, mind, soul, and spirit are depleted. Not much is known about him. Thus, why should the reader care, or become involved?

Give equal space to both. Shift from character to event: event to character. Begin with the warning, then get into character. Let his action start another event. Or reverse the order. Make sacrifices. Use only character content relevant to the story. Use only events that form a linear motion from one crisis to another. "Over-complexing" the character and overcomplicating the plot will expand the story beyond what its form was created to contain.

Delayed Insights

An effective continuity technique is one where the writer allows a character to experience a *delayed insight*. An insight is an intellectual awareness into human behavior, a relationship, an event, etc., that happens *after the fact*. With delayed insight, a character receives knowledge at one point of the novel, but only understands it fully at a later point in the book.

Example A man is at his office window looking down at the traffic. Suddenly he is flung into the air. He catches onto a flag pole and hangs on until he is rescued. Three nights later he awakens, shouting, "My God, someone pushed me."

Example Amy attends a church bingo game. Later on, she is to meet a man who will propose to her. The bingo play is stopped when five masked men with guns demand that the people line up against the wall. There is fear and hysteria. Amy notices something about one of the robbers, but it is quickly crowded from her mind. The robbers rush out with the valuables. The police arrive, ask questions. Amy leaves on time to meet the man she will marry.

Amy can experience a gamut of feelings and thoughts during the robbery, but the most prominent is her hope that she doesn't miss her date.

Eleven months later, at the end of her pregnancy, while she is being wheeled into the delivery room, her husband leans over to kiss her. She gasps "You were one of them!" Her husband is startled, "One of who?" Amy explains that when the church bingo game was held up, one of the robbers kept blinking and sniffling and nibbling his lips, "Just as you are doing now!"

The sudden realization of meaning in an insight experienced in a former scene does not have to be a physical awareness. It can be insight into someone's character, insight in a relationship, insight into a conflict, insight into an event. The value of delaying the knowledge contained in the insight is in returning a past scene into the present. It establishes a firm connection between the past and the present—providing continuity. Continuity is a unity within the story that keeps it bonded and intact.

Breaking Writing Rules

If you break a "writing rule," make it noticeable. Exploit your infraction until your personal technique becomes another rule.

A sensible rule is to not use prolonged runs of introspection because it slows the pace and stalls the action. Yet, if you have a woman aboard an ocean liner, brooding about all the men who have left her, and it is vital that she introspect about them—*pour on the introspection.*

> **Example** She dabbed the hankie to her eyes. *There must be a vileness in me, an unspeakable horror in my soul. John, John, you should have told me. There you are, John. I see you. Married, aren't you? Yes, yes. Only a fool would not marry a man like you.* "John," she spoke in her mind, savoring his name. *Remember how we danced holding filled wine glasses, and our laughter? And you, Franklin, oh Franklin, why did you desert me while thousands waited for us to marry? You said I was your true love. . . .*

Make the excessive introspection you are not supposed to use interesting. Crowd it with imagery, with recollections of former scenes, with the specifics of dead desires, fears, relationships, rage, passion. Well-written introspection uses a variety of dispositions, prose levels, inside stories, provocative inner dialogues. The only hard and fast rule a writer should follow is: *write it to be published, and read.*

A popular rule is "Don't tell it, show it!" Yet, if you have a scene with ten people who are important and you cannot devise a way to bring them all into action, then tell them—and keep on telling them.

Use visual devices. Capitalize characters' names and offer them, one at a time, as though introducing the cast of a play. Narrate them, describe them, document them, use exposition to reveal their relationships to one another—until the information is down. Tell it all—interestingly. A writer should be bold, versatile, inventive, imaginative, rebellious.

Do not break any rules at the beginning of a novel. It is advisable to allow the reader to get used to your manner of writing before you astonish them with your daring attitudes. (This is not a rule: it is a suggestion.)

Follow the Rules of the Genre

The function of writing craft is the same in all types of novels. But the specific use of craft in each individual novel form is not interchangeable. Different types of novels have their own particular techniques. The writer may adapt techniques used in other novel types, but he should arrange to have them absorbed, rather than allow them to prevail.

In the mystery novel, suspense is achieved by the complication of situations, the dispersion of clues, the danger of additional crimes. In the romance novel, on the other hand, suspense is achieved by the handicaps and hazards imposed upon the lovers before they can be brought together for an idyllic happiness.

Readers purchase specific types of novels because that is their preference. A science fiction reader will ignore a realistic novel that deals with political themes. A reader of realistic novels containing borderline pornography and big-city sleaze will rarely read novels that extol religion or the significance of an archaeological find. The writer is expected to hold true to the type of novel he is writing. It is a humane consideration.

Drawn out and heavily emotional love scenes are not appropriate in the adventure novel. They diminish the danger and deaden the pace. The love scenes should be functional, serving as pivotal intervals that heighten the pace and alter relationships. In the character or family novel, love scenes should be probing and analytical. They explore depths and motivations that cannot be revealed through scenes of pure action.

Remaining within the confines of the novel type is not a rigid rule. *There are no fixed rules in writing. There are only suggested guides.* The ultimate purpose of all novel types is to be exciting, entertaining, satisfactory. The writer may shove against the limits of the individual novel form—he may break through and establish new borders—he may write in any manner suitable to his abilities, as long as he remains dramatic, intense, fascinating, and entertaining.

First-Novel Expectations

Never depend upon the critical reception and enormity of sales of your *first novel* to "make" your career as a professional writer. Only a small percent of first novels earns back the advance given the writer. Only a few writers—the megasellers—ever have any guarantee that their next novel will also be a best seller. They did not have this guarantee on their first novel. They were where you are now. Unknown. Anonymous. Nothing has changed.

There is no readable indication, sign, or trend, that can reveal how a novel will sell *after* it is issued. There are too many public imponderables to understand and calculate. If publishers were able to even generally estimate what content creates a best seller, then at least half of what they publish would become best sellers.

Many writers have ruined their economies and gained extended depressions for depending upon their first novel to "make it big." And, naively, they relied on the promises and promotions of publishers. The raw fact is that publishers can be trusted only to the degree the contract binds them. Advertising budgets are cut, sales representatives do not hustle to get your novels prominently placed in bookstores, book-signings and radio interviews sell only a few books. Many well-known novels have achieved public acclaim, not because of the work of publishers, but because the writers, through their own efforts, devised ways of promoting their own books. Not all writers are willing or capable of doing this.

The length of the professional writer's career depends on the extent of his *vision*. If he sees himself as an immediate best seller and assumes its inevitability, his vision doesn't go past his eyelids. The vision of the writer should encompass fifty, sixty years of writing novels. It is always the next novel that must be written that keeps the writer writing. The writer must always know that being a "best-selling writer" will happen to him but he must not depend upon it.

Tense Changes In Flashbacks

Entry into the past through flashbacks, and exits from flashbacks to the present, are not difficult. Inexperienced writers are bogged down by grammatical proprieties they believe they must obey. They are so involved with past participles and pluperfects that incorrectly using such terminology becomes an accusation of ignorance.

To leave the *present* to get into the *past*—then remain in the past for the time it takes to create that flashback with its own present—then get out of the past and back into the present, requires five separate grammatical shifts. The shifts are not awesomely complicated.

Example He walked down the street. He remembered when he was thirteen years old. "Mom," he had shouted, "My pet hamster is missing. Where's the cat?" His mother called in from the kitchen, "The cat's sleeping. He looks fatter." He rushed into the kitchen and began clubbing the cat. His mother pulled the bat from his hand, scolding, "Naughty boy." The blast of a car horn jolted him from the reverie. He kept walking the street.

Break this paragraph down and analyze how it gets you from the present into the past, and then back into the present.

Example He walked down the street. (*The present*) He remembered when he was thirteen years old. (*Leaving the present*) "Mom," he had shouted, "My pet hamster is missing. Where's the cat?" (*You are into the past*) His mother called in from the kitchen, "The cat's sleeping. He looks fatter."

(*You are into the past which is the* present *for that time*) He rushed into the kitchen and began clubbing the cat. His mother pulled the bat from his hand, scolding, "Naughty boy." (*Still in the present of the flashback scene*) The blast of a car horn jolted him from the reverie. (*Leaving the past and edging back to the present*) He kept walking the street. (*You have returned to the immediate present.*)

The had had and have's, the was and were's, the did and done's, are simple to use if you view them as utilities rather than formidable fortresses impenetrable except through academic formalities.

Using Flashbacks to Foreshadow

Although most *flashbacks* are thrusts into the past of the characters' lives, they can also be used as "foreshadowing devices" for future scenes in the novel.

Often, in a novel, the present action of the story is deliberately stalled to allow some time to elapse so the characters can again become involved in new events. Flashbacks are most effective during these *passive intervals* in a character's life.

The writer places a character in a *present, but passive interlude*. Riding a stagecoach, aboard an airplane, on a spaceship going to planet 9RD-3. The writer uses an *active, action-type flashback*.

Example A professional soldier is on a train to California to join up with other mercenaries to fight in Argentina. He is thinking of the last private war he served in. Revolutionists in Santiago. He remembers how he was captured. (The flashback) While he was being tortured to tell who the rebel leaders were, he was rescued. He did not tell his rescuers that he was about to break under the vigorous torture.
Return the soldier to the train. He is touching a large ring on his finger. The ring contains a microfilmed list of all the important rebel leaders of this new war. He strokes the ring, thinking that he would not like to be captured. The train stops at the depot and the present, passive scene is over.

This active flashback enlivens the passive interlude. It reveals depths in the soldier's character that were not known before. It shows what he fears now. It also foreshadows an optional set of future scenes.

The soldier can be captured and break under torture. He can withstand the torture and grow in stature as a character. Or he need not be captured at all. The purpose of the flashback is to activate a passive interlude and to foreshadow some later, possible scenes.

What to Look For When Rewriting

When the *rewriting* process begins, the writer finally knows all there is to know about his novel. It is done. Now the writer must detect what he should not have revealed, and what he has neglected to reveal. This is the first time he has been able to see what he has written in its entirety.

Rewriting is not a theory. It is a writer's everyday reality. There are general guides and insights, learned from the rewriting experiences of other professional writers, that should be kept in mind.

Beginnings: a.) Is the setting clearly established? Does the first situation contain an external event proper for its time and capable of activating the characters? b.) Does the overall story begin immediately? Does it generate the existence of a plot line through the opening situation? c.) Is the action of the characters immediately relevant to the story? Does the initial situation begin setting up potential situations? d.) Are the major characters introduced with their conflicts, some motivation, and specific needs and relationships? e.) Are the major characters involved in high stakes, great purposes? Do they have the content and stature for great success, great failure, great tragedy, great happiness?

Middles: a.) Does the center portion of the novel bog down from lack of action? Has the "settling-in period" been extended for too long? (*Settling-in period* is that second-breath portion where some major climaxes are completed and the writer has begun preparations for launching the latter half.) b.) Have you included unnecessary summaries of what has already happened (as if the reader was not paying attention). Is there irritating dialogue recounting why all this has happened, thus far? c.) Are all the character problems, difficulties, plot lines and relationships firmly established and ready to be neatly brought together and resolved? d.) Do all the *causes* have pressure-provoking effects which bring on more pressure? Though these pressures may occur in an erratic, out-of-sequence pattern, do they happen in a manner that appears to be orderly? e.) Are the characters still conducting their lives believably? Have they experienced personal and physical changes that are coordinate with the effects of relationships, events, and passages of time?

Endings: a.) Are there specific indications (through scenes, dialogue, narrations, etc.) of how the novel will end, yet not so specific that the end is predictable? b.) Does all the plot action synchronize with the overall story line so there is no sense of separation? c.) Have there been enough dramatic moments capable of providing character-changing revelations? d.) Is there a noticeable repetition of scene settings which tend to closet and limit the expansive nature of the novel? e.) Have you begun to resolve sub-plot elements so the major plot line is not distracted? f.) If you have used any flashbacks near the three-quarter point, reduce them to fleeter recollections. g.) Have you heightened the pace—faster and faster—as you approach the conclusion?

These are only some of the areas of the novel you must consider when rewriting. They deal with the "internals" and "externals" of the work. The writer must achieve an undistracted patience when rewriting. Other areas to be viewed for the purpose of rewriting, are: 1) elimination of clichés and general phrases; 2) tightening the prose and searching for adjectival extravaganzas in description; 3) when you have cut your introspections to perfection, cut them again; 4) overlong dialogues bore more than they inform; 5) either eliminate scenes that contain only setting, or fulfill them by including character or plot information; 6) put yourself on a diet of only three "world-saving" philosophical passages; 7) check your transitions to be sure they shift the scene, time, and viewpoints smoothly.

The act of rewriting a novel consists of 85 percent administrating and 15 percent actual writing. All the subjective work has been done. The writer must now remove himself, "cut the cord," and deal with it as though appraising a raw commodity which must be refined for its highest level of marketability. This is a fact. Unless the novel is published, it does not exist.

Real Life into Fiction

The transference of real-life sensation into fictional sensation is where the writer achieves the impression of authenticity in writing.

To become a professional writer you do not have to live a particularly eventful life. Average living experiences are enough. You do not have to be a former elephant hunter, a reformed drunk, a confessed child molester writing his memoirs. You need only learn how to transpose the sensations and perceptions you have actually experienced into the lives of your characters.

Example A young woman serving as a WAC in W.W.II receives a leg injury during an enemy bombing. Her life depends upon the removal of her limb. The medical base is short of morphine. There is only enough to sedate her partially. The scene-crisis depends upon her decision. Be sedated at the beginning of the amputation, or near the end.

To create the actual agony the WAC experiences, to make the scene authentic, the writer does not have to undergo a leg amputation.

If the writer has ever had an abscessed tooth improperly pulled—a nail accidently torn from a finger—some hair yanked from the scalp during a childhood tussle—the writer can simulate the pain of a character having a leg amputated. It is a matter of dredging up the memory of a former painful experience, exaggerating its intensity, then transferring the sensations to the character.

Two irreplaceable abilities the writer must continually use are: 1.) to be in touch with his own feelings (past and present) and learn how to transpose them into an invented character and 2.) to develop a sense of *unrestrained* invention. Fiction is invention, not interpretation or the reporting of real-life events and people.

The sense of invention creates the situation. The writer's ability to transpose personal feelings into invented characters fills the content with dramatic authenticity.

Writing What You Can't Write

There are *inherent* abilities in writing, and *developed* abilities. Doing what comes naturally (in writing) continually, can be detrimental to a writer's growth. His reliance upon these natural abilities becomes a wheelchair in which he pushes himself into incompetence. Periodically, the writer should appraise his current skills in writing to know if he is training himself in additional skills that are not natural to his abilities.

Every writer has a natural ability in some dimension of the writing craft. Many writers are superb with description—imagistic, lyrical. But their dialogue is leaden, their on-scene action static. Other writers are competent in devising complicated plots but are poor in characterization. Some writers can put out reams of fascinating narration, but fail when it comes to perceptive introspection or creating a visible face, a graphic body.

The writer cannot learn from what he can already do. Eventually, his plot, conflicts, relationships, events, become unsatisfactory to him. He has pushed what he knows past its perimeter of effect. No five or six competently employed skills can sustain the multiple demands of a full novel. There are many major techniques and hundreds of subsidiary, supportive techniques that must be used in a novel. These major and secondary techniques are also blended into even more complex combinations. There is no conclusion to all that a writer must know if he is to write excellently crafted novels. What he knows now is not enough. It is never enough.

What skills the writer has now will never abandon him. They were forming in him long before he desired to become a writer. He can rely on them to function *even when he is not consciously using them*. Now he must work to reach his limitations, and extend them. Study what you can do to realize what you are not able to do. Never write through a vision of *avoidance*. Attack what you cannot write until you can write it. You progress by learning what you cannot do in writing—not by using and reusing what you have always been able to do—until even that fails you.

Your Second Novel

Writing your *second novel* will not be easier than it was to write your first novel. The novel you have already written is dead. Long live the novel you are writing! The same fears, dilemmas, and futilities will beset you. "Am I all written out?" and "Why isn't it fun anymore?" and "What if this novel takes another two years, or three? Oh God, another three years, and for what?" You will, on this second novel, have to survive the same hundreds of ugly doubts you survived before. This is the reality of being a professional writer. There is no way to escape this reality.

Do not depend upon the structure and arrangement of techniques of your first novel to support your second novel. Each novel is an independent entity. The only connection between them is that they are created by the same writer. Different characters, relationships, conflicts, stories, plot lines, backgrounds, settings, events, require other forms and other techniques. Nor are you the same person you were when you began your first novel. The experience of completing a novel has changed you. Knowing more opens you up to needing to know more. Learning draws away veils draped before all you still have to learn.

Your fears are not imaginary or neurotic. Only other writers, who experience what you are experiencing now, know you are not a moral or emotional coward.

Sustain your *faith-in-self* by remembering that once you believed it was impossible to write your first novel. You have, with tangible verification, done the impossible. There is no greater encouragement.

You are an unusual human being. You are able to turn the abstract—that which does not exist—into the readable. By the power of your talent, your passion, your skill and commitment, you are able to persuade people to participate in the world you have created. View yourself as a sponge whose full dimension and borders have not yet been reached. Your every day is a soaking up of emotion, insight, perception. You cannot be exhausted of content. You have jabbed a hole in the massive dam that holds in the world's experience. Let it pour forth and soak up its content—and write about it.

Don't Let the Detective See Clues the Reader Can't

In mystery or detective stories, readers will not appreciate deliberate evasion or subterfuge. When a detective takes an object from a room, a car, a body, etc., do not hide from the reader what he takes. Nor delay in naming the object. Do not write, *He reached under the bed and cupped his hand. He eased his palm into his pocket and kept searching for clues.* If you are not going to reveal what the detective finds, then do not let him find it.

Every object the detective takes seriously radiates outward to become a possible *solution* to problems that have not yet been *solved*. The writer does not have to enumerate the possible events the object relates to. Let the reader do the speculation, the guessing. The writer is obligated only to reveal what the object is that the detective is regarding seriously. Not revealing what the object means, either to the detective or the problem, is part of the mystery for the reader.

> **Example** Detective picks up a cracked ashtray with lipstick on the rim. (Bystander) "What is it? Is it important?"
>
> (Detective) "It is a cracked ashtray with lipstick on the rim. It could be important but, on the other hand, it could be unimportant."
>
> (Bystander) "But why is there lipstick on the rim?"
>
> (Detective) "That is a good question."

The purpose of focusing on an object the detective finds is to have that object exist for the reader. It is now part of the mystery, the puzzle. The reader should guess at its immediate significance, but never be certain the guess is correct.

The writer can mislead the reader, but should never lie to the reader. Misleading a reader is merely altering the direction of their attention. It is making a fuss over what is inconsequential so it appears significant—while what is important is diminished into appearing as trivial.

Later on, when the object becomes part of the solution, the detective will be given respect for his intuition and deductive capabilities.

You are razzle-dazzling and double-talking the reader—but you are not lying. Nor are you evading or subterfuging. You are using all that you know to create a mystery that the reader cannot quickly solve. As a person, the detective should not be superior to the reader. Only better at his profession, at that particular time. The reader should be made to feel, "Now why didn't I see that?" rather than, "How could I have known what that clue meant if I didn't see it when he found it?"

Why Autobiographical Novels Fail

Why, when writing an autobiographical novel, do the secondary characters always seem to become more interesting than the major character? A traditional insight into this condition is that the writer is too personally involved with the major character. He cannot see all of himself as he is (or was)—but he can see all of someone he is not and never was.

There are three types of autobiographical novels: (a) the true, which is created as a close facsimile to the writer's actual life, (b) the partially true, where the writer has used some of his life as the basis for the novel with the remainder being fictional and (c) the completely fictional, where events have been invented, but the story from the actual emotional and intellectual experience is true.

Even experienced professionals are unable to develop their major characters interestingly in the *true* autobiographical novel. All that the major character does, sees, feels, thinks, and is motivated by, comes through the narrow focus of the writer's self. The writer was not both watching and experiencing when it was all happening. He was not himself and others at the same time.

When writing about secondary characters, the writer is detached from them. He can manipulate them, invent them. He is in control of them. He can objectify and appraise them, to create them for their full dramatic effect. They were never alive. But he cannot alter the fact and history of his own life. Because he was not omniscient or omnipresent during the time he is writing about, he cannot know how he appeared to others. He can only speculate on how others saw him. He was never outside himself, looking in.

To write the autobiographical novel successfully, the writer must invent a person who contains what he once did. The emotional and intellectual content of the writer's life comprises the story. He fictionalizes his physical experiences into a novelistic plot line to emphasize the meaning of the events he experienced. Because he is not himself, in this novel of self, he is as interesting as the secondary characters—he actually recreates himself.

First-Person and Third-Person Viewpoints in the Same Novel

The *"first-person/third-person"* novel uses a neglected structure that should be revived because of its practicality and flexibility. It allows the reader a subjective participation in the hero's adventure, while observing all the action happening beyond the hero's personal scope. It is an excellent structure for the adventure/thriller/espionage novel.

You open with the first-person (subjective) viewpoint of the hero. He relates what has happened and is happening to him. The writer then breaks away and goes into the third-person (objective) viewpoints of other characters and their involvement IN THE SAME SITUATION.

Story A World War II submarine is sunk thirty miles off the coast of France. Forty years later military archive records reveal that U-Boat was carrying correspondence between Hitler and Churchill. They were negotiating the surrender of England. And detailed ten locations where stolen art treasures are concealed. An American agent, an expert deep sea diver, is assigned to recover the documents. Three killer mercenaries are also interested in recovering the art treasure maps. The communist leaders in England want to use the letters between Hitler and Churchill to destroy the English people's faith in their present government.

(Structure) 1. Open with the major character, in first person, to establish the importance of the danger of the assignment.

2. Going to third person, bring in the mercenaries and their plans for gaining the submarine's location and how to steal the art-treasure documents.

3. Still using third person, bring in the communists devising plans to get the heinous negotiation documents. They should have savage assassins on hand.

4. Return to first person. The major character has his opening encounter with the communists (or mercenaries) to introduce all relationships.

5. Return to third person. The mercenaries take an aggressive action against the hero. *The hero is present in their scenes, but in third person.*

6. Remaining in third person: the communists are thwarted in their attempts to stop the hero. He is forced to kill one of their assassins. *The hero is again present in the third person in the communists scenes.*

The format (structure) is now established and the writer can shift from first person to third person as the plot situations unfold to the reader.

The first-person and third-person viewpoints are used because the plot line is complicated and the hero cannot be in many places at one time. If only the main character's viewpoint is used, then what is happening outside his realm of activity becomes speculation or assumption. How are the story and plot line of the other characters unfolding? How are they affecting the major characters? The demonstration of what the other characters are doing, broadens the scope of the novel. The reader also knows more about what is happening outside the major character than the first-person narrator does. Suspense, intensity, drama, and variety of pacing is created at three levels: 1.) the resourcefulness of the hero who performs unpredictably, surprising the reader; 2.) the mercenaries who are a constant threat and 3.) the government's effort to conceal information.

This structure affords the reader many interesting "reading perspectives" not offered by more conventional novel structures. In the first-person (subjective) viewpoint of the hero the villains are seen from the personal, intimate vision of the major character—as the reader sees the major character from his own personal, intimate viewpoint. In the third-person (objective) the hero is seen in another dimension from the external viewpoints of the villains and high-ranking officials—the reader gains an "overview" of all the action.

By using the objective, detached narrative of the third person, more can be revealed about the plot than the hero can reveal through his own limited first-person viewpoint. There are also many time-spanning and space-saving devices. In the first person the hero can recount what has *already* happened. In the third person, scenes are picked up at points later on, after the hero's recounting of the events they contained. Etc.

Short Stories Are Not Novels

There are many explanations for why short stories cannot or should not be turned into novels. An obvious reason is that the content of many stories cannot be extended into a novel length: the plot line cannot be developed beyond its original limits. These deal with story and plot. There are other reasons which deal with the writer and the actual prose writing, and why some writers who excel at story writing have trouble completing a novel.

A. *The perceptive depth of the writer may be limited, shallow.*

Major characters in novels, unlike those in short stories, must be able to make acute perceptions, in order to be interesting. They must be placed both in common and unique situations. If the major character does not consistently make individual and provocative responses to the situations in which he finds himself, the unique situation becomes little more than ordinary.

Writers are people, and like people, there are perceptive and dense writers. There are clever writers and plodding writers. Desiring to be a writer or even having stories published is no guarantee that the writer is highly intelligent, remarkably sensitive, or acutely perceptive. Some writers are just limited by their perceptive depths. (The trashy best sellers do not disprove this. Many writers have learned how to successfully fake perceptions.)

B. *The quality of prose must be various and continually interesting.*

The short story is not as stringent in its demands for variable prose. It is linear in form, without many diversions. The length of the form does not demand more. Begin, keep it going for awhile, then end it. (Though many fine short story writers are admirably versatile prose writers.)

A novel requires an abundance of "manners of writing." A competently written novel may have a hundred dissimilar situations and many of them require adaptable, protean prose. Too many writers do not have this flair, this talent. This condition may be grim, but the actuality cannot be denied.

It is not the short story that stops itself from becoming a novel—it is the lack of the ability to create characters of perceptive depth and of prose versatility of the writer.

Reexamining Main Characters

After you have established a satisfactory opening to your story or novel, and your main character is functioning in relationships and plot, stop and reread what you have written. Your character is still in the early phase of development. Avoid additional work later on by determining if you have depicted your main character with thoroughness, accuracy, and clarity.

The writer should become instinctively precise about his main character's development. Thus, before bringing him into an almost irreversible status, appraise him from four levels: 1.) *physical,* 2.) *emotional,* 3.) *mental and* 4.) *unpredictable.* The main character is always growing and deepening. Prevent yourself from unknowingly or unmindfully allowing him to grow and deepen in undesirable, or unbelievable, directions.

1. *Physical:* (external descriptions must remain constant) Chubby, lean, angular, birth defects, acquired defects, athletic, fragile, runty, etc.

2. *Emotional:* (internal description) Passionate, angry, fearful, hating, impulsive, incapable of loving, adores children, reveres parents, etc.

3. *Mental:* (the caliber and level of his mind) Scholarly, illiterate, curious, indifferent to learning, intuitive rather than intellectual, an *idiot savant,* learned, facile, contemplative, plodding, etc.

4. *Unpredictable:* (the unanticipated, uncommon denominator that separates the character from stereotypes) In this unpredictable dimension the writer gains license to have the main character perform actions which may be explained later, or not at all. It is the mystery, the X-factor of human behavior that is undeterminable, inexplicable, surprising. Unpredictability is an excellent characteristic to instill in a main character. It makes him interesting, evocative esoteric.

Remaining (writing) with the main character for a long time does not automatically provide the writer with an absolute understanding of the character. It requires periodic examination of the character before this "intuitive empathy" can happen in the writer.

Reread Your Old Work

Inexperienced writers tend to appraise their growth by the *inept levels of their writing,* not upon the strength of their skill. They grieve so much over what they still cannot achieve, that they ignore what they have already accomplished. They bring an "It's beyond me" attitude to their work. They are positive they cannot write the scene.

Every writer, working to become a professional, begins blaming himself for all that he still does not know. It is as if he is responsible for his own ignorance. He believes that there is still so much to know, *that what he actually does know is inadequate.* He is only partially right. What has been learned about the craft of writing to this day is only a portion of all that must still be learned by writers.

But inexperienced writers did not create the immense amount of knowledge still to be realized and applied to the craft. It was there long before they ever considered becoming writers. Not finding the forest you are searching for doesn't mean it was not created, or that it is not *somewhere.* Every writer who desires to become a professional writer brings with him a blackboard cluttered with ignorance. Day-after-day work at writing erases the clutter. Then looking back at what you have accomplished inscribes knowledge onto the slate.

Periodically, inexperienced writers should read what they wrote six months ago and compare it to what is being written now. They will be brought

Deliberately writing for a specific "level of the public," or to fulfill the "current reading tastes" is foolish. The public mind is as stable as a drunken acrobat balanced on a furiously turning windmill. "Current tastes" are so erratic and transitory that a writer will have been passed over by ten trends before his writing is completed. A story or novel should be written because the writer cannot write anything else until that work is done, because it is time for the "work" to exist.

low by what they once produced, then elated by how much better they are writing now. Six months from now they will read the writing of today, and again feel despair, and then joy. No human has ever seen his hands grow *while they were growing*. One day he has fully-grown hands.

There is a reason why professional writers rarely read the stories and novels they publish. They know their published work is poor compared to what they are writing now. Writing every day is growing every day, *as a writer*. Some writers even grow as human beings, day after day.

Understanding Dialogue

Creating sustained dialogue is difficult for some writers. They do not have the "magic ear" or an inherent sense of speech rhythms. They cannot compose dialogue in more than its simplistic forms. Yet a contemporary novel without dialogue is like cooking an omelette with yolkless eggs. It is only by understanding the function of dialogue that a writer can overcome this deficiency. Dialogue has primary and secondary uses.

The primary function of dialogue is to inform while blending character and action. Dialogue 1.) informs, 2.) reveals attitudes, 3.) expresses responses and 4.) inquires.

1. *Information:* "I'm going downtown to buy some pickles."
2. *Attitude:* "The governor should have listened to me."
3. *Response:* "Don't you dare say that. I just bathed and perfumed."
4. *Inquiry:* "Did Pink-Nose Woodpecker really kill sweet Cock Robin?"

If the writer is not gifted in creating dialogue he should:

A. Keep the dialogue short. If a character speaks more than four sentences, *he is delivering a speech*.
B. If what the character must say cannot be done in under nine sentences, break up his dialogue. Let another character question him, respond to him. Or interrupt it with description of activity, etc.

Dialogue does not create character. Dialogue merely adds to an already created character. Nor is it the dialogue that holds the reader. It is the overall story, the plot line, the credibility and uniqueness of characters.

If a writer is limited in how he creates the impression of authentic dialogue, he is not limited in how he employs dialogue to gain its secondary benefits. Reduce the contribution of dialogue as "speaking" and use it for other purposes the reader does not know it is being used for.

By keeping the dialogue short to cover up deficiency, the writer can use it for shifting viewpoints, to change pace, to foreshadow, to break into the dulling visual effects of long narrative sections, as a replacement for lengthy exposition, to cover absences of time ("You weren't there, so let me tell you what happened to me, four days ago."), etc.

The writer is not only always in control of his material, he is also always in control of how he uses his writing craft.

"Non-Facts" in Spy Novels

There is a structural form used mainly in the spy novel which is most effective when the plot line is exceptionally exciting. It is the informative delay. It is a technique which should be in continual use throughout the novel. Its root function is to establish a prevailing credibility to cover the "incredible"—rendering the incredible action or behavior acceptably realistic. Its secondary function is to satisfy readers who also enjoy documentary types of nonfiction.

Example (general types of story) Always open with a world-wide or national threat. (a) A terrorist group has taken over the FBI computers. (b) An upper-echelon espionage agent plans to defect to another nation. (c) An agent has learned a vital secret and is trying to bring it to his government to save the country from a surprise nuclear attack.

After the story situation is established, a conference is held by high-ranking personnel and they discuss what to do. Moments before the informative delay is used, a character says, "Mr. President, I suggest that we use a Wet Team to neutralize the mole who has tapped into our computers."

"I find that a bit extreme. A Wet Team, you say. Yes, that is extreme."

The writer then interrupts the situation and explains: Wet Teams were instituted by espionage agencies in the 1950s after the Bamburgen case was given notoriety that caused the downfall of the Norwegian government. Cadres of psychologists were assigned to develop a portrait of the TKC (True Killing Character) identity. When this personality was conceived, Barth Axelrod, Commissioner of Espionage, given leave from Codes and Traffic, set about combing the agencies for men and women whose background and character were an image of the TKC identity. They were trained in all forms of exotic weaponry. . . .

This continues until the term "Wet Team" is fully explained. The writer then returns to his people and situation until another interbureau acronym or phrase is used (KGB, CIA, OSS, MI5, etc.). The story is again stopped and the writer delays the situation to provide an informative explanation of the official terms.

Training methods are often explained. Bizarre is made familiar.

Character in this type of spy novel is always subordinate to the general story and specific plot line. The people are conveyers of incident and situation, rather than representative of human characters. Some characters may be invested with humanness that is more than surface, but never with enough depth to interrupt the pace of the plot. Only the *information* of that exotic environment is allowed to *delay* the pace of plot line.

This information is vital to the spy novel. It contains the *credibility factor.* It provides authenticity to arcane government branches that are not officially sanctioned by conventional government agencies. The information also brings about the reader's belief in the impossible deeds, the inhuman suffering and fanatic patriotism these ultramagnificent agents experience and endure.

The informative delay offers authoritative documentation to the reader. It is the "high-executive" seal, the logo of certification. Without it, the reader would not believe the incredible feats conducted by the espionage agents. When the Queen of England co-signs your loan, the bank believes that you are a credible agent.

Before any feat is conducted by the agents, the novel must first provide documentation that the agents' actions are acceptable by the government. The deeds then follow. At first, they should not be overly superhuman. Then, as more documentation is offered, the deeds become more extreme, the weapons more mysterious. This constant supply of information presented in a non-fiction form interrupts the action, but is an interesting substitute. The delay is acceptable.

These human instruments (agents) of governmental destruction can decimate five brutal black-belt karate fighters with a plastic toothpick. They swim nineteen miles underwater to place tiny bombs on the hulls of deeply submerged submarines. Dum-dum bullets with poisoned tips cannot stop them. They are *übermenchen* and *überfrauen,* but unless they are accredited as superpeople through official notorization and verification, they will not be believed. You must believe in them. The government claims they are real.

Flashbacks Must Reflect Passage of Time

A common oversight in the use of flashbacks occurs when writers do not change the inner self or the appearance of their characters when returning them to the past. A flashback may return to a time of seven years ago, or seventeen minutes ago. Once the writer transports the character back into time, the character must not be the same as he is in the present. Some aspect—physical, emotional, mental, philosophical—must be different.

Example A female bank president is compelled to remember when she was only the private secretary to the chairman of the board. The content of the flashback is used to reveal her cunning manipulations to have the former private secretary disgraced, then fired.
Physical If the flashback is about five years ago, she should have a different hairdo. The dress of the other people should be compatible to the fashions of the time. The differences should be described in enough detail to make that former time appear authentic.
Emotional If she is an aggressively competitive woman in the present, give her a sentiment, an affection she was forced to sacrifice to achieve her position. The search for a father who once abandoned her.
Mental Return her to an intellectual state where she was easily provoked to suspicion by a casual remark ("There's no stopping her ambition. She's ruthless, she's cut-throat!") or she sees a common gesture (While putting on her lipstick in the restroom, through the mirror she sees two secretaries making gestures about her. One is making circles near her temple, in the common sign of "she's crazy."). Show her attending a university to learn the executive level of banking.

None of this description of past details needs be pertinent to the content or purpose for which the flashback was created. This material is there only to authenticate that the character is no longer exactly the same woman now that she was in the past. In the flashback, however, she becomes again what she once was. When she is returned to the present the changes in her are visible to the reader.

Historical Flashbacks

The *historical flashback* is similar to a background flashback experienced by a major character. Both supply information and insight that are not available from the circumstance of the present. This past history is not a space filler, nor does it appreciably slow the pace of the action. It should contain some events relevant to the story being developed.

Story Year: 1526. A monk is given the mission of delivering a holy relic to the pope who is vacationing in a palace in Urbino, Italy. The monk knows there is a great treasure hidden in the palace. It was left when a former resident was forced to flee. The monk decides that if he can locate the treasure he will leave his religious order.

Example (past history) In June of 1502, Cesare Borgia marched on Urbino and put Duke Frederick to flight. Borgia looted the Urbino treasury, carrying off 150,000 ducats which he dispatched to the Vatican. When the people of Urbino rose against the infamous duke, he conducted a series of treaties before resigning his claims on Urbino. During the lengthy negotiations he collected other treasures which he had buried. . . .

Characters, like anyone else, respond to the events of a particular time. A documented history of a particular time or place provides a special reality that details of costume or morality cannot provide. It establishes the authenticity of the time and place; it draws the reader from his own time, and fixes him into another time. It infuses credibility into the motivation of characters and their relationships. It creates a sense of continuity with the past so that when events current to that time emerge, they do not spring from a vacuum in time.

This technique of flashing back into the history of a time is not confined to the historical novel. Contemporary novels with a background of industry or politics should also incorporate this "historical flashback."

Three Types of Introspection

The type of character you are developing determines the type of *introspection* you use. There are articulate, semiarticulate, and inarticulate characters. There are three basic forms of introspection for each of these characters.

1. *Objective*: The writer articulates for the character in the writer's prose.
2. *Objective and Subjective*: A blend of the writer's prose and the character's language to reach articulation.
3. *Subjective*: Articulation gained solely through the character's inner language.

An articulate character can explain what he thinks. (*If I do not decide now, the opportunity will pass.*) A semiarticulate character can explain only some of his thoughts. (He was undecided about what to do. *If I don't act now, I'll mess up.*) An inarticulate character cannot explain himself; he needs help. (He was undecided about what to do. If he did not act now, he would lose the opportunity.)

When the writer articulates for the character (objective narration) there is analysis of the character's mind and the situation, but the character is depersonalized. The reader is placed at a distance from the character by the writer's objective prose.

When there is a blending of languages (objective and subjective, the character's language and the writer's language) there is a loss of intimacy but a gain in analysis. Though less subjective in tone, the reader is brought into greater understanding of the character by the writer's prose.

When the character's thoughts are written in the character's own language (subjective), the articulation achieved depends upon the intelligence and analytical ability of the character. If the character is smart and educated, his language can be articulate. If he is dumb and uneducated, his articulation is limited. But no matter how dumb, illiterate, or even retarded the character is, he has a language and can express himself. The information may be limited, but the sense of intimacy is intense.

The type of introspection you use depends upon the scene's pace, the depth of the thought, its sense of immediacy and how much articulation you need.

Ignore Book Reviews

When your first novel is published and reviewed, do not accept any book review as a worthy appraisal of what you have written, nor as a prophetic directional of what you will write. Unless you are in the elite echelon of the "best-selling writer"—or the large advance you were given gains you a supportive publicity and promotional campaign—the reviewer who "does your novel" will not really be qualified to make any judgments on your work.

Publishers issue first novels to newspapers and magazine reviewers in hasty, indiscriminate methods. They have no guarantees that the book will be reviewed, nor do they know or investigate the background of the reviewers. If the central action involves a bank executive, the novel might be sent to a school teacher or a librarian who once filled out a bank statement.

The majority of book reviews are not published by the mass circulation newspapers and magazines. Most first novels are reviewed through small city and small town newspapers. Many of those reviewers are "doing book reviews" because they are building up their libraries, are supplementing monthly incomes, or selling the novels to used bookstores for about 20 percent of their listed price. Many are trying to get their names in print. Some are people who once tried to write novels but abandoned the venture as being too difficult. They are all adroit in skimming. Others believe they are comedic or Oscar Wildean and use novels for inane puns, shoddy witticisms, or cynical disparagements through which they release their envy. YOU DID IT. YOU WROTE A NOVEL AND IT WAS PUBLISHED.

Others are serious but are either inexpert in understanding the depths and complexities of your novel, or are restricted from revealing anything cogent because of space limitations. The only attitude to assume when your novel is reviewed is to anticipate that whatever reviewers write about your novel will be wrong. All you can hope for is to be misunderstood favorably.

Clichés of Tradition

When possible, the writer should always use clichés of tradition to his advantage. They offer insights into human behavior that readers have been taught to accept as accurate. They *imply* meanings the writer need not openly declare through description or statement.

Example (question) A stranger strides to the door of a cabin built in an area near hostile Indian territory. Inside the cabin some dogs are barking. The man has pistols, a thick whip, a black mustache. He knocks on the door. A woman opens it. WILL HE BE A FRIEND, OR ENEMY?

The inexperienced writer uses one of two methods for revealing the stranger's character. The writer can say: *Hester was wary. She recalled rumors that a stranger was roaming the area, strangling women. "Can I help you, suh?" she said. He nodded. "Be you Hester Penn?"*

Another way is for the writer to state: *Hester sensed he was friendly.* This can be ambiguous. IS SHE RIGHT, OR WRONG? Using space to determine the stranger's attitude may not be important. He may be at the cabin for a critical reason. Description can slow the scene's urgency. Statement could be intrusive. The question that must be answered first is *Why is he there?*

In this type of circumstance, the clichés of tradition quickly define the stranger's general character so the scene can be set and the reason for the stranger's presence can be quickly answered. USE THE DOGS.

Example (menace) The dogs hunched forward, snarling. The stranger tensed. He gripped the butt of his whip.
(Friendly) The dogs bounded to him and yipped happily. He patted their backs, stroked their heads. "Be you Hester Penn?" he asked.

Every reader has been taught to believe that dogs intuitively sense the good or evil in people. It is a traditional cliché. The dogs can establish the stranger's general character quickly.

Believable Dialogue

Characters speak from what they are as people. They must speak in a manner determined by their educational, economic, and ethnic origins.

At some time before a character is given dialogue, it is advisable for the writer to prepare him for the reader, so that when he speaks, it is natural to accept his dialogue. You want to hear what he will say. Believable dialogue quickly authenticates the character.

In true life, if a university professor is taken to a police station and accused of rape, he may protest with, "Lemme outta heah, ya bums!" That may be his true-life manner of addressing his classroom. In writing, that manner of speech is unbelievable.

In writing—which is the *impression* of true life—most university professors are more believable if they protest: "Sirs, I presume your apologies will be profuse when this dreadful misunderstanding is over."

He is using language compatible to his assumed educational level. He cannot be misunderstood.

Dialogue is not only used to offer statements and information that further the situation or relationship. Dialogue is used to continually affirm the believability of the character. Unbelievable dialogue can confuse, distract, or mislead the reader.

Example In a set of quickly developed scenes, a mentally retarded criminal is seen robbing a bank, then leaping into a car to make his escape—then panicking and crashing into a police car. He is apprehended and the police see the packets of $100 bills in his pocket. "Been robbin' banks, huh Muggsy," one policeman says.

If Muggsy replies, "Officers, your accusation is an exaggeration—a gross terminological inexactitude," he is not *immediately* believable. His vocabulary is not compatible with his social and mental image. To develop him for speaking this language would take time.

Selecting a Structure

There are novel structures that do not obligate the writer to open with the major characters or their story lines. But for every conventional opening you do not use, you must substitute an opening that is equally compelling. Your purpose is to open the novel dramatically, no matter what technique you use.

Example (at police headquarters) Another Jack the Ripper is loose. Witnesses are studying mug shot books, detectives are drawing graphs for crime patterns, psychologists are guessing when the next murder will occur. No particular detective is being featured. Concentration is on the killer. Their concern creates him vividly.

In this type of novel the writer has several options for selecting a structure. His choice depends upon the best way his story and character can be emphasized and in what area of the novel the bulk of his material exists. These are some alternatives:

1. The murderer is introduced in the second chapter. He is kept on-scene for much of the novel. Reveal why, how, and when he murders. Now and then, you return to the police investigation to heighten suspense.
2. Reverse 1. In the second chapter show the murderer committing a crime. Then back to the investigation, centering on a team of detectives. Three is advisable, so none of them gets that much attention. Return to the murderer only occasionally. Sometimes open his scene while he's doing in a victim.
3. Equalize the space given to the police and the murderer. Even develop the viewpoint of some victims for pace and variety.

The strength of this novel structure depends upon how interestingly you develop the police work, how intensely you create the murderer, how sympathetically you create his victims.

A danger to be aware of is in becoming too engrossed either in the technical contrivances used for police work or in the motivational complexities of the murderer. An overuse of such content can monotonize character and deaden the pace.

No Flashbacks During Action

Do not introduce a flashback during a scene in which there is vigorous action. Whatever necessary information the flashback contains can only diminish or ruin the action scene in which it appears.

Example A woman is talking on the telephone. Her neighbor informs her that her husband intends to join a notorious gang of bank robbers. Suddenly, the woman hears her only child scream. She rushes to the window and sees the child rolling down the hill below their home. At the hill's bottom is a raging river. The mother quickly charges down the hill after her child.

Do not, as the woman is scrambling down the hill and the child is screaming, return the woman to the meaning of the telephone call about her husband—which causes her to flash back to the day she warned her husband that evil companions would cause his social downfall—at that time. Then, when the flashback is completed, return the mother to chasing down the hill to retrieve her child before the raging river claims her.

If a flashback is introduced during an action scene, it diminishes the intensity of the present situation: it does not allow for the full meaning of the flashback's content to have any impact.

Rather than being supported and deepened by the information in the flashback, the present (child falling downhill) and the past (telephone call) *clash*, and deplete each other of drama, value, and intensity.

A flashback at that time will also have a braking effect. The pace or velocity of the present scene (child rolling down hill) is halted as the reader is pulled from the present to become involved in the meaning of the past. All energy and dynamics of the action scene have to be focused on the *present action*.

Summaries

Summaries are collection boxes for inconsequential material that cannot be omitted. Shopping at the supermarket, sharpening pencils, etc. Yet there is a technique for using summaries to the writer's advantage: end a chapter with a summary; begin the next chapter with a summary. Use *mundane* material to link the end of one chapter to the beginning of the next chapter. The break between the chapters is used to change the place, the time, viewpoint and type of scene.

Story A breakthrough is being made on television components that will produce three-dimensional pictures. Petrov is being paid by a rival company to steal the secrets. The breakthrough is expected tomorrow.

Example The team of inventors assembled the FT-E4R. Petrov quickly memorized the circuits. He left the lab and phoned his contact about the approaching breakthrough. A meeting was set up for tomorrow afternoon.

The technology and mechanics of the invention are mundane and uninteresting to the general reader. The telephone procedures and clandestine meeting arrangements are also mundane and routine. Their existence as material is important, but not as material for a dramatic scene. Summarize them.

Example (summary beginning next chapter) Petrov's contact instructed him on how to pass the information when the breakthrough was reached. At 3:30 Petrov told his supervisor he had a dental appointment. He was allowed to leave. When he was in the dentist's chair, Petrov whispered, "Swallows never fly in the rain." The balding dentist nodded. Petrov began writing the complex circuitry.

The reason for not using a summary of all the material at the end of the chapter is that it appears rushed. As though the writer were in a hurry to pass over this mundane material. When one summary begins an important scene, it becomes important. The chapter break indicates that an important scene has just ended and that another important scene is just beginning.

Single vs. Multiple Viewpoints

Conducting the major character through a novel that has only his viewpoint will develop an intensity of characterization, but will also lessen the availability of devices used for creating suspense. A multiple viewpoint is more suitable for creating suspense.

In the single viewpoint, all that happens in the novel must be conducted through the major character. All situations and events are focused on his life. He cannot be absent from the novel to allow for other scenes to happen to other characters in other places. There can be no cliff-hanger scenes. No shifts to other tense situations.

Example (single viewpoint) The police sirens blared behind him. Donald jammed down the accelerator, desperately searching for a side road. The front tire suddenly burst. He fought to control the wildly spinning car. A rear tire blew, flinging the car ahead. He screamed as the car smashed through the weak shoulder guards. The police sirens stopped.

A break or a new chapter to stop the scene and hold the reader in suspense ("What happened next?") does not work here. The writer is obligated to remain in Donald's viewpoint.

Example (break) The car did not plunge off the cliff. The rear wheels caught on a cable. The police rushed over and stabilized the vehicle, then pulled Donald out.

The *break* was not a long enough departure from Donald to create suspense. The pace is drastically slowed, the excitement is stopped. The reader immediately knows what happened. He is no longer hanging on the cliff.

By using a multiple-viewpoint structure, the writer can validly "break" when Donald hits the guard rails, to pick up another character's viewpoint and situation. The writer has stalled the scene, but not the action or suspense. While wondering what has happened to Donald, the reader is also caught up in the active situation of another character. If the writer leaves the other character in a tight situation, he can return to Donald and resolve his plight—and still have the suspenseful situation of the other character to return to.

Learning from Popular Writers

There is an irony in learning the craft of writing. Reading the classics of fiction to understand techniques and structures will not offer as much as studying the hard-core contingent of professional writers whose work is so inferior. The great writers of the past were not masters of technique. They were masters at creating content. The substance of what they wrote was so penetrating and revealing about the human condition that they did not need an excess of devices to become interesting. Nor were there as many publishers, book outlets, merchandising hocus-pocus, or people who could read. The literary form was not a razzle-dazzle of gimmicks developed to promote sales against competitors. Methodology was less important than content.

The popular writers of the 80s have developed writing techniques that are complex, cunning, and cover-ups for their books' lack of content. The maze of deceptions devised to conceal a lie are always more interesting than the simple truth. Listing all the technical tricksters of the 50s, 60s, 70s, and 80s would be a vain effort. If they are remembered, it is not for their work, but for the stupefying amounts of money they earned and how wisely or outlandishly they used their celebrity. Arthur Hailey, Judith Krantz, Danielle Steel, Irving Wallace, Harold Robbins, Stephen King, Sidney Sheldon, Barbara Cartland, Janet Dailey, Louis L'Amour, Isaac Asimov, Robert Ludlum, Jack Higgins, Len Deighton, Gore Vidal, etc., are some of the writers worth studying. Overlook their often superficial content and mundane prose, and examine the methods they use for developing their novels. Whatever technique you need, they have already used it. That is another irony. Their contribution to American writing is not in the content of the package, but in the decorative wrapping.

Their contribution to the future eras of writers is notable and important. Viewing their craft techniques through an attitude of disdain is prideful and unprofitable. Any writer with a substantial range of worldly experiences, a social concern, and a passion for bringing enlightenment to his culture should not feel "above" adopting from these popular professionals.

Narrating Unbelievable Scenes

A writer often comes across events in a novel which, if they were written in a detailed scene, would be unbelievable. This imposition on the reader's credulity pulls them from the flow of the story. But if the same scene were translated into a narrative form, with an absence of details, it would be accepted as believable and the reader's involvement remains.

Example A dictator is urged to call out his troops to stop a rebellion. He tells the ambassador he must first relax before deciding. "I must first practice my bowling. My average is down." The ambassador is astounded. "Excellency, this is no time for bowling practice. The nation is being overthrown." The dictator begins polishing his special bowling ball. "I am nothing if I cannot raise my average. You will set the pins for me." This argument continues and the dictator practices his bowling.

While it may be believable that the ruler of a nation relaxes by bowling, the details of the scene render the scene too bizarre to be believed. The reader can affix a judgment upon the dictator: He's ridiculous, he's insane, to think of bowling at such a critical time. By judging the character as ludicrous, the reader is drawn from the story and participation in the events. The danger of the scene has been removed. A serious character has become a caricature. The point is to get the dictator to relax in his own believable way without damaging the scene through the reader's disbelief.

Example (narrative form) The dictator told the ambassador he would first bowl some games, to relax. Then he would give his decision. He returned from the bowling alley, grinning. "Call the troops out, now!"

The writer, by narrating the scene and leaving out the details, has avoided provoking the reader's critical sense, that might reduce the value of the scene. The writer has not omitted the scene: He has merely transposed it into another form.

"Unwritten" Scenes

Are there *unwritten* areas in a novel from which the writer can extract hidden conflicts, scenes, and information?

There are always events of a story that the writer doesn't want to cover at the time of their occurrence. The material might be distracting. The drama might be too overpowering. The information might mislead the reader. The suspense might be diminished.

> **Story** Lucille is experiencing dreadful labor pains. She must have caesarean delivery or she will die. She is taken to the hospital in frantic haste. A team of surgeons is ready to perform the operation.

The writer glibly avoids writing the delivery scene.

When Lucille is hurried into the operating room, the writer establishes a "break" and goes into the situation and viewpoint of another character. When that section ends, he follows with another character's situation and viewpoint. He then returns to Lucille's part of the story.

> **Example** It was two years since Lucille's emergency delivery. The child was born blind. Professional help was hired to raise him.

The writer can continue the story without ever referring to those "unwritten" two years. Or it is in those "unwritten" two years that the writer can find material for tangential story lines.

> **Mystery** The father believes his son was blinded because the surgeons were incompetent. He heard rumors that one surgeon was drunk.
> **Character conflict** Lucille wants to love her child but he has become a living portrait revealing her deep guilt. She had secretly taken an exotic drug to relieve her labor pains. It infected the child.

A hundred pages after the child's birth, the writer can return to that time, and write about it. The husband was outside the delivery room, waiting. He now remembers that one of the surgeons moved drunkenly.

The writer has moved back into that "unwritten" time and pulled material from it. He now has two years of former time to write about.

Horrify the Reader

All readers are human, but not all readers are humanitarians.

If you find an opportunity to frighten, terrify, or make the reader cringe with horror, grab it. Readers enjoy being scared and repulsed. First they believe the monstrous moments might happen to them, then they are exhilarated by knowing it is happening to someone else. You whet their appetites with suspense, squeeze them of emotion, then let the sense of relief whet them again.

You are writing *fiction,* not a factual documentary. You can take liberties with reality.

One basic "reader-scare" is the immediate, direct, and outrageously ugly scene.

Fright or horror cannot be induced when only trivial values are threatened. The loss of a fingernail while hanging a picture is not as awful as the loss of a hand while running a metal cutting lathe. Watching a kitten being attacked by a rabid bulldog will not frighten as much as a beloved grandmother hopelessly trapped in a burning building.

The writer must tap into the *universals* that affect all people. He must find the most primal fears in his characters which mirror the primal fears in his readers. Part of the fright or horror depends upon the circumstance; part depends upon the dramatic use of graphic details. Gang rape, the disfigurement of a fashion model, gouged-out eyes, the killing of children, drawnout deadly automobile crashes, the execution of an innocent man, branding, a vividly described ax murder.

Story A chubby senator is taken from his mistress's lavish apartment and brought to a darkened, rat-infested basement.

Example They tied him to a clammy operating table. The spotlight burned his groin. Dr. Mendella sighed, "Is your country worth your manhood? Tell me the code, or it all comes off!" The scalpel glittered. A thick faced nurse with blunt eyes slapped a bowl on his thigh. She held pads of cotton and gauze. He suddenly pleaded, "I don't know the code. I was absent from the conference." Dr. Mendella put the razor-edged scalpel on his flesh. "Tell me, now." He screamed, "I don't know," then shrieked. . . . (Depending upon the plot, the man is rescued or the doctor performs surgery.)

Do not establish your "reader-fear" scenes in settings that are compatible to the event. Finding a mutilated corpse in a city morgue is not remarkable. Hanging a horse thief from the limb of a tree is expected. Use opposites. If a vital part of the plot requires a decapitation, do it during a garden party or a high school basketball game. Have the reader watch the bloody head pop out of the rose bushes or roll and clump over the varnished court boards.

Use tastefully-selected images:

Example (1) The warty hands gripped her neck, stopping her screams. His breath smelled sewery. She was animal-wild with fear. He jammed his mouth onto her face, the long teeth biting her lips. (2) The glowing poker sizzled. He yanked back, cracking his head on the scummy wall. He strained against the chains, ripping skin. The poker jammed onto his right eye and he bucked as agony slashed into his brain. . . .

The "reader-scare" scene does not suddenly happen. The writer prepares for it by sprinkling in small human cruelties and incidental destructions before the major horror occurs. The writer cannot be inhibited by his own squeamishness. The "reader-scare" scene is an exaggeration, a frightening emphasis. The writer must write with a sense of melodrama.

A reader scare serves a dual purpose. The reader must not be allowed to "intellectualize" the nature of character or casually await the next important event. The story levels out, becomes static. The fulfillment of suspense gives the reader an emotional jolt. The raw, brutal scene heightens the reading experience. The reader acquires a sense of tension as the hero consciously rushes into peril or is unknowingly caught in danger. Then, when he is rescued or escapes, the reader is gratified. The purpose of the "scare scene" is to intensify the pace, emphasize the dramatics, and *shock the reader into feeling*.

The Greek Chorus

A technique for introducing important characters before they appear can be adapted from the playwright's craft. The introduction of these important characters is done by other characters while the major characters are still "off-stage." This technique was developed by the Greek playwrights who used the *Greek chorus*.

Before the play began, a troupe of players stood before the audience and recited the history, relationships and deeds that had *already happened* in the lives of the players who would perform the drama. Then, when the actors entered, the audience was familiar with their story. They could quickly understand the plot, the conflicts of the people. This is an effective technique which can be used in fiction—stories or novels.

Opening scene A husband and wife are standing at a window, waiting for their son who has, unexpectedly, been discharged from the army.

"He's not wounded, Sarah, I'm sure. He would have told us."

"I'm worried about the money he's been sending home for us to hold for him. Captains aren't paid that high. Either he's been gambling or—well, you know Lonny's opinion of his country. You know he hates it."

"If you think he's been selling secrets to a foreign country, I say no. He's a slick one, sure. He drinks hard and always has women, but a traitor. . . .

While this is not the most dramatic opening a writer can use, it is successful in creating a character *before he actually exists in the story*—since he has not yet appeared.

A circumstance that is unusual to an ordinary family is set up. Informative speculations *which reveal aspects of the character* are established. The questions of *why* and *who* become prevalent. The son, Lonny, is now familiar to the reader. Information into his past, his character, and even some of his future has been introduced. This "prologue" introduces the character *in a dramatic situation*. It also offers some insight into the attitudes and past of the family. Lonny does not have to stand or act to create himself when he appears in the story. He is already there.

Titles

Do not regard book titles as an important contribution to your novel. The title does not tell the reader anything about the content of the novel. To someone who is not familiar with the reputation and story of *Moby-Dick,* the title does not provide even a minor insight into the content of the novel. There is no whaling venture, no whale in the title, no madness, no soul-searching Ishmael.

What does the title of *The Red and the Black* tell anyone? Or *Flowering Judas, The Sound and the Fury, Pride and Prejudice, A Farewell To Arms, Man's Fate,* or *Gone With The Wind?* The title of a novel achieves meaning only while the book is being read, or after it is finished. The title of a novel becomes memorable only after the novel is accepted by the public as being a memorable novel. A poor novel, by any other title, is still a poor novel. It is not the title, but the content that causes the novel to be read.

Impossible Success Stories

There are two conditions the inexperienced writer should be aware of if he is to avoid horrid depressions, and to save some money. (1) A personal characteristic that inexperienced writers must never develop—or else their writing will be affected and their emotional stability shaken—is that of envying writers who claim that they never thought of writing a novel until they were sixty years old, had no idea how to start writing their first novel, never attended a class on creative writing, never went to a writing conference, or read a book on the "craft of writing," and their first novel sold 4,000,000 copies in the hardback edition. Even if they are not lying, it has no meaningful relationship to what you are writing now. These exceptions are so rare they cannot be relied upon as an actual possibility that could happen to you. Any writer who does regard such declarations as possible in his career is searching for a magic genie—not a down-to-earth publisher. (2) Save your money by not buying books on how to become a "best selling" author written by a writer nobody ever heard of.

Don't Quit Your Job

It is not always wise to quit your job to work full time at writing. There are many unpublished writers who need the stress, the pressure of writing while also working at a job. An excess of time can be more difficult to cope with than time squeezed in under pressure. It requires experience to be alone for long stretches of time, trying to write. Every uncertainty becomes magnified into a certainty of failure. Every hope slyly warps into the shape of a delusion. Irritation happens as though slews of roaches were infesting your disposition. Sometimes you become bored with yourself. You can actually be driven away from the time you have sacrificed to acquire.

Knowing you have only so much time for writing, you get to it. You may be physically tired, anxious to be with your spouse, family, friends—but the drive in your character gets you to your writing. You do more in those two concentrated hours than you would write in a leisurely time. You write because you are desperate. Remove that desperation and leisure can become lethargy.

Writing a novel under pressure helps you to work without prolonged confrontations with yourself. Living with, accepting, and appreciating yourself is not an inherent ability. It is a cultivated procedure gained a little bit at a time. Quitting your job might plunge you into depths of yourself you are either unwilling or unable to withstand. There are fathoms to the writer that the writer cannot always fathom.

Many professional writers will verify this unique condition of needing pressure until finishing their novel. It is not masochistic self-torment. Lengthy stretches of writing time can be discouraging, until you know yourself well enough to take ALL that you are as a human being. Many writers (who are now professionals) who quit their jobs to write full time, just stopped writing. The pressure of full-time writing, too early in their lives, was too much. They returned to their jobs again—so they could write again.

Intimacy vs. Distance

If the writer wants *intimacy* with the past, use a recollection. If he wants *distance* from the present, use a flashback scene.

In a recollection the writer never fully leaves the present scene. The character's consciousness is flicked from the present into another time. The remembrance is reached, its value is noted by the reader, then the character's consciousness is flicked back to the present. He does not completely "withdraw" from the *now*—the now is merely momentarily set aside.

Example Peggy leaned back in the rocking chair while Millie nursed at her breast. I am like my mother, she thought. She recalled how she had been held as an infant. Her mother rocked her and hummed softly as she was nursed. It was so pleasant. Peggy kept rocking and humming and smiled.

Peggy has not really left the present because the recollection was not long or large enough to dominate the present scene. It is a moment.

A flashback scene provides *distance* from the present so the story in the past can achieve independence. The writer wants to drop the present to emphasize the full past event. To fully create this past story it must be removed from the domineering influence of the present.

Example Peggy rocked while nursing her infant daughter. I've become as my mother was, she thought. She remembered how her mother had nursed her. The kitchen was chilly, the rocking chair squeaked. Her mother was a large woman with pendulous breasts. Her face was beginning to clutter with lines. In the apartment below, people were arguing. She placed her palm over Peggy's ears to shut out the angry voices. Someone came. . . .

As the writer reaches further into the past to create the former situation, the present becomes more remote. The purpose of the flashback scene is to emphasize the past and *diminish* the present. The purpose of the recollection scene is to quickly *add to the present* by fattening it with some of the past.

Avoid Anachronisms

Historical fact cannot be changed. Words like "superego" and "ecology" did not exist in the fifteenth century. The Duchess of Orleans cannot complain to Jean Vaillant that "The superegos of our *menues gens* are ruining our ecology with their nasty sheep." The writer must phrase the duchess's complaint in a vocabulary that was used in her time.

This logic applies to all aspects of period novels. The moral, ethnic, political, and sociological attitudes of the twentieth century cannot function *believably* in any other century. Writing must always be presented believably.

Example While kneeling in prayer in the town of Domrémy, Joan heard the voice of God speak to her. Three saints also appeared. They told her she was chosen as a divine instrument to drive the English out of France.

This is a factual account permanently fixed in its historical niche. Some fiction writers have depicted Joan of Arc as a lunatic: others, as divinely inspired; others, as a malcontent looking for an outstanding career. Inventive writers have even written what the visiting saints told Joan. Under no conditions would the following dialogue be acceptable, or believable.

> "Joan, *attention*! You have been chosen for a sacred mission."
> "God has blessed me, His humble handmaiden. What is it?"
> "The women of France have been drudges and slaves for too long. The barmaids do not earn the same wages as the barmen. Women are regarded as sexual objects, subjugated to the male whim and ego. As you go forward to defend France, you will also proclaim the liberation of women. When you have succeeded in enthroning the dauphin, you will demand equal rights for. . . .

Unless you are writing a parody on suffragettism in the fifteenth century, this dialogue will not be believed. Each century has its own morality and causes. The content of character and story must be compatible with the particular period of the novel.

Shared Images

Readers know that fiction and reality are not the same. This is emphasized in scenes of stress, sex, violence, horror, etc. Through the use of an extended, ongoing image, *shared by many people,* the writer can compel the readers to ignore their knowledge of reality and accept the fictional reality as more realistic than the actual reality.

> **Example (purpose of scene)** To develop a sequence of character vignettes that reveal the impermanence of life: to further the plot line.

> **(Situation)** Construction workers are completing the upper part of a twenty-story building. The contractor has provided concrete with more sand than cement. Suddenly, the foundation and walls begin to crack. Men begin falling into the air as the structure collapses. There are witnesses.

If all the workers fall and are killed, it is a statistical calamity. The writer wants to use the lives of the workers for his novel, but not to lose the horror of the scene. He creates an image that is appropriate to the total situation and which changes the *impossible* into the believable. "Suspended," "frozen," "glued," "slow motion." The writer must use the same image throughout the scene and within every viewpoint he explores.

Witness Myles gaped at the bodies sprawling into the air. His eyes were lenses, his mind a slow-motion camera studying a riveter spinning. . . .

Victim Ernie screamed though he felt wafted in motion, slow and gluey. *Mortgage payments, all I cared about was mortgage payments.* A jagged chunk of concrete lunged at his chest. He saw the iron rods slowly stab into. . . .

Victim Danny believed himself floating in a slow-flowing current that was cool. His shattered arm flopped as he tumbled over. He wanted to think of a deep meaning before he died. He had to leave a deep meaning. . . .

Though the image "slow motion" is opposed to the reality of "fast falling bodies," the repetitious use of the image through many viewpoints, coupled to the similarity of action, establishes another, equally credible reality. The reader does not want the workers to fall and hit the ground too quickly.

Dramatizing the Past and Future

There are times when the writer can allow the present scene to be passive and allow the *past* and *future* to contain the dynamic dramatics.

The death of an important secondary character can demonstrate this technique. The scene is written through the viewpoint of the dying man.

Story The wealthy father of adult twins is dying. They will inherit his corporation and wealth. Marjorie is a good woman. Cyril is an evil man. Cyril hates his sister. Their father's death is necessary for providing changes in the story and relationships.

It is essential that the dying man know information that has not yet been revealed through the other characters. Two transitions are necessary: into the past, into the future. The dying man is in bed, alone.

Example He could hear his own breathing. If he had not cut himself off from God, he would pray for just another year to live. He could protect Marjorie from being destroyed by her brother. He closed his eyes and saw them as they were at the age of seven. Cyril had tricked her into playing "Pioneers and Indians." But he was evil even at that age.

[The scene of the game unfolds. Cyril stalks Marjorie, then attacks. The scene ends with Cyril trying to club his sister to death. He is stopped.]

He felt his breath quicken. He wanted to leave the bed. He had to warn Marjorie to be on guard against her brother. Cyril had friends on the board of directors. He knew Cyril had been secretly buying stock through dummy corporations. He would call a special meeting of the board.

[The secret meeting begins to unfold through the dying man's viewpoint—predicting how Cyril will manipulate Marjorie from the corporation.]

He gasped painfully. His hands trembled. "Marjorie," he moaned. . . .

The dying man does nothing but lie in bed. His physical role is *passive*. His "viewpoint role" is to be a recollector of the past and a forecaster of the future. If the past and future scenes are rendered in *italics* the scenes stand out and the present scene fades even further.

Use Dialogue to Express Quick Insights

Dialogue, properly and pointedly used, is more incisive and effective than description or narration. Dialogue can be used for *quickly* giving insight into character and for *quickly* altering the meaning of a situation.

For insight into character "Just because Charlie is rich, he thinks he's also smart."

"Sure. He doesn't listen anymore. He's gotten conceited and proud."

For changing situations "You think I'm the killer, but I'm not. Start thinking about Jackson. You remember Jackson, don't you?"

"Come off it. Jackson is dead. How can a dead man be a killer?"

"Was Jackson's body ever found? Did anybody see Jackson die?"

If the above dialogues were described or narrated, they would not be emphatic. The speech of characters carries more conviction than speech described or narrated by the writer. When a character declares, "I'm innocent," it is stronger than: "He declared that he was innocent." Narration and description are muted, and always one second behind the action. Dialogue is immediately visible.

Dialogue separates the spoken from the "written prose." Prose precedes their speech, prose follows their speech—but there is no prose surrounding them. Narration and description are all prose—even the prose of speech.

Example Emma gripped the ship's railing and said she would not move. Waves slammed against the hull, causing the vessel to buck. Jim stood beside her and said he would stand with her. He braced himself when he saw another wave coming toward them.

In this scene, the motion of the ship carries equal weight with the conversation of the characters, because both are narrated by the same third-person voice. By using actual dialogue, the writer emphasizes the speech of the characters and separates the characters from the setting.

Example Jim stood beside Emma as she gripped the ship's railing.
"I'm standing here, and I won't move. Let the storm rage, let it."
"All right, darling, I'll stand here with you. I'll never leave you."
He braced himself when he saw another huge wave coming
toward them.

If dialogue is used principally for imparting information, and to give characters an added reality through speech, then the writer is truncating the full use of dialogue. The technique of dialogue is versatile.

Off-Scene Writing

An area of writing which requires no talent or skill is the writing you allow the reader to do. *Off-scene* writing is a valuable technique to learn. You avoid repetition, redundancy, irrelevance, and reader boredom.

Example The writer has just described the painstaking difficulty an artisan had working to fit the model of a Danish forty-gun frigate into an empty whiskey bottle. In the next scene, the model-in-the-bottle receives an award and the artisan, Victor, is required to deliver a speech.

If Victor uses his speech to describe the painstaking difficulty he had in getting the model into the bottle, the writer is being repetitious. The reader already knows how Victor did it. The writer should "off-scene" the speech.

Example Victor grinned at the audience and told them how painstakingly he had gotten the forty-gun frigate model into the whiskey bottle.

The reader does not have to endure the tedious hearing of what he has just read. The reader recalls the scene of how Victor got the model into the bottle, and the reader has tacitly collaborated with the writer.

Another form of off-scene writing is in *not* ever describing what is inessential and, by a reference which coincides with the reader's associative experience, letting the reader create the scene in his imagination.

Example Paul attended the local high school basketball game. The home team lost by nine points. When Paul left the gym, a light snow was falling.

The writer's object is to get the man to the basketball game, and then outside. Since the basketball game was uneventful, there is no need to write about it. It is written off-scene through the imagination of the reader.

The writer must be selective in what he decides to include in his story or novel. Not all activity must be described. If nothing dramatic or contributory happens "on-scene" then include that interval "off-scene" through a reference to it. Bring the reader into the work in a collaborative function by letting him imagine what it is not necessary for the writer to include.

Too Many Names in the Opening Chapter

Do not introduce all your important characters, their full names, and their role in the novel, in the opening chapter. They become clutter. The reader has a difficult time remembering them and sorting out their functions. Such immediate crowding flattens the various intensities and creates a sense of disorder. So much begins to happen, all at once, that the action is stalled, the pace leveled, as the reader tries to sort out the material.

Example (opening chapter situation, characters) The Orient Express is suddenly stopped inside a mountain tunnel. (1) A noted surgeon is traveling to Austria to operate on a dying monarch. (2) Two nondescript men have machine guns they plan to use for assassinating the dictator from Uganda, who is on the train. (3) Three nuns are going to set up a mission in Belgrade. One is a Russian spy. (4) An American man is carrying $4,000,000 in stolen diamonds. (5) A sexy Bavarian woman intends to seduce him and steal the jewels. (6) A Polish sailor is sick with a deadly and contagious disease. (7) Three wheels under the diner car are loose. (8) The train engineer has a heart condition which he knows is about to kill him.

If all this is introduced in the opening chapter, not enough individuality and weight can be given to individual characters and their personal situations. Readers should flow into the story, not be jammed into its forward motion. They should not be forced to focus on so many characters, events, and their portion of the story, the subsidiary plot lines—the major or secondary characters all at once. Their interest begins to flag. A "blurring condition" sets in. The reader has to keep turning back to recall which name belongs to which character, and who is involved in what situation. The mass of material prevents selective emphasis.

Use the opening chapter to name and define only the major characters and their situations, first. After clearly establishing them as individuals, merely plant the presence of the other characters who will become important. Do not name the secondary characters until their roles are included in the story and plot line.

More on Writer's Block

The writer begins a novel in possession of all "power and control" over his work. It is an authority he should never relinquish. Not even if he develops that accursed writer's block. At such a time he must use his professional privileges to decide not only to overcome the writing block, but also to use it as an opportunity for adding to the novel. DO SOMETHING—NOW:

1. Jostle the uniformity of circumstance by introducing a new character. Give him a surprising role. An enemy from the past comes to threaten the hero. Let him step into a room where a will is being read and hold up another will, canceling the old one. Don't explain him. Use him suddenly.
2. Change the physical conditions. Bring in an earthquake, a record-breaking snowstorm that endangers the characters. A flood. In a tropical climate, flash in a hurricane. A plague of tsetse flies. Any startling change that triggers more writing and brings out more of the novel.
3. Shift the time frame. A day later, three hours earlier. Or use another character's point of view. Use a transition into another locale. From a living room to a bowling alley. A church sanctuary. A recording studio.

Power and control mean mobility, choice, a varied spectrum of possibilities. Not having anything to write about means the material is gaining power and control over you. This condition must become unacceptable.

Whatever is written is not waste, though it may not appear in the novel. It is writing that has been created to produce writing that will be used. Before the curtain is raised on the opening of a play, the actors have gone through weeks of rehearsals. Though the public did not see the rehearsals, this "practice" is evident in the quality of the opening night performance. Without rehearsals the performance would be a catastrophe. The rehearsals and the writing practice are not a waste—even though it doesn't appear in the final work.

It is the same in writing a novel. The writer must DO SOMETHING—NOW! An argument against such tactics would be that they are disorderly, illogical. The argument fails. If the procedure of writing a novel was based on order and logic, only four novels would be published each year—and they would read like industrial manuals. Desperation is the parent of accomplishment.

Problems Within Problems

Never resolve a situational or character problem until you have instituted another problem *within the same situation, or character.* Plot is an ongoing progression of events and character developments that are festering with problems. When one situation or character difficulty is resolved, the plot must already have begun to produce another. Emphasis is always placed on the problem that brings the situation into existence. The secondary problem—the one that is just beginning to appear—is merely noticeable, but not yet troubling. It must remain dormant and not interfere with the problem being resolved.

Example Elroy, a former FBI agent, is in a home for the aged. He is being harassed by an attendant. Elroy reports the attendant, who is fired.

The problem is solved. If the writer is using an episodic structure with multiple viewpoint, he moves to another character and continues the plot through another viewpoint. But when it is time to return to Elroy's portion of the plot, a new problem must be created for Elroy.

The introduction of new problems requires time, space, and preparation. If a new problem already exists within the old problem which is being resolved, this time, space, and preparation are not necessary.

Example After Elroy leaves the supervisor's office, he finds his double room occupied by another elderly man. Elroy is shocked. He recognizes the man as a former Mafia don who was given twenty years for murder and tax evasion. Elroy was responsible for the Mafia killer's apprehension and conviction. The man had once sworn to kill Elroy. The man does not recognize Elroy.

When the writer leaves Elroy's situation to deal with another character, the reader is aware that Elroy has another problem. Although his initial problem has been resolved, his situational difficulty has been resolved on only one level. He has another problem which, when it is brought in later on, is quickly recognizable. There is now continuity in Elroy's plot line. There is an ongoing progression of events that will change his character.

Write Every Day

A writer must write *every day*. You may try to soften, sweeten, doctor or rationalize away the purity of this traditional verity—but the effects of not writing every day will prove its validity.

Writing every day is the writer's only protection against ignorance and failure. When the writer is separated from his work, he loses hold of his writing. He must now reach out to grasp it again. He uses time for renewing himself that he should be using for continuing.

When his writing day is over, the writer carries the lives of his characters into his own life. Their relationships and plot do not stop because he is not at his desk, or because he is working at another job. He is involved in his writing at a depth that is not perceivable to others, or even to himself. He is continuing the work; blending and bonding the novel into a compact unity. He and the novel are inseparable—they are always continuing.

When you finish your day of writing, you leave your prose in a particular disposition. When you miss a day or two of writing, you cannot recreate that same disposition again immediately. When you are writing every day you are not only working on the events and relationships in the plot, you are also mentally working ahead of yourself as you write. If you are not writing, although still involved in your work, when you return to writing you are working only from the point where you left off. You are merely catching up to your work.

There are subtle traits in character that you find when constantly writing about relationships and conflicts. When you skip some days of writing you lose contact with those subtle dimensions.

The habit of writing every day brings you to the writing even when you feel empty. If you do not write every day, gaps begin intruding into your relationship with your work. Those gaps are sneakily filled in by the doubts, uncertainties, futilities you have been able to distract yourself from through the business of writing. By writing more, you also learn more about writing. You are your own classroom. You cannot learn much during recess, or by taking too many holidays away from your work.

"Strobe-Light" Recollections

To prepare for the eventual appearance of a vital, but lengthy, flashback scene, the writer could well adapt a cinematic technique.

Film scene A character suffering from amnesia is seen on the street. He is trying to remember his past. The camera slowly moves to him for a closeup. Suddenly, the texture of the screen is altered. Another scene is superimposed onto the screen. Two men are shouting at each other. You see their faces and bodies clearly. One is the amnesia victim. Then the superimposed scene disappears.

The amnesiac gets into a taxi. Again the screen is altered. A scene is again superimposed. The two men are fighting. The major character is struck on the head. He is dazed. The scene flicks away. This superimposed flashing of a former scene happens twice more. The amnesiac leaves the taxi. Later on in the film, the viewer can be certain that when he regains his memory, *the entire scene of the past will be played out.*

This technique is compatible with the novelistic form. Using rapid recollections within a scene in the present will lead to the eventual appearance of a lengthy flashback based on those recollections.

Example (part of the novel) Julie is shown giving birth. During the terrible pain, she recollects the day during her childhood when her mother came into the bedroom to tell her she was leaving the family. Julie, only partially awake, recalls her mother telling of a hidden fortune in gold coins, and where to find the map. "So you can have a college education." During Julie's present difficult childbirth, she has an intermittent series of recollections of what her mother said before leaving. The scene ends.

Several chapters later, Julie begins putting all the recollections together in the form of a lengthy flashback which is not only vital to the remainder of the novel—but longed for by the reader.

Viewpoint in Character Novels

The character novel relies heavily on the examination of the emotions and character-consciousness of a single narrator. The plot is secondary in status. In one variation of the character novel, the writer uses both a first-person subjective narrator and a third-person objective viewpoint outside the narrator. While this type of novel concentrates on character, its unconventional structure also allows for suspense, a fast pace, excitement, and complication of plot line.

The writer uses both the first-person (subjective) and third-person (objective) viewpoints. The reader reaches an intimate connection with the major character by reading about events through that character's first-person viewpoint. Then a full objective participation in what is happening outside the major character is achieved through narration by a detached third-person viewpoint.

Story Jedro Kern is twenty-four years old and a national idol in the hard-rock realm of music. At the age of seventeen he married SueEllen, a high school girl who became pregnant. Their son is now six years old. SueEllen stays home while Jedro tours the nation. He cannot resist the groupies who give themselves to rock stars. His wife has threatened to divorce him and refuse him visitation rights to his son. Jedro loves his son, but also revels in the adoration of the female public. He tries to stop, but cannot. His wife sues for divorce. Jedro's performances suffer because of his sorrow.

In the first-person viewpoint the writer has several languages (colloquial, personal, formal) through which to convey Jedro's feelings, thoughts, and immediate responses to the events he is involved in. His depths, expectations, dilemmas are revealed through the subjective conflict within his own life. He is "confessional"—always tightly focused on self.

In his third-person viewpoint the *reader* views Jedro from the external impersonal vision. The reader sees Jedro's world and the other people as they are and what they do—not from the limitations of how Jedro sees them and relates what they do. In the third-person, the writer contributes to the reader what Jedro cannot contribute in his first-person viewpoint.

Example (third-person) Jedro stood before the thousands of people, arms stiffly upraised, sweat streaming into his grin. They began chanting, "Jedro, Jedro, Jedro!," stamping their feet, applauding. His breath was rapid, raspy, the electric guitar heavy against his thigh. The bright spotlights burned his skin. The lead drummer winked to the second guitar, "He rips'm, alla time, he rips'm." The stage manager lowered his hand toward the lightman, signaling to reduce the lights. "Jedro, Jedro, Jedro!" He began laughing. The tassels quivered on his black leather shirt, the design of sequins flashed on his legs. He did not want to leave. This was glory.

The novel is entirely Jedro's. It is all enclosed within Jedro's two viewpoints. Using another viewpoint (his wife's, his son's, a groupie, etc.) would disperse the intensity and distract the concentration of the full and deep characterization of Jedro.

The writer alternates between first-person and third-person viewpoints. Not with predictable regularity. There can be several first-person scenes, then a third-person scene, then two more first-person scenes, then three third-person scenes.

The first-person carries the character-story. It depicts the intimate scenes of Jedro's growth or deterioration, his family and social relationships in emotional intensity. He "confesses" depths that cannot be revealed through action.

The third-person viewpoint carries the plot line. It depicts the action of events and situations that authenticate the world's influence and imposition on Jedro's life, causing changes in him. The reader sees the "inside" and "outside" at different times, yet at the same time. As the character deepens the plot can become more complicated. Though character dominates, the plot line is given adequate prominence.

A Delayed Past Event

A *delayed past event* is a technique the writer uses to keep the reader guessing about character motivation, and to find answers for a present dilemma that exist only in the past. The writer uses periodic references or reminders that an important experience or situation exists in the character's past that must eventually be disclosed. The writer's timing must be precise, or else the reader will become annoyed and wonder, "What is it? What happened back then?"

Story Norman is a tough, though honorable, electronics tycoon. He is powerful and influential. His only failing seems to be with a smaller electronics manufacturer who is constantly trying to take over Norman's industry. Other people in electronics wonder why Norman does not crush or absorb the smaller rival who is becoming powerful in the field.

Much of the craft of writing is based on what the writer can legitimately postpone. Skillfully, the writer devises a series of "critical situations," which he deals with at appropriate times throughout the book. While one situation is being resolved, there is always another situation waiting to be resolved. Situations are held in reserve until a dramatic interval in the plot is reached; then they are resolved. A vital event in the character's past that happened before the novel began is one of those situations. Why does the electronics tycoon allow the smaller manufacturer to take advantage of him? While the reader knows this past event will eventually be revealed, its appearance is delayed for as long as it can sustain suspense. The past event is only referred to. Not even the victim is allowed to remember the details.

To force the past event into existence, the writer brings the electronics tycoon to a serious moral or personal crisis. If he does not stop the smaller electronics manufacturer, his industry, his family, or his life will be forfeited. It is at that moral or personal crisis which jeopardizes the tycoon's existence that the long-delayed and mysterious secret is released. The entire, detailed account of the past event is revealed in a flashback.

Example During World War II the electronics tycoon and his rival were soldiers. The tycoon abandoned his company and twelve men were killed. The rival was a survivor and he is now blackmailing the tycoon.

Make the scene dramatic!

Balancing Action and Experience

There should be a balance between the intensity of the action in a scene and the intensity of what the character is experiencing in the same scene. An imbalance of emphasis can cause the scene to become either unbelievable, or melodramatic. If what the character is experiencing is overwhelmingly dramatic (reactions and responses) the details of the action (what is happening) fade into the background. The dramatic then becomes marred, unreal, and extravagant.

Example A woman is seen racing through a dark, unoccupied park, screaming, "Help! Help!"

If the writer concentrates on exploring her fear of being raped and murdered, the presence of the pursuing assailant and the scary background of the park fades into a blur. Her fright, which is valid, is so overcharged that it seems like a caricature. She may be experiencing a delusion or some neurotic hysteria.

The action within an incident should never become more theatrical or amplified than the feelings the characters are experiencing. The reader will become so involved in the mechanics and flash of the action that the effect of the responses of the characters is diminished.

Example A woman is seen racing through a dark and unoccupied park, screaming, "Help! Help!" The writer over-details the assailant, showing him stalking the woman through the bushes. Her screams attract two policemen who charge to her aid. The assailant trips on a twig and falls into a tunnel. He rushes from the tunnel exit which is just in front of the woman. He races toward her. A gang of young muggers think the assailant is a prosperous jogger and go after him. The policemen catch up with them and start shooting. The woman thinks she's being shot at and screams louder and runs faster.

Every scene has a spectrum of values illustrated through action and character. A balance between the graphics of action and the responses of the character is essential to create the naturalness of the situation. The scene can only be comfortably absorbed by the reader if all of the material in the scene happens together, with a sense of simultaneity. The action and the character responses may share prominence at different intervals of the scene, but it is the total purpose of the scene that must dominate.

Some Contradictions Are Advisable

There are so many levels of craft in the profession of writing that sometimes the guides seem to contradict. But one guide that should always be attended to is to avoid boring the reader through character predictability.

Example Bertrum is a building contractor. At the halfway point of the novel he has had so many problems and come up with so many solutions, the reader knows that all future problems will be resolved. Only when the novel ends will Bertrum's problems stop.

A practical and effective guide in writing states that a major character without problems is either dull or not dramatic enough to be written about. But predictability also leads to boredom. Problem after problem after problem becomes a tedious reading rhythm.

Break into the rhythm with what seems to be a writing contradiction.

Allow Bertrum to reach a point in the novel where his social, marital, and spiritual life is absolutely marvelous. Even his golf score is enviable. Let him be so fulfilled that he knows his life will be perfect from this time on. Or, he feels in such a state of completion that he will be unflappable no matter what happens next. He can turn tornadoes into a zephyr and douse the fire of dragons.

The reader will not believe it. Such perfection is unbelievable.

This writing contradiction is useful for two reasons:

1. If constant pressure on a major character reveals content that cannot emerge in more casual times, then a prolonged condition of personal serenity will bring out another dimension of character content. What is Bertrum like when he is without problems?

2. Bertrum's record for having problems is so constant that the reader will not believe Bertrum is free of problems. This disbelief keeps the reader from becoming bored. While never before seen depths are emerging from Bertrum, the reader is also waiting to prove that both Bertrum and the writer are wrong.

Then distract the reader from Bertrum by writing about the plot lines of the other important characters. When you return to Bertrum, give him an unexpected and seemingly insoluble problem that drives at him. This *does not* revert Bertrum to his former predictability, because the former pattern has been broken by Bertrum's prolonged state of serenity. And the reader is delighted. *Ha!*—To think that the writer believed that Bertrum was done with having problems—*Ha!* (This is not as childish as it sounds. Readers play games with writers. If the writer can let the reader feel superior for a little while, the reader is not bored and the writer has won the game.)

Don't Read While Writing

The moment your involvement with professional writing becomes a commitment, your reading habits should undergo a transformation. You begin reading analytically to learn what other writers have done and how they have used writing techniques. You experience a loss of reading pleasure and do not realize that you are also misusing important time. When you begin writing seriously, it is wise to transform the time you use reading into time to be used for added writing.

You are in an interval of writing growth in which you must now learn from yourself. Empty yourself of what you already know about writing, by writing it out of yourself. You have been reading for many years and have absorbed and retained enormous amounts of writing technique from your reading. If you feel ignorant in comparison to what you believe you must know for what you are writing now, it is not ignorance. You are in a new dimension of feeling and thinking. You are being forced to contact what you know, and to use it creatively. You are reaching into personal resources you have never touched before. You are no longer out of your depths—you are pushing into them.

The mind of a writer, like an onion, is composed of layers sheathed around deeper layers. The writer constantly peels away the layers of knowledge to recognize more of his knowledge. During the writing of your first novel, all your efforts should be focused on getting to the core, before what you know begins to molder. Isolation from reading *while writing;* separation from the "escape" habit of reading; removal from the analysis of other people's work help you peel away the sheaths. Because no one is giving anything to you, you have to provide for yourself, from yourself, WITHIN YOURSELF.

You already contain enough writing techniques from your reading to get you through your first novel. Find them, adapt them to your needs, and they will become your own. Then return to your reading and begin preparing for your next novel.

Using Flashback to Create Suspense

A *flashback* can be used for both providing past information and for legitimately delaying the action of the plot. It can also serve as a transition which, when returning to the present, alters the mood of the present. There are intervals in a novel when the writer deliberately slows down the plot line to create suspense. He delays the reader's fulfillment without an appreciable loss of momentum. He merely uses a flashback to an exciting time in the past as a substitute for the exciting time of the present.

Example A woman and her attorney are before a judge, waiting for a decision on her divorce action. She is worried. Her husband has threatened to kill her if she leaves him. The judge is ready to hand down the decision.

The writer stops the present scene. The woman flashes back to the day her husband proposed to her. He had just been released from jail on suspicion of having murdered his first wife for divorcing him.

Example (last part of flashback) She remembers signs that prove he did kill his first wife because she divorced him. She did not want to believe it.

The writer ends the flashback to return to the present. The judge strikes his gavel for attention. He is about to offer the decision.

The suspense in the present (the divorce decision) has been delayed because of the character's return to the past. *But the past has its own suspense.* Is divorce the trigger that sets the husband into killing? This break from the present into the past has not stopped the suspense or really slowed the momentum: another dimension has been added. The suspense in the past.

A past situation has been revealed and resolved. This resolution informs the reader of actual danger to the woman, *just as she is returned to the present.* This fear leads into the present fear—her husband kills when he is divorced. Will she let the divorce go through? Will she return home to save her life? The present has been delayed by the flashback, but the pace of the plot line continues.

A transition from one time to another has been developed. When the woman is seen in the present, *she has been changed* through the flashback. She was afraid before the flashback: now she has cause for being terrified.

Mechanical Use of Writing Techniques

Do not compartmentalize the events in your chapters by using mechanical structures or static writing techniques.

Story A stage actor's career has collapsed. He climbs onto a window sill, high above the street. People rush into the room to stop him.

Example (compartmentalized scene-structure) 1.) Actor writes suicide note and goes to window. 2.) Description of height of building and city. 3.) Introspection to define motives. 4.) Details of climbing out the window. 5.) People rushing into the room. 6.) Actor resisting their pleas. 7.) Actor's introspection. 8.) Description of city and fierce wind. 9.) Policeman tries to talk him into room. 10.) His wife appears to try to talk him into room. 11.) Actor almost falling. 12.) Description of people. Etc. Etc. Etc.

In outline, this structure seems functional. But when written through this compartmentalized form, the scene reads mechanically. The writing techniques are clearly separated when they should be mixed together and used more than one at a time.

Example (the compartments) 1.) The actor's climb onto the window sill is an isolated description of movement, without introspection. 2.) The description of height of the building and the city is detailed, but the actor is not in it. 3.) When the actor introspects, all physical details and motion disappear. 4.) His climb onto the window sill is described but there is no tactile, "sense" detail of the room or city. No introspection, no sounds, no voices ready to charge into the room. It is a body without a person in it.

It is as though the writer had developed a draftsman's schematic of his story and, with mechanical skill, filled in the designed steps and stages—expecting this to create a flow of pace, mood, background, motivation, emotional responses, and the drama of human experience. Action should contain introspection, physical details, emotional responses, dialogue—all at the same time. Writing is a stream of parts blending together to become a single entity.

Example He shuffled to the window sill. Sweat banded his neck. He suddenly giggled. "This should make a four-star splash." He gripped the window hold, forcing it up. The sky was a spill of watery blue. He closed his eyes and swayed. His hands trembled. This was stupid. He could hear the rasp of street traffic. Someone knocked on the door. "John, are you all right?" He nodded. *I will be, soon.* He raised his leg to the window sill.

A description seen through the viewpoint of the character should contain background, introspection, narration, recollection, and inner dialogue.

Example He edged along the narrow concrete ledge, his palms flat against the coarse wall. The wind flailed at his clothes like crackling wires. He shuddered. He could see people through the windows of the building before him. He wanted to shout, "You're making me do this!" A jet skimmed along the sky. His father had warned him that acting would destroy him. "Pick a safe career. Actors live dangerously. They die young." He jammed his back against the wall. His face was cold. He thought of his first major part. No one believed he could play Othello. He was too young, too slight, they said. He remembered the first night reviews. "An Othello is reborn in the name of John Willis." He swayed dizzily.

Fiction writing is an undisturbed flow of language that creates the impression of a particular reality. Chapters and scenes are not read from one separate block of a type of prose to another separate block of another type until a reading structure is created. Writing is read in the concept of "all at once a little at a time." When the writer compartmentalizes the techniques of writing, keeping them separate, one doggedly following the other, he establishes form and information—but not a flow of drama. Writing techniques should be dropped into an easy-moving blender which, after it is stopped, produces a homogeneous concoction of entertainment.

Selective Emphasis

Selective emphasis is a technique for deliberately highlighting an area of a scene, an event, or a character's response that must carry more impact than the content surrounding it. Emphasis is achieved in two ways: 1.) Through *bulk*. Pushing hard to make the moment more penetrating so it will not be forgotten. 2.) By surrounding the vital moment with a run of less functional prose—scene-setting or small activity writing.

Story A youth is unhappy living in a lumber town. He has just had a fight with his father who is chief tree topper for the company.

Example (1) He had to leave Tree-Bend and its heritage of ignorance. San Francisco was the place to live. There was freedom there. People were politically active, culturally involved, socially electric. There were depths in himself he could never reach in Tree-Bend. He could find a job in advertising. Become a tycoon. Drive a Porsche, buy a lavish condominium. He did not want to become the image of his father. Felling trees and cheating on Mom with a busty hash slinger. He would die of suffocation if he did not get out, *now*. "I'm being crippled," he moaned.

Example (2) He strolled along Cedar Street, trying to feel a sense of cheer. The twelve ramshackle houses lining the main street were dark. *If I don't leave Tree-Bend now, my life is over. I'll die the same way I live—like an ignorant slug. I can make it big in San Francisco. I know I can.* He scuffed his shoe on a stone and sighed. The sky was overcast but he could see the dim blob of the moon leaking through.

Although these examples are contained within the larger text of a scene, they are isolated by the emphasis focused upon them. In one, inordinate attention is fixed on the youth's discontent. The bunching together of the reasons and prose energy stresses their importance. In the other example, the reasons for his discontent push out of the blander prose and point at the reader with *melodramatic* urgency. Through selective emphasis, what the character is feeling at the time will not be overlooked.

Sexual Problems

Normal sex problems seem so alien to contemporary fiction. Unless they are in the realm of the positional, perverse, or degenerate, average sex problems are hardly ever exploited. Heroes are always virile and can, whatever the occasion, achieve immense accomplishments and often, multiple gratifications. Heroines rarely experience a flatness of desire. The characters perform with an expertise that would turn erotic goddesses dry with envy.

> **Example** They rushed to each other, flinging clothes aside as they spanned the distance. They fell onto the fluffed rug and the furies of passion burst through them. They clutched into embrace. She shrieked her ecstasy as he thrust the power of his being into the depths of her soul. They became vibrant and thrashed into the undulations of eternal love.

In writing, sexual circumstances offer a most revealing dimension of character relationship and conflict. During sex people are unusually dramatic. Writers should accept the opportunities that a sex scene provides and use its advantages not only for extolling the superiority of heroes and heroines, but also for exposing their human frailties.

> **Example** They lay beside each other, caressing, gasping. In the darkness she could not see his tears. Soon, she whispered, "Bertrand, is anything wrong?" He edged to the bedside, unable to speak. He knew this would happen and he despised his body. He hated the desires that urged him to keep trying. But it was filth, damned, damned filth. Just as his mother said it was. He clenched the mattress and sobbed.

The object of the writer is not to create sensationalism, but to portray reality. Characters should contain all the attributes of impotence and capability that all humans contain. A sex scene crackling with excruciating dilemmas and unbearable torment is a splendid showcase for drama. It allows for the exploration of relationships that all readers can identify with and participate in. Only in real life are sexual dilemmas and doubts inconvenient and unrewarding.

Book Reviewing

An excellent "breaking-into-print" enterprise for the unpublished writer is *book reviewing*. Any effort that brings the writer's work and name into print—that gets him into the reality of publication—puts him closer to professionalism. Though it is not the speediest launch into wealth and fame, it provides proof of a ripening skill and eases some of the social pressure coming from people who disdain the validity of your ambitions. You understand some reasons for why other writers succeed, or fail. You are not only the writer, you are also the reading public.

The book review structure brings you into another facet of the writing craft. It aids in organizing writing into a compact unit, and in concentrated thinking. Writing about someone else's work forces you to be objective. The focus of insight and knowledge is fixed outside of your own content and preference. It is training in the clarity of expression.

Whatever the book reviewer writes is always too long and sprawling. The threat of non-publication if the writer exceeds a generally unalterable space, teaches him brevity. He is forced to remain centered on *topic*. Because the book-review form is not complicated, the writer must make it interesting. He learns to use a vocabulary he has neglected to employ in his own writing. He begins to read through another dimension of interest. Examination, not entertainment, is his purpose. The mystique of writing is diminished by working with the reality of what writing is, for publication.

Perhaps the greatest value gained from book reviewing is in learning that publishing is not a social philanthropy, but a business. Space and paper are money. Editors do not consider the feelings of the writer, and the power of choice belongs to them. The writer is less important than the writer's work. It has always been that way in publishing. Learning that reality will eliminate half of the "ego-superfluity" and slop in your writing. A general definition of "professional writing" is the versatility of being able to write in any writing form.

Nested Flashbacks

To shorten a scene and gain an opportunity to bring in isolated but important bits of information about a character's past, use the technique of *nested flashbacks*.

(*Concept*) You break from the present time of a character and flash back into his past. That portion of the past creates another flashback that goes even farther back into his past. The second flashback scene creates in him the need for another reach even farther back into his past.

These nested flashbacks establish a tight continuity in the character's past, while explaining (to the reader) some of the motives in his present. By returning into the character's past, then going still farther back, the writer probes deeply into the character. By using two or three flashbacks *now*—all related to the same character content, you do not have to interrupt the present action later on, to get in these explanations.

Story A police captain is demoted in rank for his gross corruptions.
The writer wants to reveal three significant phases in the captain's life to trace when the corruption began: when he was a patrolman, a college student, a high school student. These three phases of corruption will also explore three types of character traits that were not revealed before.
1. Flash back to when he was a patrolman taking a payoff from an unlicensed fruit vendor. He used authority and power to exploit the helpless, for personal gain.
2. Within the body of that flashback, flash still farther back. He used damaging photographs to blackmail a college professor into giving him a passing grade. He was indifferent to people's feelings when in a crisis of need.
3. The second flashback opens another flashback still farther back: selling the answers to high school final exams to other students. He was enterprising and not above corrupting others with his crafty immorality.

It is essential that the flashbacks deal with the same character, ON THE SAME SUBJECT: HIS OWN CHARACTER. In each flashback, identify the character through recognizable physical characteristics. Older in the first flashback, younger in the second flashback, still younger in the third flashback. When returning to the present, show what he looks like *now*.

Exotic Backgrounds

When writing about backgrounds considered exotic (compared to your own) it is advisable to use an "inverted-pyramid" structure in constructing the scene. At the top—the broadest area—you establish the presence of famous sights, quickly convincing the reader that this is the place you are writing about. Then gradually move down the pyramid and get into less exotic or known sights, until, at the base of the pyramid you are naming streets, markets, currency, costumes, and languages.

Story Ten men commit "the crime of the century." They have robbed 25 safes in New York's Diamond District. The take, in diamonds, is

$100,000,000. A team of insurance company detectives is hired to pursue them. The thieves have split up. Each one is carrying $10,000,000 in diamonds. They scatter to all parts of the world.

The task of the writer is to research these countries and find the identifying tourist sights. The most general and famous are put down as the backdrop, so the country is easily recognizable.

> **Example** Paris: Notre Dame, the Arch of Triumph, the Eiffel Tower.
> London: Houses of Parliament, Buckingham Palace, London Tower.
> Tokyo: the Ginza strip, the Imperial Palace, Tokyo Tower.
> Bombay: Marine Drive, Victoria Terminus, the caves of Elephanta.
> Rome: the Colosseum: St. Peter's, the Trevi Fountain.

Whatever country you scatter the diamond robbers to, acquire immediate identification through the *traditional sights*.

The writer does not have to scrimp and sacrifice to amass the money to visit these exotic lands, camera and notebook in hand. They are really there. Any tourist agency will provide you with brochures containing excellent photographs in vivid color. The time to travel to those lands is after you have written some best sellers.

Historical Events as Story

When historical events are used as the basis for character action, the continuing presence of those events can be considered as a subsidiary story. If the events are dropped after the story has begun, the writer loses a strong support for motivating his characters. It is like a martyr who is being burned at the stake asking himself, "I'm sure there is a reason for my being here, but I'll be burned if I can think of it."

> **Historical event** In 1209, Otho was the Guelphic emperor of Italy. A vicious political rivalry arose between Otho and Pope Innocent. Otho was excommunicated and young Frederick of Sicily became the pope's protege. The pope did not suspect that Frederick was an anti-papist. In 1211, a league composed of excommunicated leaders was formed to fight the pope.

The writer uses the events in this historical time to bring his characters into action. Their story unfolds during this eventful time.

Story (a romance) Frederick remains in the pope's good graces while serving as a spy for the excommunicated leaders. Otho's niece Stephina loves Frederick, but is betrothed to a nephew of King John in England. They are torn by their loyalties. Frederick to his cause, Stephina to her uncle. In 1213, armies are assembled for war.

If the historical events which have handicapped this romance are dropped, what prevents them from marrying? If the writer ignores the political, religious, and sociological effects of the enmity between Otho and the pope, where will he find his situations? If the writer does not place Frederick in danger of being discovered as a spy, what is there for Frederick to do? If King John does not send troops to bring Stephina to England, what makes her interesting?

In an environment where everyone is a noble, then nobility is the "norm," the common denominator of background. It is the historical events that provide the "uncommon" factors for the lovers. Otherwise they would just be "ordinary lovers" who could work their problems out on a river boat drifting down the Mississippi.

Write from Your Strengths

A writer should always write from his strengths. This does not mean that he should overuse his strengths until they become weaknesses.

Every writer is more skilled in some particular aspects of writing than in others. Some writers are masters at creating dialogue, but mechanical when fitting research into setting. Other writers are specialists in description, but shaky in developing multi-dimensional characters.

Story A child must tell his father he has stolen the family coin collection and spent it on treats and gifts for his friends.

Alternatives The writer can tell the story from both viewpoints (child and father). He can tell it from one viewpoint (child or father). He can ignore both viewpoints and narrate the scene as an objective observer.

With three such alternatives for creating a scene—and each of the alternatives could be equally effective in function—it is sensible for the writer to develop the scene through his writing strength.

If this is a "point" scene—a scene used to develop a specific change in the relationship between father and son—and the *point* in the scene is more important than the particular scene itself—the writer can also look to other alternatives

Point of scene To show the control of the father, the courage of the son.

If the writer is weak on confrontation scenes but is strong in recollections, transitions, he passes over the confrontation between father and son and picks up the scene *after the confrontation has happened.*

Example Frank opened the car door and let Joey-boy clamber to the rear seat. He was glad he hadn't slammed the boy across the face for having stolen the coins. *God, blowing all those coins on junk food for his buddies.* Frank fitted himself behind the steering wheel. *It took guts for the kid to confess it.* He turned on the motor and grinned. *I controlled myself.*

The confrontation scene is not lost, it is merely not written in on-scene details.

Sometimes professional writing is a strategy of learning how to reinterpret content and adapt it to what you know you can do *right now.* Writing what comes easily at least keeps you working until you gain skill in writing what you cannot write *right now.*

Multiple Flashbacks

Though *flashback* is an obvious intrusion into the flow of the plot's present, the writer judges it important to use. The reader must be returned to a time in the character's past to provide information that was not known before. If the writer is skilled in craft and in total control of his material, he selects the exact moment and length of the flashback:

1. When the scene which provides the flashback is dramatic enough to be picked up the moment the flashback ends—without appreciable loss to pace or intensity in the present.
2. When the dramatic dynamics within the flashback are almost equal to the dramatic dynamics in the present scene.

Having already accomplished those conditions, the writer can then not only flash back once, but twice, or even three times, in that same interval, before returning to the present.

Story Herr Otto, a chemical biologist in Argentina, discovers a serum that will cure Alzheimer's disease. He cannot make his discovery known. He is a former Nazi doctor who conducted inhuman experiments in the concentration camps.

First flashback: one page long Herr Otto strutting through the concentration camp. He is vicious, maniacal. He points a swagger stick at emaciated people and orders brutal guards to drag them into his laboratory. This flashback ends with a lead into the next flashback.

Second flashback: a half page long Herr Otto in full dress, standing before Adolf Hitler who is pinning another medal on his uniform. When they embrace, the flashback ends and the writer returns to the present.

Present: Herr Otto clenching the test tube with the serum that can cure Alzheimer's disease. There is an enraged look on his face. He must stay hidden. He pours the serum into a lab sink.

The two flashbacks are scenes moving progressively *ahead* toward the present. The second flashback is shorter than the first because it serves as a transition between the past and the present. If the writer needs still more past information, during the same flashback interval, he allows the second flashback to create a third flashback. *(Herr Otto shown frantically fleeing from the Allied soldiers searching for war criminals.)* When that shorter, third flashback is over, the writer returns to the present.

Tempo

Tempo, in a novel, is the rhythmic flow of scenes toward the conclusion. The motion of scenes can move back and forth and still sustain the impression that all is progressing forward. But tempo can be disrupted if a sequence of similarly toned scenes is used.

If the present situation is passive, do not use a flashback that is also a passive situation.

Example A woman has been hired to tutor two young boys. She is on a train traveling to her employment. While staring out the window, she recalls a time when she was able to stroll about the countryside alone.

Because the present interval and the past interval are both passive situations, inertia sets in. There is a separation in time (past and present) but no separation in tone. Although she is involved in experience (a train ride, a country stroll), these experiences develop an interval which is static. The young woman is merely on a train and is thinking of the past.

Either the present has to be active so it can absorb the past passive interval, or the past interval has to be an active situation that can enliven the present circumstance.

If there is no event in the situation, it is not a situation—it is a circumstance. Circumstance is the condition a character is in until an event happens to change it into a situation.

Though the writer may try to make the train ride sparkle with passenger dialogue, landscaping, people activity, it will remain passive until something happens.

Example A lecherous scoundrel solicits the young woman for a lower berth assignation. Fanatic terrorists take over the train and hold her hostage.

If this is not suitable to the plot line, *then activate the flashback.* During her stroll in the country she witnesses a murder. She saves a four-year-old child from drowning. A passive present scene containing a passive past scene flattens the tempo of the story.

Circumstance vs. Situation

Circumstance, by itself, is either a place where people are, or a condition people are in. Circumstance is not a *situation.*

Example of circumstance 1.) Two lovers enjoying a picnic. 2.) A stagecoach being driven through the rain. 3.) Roman gladiators poised in an arena.

When characters are fixed into an environment, in a particular condition (sick, happy, desperate, fearful, etc.) they are not yet involved in a situation. Any event which causes them to conflict with their place or the condition they are in puts them into a situation.

Whether circumstance is a place where people are, or a condition that people are in, it is always passive. Because nothing is happening to them now. They are suspended in that place or condition, waiting for something to happen NOW. What they contain as people, or what is the content of their fictional characters, is all in the past.

They are, at the moment, all that the past has brought them into becoming. They are, where they are, and what they are, and no more.

Only when something happens NOW—when they oppose the condition they are in or when an event forces their condition to be changed, and they are in a SITUATION, does their present become active. The writer is then able to bring out more of what they are as people. The writer can then shift or pivot or manipulate their plot line and intensify the relationships and conflicts.

Example of situation 1.) The lovers are attacked by wild dogs. 2.) The coach is carrying a king's messenger and it is being pursued by enemy soldiers. 3.) A gladiator suddenly charges to Nero to decapitate him.

An event that motivates characters to act within (for or against) the place or condition they are in, changes their circumstances to a situation. The focus is then directed on the situation and the circumstance becomes the setting—sometimes it is diminished into becoming the background.

Overwrite Your First Writing

In the first writing of your novel, professional writers advise that you *overwrite*. A standard assumption in fiction is that you will have to rewrite some of the original material, and reappraise *all* of what the novel contains. Overwriting, like melodramatic writing, has advantages that are not immediately obvious. It seems, at first, that you are wasting time and energy putting down content you will not use. That is a misconception.

Overwriting does not mean you are writing badly. Knowing that you will have to rewrite is not a license to write poorly. All of what you write should be written well. Overwriting means only that you are discovering and writing more than you need. Yet the content you delete in actual writing is not necessarily deleted from the content that remains. You remove what you do not need because you already have what you need. Or, what you remove is already present in what you allow to remain. It is in another form, or present through implication. You are not emptying the novel. You are tightening it: shaping it into an intense, unified form.

Content must be established in a story or plot before it can be considered a written reality. If you edit in your mind and decide what to eliminate before writing it down, you have not eliminated anything. You cannot eliminate what does not exist. If you edit it out before you write it down, you *assume* it does not belong. If you write it down, and then edit it out, you *know* it does not belong.

The procedure of discovery works in two dimensions. Discovering what you need in your novel and writing it down, then discovering what you do not need in your novel and removing it. Reducing a novel to its functional state is less troublesome than having to increase your novel because the content is inadequate. There is another serious difference between an overwritten novel and one that is inadequately filled. When you rewrite an overwritten novel, you are working from a completed novel with too much in it. When you rewrite an inadequately filled novel, your novel is not yet finished. *You are still writing your novel.*

Put Flashbacks in Passive Scenes

The point of departure from the present into a flashback must be carefully chosen. If a flashback is used during a time of action, the writer risks stopping the pace and dramatics of the action. If the character is engaged in a dialogue in which important information is being revealed, breaking into that dialogue to flash back *disconnects* the context of the dialogue. When a character in an agitated emotional/mental response to a circumstance is about to cause character-changing revelation, stalling the revelation by using a flashback disrupts the impact of the inner revelation.

Example In October, Ryan and his business partner are on the fiftieth floor of a building they are having constructed. Ryan stumbles against his partner who is flung from the platform and killed. Nine months later, Ryan is in a confessional. He is in a highly emotional state. He is remembering the accident. As the priest asks for his confession, Ryan realizes he actually murdered his partner. He deliberately fell against him, pushing him from the building. He did it so all the firm's assets could go to him.

If the moment of Ryan's revelation is interrupted by a flashback to the accident about which the reader already has read in an earlier scene, the flow of emotion is disrupted and the shock of the revelation is buffered or lost.

The time to bring in a flashback is when the character is in an *inactive, passive state*. A time when the character is doing something idle, or innocuous: changing a flat tire, cleaning laboratory test tubes, doing the laundry, putting on cosmetics, etc. The scene that causes the flashback to appear should not be a scene that must be uninterruptedly sustained. The scene should be developed to reach a point where its continuance can be interrupted with a flashback.

Note: When leaving the flashback scene, before returning to the present, reduce the intensity of the dramatics to render the past pace compatible with the passive activity of the present to which the reader is about to return.

The Flashback Story

A full story that happened in the past running parallel to the story that is happening in the present can be an interesting, suspenseful structure. The *flashback story* is an independent, associate story that happens *in its own time*. It has its own characters, conflicts, events. It is related to the story of the present through the major characters because it is the story of their past. Its content contributes to the present story.

Example Year: 1876. Robbie Ellis, the minister of a small town in Idaho, carries a terrible secret. He is a murderer who escaped from a Pittsburgh prison. He killed his older brother and is now married to his dead brother's widow. A man, once a prison guard, has moved into town. The man does not recognize Robbie. Robbie recognizes him. He is afraid.

The major story is Robbie's present. After the second chapter, the associate story begins. It is the story of Robbie's past.

Example Robbie is 19 years old. He loves Deborah. His older brother, Jimbo, wants her. Jimbo frames Robbie for a crime. He promises Deborah to get Robbie off if she marries him. She makes the sacrifice. Because Jimbo knows she still loves Robbie, he decides to kill him. There is a fight. Jimbo is killed. Robbie is imprisoned. He plans to escape.

The story of Robbie's present is the dominant story. It is interrupted at selective intervals to allow Robbie's past to unfold. Gradually the two stories begin converging to let the past catch up to the present. The past story ends *where the present story began*—when Robbie and Deborah first arrived in Idaho and he became a minister.

Long before the two stories merge to become one, the past content and events are explaining much of why the characters do and feel what they do in the present. Though the past story is an independent story, its contributions are vital to the story in the present.

Unrelated Openings

An interesting structural opening for a short story is one in which the opening scene is not immediately related to the story that follows. It is a dramatic opening meant to reach the reader quickly. Only later, when it is incorporated into the story, does it have impact and meaning.

Opening scene The Indians danced around the sheriff tied to the stake. They waved blazing torches at the dry branches piled about his legs. He pleaded, "I didn't kill the chief's daughter. It was my twin brother, Angus." The chief clapped his hands. The Indians flung the torches onto the branches. The sheriff screamed. "It was my twin brother."

This is not a "hook" opening. A "hook" opening is part of the immediate text. The hook always leads into the story.

Example The last man on earth was startled when someone knocked on the door. Quickly he hid the cans of contaminated food.

The rest of the story follows. An opening that is dramatic but not immediately related to the story is a scene within itself. It is a tight, fast, cameo story.

The story A cowboy is on the distant range, tending his cattle. His wife is at their cabin, feeding the chickens. Four men, heavily armed, ride toward her. They kidnap the woman. The cowboy, desperate to save his wife, rides off and pursues them. As he gets to them, the Indians capture them. The leader is Angus, the sheriff's twin brother. The Indians realize they had killed the wrong man. To make up for their mistake, they release the cowboy and his wife and burn the others at the stake.

After the seemingly unrelated opening scene, the writer uses a break and goes into the story that begins with the cowboy tending his cattle. The full story actually catches up to the opening. This is an effective opening because it quickly grabs the reader's attention, foreshadows the major plot line, and creates reader anticipation.

Stop the Action in Fight Scenes

An effective method for providing additional information about major characters is the *stop-the-action* technique. It is a particularly useful device in fight-to-the-death scenes. It should always be a minor, but familiar, character who is killed.

Story Bailey, a detective whose specialty is knife fighting, is amassing evidence to prosecute a ruthless business tycoon who is responsible for the death of Bailey's wife. The tycoon is always accompanied by Petey, his bodyguard. Petey is a vicious killer. Bailey leaves his apartment with conclusive evidence. Petey is waiting for him. They draw their knives.

It is at this moment that the action of the scene stops. For the first time, the writer describes the details of Petey's background. The writing is all narrative.

Example Petey would enjoy killing Bailey. The detective was the image of Clakmege who ruled the orphanage Petey lived in until he was fourteen. He had been beaten with shoe heels and mop sticks for the smallest infraction. The night he ran from the orphanage, he left Clakmege lying in his office, his throat cut with a skinning knife. He had joined a Detroit gang. . . .

The writer describes how Petey came into the life of the major villain, the business tycoon. Additional background material is learned about the tycoon. It is in that area that future scenes are implanted, foreshadowed, revealing what this villain is capable of doing when he is thwarted. Petey exists only because he is a carrier of this special information.

The events from Petey's background have to be drawn from his profession—violence, murder. His skills as a knife fighter must be extolled so when he is killed by the hero, the hero will not only appear more skilled, but will also seem to have the power of truth on his side. The content of the narration should be rendered in vigorous, strong prose.

Though the action of the fight was stopped, the fight has been postponed by equally exciting material. Then the writer picks up the hero and minor character/villain again, and the fight to the death begins.

Your Literary Heritage

Will there ever be any relief from the constant dilemma of what technique to use in your writing? Is there any source of consolation to draw from, to justify this condition of ignorance, so you can stop spending hours at your desk in a moldy blue funk? Yes. Stop your self-persecution. You are not to blame. Accuse all the writers of the past, and some in the present, who are assaulting you with their accomplishments. They are tyrannical taskmasters. They have established writing criteria and techniques and will not allow you to settle for less.

You did not create the writing problems that are distressing you. They were developed *for you* by the men and women in your literary heritage. They lived through their own moldy blue funks until they uncovered the methods for writing that you want to know now. They did not take these "craft discoveries" to their graves, to remain hidden. They left them behind for you to find. Jane Austen, Charles Dickens, Willa Cather, Thomas Hardy, James Joyce, Katharine Mansfield, William Faulkner, Ernest Hemingway, John Steinbeck, James

T. Farrell, Albert Camus—those are only a few of your persecuters.

Every advance they made in the craft of writing increased the range and complication of your present writing problems. What was already known about the conventions of writing was too limiting for them. What they were struggling to create began jamming the borders of acceptable writing. They were forced to find other techniques to accommodate the function of this overflow. They innovated, improvised, invented. And what they devised was left behind to fill your writing future. As an infant is toilet-trained by his parents, writers are technique-trained by the accomplishments of their literary predecessors.

Experience the travail of feeling ignorant, but be joyous in knowing that all the techniques you are searching for can be found. And when you find them, and they become limiting to you, become an innovator in the tradition of the masters and begin causing writing problems for the generations of writers just coming up behind you.

The Teasing Secret

There is a nasty, unfair writing device that is beginning to surface in modern fiction. It was dismissed as rude and obvious in the late 1800s because it pestered the reader to distraction. Now, in the 1980s, it has returned to agitate and taunt readers. It is the teasing secret.

Situation A chairman of the board is in trouble. He is about to be usurped by a power-obsessed executive who has sneakily purchased a majority of stock issue. The chairman is suicidal. His daughter suddenly tells him, "Dad, I can stop him." The father is skeptical but is willing to listen.

The writer then writes: "Loretta revealed her plan. Her father gasped, "No, I won't let you do it!" She gripped his hand. "It's the only way to stop him, Dad." The love he felt was a luster in his eyes. "You would do this, for me?" She kissed his wrinkled cheek, "Yes, Dad, I will. My plan won't fail. If it worked for Cesare Borgia, it will work for us."

The writer does not reveal Loretta's plan. The reader has no idea of what she intends to do. Not even while she is executing the plan is the plan understood. The writer has split Loretta's plan into seemingly unrelated parts. The reader blindly follows her plan, part after part.

Example She travels places, she bribes people, she researches facts in newspaper morgues. She buys a speed boat, some nylon rope. The father is seen, now and then, frantic with worry.

On the morning of the board meeting, she charges in with affidavits from the people she bribed, facts about the executive's past, long sheets of financial figures to prove his embezzlement. A photo of the speed boat and the nylon rope frightens him. He cringes against the wall, a broken man. He resigns from the company.

Only moments before the final crushing facts are displayed does the reader fully realize the extent of the daughter's plan. Then the writer confirms the reader's intelligence by having Loretta reveal the exact same thing. This compatibility of recognition is satisfying to the reader. It makes having read in the dark worth the strain. But the teasing secret device is risky. Too many readers will not patiently collect the parts and put them together.

On-Scene Deaths

In novels of character (where characters dominate the novel, rather than the plot line dominating the characters) the death scenes of major characters should be extended and emphasized. Readers do not like to lose their friends—or their enemies—too quickly. The death scene must become a dramatic scene, with much heart-and-soul purging and astonishing information.

Situation The elder of a family of seven, who has been the strength and guiding light of its members, suddenly collapses with a fatal illness.

Which type of death scene should be used? (1) Off-scene? (2) On-scene?
(1) The off-scene death stresses the significance and effects of the elder's death, *after the fact*. (2) The on-scene death emphasizes its immediate effects on all the members present *during* the final moments.

After the off-scene death, characters are viewed when the brunt of the effects of death have already been experienced. The characters may still be reacting with grief, but not with their original intensity. Their emotions are more reflective than immediate. The cathartic content is more recollective—they recount their experiences with his death. But the major character—who did the actual dying—is not present.

The on-scene death allows the major character to be present, and suffering. The reader can experience empathy. The reader and the characters experience a simultaneous purging. Wrench the emotions of readers, make them sob—and you have grateful readers. A writer should not be timid about using the devices of melodrama and sentimentality during a death scene. Love, hate, passion, fear, greed, lust, cunning, revenge, all this can occur in a prolonged death scene. The pace of the plot line may be slowed a little, but this is a character novel and plot is secondary. What is vital is the revelation and impact that experience has on character and relationships.

The story of someone who is dying *now,* while you are there, always carries more impact than the passive, retrospective introspection of contemplative remembrances.

Dialogue: Passive and Dynamic

Dialogue changes information from the passive to dynamic. It intensifies pace by eliminating the cumbersome word usage demanded by the propriety of grammar. It gives information the impact of intimacy.

Passive information is what the writer institutes into a scene through description (*The white window shutters were darkened from automobile exhaust fumes.*) or exposition (*The president had been warned not to ride through the Dallas streets in an open vehicle.*). This passive information is established to inform the reader. Its relevance to the characters can be immediate, or its importance can be revealed later. The characters can, but need not, know all the information included by the writer. Passive information *tells.* Dynamic information is incorporated into the scene through the characters. Dynamic information *causes.*

Example (passive) The two policemen sat in the patrol car, arguing. Miller accused Jerry of being a coward during a shootout. Jerry protested that guns did not frighten him and he had hid in the corner, relaxing until he could decide what to do. Miller brought up Jerry's father, to prove he had a history of cowardice. He called Jerry a liar.

This information, while important to the scene, merely informs the reader of what is transpiring between them and their attitudes toward it.

Example (dynamic) "Come off it, Jerry. You hid when he pulled a gun. What was a rumor is now a fact. You've done it before."

Jerry rolled down the side window and spit into the dark air, then shrugged, "You heard what I told the board, right? I stepped out of the action to think it over." He rolled the window up, and yawned. "Guns don't scare me." Miller lit a cigarette and smirked, "Sure, sure. Only in my book, you take after your father. You got a history of yellow-bellies. Added to being yellow, you're also a liar."

Information becomes dynamic when it causes characters to respond and react. Related information, presented by the writer, is passive. Its importance becomes optional because there is no immediate response or reaction to it. Information coming through characters is personalized. It does not require the formalities of grammar, the proprieties of sentence structure. It has been turned into emotion.

Prologues

There are two basic types of prologues. The *closed* and the *open*.

A prologue serves three important functions: 1.) Directly, or indirectly, it foreshadows what the novel will be about. 2.) It is a source of reference from which the writer draws material to use in the body of the novel. 3.) It establishes continuity between the past and the present.

Closed prologue Three ten-year-old orphans escape from a brutal Chicago orphanage. Before leaving, they assault the sadistic supervisor. One of them bashes his head with a heavy ashtray. They flee to the railroad yard. They swear to secrecy about the homicide and to life-long friendship. They hop onto freight trains going in different directions.

The novel must be about the three orphans, their experiences, what happens when they meet in their adulthood, how the murder affects them.

Open prologue In the years between 1562 and 1570, civil wars between Catholics and Protestants ruined the provinces of France. Charles IX, a weak monarch, feared Philip II of Spain. He negotiated alliances with Philip's enemies. These alliances caused the massacre of St. Bartholomew's Day in which 100,000 people were killed. In 1569, the prince of Condé was murdered. . . .

This prologue is "open" because its focus is on history, rather than individuals. It is meant to establish background and setting. The novel can be about Protestant and/or Catholic leaders, about the monarchs Charles IX and/or Philip II, about the peasantry, the middle class, the aristocrats, about the events leading up to the massacre, or anyone the writer creates.

The time span between prologue and novel opening can be a century, a week, an hour. It is a vignette scene, or scenes: a detailed characterization of individuals or relationships. It can be in first person, or third person. In either prologue (closed or open) the novel draws from what the prologue contains. In the closed prologue it draws from what happened off-scene (some adventures the orphans had when they escaped). In the open prologue it draws from what happened "in that time" which was not included in the prologue. A prologue serves to introduce the novel, in a particular way.

Mysteries vs. Suspense Novels

Before deciding the structure to use for either a suspense novel or a mystery novel, it would be wise to understand their conceptual differences.

While the mystery novel deals with a present investigation, it is a journey into the past. The suspense novel deals with an investigation of what is happening in the present to prevent a terrible future.

Mystery A woman has been murdered. Her husband is one of seven suspects. Heavy evidence falls on the woman's lover. He is in jail and ready to be tried. He is innocent. Will the real killer be discovered in time?

Suspense A woman believes her husband is going to kill her. Her lover guards her. He is killed in a questionable accident. A friend borrows her car and it is blown up accidentally. The woman is in constant fear. The police will not help because, thus far, no crime has been committed.

In the mystery novel the writer works backward, compiling information that leads the investigators to a solution in the present. If other murders occur they are committed to misdirect the investigators. They are used to make the mystery more complex. Although they are new crimes, they are still connected to the old crime. Additional suspects are not introduced. Some of the old suspects are killed off. It is when all the fragments of the past are brought together that the present is complete.

In the suspense novel the investigator works to learn what is ahead. *A mystery is going to happen.* If terrible accidents or other killings occur before the major character is slain, they are present only to mystify and suspend what will happen in the future. Suspense is created through the waiting for how and when it will happen. The secondary accidents and killings are treated less dramatically than the drama and horror of what it is when all the fragments of the present are brought together that the future horror is stopped from happening.

In both novel structures suspense and mystery are gained by how tightly and cleverly the writer combines the past and the present.

Readers Don't Notice Craft

Do not stop yourself from writing a scene the way you believe it should be written because you think the reader is familiar with the technique you are using. Readers are not as learned as you believe they are—nor are you as obvious as you think you are. Readers are only dimly aware of what techniques you are using. If you have written your story or novel competently and dramatically, the reader won't care if you left the center of the page blank, and wrote only in the margins. Readers buy books because they want to read.

The reader's critical level and the writer's critical level are not the same, nor does the critical focus come from the same type of vision. Readers do not read with critical magnifying glasses held over the page.

By answering the question *"What, at this time (1980s) in the history of writing, has not already been written about in such a way that its arrangement has not been noted before?,"* you are unburdened from the worry of what the reader knows. Because the answer is *"It has all already been written about in every conceivable arrangement writers have been able to devise."* Thus, you are now released to be innovative, inventive, and flagrantly melodramatic and never worry about what the reader already knows.

You must write the story or novel the way your intuitive dramatic sense and conscious sense of craft require that you write it. Your professionalism will overcome any and every aspect of writing-technique awareness the reader may possess. If people were not eager to read, then the plethora of written tripe that is published would never be set into print. Readers do not read writing—they read experience.

Your responsibility is to your profession (the craft of writing), not to the reader. The moment you write for publication, you must resolutely assume that you are taking the readers' needs into consideration. Hold to the personal integrity and craft-criteria you have developed through the experience of writing. Readers want solid and compellingly written stories peopled with interesting and dramatic characters. That is your focus; allowing yourself to be distracted and/or directed by the reader is disastrous.

Universal Symbols

Writers should take advantage of the meanings contained within *universal symbols*. A universal symbol is any object that conveys two meanings: 1.) what it is in itself and 2.) what tradition has caused it to suggest. Universal symbols not only establish setting, but also save on tedious descriptions.

Example a.) A flag is a tailored, colored piece of cloth. But a flag also suggests a particular nation. b.) Bars across a window are used to prevent entry or exit through that window. But bars across a window also suggest the existence of a prison.

Universal symbols are objects which all readers recognize, not only for what they are in themselves, but for what the reader has been conditioned to assume they suggest or imply.

Example A musketeer for the king is captured by an opposing revolutionary party. He is chained to a wall in a dungeon.

To quickly establish the menace and discomfort of the dungeon, include a family of sag-bellied, fat-tailed rats. To indicate what might happen to the musketeer, let him detect the odor of burning flesh. Have another prisoner, somewhere in the catacomb of dungeons, let out an agonized scream. Every reader knows that the presence of rats suggest dirt, disease, that they nibble on human flesh when the person is asleep. Someone screaming, with the accompanying odor of burning flesh, suggests that someone is being tortured.

On one level, the rats, the odor of burning flesh, the scream, are part of the setting. This dungeon is not a wholesome place to be. On the "universal" level—when the reader sees beyond the literal presence of these objects—much more is suggested. The writer describes only the literal object; the reader brings into that description a deeper level of suggestion.

A non-universal symbol would be a discarded scarf, a bone-china tea cup with a broken handle. These objects require explanation. Because they do not carry "universal suggestions" they must be further explained.

Theme

At some time during the writing of a novel a writer experiences a degree of panic and believes the reader will not clearly perceive the meaning of his *theme*. This need to openly reveal a theme is not an inherent trait of talent. It is a tradition promoted by some schools of writing. Literary critics and *hypostatizers* have analyzed and reanalyzed the themes of the great books with such masticating persistence, that writers have come to believe that without a statement of a theme, *the theme will either be missed or will not appear to exist*.

A theme is a prevailing idea that overlays, in an unstated, tacit manner, the entire novel. It is an abstraction given communicative solidity by the body of the novel, through the action, characters, relationships, and the conclusion.

It is usually a meaningful perception about "living experience" that the writer has garnered from his existence.

Themes can be stated in one sentence. Often, they read like adages. "Good will triumph over evil." "Holiness is the regeneration of corruption." "If we run from our pasts we reach an uncertain future." "Tomorrow will be better." "You cannot rush time—it unfolds one day at a time."

If you must blatantly include your theme in the novel before the novel is concluded, then do it in a small scene. If it is more than a typewritten page, you are writing a lecture. Do it through dialogue, narration, or introspection. Any action or dramatic content will quickly dominate the thematic material and it will remain unnoticed. Action and drama are realities—theme is philosophical abstraction. Find an area in the novel where all action, plot, characterization, and relationships can be stopped without a serious loss of pace and intensity, and get it over with—state your theme.

If a novel can be encapsulated in only one theme, the writer has not created a various and complex work. A novel should contain many themes—which only the literary critics will care to find. One of them should be: "After creating a novel the writer should find his theme and claim he knew it all along."

Symbolism

Be wary of using *symbolism* in your stories or novels. If you believe you need a symbol to add undercurrents of meaning, then trust that your intuitions have already produced them. This is not mystical or romantic. Symbols are all part of the content you are writing. What you emphasize and continue (like a thread through a large tapestry) turns into the symbolic.

In fiction, a symbol is any object, character, place, gesture, color, smell, etc., that carries meaning, not only for what it is, but also for what it implies. White is not only a color, it also implies purity, virtue, innocence, goodness. Though a space ship is used as a vehicle, it can also symbolize scientific progress. A symbol (flag, star, ashtray, pencil, river, hurricane, etc.), *by itself,* is only an object represented by the identifying name it bears. To become a functioning symbol, the object must be contextual, an inherent part of the content. When symbols are forced into the work, they are either intrusive, or amateurish.

Example Archaeologists notice a twenty-three-foot-high statue of the human tongue on the jungle island of Fricative. The archaeologists photograph the statue, then go further into the jungle.

Identified only as one of many other jungle features and native objects, the giant statue is simply part of the primitive, savage setting. When the writer emphasizes the statue's presence, it then implies pagan ritual and idol worship. Why the natives worship the tongue statue is important to the plot. The archaeologists must learn its meaning. When an object is used as a symbol, its meaning is hidden in its existence. It is *tacit*. It becomes a true symbol only when the reader identifies its meaning.

The effectiveness of a symbol depends upon how subtly the writer leads the reader into discerning the undercurrent of its meaning. Some symbols are universal, others change from era to era. But all symbols are subjectively interpretive. They are quixotic, untrustworthy. They are scented with formalism. Use them wisely or they will be smelled out, and will fail.

Novels Must Be Published

There are only two unarguable and never-changing rules in the profession of writing. (1) Novels are not written until they are totally written—completed, and with "The End" on the last page. (2) What you write must be submitted for publication.

Unfinished novels by previously unpublished writers are never "suddenly discovered" and published. That is a romantic fantasy founded on public legend based on addled hearsay started by semiliterate idlers. A work must be finished and submitted before it can be published. And anyone who writes for "this time" or "the ages" and does not submit the writing for publication will not even achieve momentary recognition.

There is an attitude that inexperienced writers should keep in mind when they have written a work that is within the realm of possible publication. "Don't run scared!" Publishing houses are power bullies who make enormous sums on inexperienced writers who allow themselves to be cowed. The hungrier you look, the less you will be fed. The more desperate you seem, the more you will be exploited. If the first offer of an advance is meager, ask for more. ALWAYS ASK FOR MORE. Publishers are not idealists, they are merchants. Most publishers today are not even people—they are corporations.

Also never rewrite from editorial dictates or suggestions until you are under contract and have been paid your advance. If an editor believes you have written a publishable book, but "only with rewriting and revisions," let him prove his sincerity with money. In publishing, money is the criterion that proves respect. If your manuscript is returned to you with accolades AND a list of suggestions for rewrites and revisions BEFORE it can be considered for publication, ignore the editor and submit it to another publisher. Long before you have completed the rewrites and revisions, chances are that that editor will have left that publisher and the replacement editor will have other suggestions AND YOU STILL HAVEN'T BEEN PAID FOR YOUR WORK. *Don't run scared.* A competently written novel with commercial properties WILL BE PUBLISHED. Take heart, and hold out!

INDEX

INTROSPECTION AND INSIGHT

INVENTION AND IDEAS

LANGUAGE AND TONE

OPENINGS

PLOT

POINT OF VIEW

PUBLISHING

REWRITING

SCENE STRUCTURE

SETTING AND DESCRIPTION

STRUCTURE

SYMBOL AND THEME

WRITER'S EDUCATION

Other Books of Interest

Annual Market Books
  Children's Writer's & Illustrator's Market, edited by Lisa Carpenter (paper) $17.95
  Guide to Literary Agents & Art/Photo Reps, edited by Robin Gee $15.95
  Humor & Cartoon Markets, edited by Bob Staake (paper) $16.95
  Novel & Short Story Writer's Market, edited by Robin Gee (paper) $19.95
  Photographer's Market, edited by Sam Marshall $21.95
  Poet's Market, by Judson Jerome $19.95
  Writer's Market, edited by Mark Kissling $25.95
General Writing Books
  Beginning Writer's Answer Book, edited by Kirk Polking (paper) $13.95
  Discovering the Writer Within, by Bruce Ballenger & Barry Lane $17.95
  Freeing Your Creativity, by Marshall Cook $17.95
  Getting the Words Right: How to Rewrite, Edit and Revise, by Theodore A. Rees Cheney (paper) $12.95
  How to Write a Book Proposal, by Michael Larsen (paper) $10.95
  Just Open a Vein, edited by William Brohaugh $6.99
  Knowing Where to Look: The Ultimate Guide to Research, by Lois Horowitz (paper) $16.95
  Make Your Words Work, by Gary Provost $17.95
  Pinckert's Practical Grammar, by Robert C. Pinckert (paper) $11.95
  12 Keys to Writing Books That Sell, by Kathleen Krull (paper) $12.95
  The 28 Biggest Writing Blunders, by William Noble $12.95
  The 29 Most Common Writing Mistakes & How to Avoid Them, by Judy Delton (paper) $9.95
  The Writer's Book of Checklists, by Scott Edelstein $16.95
  The Writer's Digest Guide to Manuscript Formats, by Buchman & Groves $18.95
  The Writer's Essential Desk Reference, edited by Glenda Neff $19.95
Nonfiction Writing
  The Complete Guide to Writing Biographies, by Ted Schwarz $6.99
  Creative Conversations: The Writer's Guide to Conducting Interviews, by Michael Schumacher $16.95
  How to Do Leaflets, Newsletters, & Newspapers, by Nancy Brigham (paper) $14.95
  How to Sell Every Magazine Article You Write, by Lisa Collier Cool (paper) $11.95
  How to Write Irresistible Query Letters, by Lisa Collier Cool (paper) $10.95
  The Writer's Digest Handbook of Magazine Article Writing, edited by Jean M. Fredette (paper) $11.95
Fiction Writing
  The Art & Craft of Novel Writing, by Oakley Hall $17.95
  Characters & Viewpoint, by Orson Scott Card $13.95
  The Complete Guide to Writing Fiction, by Barnaby Conrad $17.95
  Cosmic Critiques: How & Why 10 Science Fiction Stories Work, edited by Asimov & Greenberg (paper) $12.95
  Creating Characters: How to Build Story People, by Dwight V. Swain $16.95
  Creating Short Fiction, by Damon Knight (paper) $10.95
  Dialogue, by Lewis Turco $13.95
  The Fiction Writer's Silent Partner, by Martin Roth $19.95
  Handbook of Short Story Writing: Vol. I, by Dickson and Smythe (paper) $10.95
  Handbook of Short Story Writing: Vol. II, edited by Jean Fredette (paper) $12.95
  How to Write & Sell Your First Novel, by Collier & Leighton (paper) $12.95
  Manuscript Submission, by Scott Edelstein $13.95
  Mastering Fiction Writing, by Kit Reed $18.95
  Plot, by Ansen Dibell $13.95
  Spider Spin Me a Web: Lawrence Block on Writing Fiction, by Lawrence Block $16.95

Theme & Strategy, by Ronald B. Tobias $13.95
The 38 Most Common Writing Mistakes, by Jack M. Bickham $12.95
Writer's Digest Handbook of Novel Writing, $18.95
Writing the Novel: From Plot to Print, by Lawrence Block (paper) $11.95

Special Interest Writing Books

Armed & Dangerous: A Writer's Guide to Weapons, by Michael Newton (paper) $14.95
The Complete Book of Feature Writing, by Leonard Witt $18.95
Creating Poetry, by John Drury $18.95
Deadly Doses: A Writer's Guide to Poisons, by Serita Deborah Stevens with Anne Klarner (paper) $16.95
Editing Your Newsletter, by Mark Beach (paper) $18.50
A Guide to Travel Writing & Photography, by Ann & Carl Purcell (paper) $22.95
Hillary Waugh's Guide to Mysteries & Mystery Writing, by Hillary Waugh $19.95
How to Pitch & Sell Your TV Script, by David Silver $17.95
How to Write & Sell True Crime, by Gary Provost $17.95
How to Write Horror Fiction, by William F. Nolan $15.95
How to Write Mysteries, by Shannon OCork $13.95
How to Write Romances, by Phyllis Taylor Pianka $15.95
How to Write Science Fiction & Fantasy, by Orson Scott Card $13.95
How to Write Tales of Horror, Fantasy & Science Fiction, edited by J.N. Williamson (paper) $12.95
How to Write the Story of Your Life, by Frank P. Thomas (paper) $11.95
The Magazine Article: How To Think It, Plan It, Write It, by Peter Jacobi $17.95
Mystery Writer's Handbook, by The Mystery Writers of America (paper) $11.95
The Poet's Handbook, by Judson Jerome (paper) $11.95
Powerful Business Writing, by Tom McKeown $12.95
Successful Scriptwriting, by Jurgen Wolff & Kerry Cox (paper) $14.95
The Writer's Complete Crime Reference Book, by Martin Roth $19.95
The Writer's Guide to Conquering the Magazine Market, by Connie Emerson $17.95
Writing Mysteries: A Handbook by the Mystery Writers of America, Edited by Sue Grafton, $18.95
Writing the Modern Mystery, by Barbara Norville (paper) $12.95

The Writing Business

A Beginner's Guide to Getting Published, edited by Kirk Polking (paper) $11.95
The Complete Guide to Self-Publishing, by Tom & Marilyn Ross (paper) $16.95
How You Can Make $25,000 a Year Writing, by Nancy Edmonds Hanson (paper) $14.95
This Business of Writing, by Gregg Levoy $19.95
Writer's Guide to Self-Promotion & Publicity, by Elane Feldman $16.95
Writing A to Z, edited by Kirk Polking $22.95

To order directly from the publisher, include $3.00 postage and handling for 1 book and $1.00 for each additional book. Allow 30 days for delivery.

Writer's Digest Books
1507 Dana Avenue, Cincinnati, Ohio 45207
Credit card orders call TOLL-FREE
1-800-289-0963
Prices subject to change without notice.

Write to this same address for information on *Writer's Digest* magazine, *Story* magazine, Writer's Digest Book Club, Writer's Digest School, and Writer's Digest Criticism Service.